Practical Forensic Analysis of Artifacts on iOS and Android Devices

Investigating Complex Mobile Devices

Mohammed Moreb

Apress®

Practical Forensic Analysis of Artifacts on iOS and Android Devices:
Investigating Complex Mobile Devices

Mohammed Moreb
Palestine Hebron Halhul, Palestine, State of

ISBN-13 (pbk): 978-1-4842-8025-6   ISBN-13 (electronic): 978-1-4842-8026-3
https://doi.org/10.1007/978-1-4842-8026-3

Managing Director, Apress Media LLC: Welmoed Spahr
Acquisitions Editor: Aaron Black
Development Editor: James Markham
Coordinating Editor: Jessica Vakili
Copyeditor: Brendan Frost

Distributed to the book trade worldwide by Springer Science+Business Media New York, 233 Spring Street, 6th Floor, New York, NY 10013. Phone 1-800-SPRINGER, fax (201) 348-4505, e-mail orders-ny@springer-sbm.com, or visit www.springeronline.com. Apress Media, LLC is a California LLC and the sole member (owner) is Springer Science + Business Media Finance Inc (SSBM Finance Inc). SSBM Finance Inc is a **Delaware** corporation.

For information on translations, please e-mail booktranslations@springernature.com; for reprint, paperback, or audio rights, please e-mail bookpermissions@springernature.com.

Apress titles may be purchased in bulk for academic, corporate, or promotional use. eBook versions and licenses are also available for most titles. For more information, reference our Print and eBook Bulk Sales web page at http://www.apress.com/bulk-sales.

Any source code or other supplementary material referenced by the author in this book is available to readers on the Github repository: https://github.com/Apress/Practical-Forensic-Analysis-of-Artifacts-on-iOS-and-Android-Devices. For more detailed information, please visit http://www.apress.com/source-code.

Printed on acid-free paper

This book is lovingly dedicated to God Almighty, and to my parents, Adnan and Hana Moreb.

To my lovely family—Amany, Lotus, Lojen, Adnan, Majdy—who have been our constant source of inspiration. They have given me the drive and discipline to tackle a task with enthusiasm and determination. Without their love and their support, this book would not have been possible.

Table of Contents

About the Author

Mohammed Moreb, Ph.D. in Electrical and Computer Engineering. Expertise in Cybercrimes & Digital Evidence Analysis, specifically focusing on Information and Network Security, with a strong publication track record, both conceptual and practical record built up during work as a system developer and administrator for the data center for more than 10 years; config, install, and admin enterprise system related to all security configurations. He improved his academic path with international certificates such as CCNA, MCAD, MCSE; and he teaches graduate-level courses such as Information and Network Security, Mobile Forensics, Advanced Research Methods, Computer Network Analysis and Design, and Artificial Intelligence Strategy for Business Leaders.

Dr. Moreb recently founded a new framework and methodology specializing in software engineering for machine learning in health informatics named SEMLHI, which investigates the interaction between software engineering and machine learning within the context of health systems. The SEMLHI framework includes four modules (software, machine learning, machine learning algorithms, and health informatics data) that organize the tasks in the framework using a SEMLHI methodology, thereby enabling researchers and developers to analyze health informatics software from an engineering perspective and providing developers with a new road map for designing health applications with system functions and software implementations.

ABOUT THE AUTHOR

Mobile forensics team members who participated in practical forensics experiments to prepare chapters or parts of chapters are the following:

Ammar Naser

Derar Abu Sheikha

Layth Abu Arram

Rawan Samara, Mohammed Dweekat

Ibrahim Shawahni

Ahmad Abu Eisheh

Firas Abu Hasan, Bashar Jaber

Asad Salem

Mohammad Shadeed, Shadi Younis, Aref Khalil

Sajida Qadan, Safa' Siam, Ibrahim Abubaker, Shadia Jayyosi

Bushra Ayyash

Ahmad Hammoudi

Iyad Ramlawy, Maryam Abu Safeia

Zaer Qaroush

About the Technical Reviewer

Wesley Matlock is a published author of books about iOS technologies. He has more than 20 years of development experience in several different platforms. He first started doing mobile development on the Compaq iPAQ in the early 2000s. Today Wesley enjoys developing on the iOS platform and bringing new ideas to life for Major League Baseball in the Denver metro area.

Acknowledgments

I would like to express my profound gratitude to the mobile forensics team who participated in practical forensics experiments to prepare cases.
I wish to express my deep appreciation to my family, particularly my wife Mrs. Amany Isead, and my children—Lotus, Lojin, Adnan, and Majdy—for their unwavering support and encouragement with the editing of this book, and for their patience and support, which was freely given during the last years of nights and weekends that were needed to complete this research.

I would also like to extend my heartiest thanks to my father, Mr. Adnan Moreb; to my mother, Mrs. Hana Abid Alkader; to my brothers for their big support during my initial research; to Mr. Majdi and Mr. Mamoun; and finally to all my friends who supported me during this book journey.

What This Book Covers

This book is written to represent a natural flow in the e-discovery process, covering all mobile forensics stages from seizing the device to acquiring the data and analyzing evidence using different tools. The book covers basic handling, acquisition, and analysis techniques for the most popular mobile iOS and Android devices. The following topics are covered in detail:

Chapter 1, "Introduction to Mobile Forensic Analysis." This chapter introduces the reader to practical mobile forensic analysis by explaining challenges for the use of different models, and how forensically sound investigations are applied in the forensic community to select tools for the forensic process.

Chapter 2, "Introduction to iOS Forensics." This chapter provides an overview of iOS devices such as iPhones and iPads, as well as an overview of the operating systems and file systems they run. Many forensic tools are used in forensic science; these tools are concerned to handle all forensic process activities. Digital forensics has three types: manual (i.e., opening a PC, removing storage), logical, and physical. After completing this chapter, you will have learned about various third-party tools used for iOS forensics, and will be able to answer three questions: the difference between acquisition and backup, how to measure and check the effect of jailbreaking on an iOS device, and the differences between third-party tools used in the forensic analysis process.

Chapter 3, "Introduction to Android Forensics." This chapter covers everything you need to know about practical forensics on Android devices. We will start by understanding the Android platform and its file system and then cover the topics of setup, acquisition, extraction, and recovery.

We will also learn how to connect devices using ADB tools and back them up and how to use SQLite files for the acquisition process.

Chapter 4, "Forensic Investigations of Popular Applications on Android and iOS Platforms." Since the last century, because of the growth in social media, online resources, and websites such as Facebook, there has been a huge number of users who have been sharing huge amounts of private data such as texts, pictures, videos, and calls on the Android and iOS platforms through instant messaging applications like Messenger, WhatsApp, and so on. In this chapter, we'll investigate how much privacy these applications can provide for users, and how much information can we get through forensic investigation using digital forensic programs like FINALMobile forensics.

Chapter 5, "Forensic Analysis of Telegram Messenger on iOS and Android Smartphones Case Study." Mobile digital forensics science is developing daily, and every day there is a new tool introduced and a new challenge as well. This chapter is to get hands-on with all available forensics tools, to identify the benefits of using each tool, to practice with them to get results faster, and to determine the most suitable tool to get accurate results in a relatively short time in different situations. The chapter uses two images of evidence to assess the ability of different tools to extract the results and build a strong case when it comes to Telegram Messenger investigation on iOS devices.

This chapter discusses in detail the set of user tools for each operating system. While they can be used interchangeably in most cases, it's still up to the investigator to know which tool to use.

Chapter 6, "Detecting Privacy Leaks Utilizing Digital Forensics and Reverse Engineering Methodologies." Most commercial iOS forensic & data acquisition tools will effectively do the job in general, but in cases of data leaks as presented in this chapter, we need to look between the lines to extract all related logs and API communication that occurred inside the mobile system. Thus, we need to investigate the most recent updated tools and use more and more tools to have better evidence about our case.

Chapter 7, "Impact of Device Jailbreaking or Rooting on User Data Integrity in Mobile Forensics." This chapter covers with practical uses cases how jailbreaking techniques affect user data integrity by comparing the hash values for extracted data before and after jailbreak. It was found that the hash values are the same, hence data integrity is not affected by jailbreaking an iPhone device, and investigators can use the jailbreaking technique to acquire data for suspected iPhone devices, which allows a deeper level of data acquisition, which can be used to support the case.

Chapter 8, "The Impact of Cryptocurrency Mining on Mobile Devices." This chapter analyzes the cryptocurrency mining application installed on the mobile device and how it affects the tools to use. Our experiment uses two devices: iOS and Android.

Chapter 9, "Mobile Forensic Investigation for WhatsApp." The rapid and exponential development in communication technology and the Internet also accelerated development in smartphones and their data connectivity (e.g., 3G and 4G). Social networking and instant messaging (IM) companies developed their mobile applications. Other IM mobile applications were developed, such as WhatsApp (WA), Viber, and IMO. WA is considered the most popular IM application.

While the messages, exchanged files, and call logs are stored in smartphone memory, WA usage leaves different types of artifacts that can be extracted and analyzed to determine the digital evidence. Besides, the iOS platform is one of the most used smartphones. Therefore, forensic investigation tools and methods are required for the investigation process.

Chapter 10, "Cloud Computing Forensics: Dropbox Case Study." In our digital world and with many services provided through the Internet, many consumers use online services to store their data or share it online, which means that important data is still stored online and it still at risk to be affected by criminal activities. One of these online services is cloud computing, which provides a set of services including storage. This chapter will illustrate more about cloud computing forensic artifacts, especially with Dropbox cloud storage service analysis as a case study. Dropbox analysis will indicate the forensics artifacts that can be acquired from the cloud and also from mobiles to find the different artifacts that may be acquired using different evidence sources and different forensic tools. In this chapter, we will use iOS and Android mobile to experiment and find results. This analysis and study of new versions of the Dropbox app with different versions of Android OS and iOS will increase the knowledge pertaining to cloud storage forensics artifacts. In addition, it will help investigators to use it in investigations of criminal activity that took place on them.

Chapter 11, "Malware Forensics for Volatile and Nonvolatile Memory in Mobile Devices." Day after day, malware and malicious programs are spreading continuously, especially for unprotected mobile devices. Malware in the mobile device can reside in the nonvolatile memory, or it can hide behind some process in the RAM, and so, in the latter case, there is no need for any file in the mobile storage to perform its tasks. Mobile memory forensics tasks can help investigators to extract interesting information from the two types of mobile memory, such as detecting some of the resident malware and its related details, which traditional techniques (like antivirus software) might or might not be able to detect. There are several approaches used by different investigators in analyzing mobile memory to detect malware, such as static memory analysis, dynamic memory analysis, hybrid memory analysis, and automated systems for detecting mobile malware. This chapter depends on iTunes and 3uTools for the iOS device backup process, and FINALMobile, Magnet AXIOM, MOBILedit, and Belkasoft forensic tools for logical and physical acquisition and malware analysis. Also, a bootable copy of Checkra1n is used to jailbreak the iPhone device

Chapter 12, "Mobile Forensic for KeyLogger Artifact." This chapter investigates mobile forensic investigation for the KeyLogger application installed on iOS or Android, and introduces and helps the investigator to discover traces of a spy application case, to determine which tools were used to investigate and search for various spy programs, and to learn how to report results obtained from the iPhone spy program that was installed and used for espionage and gaining access to sensitive data.

Chapter 13, "Evidence Identification Methods for Android and iOS Mobile Devices with Facebook Messenger." Facebook Messenger (FBM) is widely used by most mobile users. FBM is used for normal communication in addition to its involvement in criminal cases. Following a scientific mobile forensic analysis approach keeps the evidence admissible. This chapter follows the NIST mobile forensic process to retrieve data from FBM. Students will provide several methods for device identification, data acquisition, and analysis of FBM data. Several tools are used for acquisition, including Libimobiledevice, iTunes, Belkasoft, and AXIOM. Additionally, several tools are used for data analysis, including AXIOM Examine, Belkasoft, and DB Viewer for SQLite. This study concludes that the appropriate forensic tool for FBM analysis is AXIOM based on the results of analyzing encrypted iTunes images for iPhone 6s with iOS 14.6 and Android 10.

Chapter 14, "Mobile Forensics for iOS and Android Platforms: Chrome App Artifacts Depending on SQLite." This chapter firstly compares and contrasts the architectures of Android and iOS as discussed in the first chapter; as a result, we implement and utilize mobile forensics methodology to analyze SQLite files from the application that installs on the mobile device, and we discuss some of the techniques and tools used to extract information, as well as a case study of Chrome application. In terms of forensic analysis, the chapter will also emphasize the necessity of examining all SQLite files that come under the apps to extract the most digital evidence feasible. We investigated practical forensic analysis for the Chrome app for iOS and Android, and forensic procedures were carried out using the three phases (seizure, acquisition, examination & analysis) methodology. This chapter aims to extract artifacts from Chrome applications using many tools such as iBackup, iExplorer, iTunes,

Belkasoft, and FINALMobile software for iOS. We use ADB, Belkasoft, Axiom, FINALMobile and MOBILedit for Android. SQLiteStudio is used to view SQLite database files extracted from both Android and iOS.

Introduction

This book is intended for forensic examiners with little or basic experience in mobile forensics or open source solutions for mobile forensics. The book will also be useful to researchers who have previous experience in information security, and anyone seeking a deeper understanding of mobile internals. This book will provide you with the knowledge and core skills necessary for trying to recover accidentally deleted data (photos, contacts, SMS, and more).

The book includes practical cases and labs that will involve certain specialized hardware and software to perform data acquisition (including deleted data) and the analysis of extracted information.

This book is designed as an advanced book in computer forensics focusing on mobile devices and other devices not classifiable as laptops, desktops, or servers. The goal of practical forensic analysis of artifacts on iOS and Android devices is to develop the critical thinking, analytical reasoning, and technical writing skills that are necessary to effectively work in a junior-level digital forensic or cybersecurity analyst role. This is accomplished through utilizing industry-standard tools and techniques to investigate labs and cases based upon real-world investigations.

This book takes a hands-on approach to provide students with foundational concepts and practical skills in practical mobile device forensics using case studies, which can be leveraged to perform forensically sound investigations against crimes involving the most complex mobile devices currently available in the market. Using modern tools and techniques, students will learn how to conduct a structured investigation process to determine the nature of the crime and to produce results that are useful in criminal proceedings. The book will provide a walkthrough on various phases of the mobile forensics process for both Android- and iOS-based devices, including forensically extracting, collecting, and analyzing data and producing and disseminating reports. The book includes practical cases and labs that will involve certain specialized hardware and software to perform data acquisition (including deleted data) and the analysis of extracted information.

Upon completing this book, the reader will be able to:

- Analyze the need for and types of digital forensics.

- Explain and critically analyze a variety of digital forensics.

- Propose appropriate mobile forensic investigation mechanisms to detect digital evidence.

- Critically analyze the basic mobile forensic type.

- Present a real-world case of a mobile forensics investigation.

- Understand what data can be acquired from mobile devices and be able to acquire and investigate data from mobile devices using forensically sound and industry-standard tools.

- Understand the relationship between mobile and desktop devices in terms of criminal and corporate investigations.

- Analyze mobile devices, their backup files, and artifacts for forensic evidence.

CHAPTER 1

Introduction to Mobile Forensic Analysis

In this chapter we'll introduce mobile forensics by using different programs and tools to acquire from iOS (iPhone8) and Android (Samsung Galaxy S7) devices. We'll then use the forensic tools to make several backup copies of the iPhone 8, and analyze results from those files. The goal is to see if it is possible to recover and extract the deleted files. The forensic tools will be put to use in later chapters as well.

In this chapter, we will cover the following topics:

- The Importance of Mobile Forensic Analysis

- Understanding Mobile Forensics

- Digital Investigation Process

- Rules of Evidence

- Tools Used for Mobile Forensics

- The Mobile Phone Evidence Extraction Process

- Mobile Forensic Challenges on iOS and Android

© Mohammed Moreb 2022
M. Moreb, *Practical Forensic Analysis of Artifacts on iOS and Android Devices*,
https://doi.org/10.1007/978-1-4842-8026-3_1

The Importance of Mobile Forensic Analysis

While mobile devices have become a necessity for everyone, smartphones are the most used devices in our daily lives. There are many operating systems used by smartphones and one of these systems is the iOS. These phones are widely used in many fields such as making calls, email, communication through social media, and payment and purchase through the Internet (Kuittinen, 2013). Mobile forensics is a branch of science that is concerned with retrieving digital evidence from mobile devices using reliable and appropriate forensic tools (Riadi, Umar, & Firdonsyah, 2017). Because of the increasing demand for smartphone-based services and the increasing number of its users, mobile forensic science has become a necessity because of the proliferation of services, facilities for users, and the spread of the Internet of things technology that requires a device connection; there is also a popular tendency for people to use mobile phone transactions during their daily dealings (Al-Dhaqm, Razak, Ikuesan, Kebande, & Siddique, 2020).

Mobile forensics is the science of obtaining evidence from portable devices under forensically sound conditions utilizing acknowledged strategies, while mobile device forensics is a branch of digital forensics that entails gathering evidence from mobile devices under forensically sound conditions. Preservation, acquisition, examination, analysis, and reporting are the five phases of mobile forensics. Seizing and safeguarding suspect mobile devices without affecting the contents of stored data is preservation. The term "acquisition" refers to the process of recovering data from a computer. The term "cloud computing" refers to "the application of digital forensic science in cloud computing environments."

Recent years have revealed the generation of behavior and exploitation of modern crimes through the Internet that was not known before, which led to these crimes threatening the security and safety of individuals and institutions; with the increasing use of the Internet in ecommerce operations, the types of these attacks and threats will increase, which prompted us to acknowledge the existence of this type of crime and be alerted to its seriousness and the need to take a strict stance to fight it and find appropriate solutions to it.

During this case study, we will focus mainly on iOS, which is one of the worldwide operating systems; we will use an iPhone 8 (A1905) device as a sample for one of the types of devices that use the Apple file system, and we will do an acquisition for this device. The acquisition passes through several promising stages. Through this research, we will learn about the most important challenges that we face while extracting and restoring files for Apple devices in general and for iPhone 8 devices in particular.

Understanding Mobile Forensics

Mobile forensics is defined as the science of obtaining and handling digital evidence from portable devices by use of techniques similar to digital forensic investigations. Mobile device models, depending on where the storage is located so that it can be stored on the internal or external memory card, and the phone memory may be volatile or nonvolatile.

Digital forensics can be defined as an applied and practical use of reliable and proven methods for digital devices, and this action has been done in several ways, the most important of which are verification, identification, analysis, and interpretation; then, the digital evidence that has been derived from digital data is presented. It is the reconstruction of the events that show the crime or that help in the anticipation of unauthorized procedures. With the ever-increasing popularity of smartphones and people's reliance on instant messages in their everyday lives, quick updates of instant messages increase the features of the application and entice users to continue using their product. On the other hand, the majority of these characteristics will provide a significant challenge to digital forensic practitioners and specialists. Many studies have been done to acquire data from older versions of the WhatsApp apps. Many security measures arose with the introduction of new versions of WhatsApp, making it difficult for mobile forensic practitioners to gather information and evidence that live in internal storage.

Digital Investigation Process

Obtaining digital forensics data from mobile devices must include the use of the two main technologies, mainly logical acquisition and physical acquisition, and each of these features has its advantages (Anwar & Riadi, 2017); taking a logical copy of the device may not need to root the device, and it can give us the virtual files of the stored data on the memory, while the physical version (bit by bit) needs to root the device and may cause problems on mobile devices.

To pursue and achieve the goal in this practical case, we will conduct a forensic investigation into the iPhone, and we will also assume a scenario to simulate the case and apply all the mobile forensic stages. In terms of seizing, acquisition, extracting, analyzing, we will finally write the report on this phone.

We'll assume a scenario in which there is a drug dealer, where this person takes pictures of narcotic substances and sends the drug pictures to his friends, along with audio recordings to tell them the prices through social networking sites, and then deletes these pictures and recordings from his phone and social media sites.

The digital forensic officer must take all safety measures for the seized phone to preserve the data and follow the official and legal procedures to check the phone without destroying the data and to present their final report to the court.

In 2006, NIST recommended a process that goes through four steps for conducting digital forensics, as shown in Figure 1-1:

1. **Collection** - Identify, acquire, and protect the data collected at the crime scene.

2. **Examination** - Process the collected data/evidence and extract relevant information.

3. **Analysis** - Analyze the extracted information to connect the dots and be able to build a robust and admissible case.

4. **Reporting** - Present the findings of the analysis stage into an admissible and understandable format.

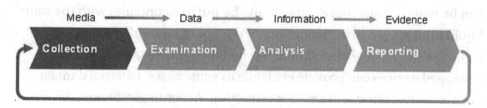

Figure 1-1. *Digital forensics process steps*

Evidence and Scene Security

Evidence preservation failure may make it inadmissible by a court or even less-formal parties; the preservation stage involves locating the evidence and identifying it including any related digital equipment. Additionally, it deals with securing, evaluating, and documenting the evidence and the scene; securing the evidence involves its isolation and packaging. Procedures should be followed also during evidence transportation and archiving.

During the seizure process, not handling the device properly may cause data loss or damage the evidence. Far away from digital forensics, some cases may require biological forensics involvement to extract DNA or fingerprints from the device. This is to relate the evidence to its owner or user. Evidence contamination can destroy the relationship of the evidence to the owner and lose evidence. Accordingly, it is necessary to wear gloves all the time while working on the device.

The scene should be searched carefully not to miss any evidence-related equipment; this includes cables, power adapters, memory cards, and other accessories related to the mobile device. Computers at the scene may provide valuable help if the mobile was synced with them; in a few cases during the seizure process, the evidence may be found at the scene in a seemingly unusable condition, such as having sunk in liquid or having broken parts. If the liquid is water or another harmless liquid, the battery can be removed, and the device should be put in a container with the same liquid until moved to the laboratory. If the liquid is blood or a dangerous explosive liquid, an expert should be consulted before taking action. Damaged devices can provide evidence in some cases. External damage does not necessarily prevent data extraction. Accordingly, broken devices should be seized too.

Scene Documentation

The entire crime scene should be photographed as well as each digital device with its accessories; a record of all digital devices found should be made including identification and state description for each one. Related nondigital documents, notes, and manuals should be collected; they may contain information about unlocking the device, its storage size, related capabilities, and any other information that may help during the examination. Running devices on the scene should be photographed while they are running; this is to record contents appearing on them including time. Also, any changes or actions made on the device should be recorded, including connecting the device to power adaptors or other devices; these records and photographs provide information if the court asks about the evidence environment.

Evidence Isolation

Mobile device isolation is very important to avoid data loss or change; factory reset commands can be sent remotely to the device and wipe all data; evidence can also be changed if the mobile receives an SMS or a call; and isolation is also required to prevent sending data from the device such as its geolocation. Isolation can be performed in different ways: the first method is disabling the communication through putting the device in Airplane mode. Enabling Airplane mode involves using the device, and thus is not preferred; but if it is used, it should be recorded and pictured. Another concern with using Airplane mode is that it does not prevent all services on the device such as geolocation. The second isolation method is by turning the device off. The availability of the unlock code should be considered in this case. The unlock code will be required when turning the device on for examination. Some services can still run even when the device is off such as alarms in some models. The third method that can be used involves isolation containers such as Faraday containers. In this case, the device will be kept on. This will increase the network signal and drain the battery quickly. Faraday containers should be sealed very well. There is a risk of communication success if it is not completely locked. Power-saving mode can be activated before putting the device in the Faraday container.

Prepare for Acquisition

The acquisition is imaging the mobile device or else getting evidential information from it or its related media; examination starts with identifying the seized mobile device. Learning the device model and hardware characteristics helps determine the method of acquisition and forensic toolkit choices. This will be discussed in the next subsections for Android and iOS devices.

Mobile forensics is a wide field that aims to extract digital evidence from mobile devices running different operating systems. All the previous stages are within the digital investigation process, as the nature of the seized material determines what the digital investigator focuses on, establishes hypotheses about what happened, and verifies any information that proves or clarifies the case. As digital investigators, we always assume that any digital device may contain the required digital evidence, so it is important to adhere to these stages to protect and save all seizures.

Figure 1-2 shows the most common types of mobile phones in terms of operating systems, and the most devices used in the smartphone's world. It also shows the most widespread tools in mobile digital forensics.

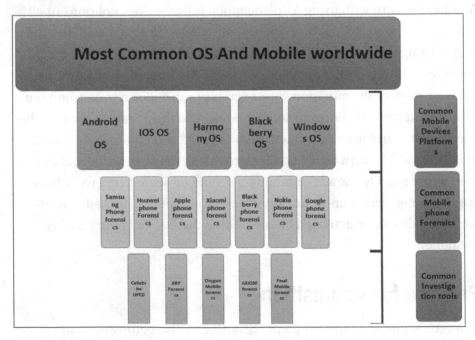

Figure 1-2. *Mobile forensic investigation processes for different mobile devices*

In the next section, we extracted data from the Apple iPhone using various tools, where we jailbreak an iPhone 8 and display the images including the results obtained through the use of different tools.

The Identification Phase

The first step for the digital forensic investigator is to identify the device model. This is important to help the investigator recognize the possibilities of recovering the evidence. Another value of knowing the device model is to be able to identify the appropriate and compatible tools and methodologies supporting that model. Additionally, this will provide information about the internal storage size of the device to ensure that there is enough space to store the forensic image. The following provides an example of an identification case for the practical case we use in this chapter.

- **Agency:** Digital Forensics Lab, Cyber Crime Department, Palestinian Civil Police – PCP.

- **Case identifier:** Investigative Case Number: 75/2021 – Ramallah Prosecution (fake case Number) Police Case Number: 127.

    Based on: Article (22,39) of Law No. (10) of 2018 regarding cybercrime, a Permission warrant was issued for the aforementioned case.

- **Investigator:** Eng. Ammar Dawabsheh – Digital Forensics Expert. Specializing in cybercrime and digital evidence in a joint program between Khadouri University and the Arab American University, and he works at the Cyber Crime Department in the Digital Evidence Laboratory of the Palestinian Civil Police (PCP) from 2015 until now (2021).

- **Submitter identity:** The seized phone was sent by the Public Prosecution - Ramallah, where the phone belongs to the suspect, M***** H***** (assumed name).

The Collection Phase

The collection phase includes a description of the device details that we use in our practical case; Table 1-1 shows that we use a set of tools such as iTunes, iBackup, and iExplorer as described in the next section, but the main tool we use is XRY FINALMobile.

XRY is a powerful, intuitive, and efficient software application that runs on the Windows operating system. It lets you securely extract more high-quality data in less time than ever before, while at all times fully maintaining the integrity of the evidence.

FINALMobile forensics offers one of the most advanced and easy-to-use data carving tools for the mobile forensic community. It captures/analyzes the mobile device's raw data and uses a database wizard to streamline the acquisition procedure, providing greater acquisition of "deleted" and "live" data that can be undetected with a logical file acquisition.

Table 1-1. *Specification for Seized iOS Phone*

Brand	iPhone	Model No.	Apple iPhone 8 TD-LTE (A1905)
IMEI1	123123123123	Color	White
Jailbroken	Yes.	SIM	Jawwal
Storage	64 GB	Phone lock	Yes (password:000000)
iOS Version	13.5.1	Battery Percentage	82%

Other Notes:

- available storage 42.5 GB.

- there is a break in the protection screen.

- the device was powered on.

- the suspect provided us the password with the search warrant, which is 000000.

Mobile photos:

attached with the report

Tools Used for Mobile Forensics in Examination Phase

iPhone Acquisition Using XRY

When we connect the iPhone to XRY, the devices are added and verified as shown in Figure 1-3.

Figure 1-3. *XRY main menu*

Then we choose the action we want (logical) and press "next"; after this stage we can choose if we want to jailbreak the phone to extract the deleted files, or just choose a logical acquisition to read the live mobile files as shown in Figure 1-4.

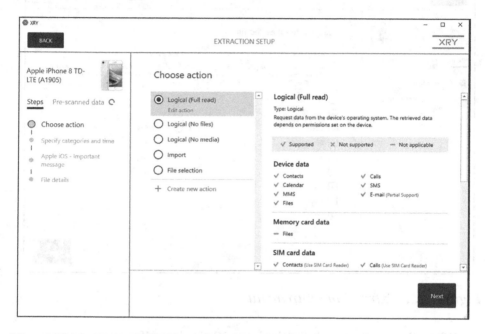

Figure 1-4. *Logical (full read acquisition)*

Now, we can choose what artifacts we want to search because of the privacy of the suspect. Figure 1-5 identifies what artifacts we can choose:

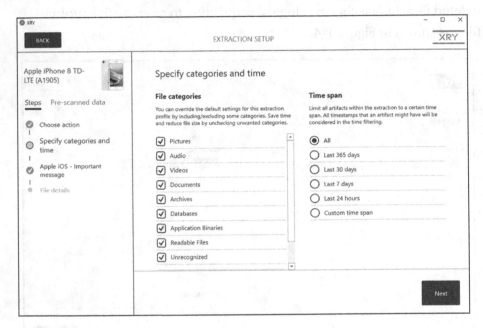

Figure 1-5. *Extraction setup menu*

When the acquisition is finished, the XRY asks us if we want to open with the XRY reader or the XAMN reader, and when we choose XAMN (one method), it will display this summary about our case as shown in Figure 1-6 for the extracted artifacts, and also, the recovered files and artifacts as shown Figure 1-7:

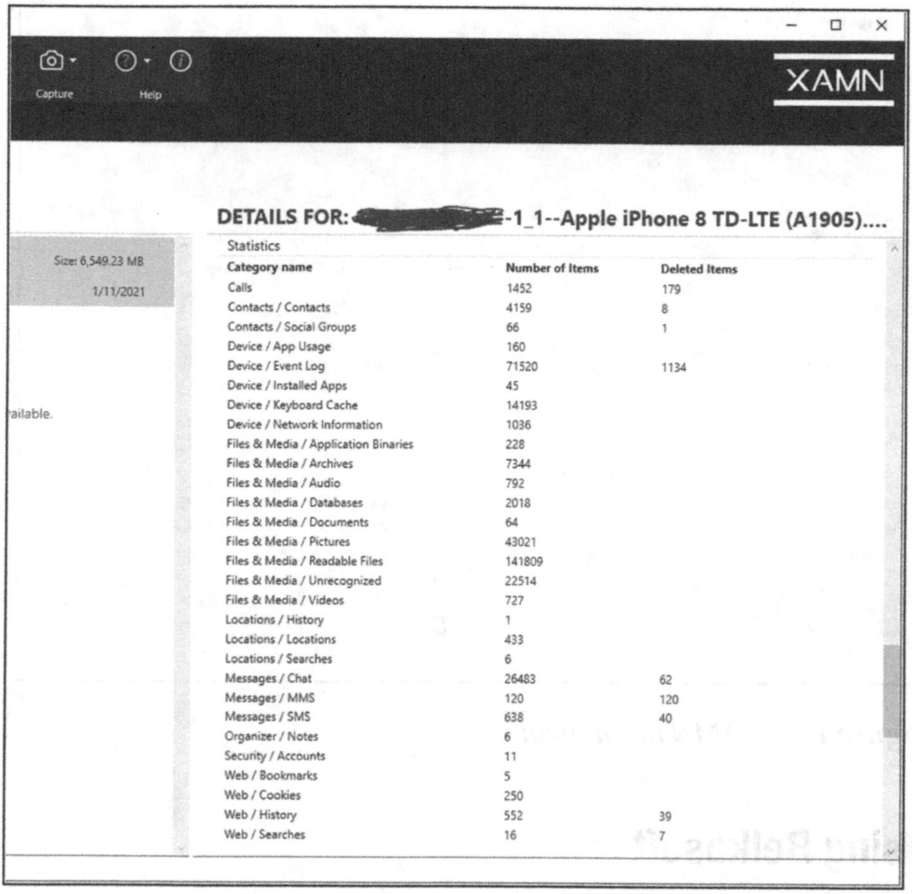

DETAILS FOR: ████████-1_1--Apple iPhone 8 TD-LTE (A1905)....

Statistics

Category name	Number of Items	Deleted Items
Calls	1452	179
Contacts / Contacts	4159	8
Contacts / Social Groups	66	1
Device / App Usage	160	
Device / Event Log	71520	1134
Device / Installed Apps	45	
Device / Keyboard Cache	14193	
Device / Network Information	1036	
Files & Media / Application Binaries	228	
Files & Media / Archives	7344	
Files & Media / Audio	792	
Files & Media / Databases	2018	
Files & Media / Documents	64	
Files & Media / Pictures	43021	
Files & Media / Readable Files	141809	
Files & Media / Unrecognized	22514	
Files & Media / Videos	727	
Locations / History	1	
Locations / Locations	433	
Locations / Searches	6	
Messages / Chat	26483	62
Messages / MMS	120	120
Messages / SMS	638	40
Organizer / Notes	6	
Security / Accounts	11	
Web / Bookmarks	5	
Web / Cookies	250	
Web / History	552	39
Web / Searches	16	7

Size: 6,549.23 MB

1/11/2021

Figure 1-6. XAMN summary

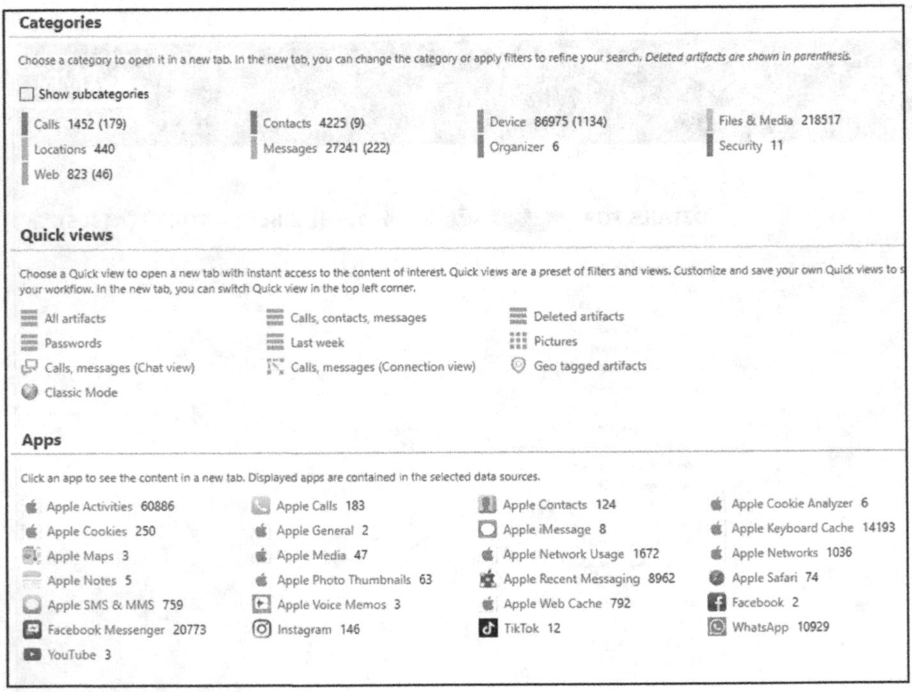

Figure 1-7. *XAMN main menu*

Using Belkasoft

Now we went to try the previous steps with the Belkasoft tool trying
to extract files and artifacts from the same iPhone (iPhone 8). In the
beginning, we tried to choose a full logical backup, but we got the problem
shown in Figure 1-8, which is what Belkasoft needs to make a jailbreak for
the phone with an external tool.

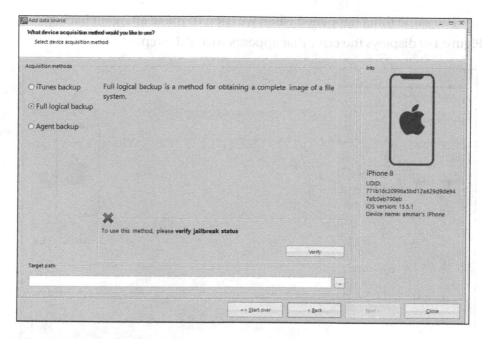

Figure 1-8. *Belkasoft full logical backup*

The same thing happened when we tried to make an Agent backup. Figure 1-9 displays the error that appears with this step:

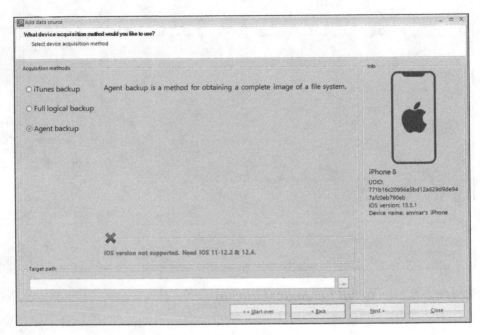

Figure 1-9. *Belkasoft Agent backup*

So, we finally chose the iTunes backup to get the extracted files shown in Figure 1-10.

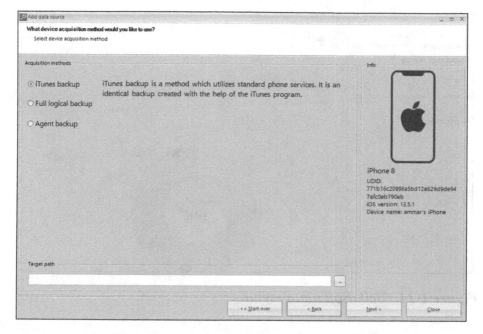

Figure 1-10. *Belkasoft iTunes backup*

As we see from the preceding figures, the Belkasoft tool could not recover deleted files from the selected phone, and the tool succeeded only in getting an iTunes acquisition. Figure 1-11 shows the results of the Belkasoft tool.

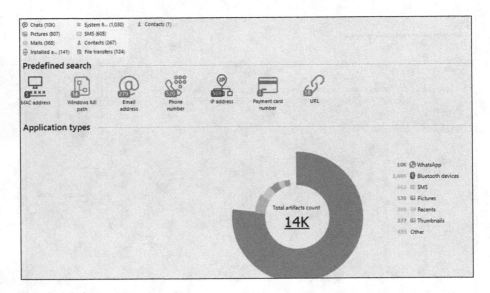

Figure 1-11. *Belkasoft main menu*

Using FINALMobile

Now we went to try the previous steps with the FINALMobile tool, trying to extract files and artifacts from the same iPhone (iPhone 8). FINALMobile succeeded in extracting files from the iPhone with logical image acquisition, but it also needed an external tool to jailbreak and get the deleted files, as shown in Figure 1-12 and Figure 1-13.

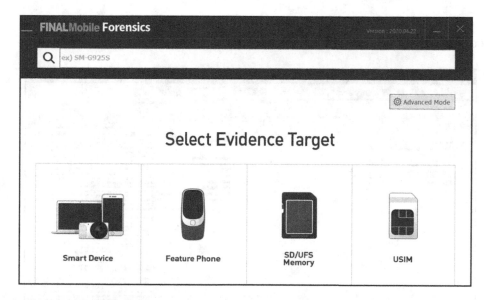

Figure 1-12. *FINALMobile main menu*

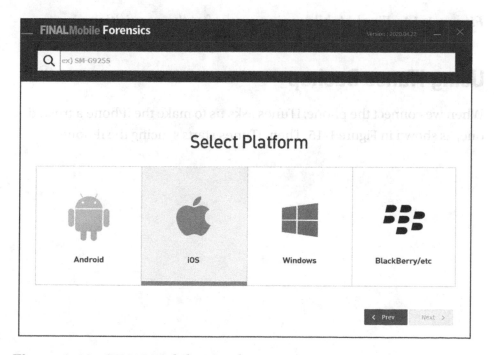

Figure 1-13. *FINALMobile OS selection*

Figure 1-14 shows the extracted artifacts from FINALMobile that contain the nondeleted files.

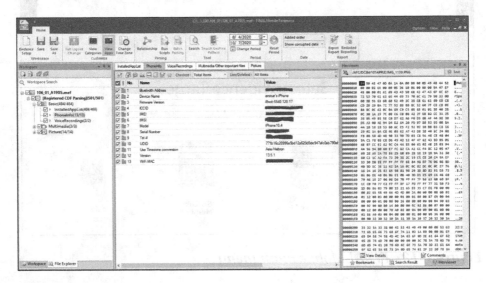

Figure 1-14. *Final Mobile main menu after the acquisition*

Using iTunes Backup

When we connect the phone, iTunes asks us to make the iPhone a trusted one, as shown in Figure 1-15. Then, iTunes starts syncing the iPhone:

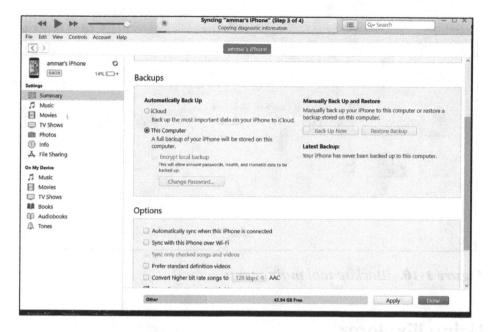

Figure 1-15. *iTunes backup*

Using iBackup

When we open the Backup using iBackup we get the data shown in
Figure 1-16.

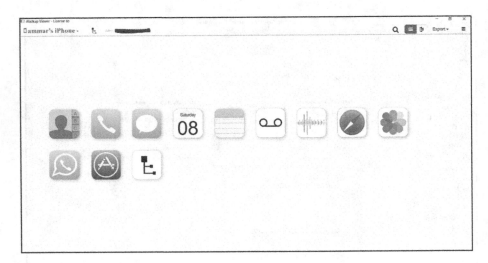

Figure 1-16. *iBackup tool main menu*

Using iExplorer

When we open the backup using iExplorer, we get the data shown in
Figure 1-17.

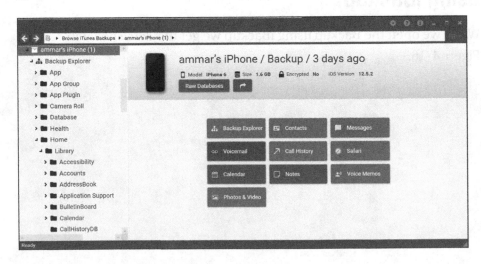

Figure 1-17. *iExplorer main menu*

SQLite Database

According to SQLite, XAMN and some other tools have an external SQLite viewer as shown next; we note that both Belkasoft and XRY can export the database and view it in DB viewer as shown in Figure 1-18.

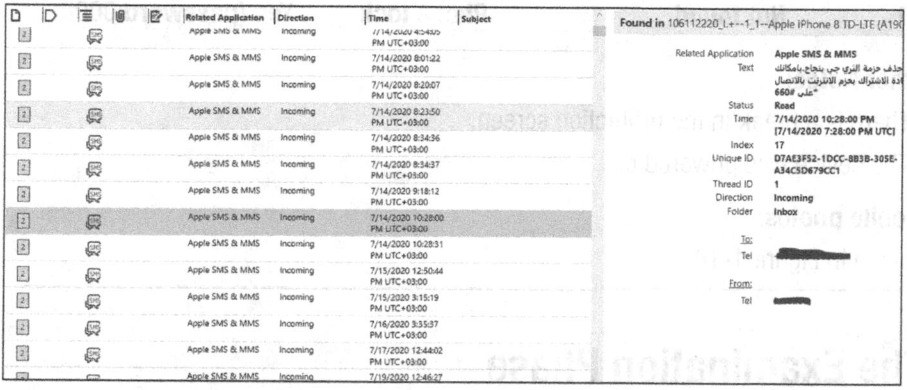

Figure 1-18. SQLite XAMN

Evidence Extraction Process for Android Mobile Phone

In this section, we performed the process of extracting data from an Android phone using multiple tools, after we rooted the device, as we rooted a Samsung Galaxy S7 phone, and we displayed the images and results obtained by using different tools.

The Collection Phase

The collection phase for Android devices describes the details used in our practical case as described in Table 1-2.

Table 1-2. *Seized Phone Specifications*

Brand	Samsung Galaxy S7	Model No.	SM-G930F
IMEI1	532587624892	Color	Gold
IMEI2	532587612891	SIM	Jaw*al
SD	Not found	Phone lock	Yes (password:0000)

Other Notes:

- There is a break in the protection screen.

- The device was powered on.

Mobile photos:

Shown in Figure 1-18.

The Examination Phase

In this section, we will introduce how to examine the mobile device for Android OS, to reach the desired goal of our practical case, which is to find challenges for the work of digital investigators. The first thing we want to root the device; Figure 1-19 shows the verified root for the Samsung S7 device.

Figure 1-19. *Unrooted Android device*

To make the root in this device, we use Odin3 software with a custom ROM for Samsung Galaxy S7 SM-G390F devices. After using Odin3, we get a rooted device as shown in Figure 1-20:

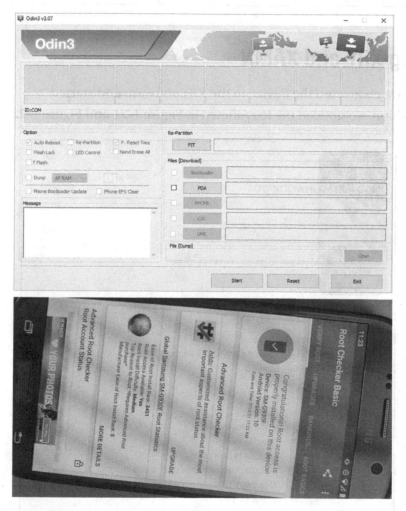

Figure 1-20. *Rooted device*

Note   When we root the device, a new firmware is installed on the device, all applications are gone, and a new ROM is also installed.

Using XRY and XAMN

When we connected the device to the XRY software and started acquisition, we noticed the logs shown in Figure 1-21 and Figure 1-22.

Figure 1-21. *General information about the device*

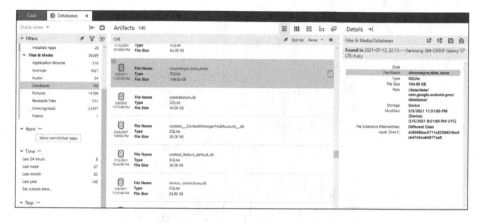

Figure 1-22. *Some of the databases found in the phone*

Using ADB Command

In this section, we will explain how to use the Platform tools shell to obtain a lot of information and data and access to the phone. Figure 1-23 shows many of the operations that can be done through this tool.

```
C:\platform-tools>adb.exe devices
List of devices attached
2b2a08ce9805    device
```

Figure 1-23. *Connected device in ADB shell*

Using FINALMobile

The investigator team can use FINALMobile, which includes a set of integrated tools such as file explorer and SQLite database within the main screen, as shown in Figure 1-24.

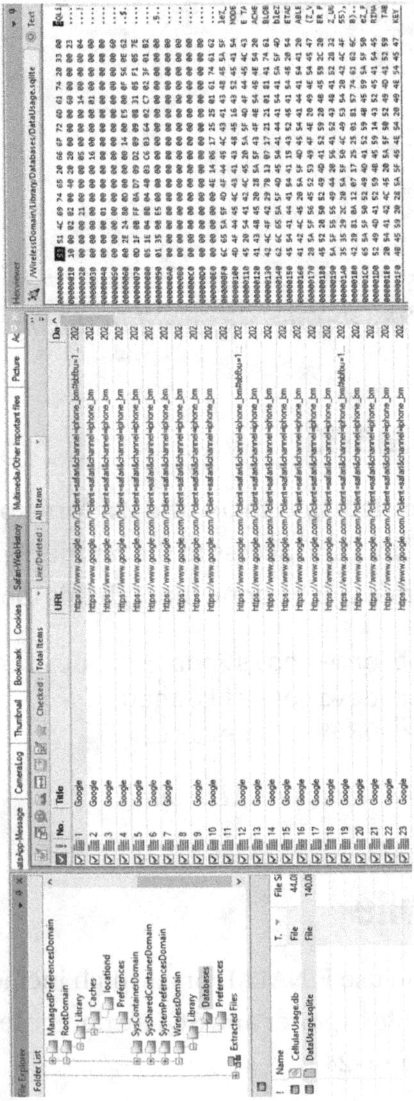

Figure 1-24. File explorer and SQLite database

Mobile Forensic Challenges on iOS and Android

Considering all the previously described software and tools and after testing various versions of iOS and Android devices, we can summarize most of the challenges we faced through our implementation and through extracting digital evidence from the devices: it can be said that the XRY tool is the only tool that was able to jailbreak the phone without using any external tool or external source. Moreover, the tool was able to extract and retrieve all the files that were deleted from the phone. As for the other tools, they were able to extract all the data and files from the device but were not able to recover the deleted files, as the Belkasoft tool requires the use and download of a tool to complete the work and extract and retrieve the deleted files. The others were able to extract the files on the "Logical Copy" phone without recovering the deleted files. Table 1-3 summarizes a comparison between the tools we used.

Table 1-3. Comparison between Tool Results for iOS Implementation

Used Tool	Logical Image	Required Jailbreak	Internal/external Jailbreak	Export Files	Deleted Files	View Hex Dump	Geolocation	Accounts
XRY	✓	✓	Internal	✓	✓	✓	✓	✓
Belkasoft	✓	✓	External	✓	✓	✓	✓	✓
Final Data	✓	✓	External	✓	✓	✓	✓	✓
iBackup	--	--	--	✓	--	✓	✓	✓
iExplorer	--	--	--	✓	--	✓	✓	✓
XAMN	--	--	--	✓	--	✓	✓	✓

Related to Android devices, we have used many tools to extract data for third-party applications and try to recover deleted data from phones. Table 1-4 represents a comparison between the applications that were used and retrieved some of the deleted data even though they needed to be rooted or not.

Table 1-4. Comparison between Tool Results for Android Implementation

Used Tool	Logical Image	Physical Image	Root Required	Export Files	Deleted Files	View Hex Dump	Geolocation	Accounts
XRY	✓	✓	✓	✓	✓	✓	✓	✓
Belkasoft	✓	✓	✓	✓	✓	✓	✓	✓
Final Data	✓	✓	✓	✓	✓	✓	✓	✓
ADB command	✓	✓	✓	✓	✓	✓	✓	✓
XAMN	--	--	--	✓	--	✓	✓	✓

Summary

In this chapter, we have introduced mobile forensics by using different programs and tools to acquire the data from iOS or Android devices for both rooted and jailbreak mobile; the XRY software tool ranked first in terms of its ability to recover deleted materials. As for the rest of the programs, although they were able to extract all the data from the phone, they were not able to retrieve deleted data because the iPhone has not been jailbroken. In addition, the XRY tool jailbreaks the phone without using any third-party software or tool. Rather, through the tool itself, the phone was successfully jailbroken, and all its data was retrieved and extracted. As for using other tools and programs, it requires jailbreaking the phone using external tools to be able to complete the extraction process.

References

[1]. Al-Dhaqm, A., Razak, S. A., Ikuesan, R. A., Kebande, V. R., & Siddique, K. (2020). A Review of Mobile Forensic Investigation Process Models. *IEEE Access*, 8(September), 173359–173375. https://doi. org/10.1109/ACCESS.2020.3014615

[2]. Anwar, N., & Riadi, I. (2017). Analisis Investigasi Forensik WhatsApp Messanger Smartphone Terhadap WhatsApp Berbasis Web. *Jurnal Ilmiah Teknik Elektro Komputer Dan Informatika*, 3(1), 1. https://doi.org/10.26555/jiteki.v3i1.6643

[3].   Kuittinen, T. (2013). Exclusive New Survey Shows
       BlackBerry's BBM Beating WhatsApp And SnapChat
       In Key Markets. Available at www.forbes.com/
       sites/terokuittinen/2013/11/26/exclusive-
       newsurvey-shows-blackberrys-bbm-beating-
       whatsapp-and-snapchat-in-keymarkets/
       #4a0055b92dd8

[4].   Riadi, I., Umar, R., & Firdonsyah, A. (2017).
       Identification Of Digital Evidence on Android's
       Blackberry Messenger Using NIST Mobile Forensic
       Method. *International Journal of Computer Science
       and Information Security, 15*(5), 3–8.

CHAPTER 2

Introduction to iOS Forensics

This chapter will provide you with an overview of iOS devices such as iPhones and iPads, as well as an overview of the operating systems and file systems they run. There are many forensic tools that are used in forensic science; these tools are able to handle all forensic process activities. Digital forensic tools for data extraction are categorized into three types: manual, logical, and physical. You will learn after completing this chapter about various third-party tools used for iOS forensics, and you will be able to answer questions about three important topics: the first topic aims to find the difference between acquisition and backup, the second measures and checks the effect of jailbreaking on an iOS device, and the third illustrates the comparison between third-party tools during forensic analysis process.

In this chapter and practical experiment, we will introduce an acquisition for iPhone 6s, and the focus will be on it, as it works on the iOS system. We will use the various forensic tools to try to take several copies of the iPhone 8, analyze the results that can be obtained and the data available from these tools, and see if it is possible to recover and extract the deleted files.

In this chapter, we will cover the following topics:

- iOS Boot Process

- iOS Architecture

© Mohammed Moreb 2022

M. Moreb, *Practical Forensic Analysis of Artifacts on iOS and Android Devices,*
https://doi.org/10.1007/978-1-4842-8026-3_2

- iOS Security

- iOS Data Extraction Techniques

- Understanding Jailbreaking

- Data Acquisition from iOS Devices

- Data Acquisition from iOS Backups

- iOS Forensic Tools

- iOS Data Analysis and Recovery

- Mobile Forensics Investigation Challenges on iOS

iOS Boot Process

The use of the mobile phone has become more common, so you can conduct your banking and money-related operations on it, which has prompted some people to hack phones to steal sensitive information. Therefore, forensic analysis is considered one of the important skills that an IT employee must have to be able to investigate the crimes committed in Palestine. There are laws to reduce, criminalize, and punish electronic crimes.

This chapter will use a real practical case study related to child pornography to introduce iOS forensics. Child pornography is regarded as a crime punishable under the law in Palestine and elsewhere in the world because it is an immoral act designated to sexually exploit children over the Internet, by which criminals send and receive photos and videos of children. This is a criminal offense.

The Palestinian Cybercrime Law, established in 2018, is based on the Jordanian Cybercrime Law, and it constitutes a line of defense and a deterrent to acts violating the law committed through the Internet using a computer, mobile phone, or any technological means, but there is a gap in the law as penalties and fines do not constitute a deterrent to criminals. In this chapter, we will present some laws related to the sexual exploitation of children and their punishment according to the Cybercrime Law in Palestine [1]. In addition to that, we will present some of the laws related to the sexual exploitation of children stipulated in the Electronic Crimes Law in Palestine, and we will also present a case study that some researchers will address related to the sexual exploitation of children via mobile phone.

Before testing the iPhone, it is necessary to identify the correct hardware model and firmware installed on the device. There are several ways in which you can identify the hardware for a device that is a tool that is a recommended libimobile device. The iPhone is a group of modules, chips, and electronics of various manufacturers. Because of the complexity of the iPhone, the list of hardware parts and internal components for each device is extensive.

iOS Architecture

In this practical case, we will start our investigation on iOS, known formally as the iPhone Operating System. Also, we have to know that the iOS is derived from Mac OS, which in turn is based on UNIX- OS. iOS was at the early stage of the development of a famous application, which is the iPod as the digital storage and application to run music. Later, the development became fast with very common applications like mail, in a browser known as Safari.

To start investigations in mobile, the investigators should have good knowledge of the architecture of the mobile systems. Figure 2-1 illustrates the architecture of the mobile, which consists of three main module layers: the presentation layer, which contains UI components; the business layer, which is composed of business entities and workflow; and the data layer, which contains data access components, data utilities, and service agents (mobile app architecture, e.g.). And it is important to differentiate between the iOS architecture and the Android architecture: although they are both operating systems that have the same architecture, they do have not the same functionality. Android works under Linux kernel, whereas iOS works under BSD-derived kernel, so both of them are Unix based.

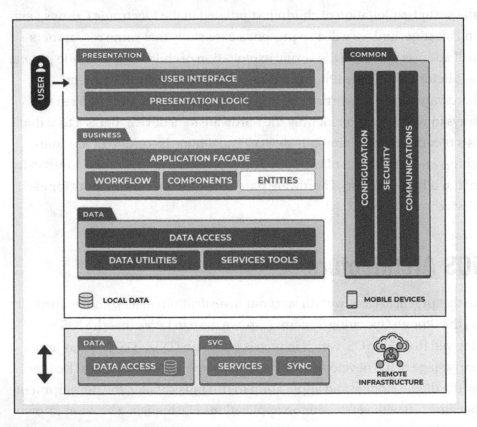

Figure 2-1. *iOS architecture*

iOS is the operating system that runs on a variety of Apple devices as illustrated in Figure 2-1, the iPhone being one of the most popular. In 2007, Apple debuted the iPhone, which revolutionized the smartphone market. It had a huge touch screen as well as remarkable technical characteristics, at least at the time. The Cocoa Touch library is used to develop iOS applications in Objective-C. Objective-C is a C language extension, whereas Cocoa Touch is a collection of classes. While the syntaxes of C# and Java (used for Android and Windows Phone development) are similar, the Objective-C library offers a unique option. Object-oriented programming is supported by Objective-C, as the name indicates. The language and platform have steadily improved over time, with the advent of ARC (Automatic Reference Counting) being a particularly notable advance. As a result of the automated memory management, the amount of boilerplate code was decreased, and memory leaks were minimized in general. A Mac machine is required for iOS development. Xcode is the most often used program for developing iOS apps. It comes with a robust editor, an analytical tool, an iOS emulator, and the SDK (Gronli, Hansen, Ghinea, & Younas, 2014).

As the operating system developed by Apple, iOS constitutes the primary platform for Apple mobile devices (Gyorödi, Zmaranda, Georgian, & Gyorödi, 2017). This system controls all services and parts of Apple devices. The iOS operating system was launched for the first time in 2007 with the launch of the first iPhone device, where the name of the operating system was OS X; the name was changed to iOS in 2010 (Aleem, 2019). The iOS operating system architecture has four layers: the core OS, core services, media, and the Cocoa Touch layer (Yates, 2010).

The iPhone is a collection of modules, chips, and electronic components from different manufacturers. Due to the complexities of the iPhone, the list of hardware components is extensive, and each device should be researched for internal components: for example, iPhone 11 has an A13 Bionic processor; storage (64 GB, 128 GB, or 256 GB); 4 GB of RAM; a 6.1-inch Liquid Retina liquid crystal display (LCD); and a dual-lens 12 MP, rear camera array. As with the iPhone, not all versions of the iPad are supported for file system acquisition; Apple changes data storage locations in iOS versions, which affects iPad devices as well, and so you must be aware of the different models, the released and currently installed iOS version, the storage capability, and the network access vectors. Internal images for all iPhones can be found in the teardown section of https://www.ifixit.com/Device/iPhone.

Just like the iPhone, the iPad is also a collection of modules, chips, and electronic components from different manufacturers. The internal images for all iPads can be found in the teardown section of `https://www.ifixit.com/Device/iPad`.

The iOS operating system acts as an intermediary between the applications running on the screen and the hardware components of the device. The iPhone has two partitions, the iOS system partition and the iOS data partition (Höne, Kröger, Luttenberger, & Creutzburg, 2012). The contents of the iOS system partition, which is used for the operating system and read-only for the user, may not be evidentiary, but it may be necessary to examine it (Höne et al., 2012). The iOS data partition is used as a read/write for the user and the applications so the evidence can be acquired from this partition (Höne et al., 2012). iOS performs its roles through four layers (Aleem, 2019), as shown in Figure 2-1.

iOS Architecture Layers

1. **Cocoa Touch Layer:** The top layer of the iOS architecture, this layer consists of a set of basic frameworks for developing the visual interface and providing the basic infrastructure for applications on the iOS system such as touch, multitouch, input services and processes, and high-level tasks (Aleem, 2019).

    2. **Media Layer:** This application consists of basic multimedia frameworks such as audio, video, and graphics. This layer provides an aided environment for programmers to create applications with a distinctive graphic appearance (Aleem, 2019).

    3. **Core Service Layer:** This layer works to provide the basic services required for applications on the system, such as location services, communication services, and iCloud services (Rupesh, 2017).

4. Core OS Layer: This layer is located directly above the device's hardware, and it deals with basic, low-level functions in the device, such as memory management, file system, communication, and networking (Aleem, 2019).

The iOS system enjoys high protection, and with the development of this system, the protection from the company has increased to the point that Apple offers huge rewards every period for those who can penetrate this system and find a loophole in it. If this indicates something, it indicates the extent of Apple's confidence in its system and the level of protection it has in it.

The HFS Plus and APFS File Systems

To accommodate the storage of large datasets, Apple has developed a new file system, HFS, as illustrated in Figure 2-2. The HFS Plus file system supports larger sizes of files, and the HFS Plus volume includes a number of internal structures for data management. The volume of HFS Plus contains a multilayer of internal structures that are used to manage the organization of data. Such structures include header, an alternate header, and five special files: the allocation file, the extents overflow file, the catalog file, the attributes file, and the startup file. Of these five files, three (extents overflow file, catalog file, and attributes file) use the B-Tree structure.

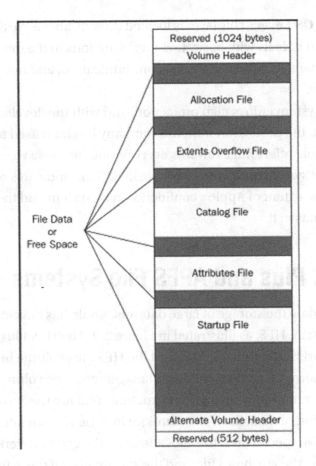

Figure 2-2. iOS file system

Assume that a law enforcement official legally seizes a certain number of suspicious smartphones during a criminal investigation, which could be analyzed on smartphones using child pornography. The difficulty of identifying and verifying the existence of hidden child pornography on any particular phone is increasing as a result of the ever-increasing number of smartphones and law enforcement files [1]. Some of the forensic equipment on the market is currently being researched. Although many human interventions and manual tasks are required to limit the efficiency of crime scene evidence collection, the Access Data Forensic Toolkit and Guidance Encase are primarily used for collecting information from storage devices. The most common tools for analyzing and detecting nude images are the Paraben Porn Detection Stick and the SDK (Software Analyzer) [2].

The iPhone APFS is a state-of-the-art file system for iOS, macOS, tvOS, and watchOS. It is basically a 64-bit file system that supports over 9 quintillion files on one single volume. APFS is structured in one single container that may contain one or more volumes. Every structure of the APFS file system begins with a block header. The BH starts with a checksum (used Fletcher's checksum algorithm). The entire block also contains the version of a copy-on-write block, the block ID, and the block type.

iOS Security

Apple iOS devices, like iPhone, iPod, and iPad, have been designed with several layers of security. The low-level security layer consists of hardware features that safeguard from malicious attacks, and the high-level security layer protects OS features from unauthorized access and use. Features provided in the following image are considered the main iOS security features:

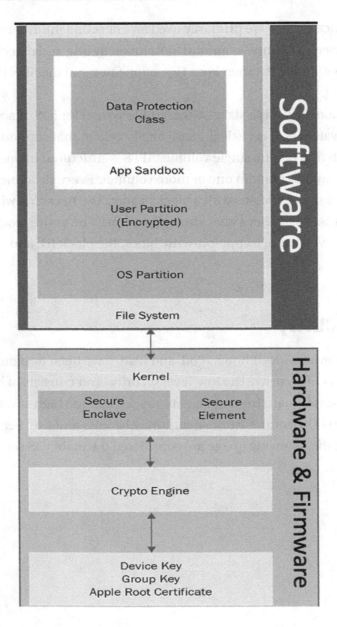

- **Passcodes, Touch ID, and Face ID**

  - iOS 9 released the option to use a six-digit simple passcode instead of the legacy four-digit option.

- **Code signing:** prevents users from downloading and installing unauthorized applications on the device.

- **Sandboxing:** post-code-execution exploitation by placing the application into a tightly restricted area.

- **Encryption:**

  - On iOS devices (starting with the iPhone 4), the entire file system is encrypted with a file system key, which is computed from the device's unique hardware key. This key is stored in effaceable storage, which exists between the OS and hardware levels of the device.

  - This is the reason that Joint Test Action Group (JTAG) and chip-off methods are not useful acquisition methods, as the entire data dump will be encrypted.

- **Data protection:** designed to protect data at rest and to make offline attacks difficult, hardware encryption, strong encryption key.

- **Address Space Layout Randomization (ASLR):** introduced with iOS 4.3. ASLR randomizes the application object's location in the memory, making it difficult to exploit the memory corruption vulnerabilities.

- **Privilege separation:**

  - iOS runs with the principle of least privilege (PoLP). It contains two user roles: root and mobile.

47

- The most important processes in the system run with root user privileges.

- All other applications to which the user has direct access, such as the browser and third-party applications, run with mobile user privileges.

- **Stack-smashing protection:** protects the device against buffer overflow attacks by placing a random and known value (called a stack canary) between a buffer and the control data on the stack.

- **Data Execution Prevention (DEP):** portions of memory that are executable code from data.

- **Data wiping:** erase all content and settings

- **Activation Lock**

iOS provides advanced security features, many of which are enabled by default; users don't need to perform extensive configurations. The key security features are not configurable, so users cannot disable them by mistake. The security features that will be addressed in this study are the code signing and privilege separation features, which get affected by jailbreaking an iPhone.

Code signing: the process by which a compiled iOS application is sealed and users are assured that it is from a known source and has not been tampered with since it was last signed with a certificate issued by Apple. This would prevent Apple users from downloading and installing unauthorized applications on jailed iPhone devices.

Privilege separation: "iOS runs with the principle of least privilege (PoLP). It contains two user roles: root and mobile. The most important processes in the system run with root user privileges. All other applications to which the user has direct access, such as the browser and third-party applications, run with mobile user privileges".

iOS Data Extraction Techniques

Identifying the device model helps forensic examiners to choose the appropriate forensic tool and methods of data acquisition. It is about digitally imaging the mobile device and getting the information from it and its related storage locations. Three main acquisition methods are available for mobile devices: manual, logical, and physical, or file system for iOS.

1. Manual Data Extraction: This method is navigating the device as a normal user and taking screenshots of the found evidence. It is not a recommended acquisition method since it involves a high risk of human errors. This might affect the evidence state by accidental deletion of or changes to data. This is a very simple process and shows only what is seen on the device. Can be used only to validate the previous methods' outcomes in some cases.

2. Logical Data Extraction: Logical acquisition is the second-best recommended acquisition method. It involves copying what the user has access to on their mobile, which means that it is equivalent to iTunes backup. This method requires the device to be unlocked. This method provides readable data, unlike some encrypted parts in the physical image. Recovering data from unallocated space is limited to data recovery from unallocated SQLite records.

3. Physical Data Extraction: This is the best-recommended acquisition method. The copying process in this method includes the device storage and the file system. The copying is done on the bits level acquiring all data. This includes deleted data

and the ability to access the unallocated space.
Physical acquisition is not useful for iPhone 5s and
later. This is due to the Secure Enclave hardware
feature in Apple devices. It provides an additional
layer of security by its isolation from the main
processor. This security mechanism keeps the user
data encrypted even if the OS is compromised.
This is the reason why physical acquisition will not
be useful for iOS devices since the iPhone 5s. File
system acquisition now is used for iOS devices.
File system acquisition for iOS devices requires a
jailbroken device. Applying a jailbreaking technique
on the device will change the original data on the
device. Jailbreaking is not a reversible change.

Data Acquisition from Backup Devices

Copying the whole contents of a file system to a backup medium is
the easiest technique to secure a file system against disk failures or file
corruption. A full backup is a name given to the generated archive. A file
system can be recreated from a full backup onto a new disk if it is lost later
due to a disk failure. It is also possible to recover individual files that have
been misplaced. Full backups have two drawbacks: reading and writing
the complete file system takes a long time, and keeping a copy of the file
system takes up a lot of storage space on the backup media.

An incremental backup strategy replicates just those files that have
been created or updated since the last backup, resulting in faster and
smaller backups. Because only a tiny fraction of files change on any given
day, incremental backups are smaller. A common incremental backup
strategy combines complete backups with regular incremental backups.
In an incremental backup system, restoring a deleted file or an entire file

system takes longer; recovery may entail examining a chain of backup files, starting with the most recent complete backup, and applying changes recorded in one or more incremental backups. Backup is a method of backing up a device's contents, which includes only the files currently loaded on the device and excludes deleted files. Logical acquisition is the name of this procedure (Chervenak, 1998). Most of these products have been operating independently, and no forensic tool provides more than a technical framework for detecting child pornography. Through careful education, log analysis, file names, and cell location analysis, the proposed design model proposes a method for automatically collecting and processing image films on smartphones to detect child pornography images quickly. This will reduce the amount of human intervention and handling of materials collected and processed by law enforcement officers, as well as speed up investigations.

WhatsApp Messenger is the world's most popular multiplatform instant messaging app, allowing users to exchange text, images, video, and audio for free. The Jamaican police, for example, use WhatsApp to prevent child exploitation via social media. Before law enforcement can determine which CSA images are stored on suspicious smartphones, the logical flow of image creation, dispatch, and deletion in WhatsApp must be understood [1]. This practical case was carried out using two iPhones as depicted in Figure 2-3.

(1).   Phone A: Unjailbroken iPhone 4S (iOS 8.4.1).

(2).   Phone B: Jailbreak iPhone 5S (iOS 9.3.3).

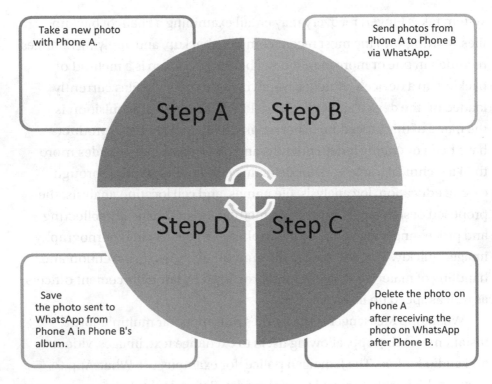

Figure 2-3. Steps for iOS investigation

Later, the two phones will be double-checked to see whether images were still stored in a media archive via WhatsApp using the four following steps:

- Step A: Take a new photo with Phone A.

- Step B: Send photos from Phone A to Phone B via WhatsApp.

- Step C: Delete the photo on Phone A after receiving the photo on WhatsApp Phone B.

- Step D: Save the photo sent to WhatsApp from Phone A in Phone B's album.

Identification by automatic CSA image recognition of child pornography files has been demonstrated in practice. As shown in Figure 2-3, the four steps allow the investigator to quickly analyze the crime scene and identify the main steps to investigate illegal images or actions using cell phones for the following evidence:

- Acquiring a physical image of an Android device

- Imaging the memory card

- Create the disk image: dd image of memory

- Recovered documents

- Examination of memory

Data Acquisition from iOS Devices

This section introduces the data acquisition and analysis of the Result using two tools: Belkasoft Evidence Center (BEC) and Magnet Axiom. BEC is an all-in-one forensic system for obtaining, finding, extracting, searching, analyzing, storing, and sharing digital evidence saved on mobile and computer devices, as well as in RAM and the cloud. It may extract digital evidence from a variety of sources, with the most forensically significant artifacts being chosen for the investigator to study, study further, and report on. For a thorough analysis, this tool searches for hidden places and encrypted information, as well as carving out damaged or destroyed data. BEC is capable of completing the following tasks:

- obtaining a device, RAM, or cloud forensically;

- examining the device's file system, deleted data, and unique locations;

- conducting communication, documents, and media searches;

- locating items that were removed on purpose;

- detecting implicit traces if artifacts are robustly eliminated;

- locating and decrypting encrypted data;

- thoroughly examining the SQLite database.

In our case study, a child pornography viewer was sent a child pornographic image from the computer using WhatsApp web to iPhone 6s; the user of the iPhone downloaded the image and then deleted it. We are trying to investigate if mobile digital forensics tools can recover this image, and evaluating this tool based on the result we additionally found that we could also use SQLite to see deleted records, since a backup was taken from this iPhone using iTunes software, after the image was deleted. Information about the device is described in Table 2-1.

Table 2-1. *Specification for Seized iOS Phone*

Brand	iPhone	Model No.	Apple iPhone 6s
IMEI1	123123123222	Color	White
Jailbroken	No.	SIM	Jawwal
Storage	32 GB	Phone lock	Yes (password:00000)
iOS Version	11	Battery Percentage	72%

Other Notes:

- The device was powered on.
- the suspect provided us the password with the search warrant, which is 00000.
- Height: 5.44 inches (138.3 mm)
- Width: 2.64 inches (67.1 mm)
- Depth: 0.28 inch (7.1 mm)
- Weight: 5.04 ounces (143 grams)

Touch ID:

Fingerprint sensor built into the Home button.

The following are the steps to create a backup of iPhone 6s using iTunes. First, connect the iPhone to your computer using the cable. Second, unlock iPhone by typing the passcode to access the phone. Third, open iTunes and click on backup. There will be two options: encrypted backup and unencrypted backup. The encrypted backup will encrypt the data with a private key and password, and additional information will be retrieved such as WIFI setting. In this chapter, we have done an unencrypted backup since we are interested in images and deleted images. Fourth, after the backup is done, the file of the backup will found in the backup folder as shown in Figure 2-4.

| dc6cf27ae2a61c1b00cc58d2fbfce38a02b0... | 6/11/2021 06:33 PM | File folder |

Figure 2-4. *Backup file*

Jailbreaking

Jailbreaking simply means removing limitations imposed by Apple's mobile OS through the use of software and hardware exploits; this will permit unsigned code to run and gain root access on the OS. The most common reason for jailbreaking is to expand the limited feature set imposed by Apple's App Store and to install unapproved apps.

Jailbreaking can aid in forensic acquisition but will void the user's warranty, potentially brick the device, and may not support being restored to the factory settings. Table 2-2 summarizes many publicly available jailbreaking tools such as Cydia, Pangu, TaiG, Electra, and UncOver, and specifies the recommended tool according to the device you have with iOS version.

Table 2-2. *Jailbreak Tool According to the Device Model and iOS Version*

Version	Release date	Tool
iOS 1.0	June 29, 2007	(no name)
iOS 2.0	July 11, 2008	PwnageTool
iOS 3.0	June 17, 2009	PwnageTool
iOS 4.0	June 21, 2010	PwnageTool
iOS 5.0	October 12, 2011	redsn0w
iOS 6.0	September 19, 2012	redsn0w
iOS 7.0 - 7.0.6	September 18, 2013	evasiOn7
iOS 7.1 - 7.1.2	May 29, 2014	Pangu
iOS 8.0 - 8.1	September 17, 2014	Pangu8
iOS 8.1.1 - 8.4	November 17, 2014	TaiG, PP Jailbreak
iOS 8.4.1	August 13, 2015	EtasonIB
iOS 9.0	September 16, 2015	Pangu9
iOS 9.1	October 21, 2015	Pangu9
iOS 9.3.5	August 25, 2016	Phoenix
iOS 10.0 - 10.1.1	September 13, 2016	Yalu
iOS 11.0 - 11.1.2	September 19, 2017	LiberiOS, Electra1112
iOS 11.0 - 11.4.1	July 7, 2018	Electra1131
iOS 11.0 - 11.4.1	October 14, 2018	UncOver
iOS 12.0 - 12.2, 12.4 - 12.4.2	September 17, 2019	Chimera, UncOver

Steps for Boot-Based Jailbreak

1. Download appropriate iOS firmware image from Apple (called IPSW)

2. Download jailbreak software

3. Connect iDevice to computer via USB

4. Launch the jailbreak app on the computer

5. On the computer, select the IPSW file

6. Put iDevice into Device Firmware Update (DFU) mode

7. Wait

8. Jailbroken iThings now have Cydia.

iOS Forensic Tools

This is a set of tools available for the forensics investigation process, such as iTunes, iBackup viewer, and XRY. Each of the tools can work for a specific task or set of tasks, and Table 2-3 summarizes the forensic tools related to iOS devices.

Table 2-3. *Forensic Tools Comparison Related to iOS Work*

Forensic Tool	Purpose/Use	Results
BEC	Logical acquisition and database opening	Acquisition succeeded, database file opened and examined
Magnet Axiom	Logical acquisition and database opening	Succeeded
Mobiledit Forensic Express	Logical acquisition	No valuable results
iBackup Viewer	Data extraction from backup	Data have been extracted
Elcomsoft Phone Viewer	Viewing backup artifacts	Artifacts were viewed
DB Browser	Viewing and analyzing database files	Db files were viewed and analyzed

iOS Data Analysis and Recovery Using Belkasoft Tool

Now we are ready to use one of the most common mobile forensics tools called Belkasoft; it has SQLite integrated with this tool so we need to install SQLite separately. First, we create a case as shown in Figure 2-5.

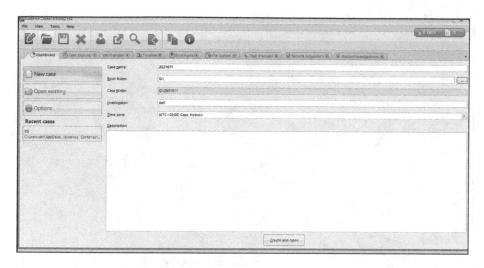

Figure 2-5. *Create case by Belkasoft*

Second, we select the folder that was created by iTunes (backup folder in Figure 2-3) as shown in Figure 2-6.

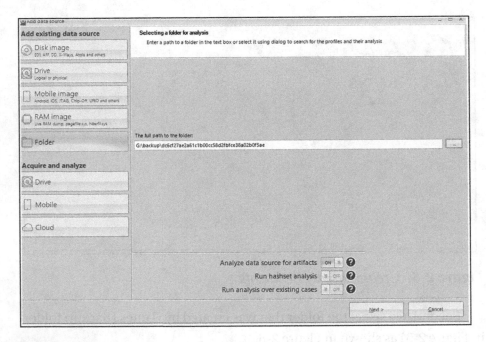

Figure 2-6. *Choose the backup folder*

Third, we select a set of artifacts to investigate as shown in Figure 2-7.

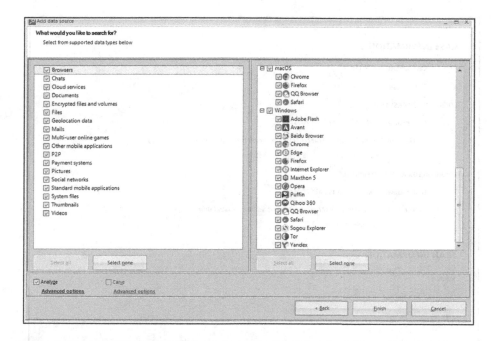

Figure 2-7. *Belkasoft artifact*

Fourth, after analyzing the artifacts on Belkasoft for "Child-pn", which is a child pornographic image, the result we get using this tool indicated that the image was not found.

iOS Data Analysis and Recovery Using Axiom Tool

The second tool is Magnet Axiom; it's a common tool used for mobile forensics. First, create a case using Magnet Axiom: the case number is 2021116, as shown in Figure 2-8.

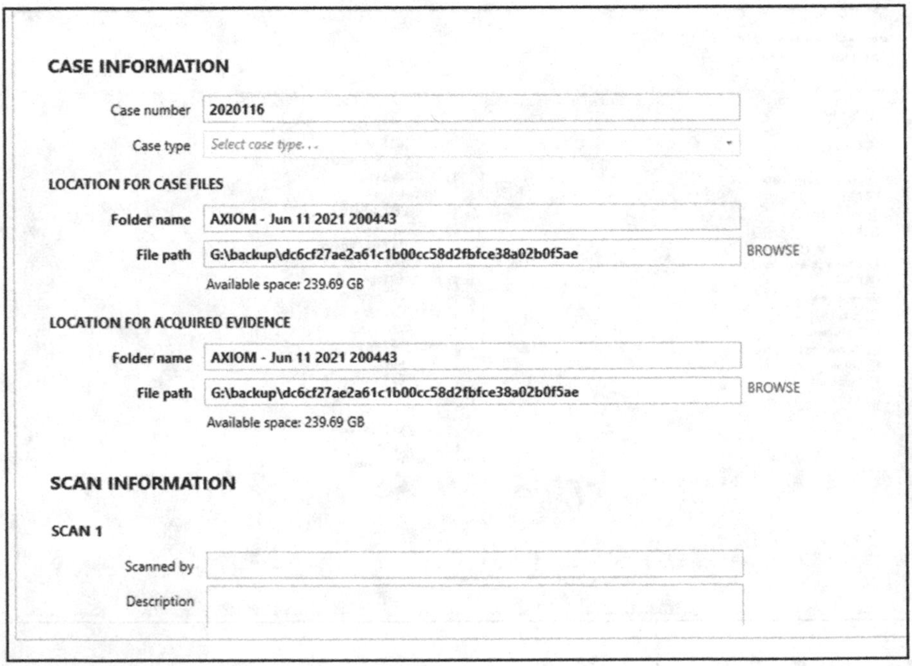

CASE INFORMATION

Case number   2020116

Case type   *Select case type...*

LOCATION FOR CASE FILES

Folder name   AXIOM - Jun 11 2021 200443

File path   G:\backup\dc6cf27ae2a61c1b00cc58d2fbfce38a02b0f5ae   BROWSE

Available space: 239.69 GB

LOCATION FOR ACQUIRED EVIDENCE

Folder name   AXIOM - Jun 11 2021 200443

File path   G:\backup\dc6cf27ae2a61c1b00cc58d2fbfce38a02b0f5ae   BROWSE

Available space: 239.69 GB

SCAN INFORMATION

SCAN 1

Scanned by

Description

Figure 2-8. *Create case using Axiom*

Second, choose artifact (what is important in our case study is images) as shown in Figure 2-9.

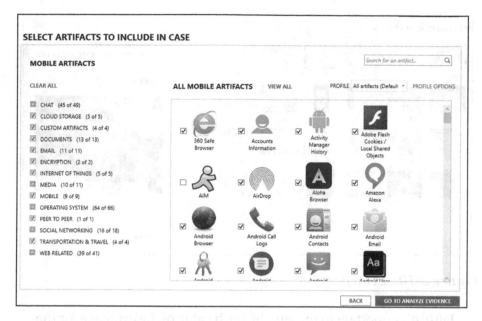

Figure 2-9. *Axiom artifact*

Third, after analyzing all artifacts, we checked the images, and fortunately we found the evidence, which is a child pornographic image as shown in Figure 2-10.

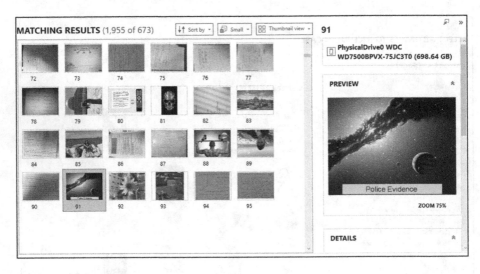

Figure 2-10. *Evidence*

Fifth, it's important to present the hash value of the evidence for the purpose of integrity, as shown in Figure 2-11.

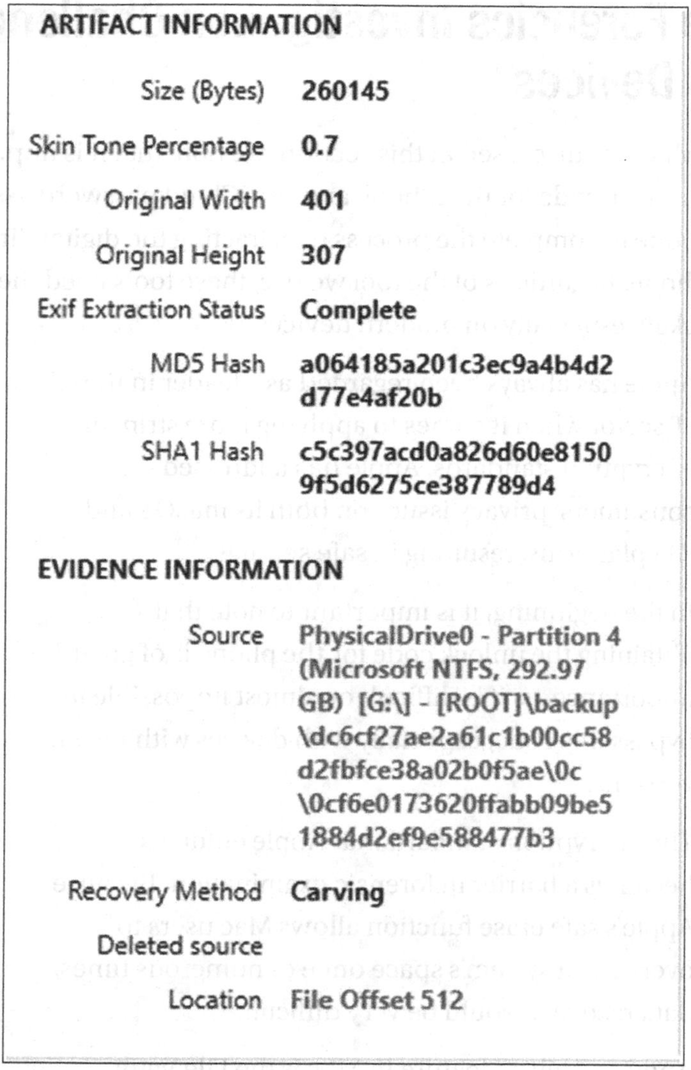

ARTIFACT INFORMATION

Size (Bytes)	**260145**
Skin Tone Percentage	**0.7**
Original Width	**401**
Original Height	**307**
Exif Extraction Status	**Complete**
MD5 Hash	**a064185a201c3ec9a4b4d2 d77e4af20b**
SHA1 Hash	**c5c397acd0a826d60e8150 9f5d6275ce387789d4**

EVIDENCE INFORMATION

Source	**PhysicalDrive0 - Partition 4 (Microsoft NTFS, 292.97 GB) [G:\] - [ROOT]\backup \dc6cf27ae2a61c1b00cc58 d2fbfce38a02b0f5ae\0c \0cf6e0173620ffabb09be5 1884d2ef9e588477b3**
Recovery Method	**Carving**
Deleted source	
Location	**File Offset 512**

Figure 2-11. Hash value

Mobile Forensics Investigation Challenges on iOS Devices

Based on what was discussed in this section, we note that it is important to obtain the unlock code for the iPhone and the iCloud password associated with the phone to complete the process of extracting the digital directory from the phone. Regardless of the tool we use, these tools need the phone to be unlocked, especially on modern devices.

1. Apple has always been regarded as a leader in the IT sector when it comes to applying more stringent encryption standards. Apple has addressed consumers' privacy issues on both its macOS and iOS platforms, resulting in safe settings.

2. In the beginning, it is important to note that obtaining the unlock code for the phone is of great importance, as it is difficult or almost impossible to bypass this code, especially with devices with recent versions.

3. The encryption standard that Apple enforces becomes a barrier in forensic examination. Because Apple's safe erase function allows Mac users to overwrite a system's space once or numerous times, data recovery would be very difficult.

4. Another built-in feature in Mac is the File Vault, which gives users a safe and secure place to keep their data. The File Vault can only be opened if the encryption is broken or if the password is obtained. Forensic investigators have no access to the data stored in the File Vault unless it is deactivated.

5. Finally, users can back up their device data to
    Apple's iCloud platform. Every iCloud user is
    granted an account. They may use their Apple
    ID to sync, upload, and retrieve data from the
    iCloud, including all of their Mac products, like the
    MacBook, iPhone, and iPad.

6. If a forensic investigator can get the Apple ID and
    password, they will have access to all information
    and data connected with all synced devices
    (Reddy, 2019).

Summary

With the first-generation iPhone in June 2007, iPhone forensics became
more challenging when it comes to dealing with file system forensic
acquisition methods, as there is no method or tool available to physically
recover data from these devices unless they are jailbroken, while the
logical acquisition can be obtained if the iPhone is unlocked.

Axiom and Belkasoft are two of the best and most powerful programs
in the process of forensic analysis of mobile phones; they both support
mobile phones and computers, and this is a good thing. The Belkasoft
can retrieve about 700 artifacts. It is easy to use, and it has an easy-to-use
scripting module you can write your scripts with, but it is not free and the
price may be high. As for Axiom, it can recover about 500 different artifacts
and is also not free, but a trial version is available. Axiom is a consumer of
computer resources, and it is generally slow and does not respond quickly.
In this case, we chose the Belkasoft program for speed because we are at
the airport, and we only have two hours. We want a fairly fast program.
What is important in our case study is that Belkasoft failed in retrieving
deleted images that were downloaded using WhatsApp, in contrast to

Magnet Axiom, which successfully retrieved the child pornographic images. Magnet Axiom used a carving method to retrieve the images; this method also exists in Belkasoft but can't be applied for some reason.

In the end, the Axiom program showed its superiority over Belkasoft, although it was somewhat slow. It succeeded in recovering the deleted image, and it was able to recover the deleted image on the iOS system without jailbreaking.

Practical Lab 2.1

In this lab, the investigator will learn how to connect iOS devices with workstations and identify the iPhone model and its iOS version for the connected device, by applying the following steps:

1. Download the libimobiledevice library to access iOS devices with the latest binaries from the following link: `https://www.quamotion.mobi/`.

2. Unzip the archive with x86 or x64 binaries, depending on your workstation's version.

3. Open the command prompt and change the directory to the one with binaries (use the cd command for this).

Connect the iPhone to your workstation using a universal serial bus (USB) cable (for the latest iOS versions, the passcode is also required), and run the ideviceinfo command with the -s option (*$ ideviceinfo -s*), as shown in Figure 2-12.

```
C:\Users\0136\Desktop\binaries\libimobiledevice.1.2.1-r419-win-x64>ideviceinfo.exe -s
BasebandCertId: 524245983
BasebandKeyHashInformation:
 AKeyStatus: 64
 SKeyStatus: 2
BasebandSerialNumber: sHODAZgntV0AAAAA
BasebandVersion: 1.02.14
BoardId: 4
BuildVersion: 17B84
CPUArchitecture: arm64e
ChipID: 32816
DeviceClass: iPhone
DeviceColor: 1
DeviceName: OlegтAЩs iPhone
DieID: 8563692629688366
HardwareModel: N104AP
HasSiDP: true
PartitionType: GUID_partition_scheme
ProductName: iPhone OS
ProductType: iPhone12,1
ProductVersion: 13.2
ProductionSOC: true
ProtocolVersion: 2
SupportedDeviceFamilies[1]:
 0: 1
TelephonyCapability: true
UniqueChipID: 8563692629688366
UniqueDeviceID: 00008030-001E6CA21128802E
WiFiAddress: f8:87:f1:f2:b0:78
```

Figure 2-12. *ideviceinfo command output*

References

[1]. L. Abu Arram and M. Moreb, "Cyber Security In
      Mobile Apps And User CIA," 2021 International
      Conference on Information Technology (ICIT), 2021,
      pp. 7–12, doi: 10.1109/ICIT52682.2021.9491657.

[2]. Gronli, T. M., Hansen, J., Ghinea, G., & Younas,
      M. (2014). Mobile Application Platform
      Heterogeneity: Android vs Windows Phone vs
      iOS vs Firefox OS. *Proceedings - International
      Conference on Advanced Information Networking
      and Applications, AINA*, 635–641. https://doi.
      org/10.1109/AINA.2014.78

[3]. Gyorödi, R., Zmaranda, D., Georgian, V., &
      Gyorödi, C. (2017). A Comparative Study between
      Applications Developed for Android and
      iOS. *International Journal of Advanced Computer
      Science and Applications, 8*(11). `https://doi.`
      `org/10.14569/ijacsa.2017.081123`

[4]. Höne, T., Kröger, K., Luttenberger, S., & Creutzburg,
      R. (2012). iPhone Examination with Modern
      Forensic Software Tools. *Mobile Multimedia/
      Image Processing, Security, and Applications
      2012, 8406*(May), 84060R. `https://doi.`
      `org/10.1117/12.921453`

[5]. Reddy, N. (2019). *Practical Cyber Forensics.*
      `https://doi.org/10.1007/978-1-4842-4460-9`

[6]. Rupesh. (2017). *iOS Layered Architecture*, 1 Jan.
      1970, `https://codeingwithios.blogspot.`
      `com/2017/09/ios-layered-architecture.html`.

[7]. Yates, M. (2010). Practical Investigations of
      Digital Forensics Tools for Mobile Devices.
      *Proceedings of the 2010 Information Security
      Curriculum Development Annual Conference,
      InfoSecCD'10*, 156–162. `https://doi.`
      `org/10.1145/1940941.1940972`

CHAPTER 3

Introduction to Android Forensics

This chapter will cover everything you need to know about practical forensics on Android devices. We will start by learning about the Android platform and its file system and then cover the topics of setup, acquisition, extraction, and recovery. We will also learn how to connect devices using ADB tools and back them up and how to use SQLite files for the acquisition process.

Recently, smartphones have developed tremendously; in each period of development, a new company has appeared to enter the global market competition to impose itself, and this is directly proportional to the emergence of new applications every day for various devices. In addition, the field of cyber security has several aspects, including smartphones; especially with the exploitation of the huge number of users, many immoral hackers have been greedy to exploit these applications for their interests, either theft, destruction, plagiarism, or many others. This chapter shows how these applications are exploited, especially in Android devices; how to explore the backups; how the company Evina found some apps that used phishing attacks to steal users' accounts using a quantitative methodology; and data analysis and results from the Android presentation.

© Mohammed Moreb 2022
M. Moreb, *Practical Forensic Analysis of Artifacts on iOS and Android Devices*,
https://doi.org/10.1007/978-1-4842-8026-3_3

In this chapter, we will cover the following topics:

- Understanding Android

- Application Framework

- Android Runtime

- HarmonyOS

- Linux Kernel

- Android Forensic Setup and Pre-Data Extraction Techniques

- Android Data Extraction Techniques

- Android Data Analysis and Recovery

- Android App Rooting Process and Techniques

Introduction

Increasingly, many devices do much more than receive a telephone call occasionally. These devices are becoming more and more capable, and the number of people using them has increased accordingly. With the increasing availability of these powerful devices, criminals can also use this technology. Criminals might use smartphones for several activities, such as email fraud, textual harassment, trafficking in child pornography, communication for narcotics trafficking, and so on. Analysts can be extremely helpful in the investigation by storing data on smartphones. Mobile equipment already shows a large amount of data connected to a person with a basic telephone history, contact information, and text information; even more useful information such as email, browser history, and chat logs is provided by smartphones. Mobile devices probably display more proof of byte connectivity than most computers – and it may be harder to collect forensically. Part of the problem is that there is plenty of available hardware, software, and/or interfaces. These differences vary between media, in which data is stored in the operating system and the file system, and the efficiency of specific instruments. Even different cellular models manufactured by the same manufacturer may need cables and software for access to telephone information [8].

In recent days, the popularity of Android OS has grown. It has almost the same features on desktop/laptop computers. Users can create documents, access the Internet, read and forward email, call, text and MMS, and maintain confidential information in many different ways. You can access the information via the Internet. These Android devices and apps make it easy for friends, family members, and groups to communicate on the web and socially. For many cybercrime investigations, a forensic smartphone exam is necessary to determine a range of suspected activities. Advanced cells contain a lot of information, which is extremely useful to investigators in the exploration cycle. Cell phones give significantly more valuable data, for example, talk logs, messages, individual data, and program history. These incorporate the major history of your phones, texts, and contacts. In this chapter, strategies for and instruments of scientific seizure of the specified instrument and the investigation of crimes is analyze [9].

When reading cutting-edge Android forensic approaches, particular writing or techniques about rooting were used to achieve root user privileges because of the device. The largest user privilege is to show the partition and wreath over the gadget with the aid of "dd" (ADB). The images received are analyzed using common forensic commercial enterprise tools [10]. The creator talked otherwise concerning the fast imaging and analysis information partition area based on Yaffs2 Android. Even without a precise tool and system, a wealth of pertinent information has been recovered forensically [11].

Android File System

Most Android users just use their Android phones for telephone, text messaging, browsing, and basic apps, but for development prospects, we should know the Android internal structure. To organize files and folders on your device (for example booting, systems, recovery, data, etc.), Android uses multiple parts just like Windows OS. This is a feature for each partition, but the meaning and content of each partition are unknown to most of us [13].

As mentioned previously, Android is based on the Linux kernel. Accordingly, Android uses the same file hierarchy technology with a customized version based on the mobile device manufacturer. The file hierarchy in Android is a tree structure with the root (/) at the top of the tree. Under the Android file structure, there are seven main partitions common between all Android devices including the SD card partition [14]. These partitions are located under the root. They are the following:

- **/boot:** has the files and information needed for the phone to boot after power on. It contains the kernel and RAM, which have forensic value and should be captured in some cases.

- **/system:** contains the ROM OS files other than those in /boot. ROM files include the Android user interface files and preinstalled apps.

- **/recovery:** tools in this partition help the user to back up and restore other partitions. Additionally, this partition contains the files needed to enable the device to boot in recovery mode.

- **/data:** applications data are stored in this partition. This includes the data of all user-installed apps and preinstalled apps like contacts, call history, SMS, and others. This partition is accessible on the user level through a data connection to a computer. Factory reset deletes this partition removing all user data.

- **/cache:** contains the frequently accessed data and applications parts for increasing the performance of referencing these data. Contents of this folder can be deleted; it will be rebuilt during normal use of the phone.

- **/misc:** contains system and hardware settings information. These mostly describe the on or off state of the devices.

- **/sdcard:** a user-accessed partition. It contains the information on the SD card. It can hold pictures and user files of different formats.

Android file systems handle the data storage techniques, organization, and retrieval from the disk volume. Android has several file systems. The volume can have several partitions where each partition can be managed separately by a different file system. The file system can be attached as an additional file system to a partition when it is mounted. File system type may affect the analysis process for the targeted partition, so it is forensically important to know the file system used on the partitions of interest. Android file systems are organized into three main categories [15]: flash memory file systems, media-based file systems, and pseudo file systems.

Flash Memory File Systems

File systems in this category support nonvolatile memory (NVM). Data is not lost in NVM when the power supply is absent.

[1].   Extended File Allocation Table (exFAT): invented
by Microsoft for flash drives. exFAT is not part of
the Linux kernel. Some manufacturers still support
Android with the exFAT file system.

[2].   Flash-Friendly File System (F2FS): an open source
Linux file system utilizing log-structured methods.
F2FS for Android was introduced by Samsung
in 2013.

[3].   Yet Another Flash File System (YAFFS2): a relatively
old file system. New kernels do not support it
anymore with a few exceptions. It is a single-
threaded file system based on log-structured
methods.

[4].   Robust File System (RFS): like the File Allocation
Table (FAT 16, FAT 32) file systems with journaling.
It may slow down some Android features.

Media-Based File Systems

Android devices support the following media-based file systems:

1.   Extended File System (EXT): introduced as one of
the first Linux-supported file systems in 1992. Now,
it has subsequent versions, namely, EXT2, EXT3,
and EXT4. EXT4 gets the advantage of supporting
multiple processors.

2.   Virtual File Allocation Table (VFAT): an extension for
FAT 16 and FAT32. Most operating systems support
FAT32. Additionally, most SD cards are formatted
with FAT32. VFAT makes it easy to support file
operations on FAT32 partitions in Android.

Pseudo File Systems

This category includes nonactual file systems that nevertheless present a logical grouping of files.

1. rootfs: the root mount point in which the boot process starts. It is the base file system in which other file systems can be mounted. It is mounted at the root /.

2. sysfs: contains information about device configurations. It is mounted on /sys partition.

3. devpts: mounted on /dev/pts. It creates a node for each shell connection made to the device.

4. cgroup: control groups are used to track the tasks of the Android device.

5. proc: mounted on /proc. This file system contains information about the kernel processes and other system information. The list of supported file systems can be retrieved from /proc/filesystems.

6. tmpfs: temporary storage file system to store files in RAM. Data in RAM will be lost upon device reboot or power off.

Android System Architecture

Android OS is based on Linux OS, and it is an open source platform from Google for mobile devices. Since Android is open source, it is easy to view code and update it as needed. The native code of Android is set up the way it is because other operating systems must talk with hardware as a sequence of layers, as shown in Figure 3-1.

There are various components for all Android apps in Android's architecture. There are many C/C++ libraries exposed by the application framework services within an open source kernel of the Android software of Linux [14].

The Android architecture is shown in Figure 3-1. The main components are as follows:

- Applications

- Application Framework

- Android Runtime

- Platform Libraries

- Linux Kernel

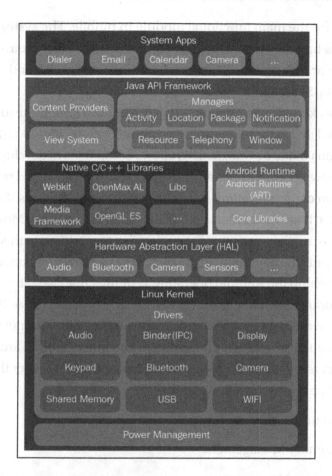

Figure 3-1. Android architecture

The starting point is the **Linux kernel layer**, which acts between hardware and Linux. The **hardware abstraction layer** (HAL) consists of several libraries and interfaces for a specific type of hardware, allowing hardware companies to develop functionality without altering system components. **Libraries** include all programming packages interacting between HAL and Java API layers. The **Java API framework layer** is responsible for the main functional module in mobile. The **system apps layer is** basically where the user can work with either preinstalled applications or new ones such as social media, email client, and others (Rohit T., Oleg S., Heather M., Satish B., 2020).

The Linux kernel layer represented in the bottom layer is the foundation of the Android architecture. Android OS is built over the Linux kernel with customizations made by Google. This allows companies to develop drivers for a well-known portable operating system. The Android kernel represents an abstraction communication layer between the applications software and the device hardware. When a picture is taken by Facebook Messenger (FBM), the instructions are sent to the related camera driver in this layer. The driver sends the command to the hardware camera. The Linux kernel is the brain behind the Android operating system: it manages all accessible drivers, including display and camera drivers. It is possible to use Bluetooth controllers, memory drivers, and audio controls. The Linux kernel provides a layer of abstraction between the hardware and other Android architectural aspects. It oversees storage, power, and equipment, among other things. The Linux kernel performs the following tasks:

- Security

- Memory Management

- Process Management

- Network Stack

- Driver Model

The second layer is HAL, which presents the hardware capabilities of the device through standard interfaces to the higher-level API framework. HAL consists of library modules. These libraries implement interfaces for hardware components. When taking a picture from an application, the API needs to access the hardware camera. Accordingly, the OS loads the related library modules for the camera. The next layer is the Android Runtime (ART), which is one of Android's most important components.

The main components of this layer are Just in Time (JIT) and Ahead of Time (AOT) compilers. JIT executes the frequently used codes of identified operations and compiles them to machine code. This improves the performance of the most used operations. AOT compiles the entire application into machine code. This is done once the application is installed. This will result in reducing power consumption and increasing performance. Accordingly, FBM DEX files will be compiled and converted to executable code. Dalvik includes essential libraries and a virtual chin, among other things (DVM). It primarily serves as the foundation for the app frame and makes use of key libraries to make our application more user-friendly. Dalvik virtual machine (DVM), like Java virtual machine (JVM), is an Android-based virtual machine that runs on a registry that has been carefully developed and optimized for performance. The threading kernel and low-memory management will be crucial to the Linux layer. For Android apps, we employ the mainstream Java and Kotlin programming languages in our core libraries.

Platform Libraries: The collection comprises some Native C and C++ libraries (such as media, graphics, Surface Manager, OpenGL, etc.) from the next layer in Android architecture. Some of these libraries can be accessed using Java framework APIs provided by the Android platform. Some of the Android components are built using Native C and C++. This is like the ART mentioned in the previous layer. Additionally, any application developed using native C and C++, in case they need to reference the related code libraries, will be provided by this layer. Above the libraries and ART layers, there is the Java API framework layer. It is responsible for providing Java APIs to handle the basic phone services and OS features. Developers can use these APIs as building blocks for their apps to use the core components and services of Android.

The last layer, the system apps layer, supports the direct user interaction with the device. This layer has a set of core apps such as a calendar, browser, email app, and others. Only this layer will be installed in preinstalled apps like home, contacts, camera, gallery, and so on, as well as third-party apps downloaded from the Play Store. It operates within Android times with the help of classes and services provided by the app framework. Developers can utilize these apps. This layer manages the default app to be used, which can be a native app or a user-installed app. User interaction with some installed apps, such as writing and sending messages, involves the direct use of the system apps layer.

Android System Permission Model

Android applications need to be granted explicit permission by users to be able to access sensitive functionality and certain services of the MD, such as the Internet, call lists, contact details, and so on (Almomani & Khayer, 2020). This provides the opportunity for users to know beforehand what the functionality is and which running services are on a device accessed by the application. Thus, it requires a user's explicit permission to be able to perform any type of malicious activity like stealing identity, stealing data, or compromising the system. In devices running Android 6.0 and prior versions, the users needed to explicitly grant the permissions while the app was installed.

Users have the choice of either accepting the entire permissions or not installing the entire application at all. Starting from devices running Android 6.0 and later versions, users can grant permissions to the applications at the running status. This new permission model also increases user control over the application's functionality and running services by allowing the user to be able to grant any appropriate and selective permissions (Talegaon & Krishnan, 2020). Thus, users can deny particular application access to their location, but are able, meanwhile, to provide access to the Internet services. From a mobile forensic point of view, this means that the type and amounts of information capable of being extracted from MD not only depends on the device and the installed applications but also depends on the permissions granted and configured by the user.

The app authorization model described in Figure 3-2 governs how applications access such sensitive resources, such as personal data of users or sensor data (e.g., camera, GPS, etc.). For example, to read entries on a user's phone, an application must have READ CONTACTS permission. Device permissions are split into four levels of protection: standard and dangerous permissions are the two most important levels to this manuscript.

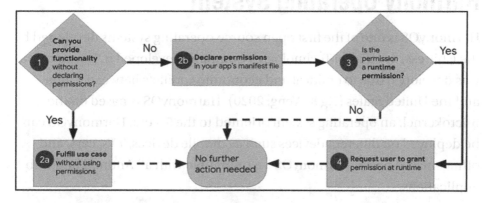

***Figure 3-2.** The workflow for using software permissions on Android*

Standard permissions require access to data or resources beyond the sandbox of the app, but there is very little risk to the privacy of the user or the operation of other applications. Permission to set the alarm, for instance, is an example. Dangerous permissions are needed if the app wants information or services that include the private information of the user or that could potentially impact the stored information of the user or the activity of other apps. For instance, dangerous permission is the ability to read user contacts.

To limit the usage of components in an application that can perform critical tasks, applications can also specify their permissions. The third level of authorization is signature permission, which developers use to move resources and data between their applications while protecting them from other developer applications. Finally, there is high-level signature or system authorization, which involves modifying security settings, downloading an application, and so on. OS developers and manufacturers retain these permissions. The system grants these applications either found in the system image or signed by the same certificate as the system image (Bhandari et al., 2017).

Harmony Operating System

HarmonyOS is one of the first open source operating systems developed by the Chinese, as Huawei Technologies Company developed it. HarmonyOS was developed due to political and economic conflicts between China and the United States (Ng & Weng, 2020). HarmonyOS is based on the microkernel, an operating system oriented to the 5G era. HarmonyOS can be deployed on different devices such as mobile devices, TVs, cars, and other smart devices. HarmonyOS is compatible with all Android and web applications.

HarmonyOS Architecture

HarmonyOS is designed with a layered architecture, which from bottom to top consists of the kernel layer, system service layer, framework layer, and application layer as shown in Figure 3-3. System functions are expanded by levels, from system to subsystem, and further to function/module. In a multidevice deployment scenario, unnecessary subsystems, functions, or modules can be excluded from the system as required. Figure 3-3 shows the technical architecture of HarmonyOS.

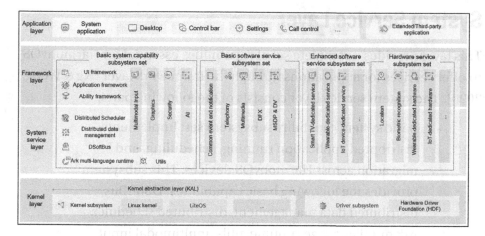

Figure 3-3. *HarmonyOS architecture ("About HarmonyOS," 2021)*

Kernel Layer

- Kernel subsystem: HarmonyOS uses a multikernel design so that appropriate OS kernels can be selected for devices with different resource limitations. The kernel abstraction layer (KAL) shields differences in kernel implementations and provides the upper layer with basic kernel capabilities, including process and thread management, memory management, file system, network management, and peripheral management ("About HarmonyOS," 2021).

- Driver subsystem: Hardware Driver Foundation (HDF) lays the foundation for an open HarmonyOS hardware ecosystem. It allows unified access from peripheral devices and provides the foundation for driver development and management (Ng & Weng, 2020).

System Service Layer

This layer provides a complete set of capabilities essential for HarmonyOS to offer services for applications through the framework layer (Ng & Weng, 2020). The system service layer consists of the following parts:

- Basic system capability subsystem set: Implements distributed application running, scheduling, and migration across HarmonyOS devices. This subsystem provides the following basic capabilities: DSoftBus, distributed data management, distributed scheduler, Ark multilanguage runtime, utils, multimodal input, graphics, security, and AI. Among them, the Ark runtime leverages the C, C++, and JS runtimes and provides basic system class libraries. It also provides the runtime required for Java programs statically compiled by the Ark compiler (Ng & Weng, 2020).

- Basic software service subsystem set: Provides HarmonyOS with common and universal software services, including common event and notification, telephony, multimedia, Design For X (DFX), as well as Mobile Sensing Development Platform (MSDP) & Device Virtualization (DV) (Ng & Weng, 2020).

- Enhanced software service subsystem set: Provides HarmonyOS with differentiated and enhanced software services, including those dedicated to smart TVs, wearables, IoT devices, and more (Ng & Weng, 2020).

- Hardware service subsystem set: Provides HarmonyOS with hardware services, including location and biometric recognition, as well as those dedicated to wearables and IoT devices (Ng & Weng, 2020).

The basic software service, enhanced software service, and hardware service subsystem sets can be tailored by subsystems, and each subsystem can be tailored by functions, depending on the deployment scenario for a particular device form (Ng & Weng, 2020).

Framework Layer

This layer provides what you need to develop HarmonyOS applications: application framework and ability framework, specific to multiple languages (like Java, C, C++, and JS), Java and JS UI frameworks, as well as multilanguage APIs for hardware and software services. The APIs available for different HarmonyOS devices vary according to component-based tailoring ("About HarmonyOS," 2021).

Application Layer

This layer consists of system applications and third-party applications. Each HarmonyOS application is powered by one or more Feature Abilities (FAs) or Particle Abilities (PAs). An FA provides a UI for user interaction. A PA has no UI and provides background task processing as well as data access. During user interaction, FAs may need to retrieve background data from PAs. Applications developed based on FAs and PAs implement specific business characteristics and achieve cross-device scheduling and distribution, delighting users with a consistent and efficient experience ("About HarmonyOS," 2021).

Data Extraction Techniques on Android

We refer to manual, logical, and physical acquisition by one of three methods when we speak of extracting the data from an Android device, due to the sensitivity of mobile evidence, which constantly requires particular treatment to avoid contamination or loss of evidence. The weakest mobile forensic procedure is acquiring digital evidence (Ashawa & Ogwuche, 2017). Data collection is a crucial stage in mobile forensics for retrieving both deleted and undeleted data, as well as discovering and finding relevant artifacts to create significant evidence (Al-Sabaawi & Foo, 2019). There are five tiers of acquisition data techniques, according to Sam Brothers' classification, to separate the tool's capabilities from the data they can collect (Chernyshev, Zeadally, Baig, & Woodward, 2017). Table 3-1 shows different levels of acquisitions, advantages, and disadvantages of each level.

Table 3-1. *Acquisition's Levels, Advantages, and Disadvantages [3]*

No	Data acquisition method	Advantages	Disadvantages
1	*Manual extraction* Standard interfaces such as touch controls, screen controllers, and keyboards are used to access the information stored on the device and to record input directly from the screen.	There are no special tools necessary, and the technical difficulty is modest.	Large amounts of data will be exhausted over time; there is a risk of data adjustments being made by mistake; it does not restore data that has been erased. It will certainly be impractical if the hardware is destroyed.
2	*Logical extraction* A standard interface between the workstation and the device must be built utilizing USB, Wi-Fi, or Bluetooth to send device data to the workstation.	Technical complexity is minimal, while data abstraction is high.	Unintentional data changes may occur, and data access is restricted.

(continued)

Table 3-1. (*continued*)

No	Data acquisition method	Advantages	Disadvantages
3	***Physical extraction or Hex dumping*** The device should be in diagnostic mode and downloading its flash memory.	It's possible to do with conventional interfaces; it works with devices that have little damage; data access is still possible.	Data analysis and decoding might be difficult. It is not assured that you will have access to all partitions. Invasive device access (JTAG) necessitates extensive training.
4	***Chip-off*** After removing the device's physical flash memory, extract a binary image.	Provides a complete binary image suitable for more traditional analysis.	Possibility of causing physical harm; much training is necessary.
5	***Micro read*** Using an electron microscope to examine logic gates on a physical level and then turning these observations into readable, comprehensible data requires a high level of technical skill.	Last option that is applicable.	Resource-intensive and technically challenging.

Manuel Data Extraction

Manual acquisitions take place with the investigator facing the phone's user interface. This is an excellent way for investigators to scroll via a phone that usually works and allows them to document what they see. Data can be detected by researchers only when clicking a call log, text messages, a photo scan, or a browser history, and data are sorted for other applications like Facebook. The photos/screenshots of the valuable data on the telephone are evidence. Manual removal is a simple and quick way to scan Android contents but involves many challenges. This enables us to check data available only at the moment. Researchers or investigators are at risk of accidental deletion or compromising the integrity of the device or its contents.

The first method in mobile forensics is manually checking the phone, and the first stage is to bypass the lock screen. In this case study, the Samsung Galaxy Note 9 doesn't have any lock screen or any protections; someone sent a child pornographic image using WhatsApp and the criminal opened the photo. Once they saw it, they deleted it. What the criminal didn't know was that there is a bin and when an image is deleted it is moved to the bin folder instead of being permanently deleted. We successfully found the porno image in the bin folder (trash); however, it will last for only 30 days in the trash. After that, it will be deleted permanently.

Logical Data Forensics

The logical acquisition enables the analysis of data on the Android device to be made more thorough and is the first way to use data 'extraction' for a separate review. This means connecting the device to the forensic workstations by wired or wireless. It also means accessing your phone file system and obtaining a copy of the backup information, for example, ADB pull data extraction. In our practical case for this chapter, the logical forensic analysis will be done to Samsung Galaxy Note 9 without rooting.

Method 1: Using ADB Pull Command:

The first step is to enable developer options.

The second step is to enable debugging mode as Figure 3-4 shows.

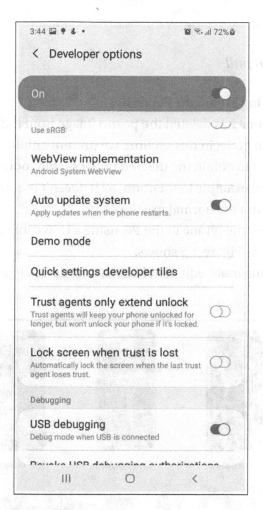

Figure 3-4. *USB debugging mode*

The third step is to go where ADB is located: "C:\Users\full\path\Local\Android\Sdk\platform-tools".

The fourth step is to run ADB pull data\data "path". As shown in Figure 3-5, no output was found, because the device is not rooted.

```
C:\Users\dell\AppData\Local\Android\Sdk\platform-tools>Adb pull /data "C:\Users\dell\Desktop\logical forensic"
/data/: 0 files pulled.
```

Figure 3-5. *ADB pull*

Method 2: Using Mobiledit Forensics

Now the criminal has deleted the porno image from the gallery and
also from the trash cycle; in this section, we present another method
of mobile forensics to obtain the deleted images (child pornography).
Mobiledit is a good example to mention, as it doesn't require rooting and it
can collect data from the normal privileges.

Step 1: Connect the phone to the PC using a USB cable and enable
debugging mode, as Figure 3-5 shows.

Step 2: From the mobiledit panel choose the device type, as
Figure 3-6 shows.

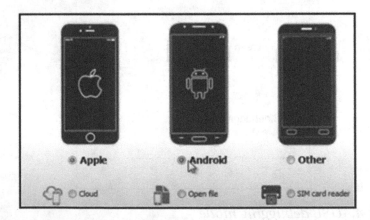

Figure 3-6. *Main screen for deceive select on mobiledit*

Step 3: Choose the connection type, as Figure 3-7 shows.

Figure 3-7. *Connection type*

Step 4: Analyze the data that is extracted, as Figure 3-8 shows.

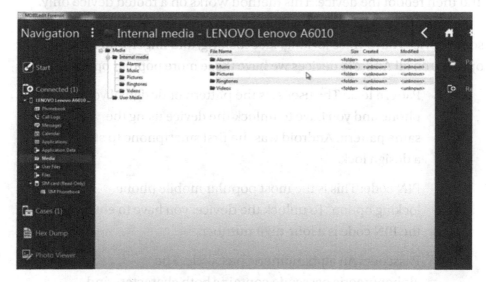

Figure 3-8. *Media*

After examining and analyzing the data that was extracted by mobiledit, we can see that the program has the advantages that the phone doesn't require root, and it's good for analysis of nondeleting media, but it doesn't get any deleted data, which means that the data extracting is not bit by bit; it's only for existing data.

Screen Lock Bypassing Techniques

Based on the lock technology used, the key file will be named. The naming of the key file depends on the manufacturer too. In this experiment the key files were located under /data/system partition. Names of the key files are gatekeeper.password.key for password or passcode lock and gatekeeper, pattern key for the pattern lock. To bypass the lock, delete the mentioned key files using the rm command with superuser privilege and then reboot the device. This method works on a rooted device only.

Three types of locking mechanisms are available for Android. While some devices have voice locking, face locking, and fingerprint locking options, on all Android devices we have three more popular options [16]:

✓ Pattern lock: The user sets the pattern or design of your phone and you have to unlock the device using the same pattern. Android was the first smartphone to start a design lock.

✓ PIN code: This is the most popular mobile phone locking option. To unlock the device, you have to enter the PIN code is a four-digit number.

✓ Passcode: An alphanumeric passcode. The alphanumeric passcode contains both characters and numbers, contrary to the four-digit PIN.

There are also some popular methods and tools to bypass the screen lock, such as the following:

- ADB: When you connect to ADB via a USB connection on an Android device, it's best to take advantage of USB debugging.

- The gesture is deleted. Key File: The gesture is taken away. The device pattern lock is deleted from the key file.

- Lock screen removal: Dr.Fone from Wondershare.

The update settings.db file technique requires accessing a rooted device from the shell. This can be done from the ADB shell. The settings file is located under */data/data/com.android.providers.settings/ databases*; using `sqlite3` you can update by setting the lock screen values to 0.

Rooting the Devices

Rooting any device usually involves exploiting a security bug in the device's firmware, then copying the su (superuser) binary to a location in the current process's path (*/system/xbin/su*), and granting it executable permissions with the chmod command. Rooting Android phones has become a common phenomenon, and you can expect to encounter rooted phones during forensic examinations, and you may also need to root the device in order to acquire data for forensic examination. The root user has the power to start/stop any system service, edit/delete any file, and change the privileges of other users. Rooting an Android phone is all about gaining access to the device to perform actions that are not normally allowed on the device; most rooting of Android devices is done to allow superuser capabilities and provide open access to the Android device.

In order to make a bit-by-bit image, a root of the device must be taken; as we saw in the manual, if the criminal deleted the child porno image from the trash it would be possible to track him. As for logical forensics, if it's impossible to get the deleted media such as images, then the last weapon is to try physical forensics, but first the root should be done to make it available to physical forensics. Rooting the Android is done using Odin3 software for Samsung Galaxy Note 9.

1. Connect the phone by USB cable.

2. Download the firmware from sammobile.com or
    halabtech.com.

3. Check the model number if it's supported and
    download the firmware as shown in Figure 3-9.

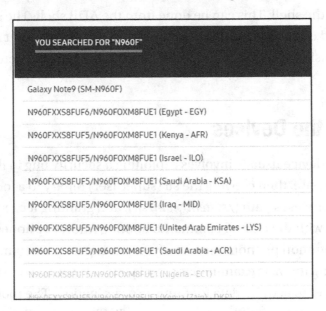

YOU SEARCHED FOR "N960F"

Galaxy Note9 (SM-N960F)

N960FXXS8FUF6/N960FOXM8FUE1 (Egypt - EGY)

N960FXXS8FUF5/N960FOXM8FUE1 (Kenya - AFR)

N960FXXS8FUF5/N960FOXM8FUE1 (Israel - ILO)

N960FXXS8FUF5/N960FOXM8FUE1 (Saudi Arabia - KSA)

N960FXXS8FUF5/N960FOXM8FUE1 (Iraq - MID)

N960FXXS8FUF5/N960FOXM8FUE1 (United Arab Emirates - LYS)

N960FXXS8FUF5/N960FOXM8FUE1 (Saudi Arabia - ACR)

N960FXXS8FUF5/N960FOXM8FUE1 (Nigeria - ECT)

Figure 3-9. *Firmware*

4. Turn off the phone and hold the volume-down
    button and the Bixby button, then fill the (BL, CP,
    CSC, and AP) as Figure 3-10 shows, and then click
    start, and the phone will be rooted.

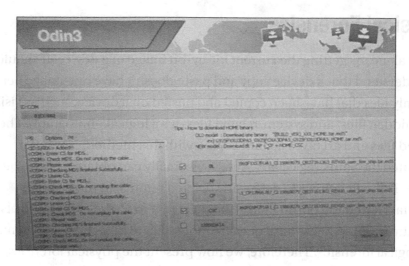

Figure 3-10. *Odin3*

Advantages of rooting

- Rooting allows modification of the software on the device to the deepest level—for example, you can overclock or underclock the device's CPU.

- It allows restrictions imposed on the device by carriers, manufacturers, and so on to be bypassed.

- For extreme customization, new customized ROMs can be downloaded and installed.

Disadvantages of rooting

- Rooting a device must be done with extreme care as errors may result in irreparable damage to the software on the phone, turning the device into a useless brick.

- Rooting might void the warranty of a device.

- Rooting results in increased exposure to malware and other attacks.

Physical Forensics

Physical means getting the current bit-by-bit image of a device. It should be understood that a device copy and paste doesn't have one image per bit. Only files that have been copied and pasted on a device, such as visible files, hidden files, and system-related files. It's a logical photograph. The deleted files and archives are not copied with this method. Now after we rooted the Samsung Galaxy Note 9, we finally can obtain a bit-by-bit image. This will help us to detect any deleted photos; in our case the criminal viewed the porno image and deleted it from the gallery and also from the trash, so it was hard or even impossible to detect it using manual and logical forensics. Therefore, we now present the physical forensics, which is getting a bit-by-bit image.

Back to logical extraction: now we will use ADB tools to create bit-by-bit images.

Step 1: Go to where adb is located: "C:\Users\dell\AppData\Local\Android\Sdk\platform-tools"

Step 2: You can use the dd command for creating a raw image of the device. This command helps us create an Android image bit-by-bit by copying low-level data.

Step3: After copying all data, it will be shown as a .dd file extension as Figure 3-11 shows; this file extension is supported and can be opened by Magnet Axiom toolkit and many forensic toolkits.

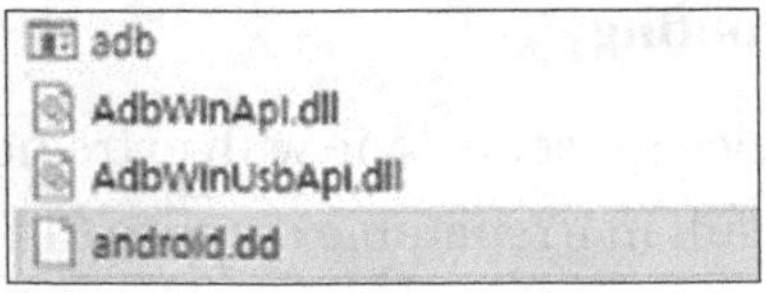

Figure 3-11. .dd image

Step 4: Open autopsy and analyze the file.

Step 5: After we analyzed the mobile data, we finally found the child porn image after the criminal deleted it from the gallery and the trash, as Figure 3-12 shows.

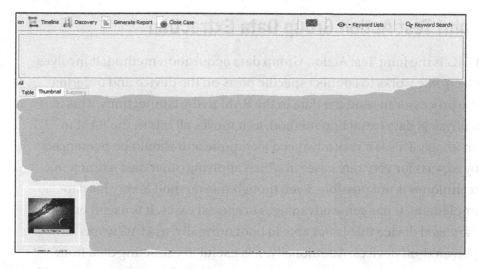

Figure 3-12. *Autopsy*

In some cases, we can flash the recovery partition that was used to replace the recovery partition on the Android device with previously stored images from a computer (backup image). This works if the bootloader is not locked on the device. The flashing is made through the `fastboot` diagnostic protocol, which comes with the Android SDK. To apply this method, reboot the device in the boot loader mode. Use a set of commands from the shell to flash or write over the recovery partition. After the process finishes, reboot the device in recovery mode. From the recovery mode shell, mount /data and /system partitions. Investigators can use the ADB bypass method on the mounted partitions. This technique makes unrecoverable changes to the evidence. The alternative approach supported by `fastboot` is to boot a temporary recovery image without changing the original recovery partition.

Other advanced physical data extraction techniques are JTAG and chip-off. Note that these techniques will not work on devices with full desk encryption enabled.

Joint Test Action Group Data Extraction

JTAG is the Joint Test Action Group data acquisition method. It involves electronic works to connect specific ports on the device and ordering the processor to send the data in the RAM to the connections. This is a physical data extraction method, as it moves all bits in the RAM to an image. This is a very advanced technique and should be referenced by experts for very rare cases in which applying other data extraction techniques is not possible. Even though this method is very hard to implement, it has some advantages in special cases. It is useful on a damaged device that is not able to boot normally, as JTAG works on powered-off devices. Additionally, it is useful in extracting data from locked devices without the need for root or USB debugging mode enabled. It should be noted that this technique may result in damages to the device and losing all data.

Chip-Off Data Extraction

This technique involves detaching the NAND flash electronic chips from the device and attaching them to a specific device to extract the data. Chip-off has the advantages of JTAG in accessing unlocked, damaged, or unrooted devices. On the other hand, it has an extremely high risk of damaging the device. This is due to the very delicate chip-detaching process. Additionally, it is much more difficult to reattach the removed chips back to their place. Accordingly, the device after this process should be considered unrecoverable.

Mobile Forensics Investigation Challenges on Android Devices

With the rapid evolution of smartphones, mobile forensics is more difficult than ever. Every new Android version introduces new features and security enhancements, which might obstruct the forensic procedure. Based on what was discussed during this section and the previous section, the problems and difficulties that exist in Apple devices are the same as the difficulties found in Android devices. Add to this that Android devices are witnessing a great development in the field of security and encryption. Moreover, phones that run on the Android system are multiple, and we witness many versions from companies and multiple versions that are very difficult to follow:

1. Apart from software, a forensics analyst may come across many sorts of hardware due to a large number of competitors in the market. Device requirements have gotten increasingly complicated, and they differ from one company to the next. This adds to a forensic examiner's preparation work since they require the right tools to access the hardware.

2. Manufacturers have begun to enhance their security modules, which the consumer appreciates. Such a high degree of protection has become a major roadblock for forensic examiners since it is extremely difficult to get beyond the device's security. While older Android devices may still be accessed in various ways, newer smartphones sometimes lack support from even commercial software.

3. For smartphone users, cloud storage has become a popular and preferred alternative. Manufacturers provide enticing packages to entice customers to store their data on the cloud, and customers find it to be quite handy.

4. Advanced forensics techniques like JTAG, chip-off, and micro-read, in addition to the logical and physical acquisition, are very intrusive and need thorough understanding and specialized training. These methods are also highly expensive, and only a few firms provide these services, so they are not available to everyone.

5. There are many things that are important to mention that are available in Xiaomi phones and some other Android devices, as these things are considered among the distinctive characteristics of users in terms of safety. (Reddy, 2019)

6. At the same time, these matters are considered among the great challenges facing the digital investigator, and these characteristics include:

   – Two spaces in the same device. Figure 3-13 shows how the second space can be created in Xiaomi devices.

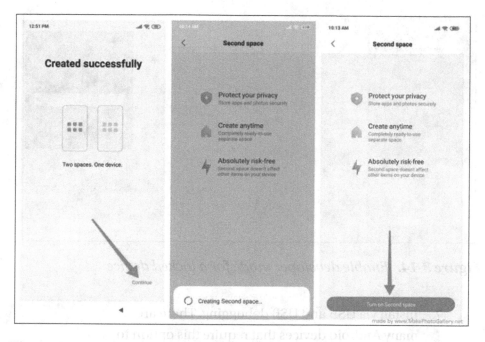

Figure 3-13. *Two spaces in Xiaomi devices*

When the user creates a second interface in the device, it seems that it is another phone in the same phone; when an investigator tried to acquire the second space, it wasn't included in the acquisition copy because it is a separate space. Figure 3-14 shows that even if we get inside the second space we can't extract the third-party apps because we need to enable the developer mode and we can't make this happen because of device security (MIUI, 2019).

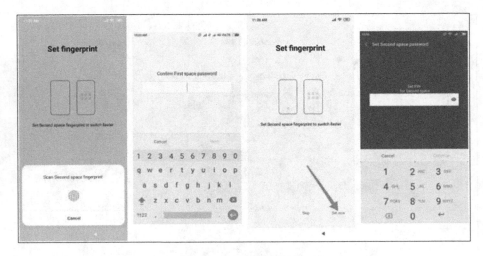

Figure 3-14. *Enable developer mode for a locked device*

7. Install via USB and USB debugging. There are many Android devices that require this option to be activated in order to install and extract data from third-party applications such as WhatsApp. Unfortunately, activating this option requires an Internet connection, and doing this step on the digital directory will expose the digital directory to the risk of losing data or damage to the phone.

8. Since many phones can be formatted remotely through the Internet, it is also possible to lose open accounts if the account holder locks them or changes the open sessions by changing passwords (Xiaomi, 2019).

Summary

The iPhone 6s was backed up by the iTunes program, and we were able through this backup to get the porno picture using Magnet Axiom. However, the Belkasoft program could not get the porn picture; we note that the iPhone has not been jailbroken, so we were able to get the image after deleting it, unlike the Samsung Note 9. I browsed the device manually and found the image in the trash file, but when we deleted the image from the trash file, we made a logical image without rooting the device, but we were unable to get the deleted image. So we did a physical image and rooted the device, and after that, we were able to get the deleted image. In the end, the forensic investigation of the iPhone was easier than the forensic process for the Samsung phone.

Practical Lab 3.1

Access the device using ADB (developer.android.com) by enabling USB debugging as described from step 1 to step 7, then type the command *ADB devices* in step 8.

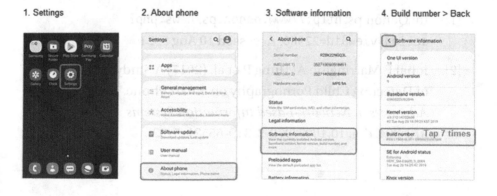

5. Developer options

6. USB debugging

7. OK

8. Type command using cmd.

```
C:\android-sdk\platform-tools>adb.exe devices
List of devices attached
* daemon not running. starting it now on port 5037 *
* daemon started successfully *
4df16ac3115e5f05          device
```

References

[1].   In: Qanon.ps. http://www.qanon.ps/news.php?
        action=view&id=22980. Accessed 10 Aug 2021

[2].   Iqbal F, Marrington A, Hung P et al. (2017) A Study
        of Detecting Child Pornography on Smart Phone.
        Advances in Network-Based Information Systems
        373-384. doi: 10.1007/978-3-319-65521-5_32

[3]. Polastro M, da Silva Eleuterio P (2010) NuDetective: A Forensic Tool to Help Combat Child Pornography through Automatic Nudity Detection. *2010 Workshops on Database and Expert Systems Applications*. doi: 10.1109/dexa.2010.74

[4]. Garcia N (2018) Digital Steganography and Its Existence in Cybercrime. *Scientific and Practical Cyber Security Journal* 2(2): 18-24.

[5]. In: Ro.ecu.edu.au. `https://ro.ecu.edu.au/cgi/ viewcontent.cgi?article=7480&context=ecuworks`. Accessed 10 Aug 2021

[6]. Al Mutawa N, Baggili I, Marrington A (2012) Forensic Analysis of Social Networking Applications on Mobile Devices. *Digital Investigation* 9:S24-S33. doi: 10.1016/j.diin.2012.05.007

[7]. D'Orazio C, Ariffin A, Choo K (2013) IOS Anti-Forensics: How Can We Securely Conceal, Delete and Insert Data? *SSRN Electronic Journal*. doi: 10.2139/ssrn.2339819

[8]. Lessard J, Kessler G (2010) Android Forensics: Simplifying Cell Phone Examinations.

[9]. Rao V, Chakravarthy A (2016) Forensic Analysis of Android Mobile Devices. 2016 International Conference on Recent Advances and Innovations in Engineering (ICRAIE). doi: 10.1109/icraie.2016.793954s

[10]. Lessard J, Kessler G (2010) Android Forensics: Simplifying Cell Phone Examinations.

[11]. Lamine A, Kechadi T (2012) Android Forensics: A Physical Approach.

[12]. L. Simao A, CausSicoli F, Melo L (2011) Acquisition of Digital Evidence in Android Smartphone.

[13]. Anglano C (2014) Forensic Analysis of WhatsApp Messenger on Android Smartphones.

[14]. Wiley J (2012) Beginning Android™ 4 Application Development.

[15]. Farooq U (2018) Android Operating System Architecture.

[16]. Tamma R, Skulkin O, Mahalik H, Bommisetty S. Practical Mobile Forensics - Fourth Edition.

CHAPTER 4

Forensic Investigations of Popular Applications on Android and iOS Platforms

Since the turn of the 21st century, because of the tremendous growth in social media, online resources, and websites such as Facebook, there has been a vast number of users who have been sharing a huge amount of private data such as texts, pictures, videos, and calls on the Android and iOS platforms through instant messaging applications like Messenger, WhatsApp, and so on. This chapter investigates how much privacy these applications can provide for users, along with how much information can we get through forensic investigation using digital forensic tools like FINALMobile, Mobiledit, and so on.

© Mohammed Moreb 2022
M. Moreb, *Practical Forensic Analysis of Artifacts on iOS and Android Devices*,
https://doi.org/10.1007/978-1-4842-8026-3_4

In this chapter, we will cover the following topics:

- Introduction to Investigations of Popular Applications

- Extracting Data of the Activities of the Instant Artifacts

- Details of Device Seized for Examination

- Gmail Application Artifacts

- Gmail App Seizure Device Information for iOS
  and Android

- Gmail App Physical Extraction

- Mobile Forensics for Google Drive

Extracting Data of the Activities of the Instant Artifacts

In previous chapters, we introduced the Android and iOS architecture. The
iOS architecture includes an intermediate layer between the programs and
the hardware such that they do not communicate directly. Also, the lowest
levels provide fundamental services, while the upper layers give the user
interface and advanced visuals. The Android architecture incorporates
a variety of components to support the demands of any Android device.
Android software has an open source Linux kernel that includes a
collection of C/C++ libraries that are accessed via application framework
services.

This chapter is divided to three sections: the first section introduces
the process of extracting the data remaining from instant messaging and
other applications on an Android and iOS platforms. The second section
extracts data from Gmail application artifacts using both the recent iPhone
operating system and Android 10, and describes the proliferation of
mobile phone industries, which caused an increase in the opportunities

110

for the intruder's chance to do their activities beyond the challenges of the new techniques. The third section explains how to analyze evidence from Google Drive by applying a mobile forensic method on an Android smartphone on which the Google Drive application is installed.

Implementation and Examination Details

This study uses two smartphones with an installation of Facebook Messenger, WhatsApp, and so on. It focuses on extracting the data remaining from instant messaging and other applications on Android and iOS platforms. This chapter studies the user's behavior, including logging on to these applications, uploading images, exchanging information, and so on. All the experiments are conducted on real systems and iTunes backup files. It performs on OPPO Reno5 F under the Android operating environment and on IPhone7 under the iOS platform; instant messaging applications are already installed in all cases.

We try to collect and gathered data such as call logs, deleted items, images, Internet connection logs, lock codes, memos, MMS, phonebooks, SMS, system files, video clips, and voice files; all the specifications of the tools that used are listed in Table 4-1.

- Details of the reporting agency: Dr. Mohammed Moreb

- Case identifier: 741994

- Date of evidence receipt: 24th April 2021

- Identity of the submitter: PalMobileCenterTest

- Forensic investigator: Rawan Samara

The first step is to find the details about the device seized for examination like brand name, model, serial number, IMEI number, and so on. There are two methods. Firstly, searching the phone for labels that contain some information like IMEI number will be very useful because there are many websites that can show all the details about the seized device like `https://www.imei.info/`. Secondly, use the tools that are introduced in Chapter 2. We used *Libimobiledevice* for iPhone 7 and *HalabTech* tool for OPPO Reno5 F, as shown in Figure 4-1.

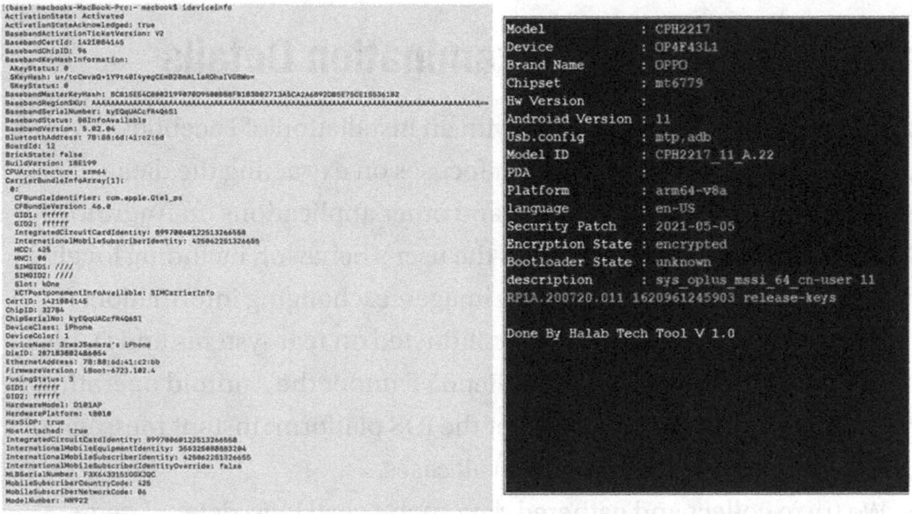

Figure 4-1. *Details of the device seized for examination*

Then, we create an image file for the physical memory of the smartphones and use forensic tools to extract and analyze the data extracted from the image files. After that, extract data and create image files from physical memory by connecting the mobile phone with the computer by using the phone cable after enabling developer options and allowing connection via USB (introduced in Chapter 2). Following that, when the two devices are connected, we use forensic tools and continue with the device connection, user settings, acquisition, examination, analysis, and reporting. During the acquisition for the iPhone7, there were some additional difficulties over what was seen during the acquisition for the OPPO mobile, namely, requesting the iTunes program to be open in the PC, needing the iTunes backup password, and being locked out of the iPhone multiple times.

Results and Analysis

Every operating system has its pros and cons; for example, iOS was very
difficult in the acquisition process especially without jailbreak, and the
process required a lot of time, authentications, and passwords, but on
the other hand the iTunes backup folder was very helpful, and it could
have a lot of valuable data without undergoing the jailbreak process. Also,
the jailbreak is not an easy task, and it has many disadvantages, of which
voiding the warranty is just one. As for Android, the problem was that
without rooting, the data was not enough, but with rooting, there are a
lot of disadvantages (e.g., Installing incompatible apps, It can brick your
device, No more warranty, Tweaking risks, and Update problems) and the
rooting process itself is very difficult and complicated especially with the
new versions of Android. However, if rooting were to be done, which we
couldn't do in our situation, it would allow access to important files, which
would have made the acquisition much easier and would have produced a
lot of data, but this is for future work.

Acquisition for iOS - iPhone 7

- **Normal acquisition without jailbreak:** We tried to do
  normal acquisition using FINALMobile4 and Belkasoft
  without jailbreaking for the iPhone but it was not
  successful, because it got an extremely limited data
  (some images, videos, and device information).

- **Acquisition using the database stored in iTunes
  backup folder:** Using this method was the most
  suitable solution to extract a lot of data for a
  nonjailbreak iPhone; although the acquisition took
  a lot of time compared to the normal acquisition,
  the results were amazing, from passwords, notes,
  contacts, call logs, chats on SMS, Instagram, Facebook,

Messenger, WhatsApp, and so on. Of course, the
result was different in every program as shown in the
following:

- **Belkasoft:** We used Belkasoft Evidence Center X, and
  it extracted a lot of data compared to other programs
  and other features like charts. It extracted data like
  pictures, videos, call logs, notes, chats from WhatsApp,
  Messenger, SMS, and so on. Also, it extracted a lot of
  data that did not show in other programs like audio
  files, calendars, visited websites, chats in TikTok, files
  in DropBox and GoogleKeep, documents, emails,
  passwords, and deleted files.

- **FINALMobile Forensics 4:** This program was
  remarkably effective in extracting all types of data
  like GoogleKeep, cloud documents, Google translate
  history, notes, account details, pictures, videos, and
  contacts, call logs, and chats for Facebook, Instagram,
  WhatsApp, and account details for Snapchat and
  LinkedIn, except data from SMS like messages, contacts
  and call logs, documents, device information, calendar
  and web browser information like accounts and
  history. Unfortunately, FINALMobile did not support
  SQLite analysis.

- **Magnet Axiom:** There is a specialty in Axiom that does
  not exist in other programs: the real-time preview for
  chats, documents, and everything exactly as you see
  in your smartphone. In addition, the extracted data
  was incredibly good; it also was the only program that
  extracted data from Zoom, Skype, and iOS call logs. It
  did extract data from Tok-Tok, WhatsApp, Messenger,

Instagram, notes, documents, audio, pictures, and videos, but very little data from Safari. Also, it does SQLite analysis.

- **Mobiledit Forensic:** This program was the most amazing one because it extracted every tiny detail in the phone with a report with 1,2435 pages; it holds everything and every detail in the phone, even the deleted data and the previous accounts. No SQLite was found but there were XML files and Excel files with data.

- **IExplorer:** This was the best program for investigating the device's built-in apps and data like contacts, messages, notes, calendar, call logs, Safari history and bookmarks, photos, and videos.

- **SQLiteSpy:** The whole Apple device line relied heavily on SQLite databases to store data. Most built-in iOS applications, such as messages, phone, mail, calendar, and notes, save data in SQLite database tables. In addition, many third-party programs running on mobile devices use SQLite databases to store data. Databases are commonly given the SQLite db or ".db" file extensions, as well as other extensions and file formats.

Acquisition for Android Device - OPPO Reno5 F

- **Logical acquisition (Nonrooted device):** We used this method on OPPO Reno5 F using many challenges as follows:

- **Mobiledit:** Unfortunately, no data was extracted from
  any application in the device. The only information we
  got is the permissions that the device granted for every
  application.

- **FINALMobile:** This program was one of the best when
  dealing with Android without rooting. It extracted
  a good amount of data like Messenger, Twitter, and
  Instagram chats. Also, it detected the true caller, which
  was a bonus.

- **Belkasoft:** We used another version of Belkasoft with
  Android (the crack version of Belkasoft evidence
  center), which is not as good as Belkasoft X. Also, the
  fact that the device is unrooted reduces the amount
  of data extracted. This version extracted only the
  image, audio, video, document, location, and device
  information.

- **Axiom Magnet:** It was the worst in extracting data.
  There was a problem with the application when it was
  installed on a nonfunctional phone which does not
  run, and I think the agent that uses it is not compatible
  with OPPO devices.

- **DB Browser (SQLite):** The SQLite database is a free
  and open source database engine that is used as an
  in-process systematic library to deploy transactional
  SQL databases. The SQLite database is a full database
  that has multiple tables, programmable triggers, and
  data views in a single platform file. Because SQLite is a
  dependable, portable, and lightweight database format,
  it is the most often used database format in many
  mobile environments. Several attempts to root the

phone (Redmi Note 7) were made using XRY, TWRB,
MI Flash, and other tools as shown in Figure 4-2,
but there was a problem when the app (find device)
couldn't activate the SIM card that associated with the
MI account, which meant that we couldn't unlock the
bootloader to continue rooting. We also tried recovery
boot and a variety of other approaches, but none of
them worked. More research and study are needed
on this subject to complete, as we explain in the next
chapters. For the screen lock bypassing technique,
there's a Halab Tech tool that can remove the lock
screen, but the device must be rooted.

Figure 4-2. *Acquisition data using different tools*

Gmail Application Artifacts

This section will introduce the process of Gmail investigation artifacts
on both operating systems: iOS and Android. The revolution of the
development of smartphones in the last few years, especially the variation
in developed applications, has made life easier, and such applications are
fast enough to handle such problems in real life. The statistics show that
the number of smartphones running worldwide is 3.6 million in 2020, and
the expectation in 2023 to be 4.3 million (Statista, 2021).

Here is a brief introduction to a famous artifact on mobile devices
that may help make the overall picture of mobile investigations more
easily understood. A mobile web browser is an application used to
access the Internet. Using a web browser, a user can search information,
communicate with others using social networks, send/receive emails,
and so on. The forensic artifacts that are left by a web browser like Google
Chrome as a session ends are not only website visits, downloads, and
cookies, but other artifacts like time of access and some keywords. Web
browsers store a large amount of data on the user's hard disk, and either
Safari or Google Chrome stored data about the user such as usernames,
emails, downloads, temp files, and cache in a database of SQLite at the
user's side. Investigations on mobile web browsers are also known as
mobile forensics, which is divided into two techniques: live and static
(Sariboz, E., & Varol, C., 2018).

A technique that allows investigators to restore deleted files is relying
on the journaling file system in iOS. The forensic analysis to confirm
the suggested technique (A. Ariffin, C. D'Orazio, K. R. Choo, and J. Slay,
2013). In addition to that, there are multiple methods for collecting data
and extracting evidence, as well as corresponding policies. However,
combined with rapidly changing technology, many challenges in the
forensic investigation process. In iTunes backup utility the data of forensic
value like email messages, text, and messages, calendar, browsing history,
call history, and others may be found using iPhone capture dump.
Despite their research professionalism they did not mention live data
forensics (Bader, M., Baggili, I., 2010). Android forensic for extracting
Gmail data from mobile device has received recent attention: researchers
have successfully found extracted data from the database of the Gmail
application under */data/data/com.google.android.gm directory*. The one
thing that has not been solved is how to find the encrypted files residing in
the database directories for Gmail (Kim, D., & Lee, S., 2020).

International cooperation in cybersecurity law is taking place in constituencies to bring international support to cybercrime issues. International Telecom Union (ITU) in 2014 in WASIS initiated an initiative in cybercrime cooperation in five regions worldwide (ITU Cybersecurity Activities, 2020).

On May 25, 2018, the European Union (EU) launched the General Data Protection Regulation (GDPR), which is security and privacy law (What is GDPR, 2019). On the other hand, in June 2017 the Republic of China approved the cybersecurity law addressing most features of security, but there is not one single word regarding mobile security (Translation: Cybersecurity Law of the People's Republic of China, 2017), which is a weakness in this law. The Budapest Convention against Cybercrimes, the first convention related to digital crimes, took place in the Hungarian capital Budapest on November 23, 2001. It highlights the cooperation and international solidarity in combating cybercrime. The signing of that international convention is the first step in the field of building international solidarity against those crimes that take place through the Internet (Budapest Convention and Related Standards , n.d.).

In this section, the main goal is to achieve the best practice method in investigating the Gmail application, which runs on both iOS iPad 10.5 version 14.4 and Android 10. The analysis will be on both OS for seizure, acquisition, analysis, and reporting as shown in Figure 4-3.

Figure 4-3. Mobile forensic process

In this section, experiments with both iOS and Android will take place with all stages of the forensic life cycle as described next.

iOS Seizure Device Information

In this section, we will obtain all information about the iOS device, which is the iPad; Table 4-1 describes all information about the iPad's status to emphasize the health of the device before the case investigation.

Table 4-1. *iPad Obtained*

Color	Gold
Scratches	No scratches found
Wallpaper	Default Apple wallpaper
Accessories	Just cover
External storage	Not found
SIM card	No

[1]. **Isolation:** Before starting acquisition, and because we did not have a box for isolation such as a Faraday box, we did isolation for the device from other external connections, putting the device in Flight mode to disconnect it from Wi-Fi, Bluetooth access, or cabling. This operation is done on all devices in both iOS and Android.

[2]. **Acquisition:** To acquire mobile phones, there are three types of extractions used: manual, logical, and physical extractions.

[3]. **Manual Acquisition:** This method of extraction is used to verify the accuracy after the physical extractions for both iOS and Android OS. It is done simply to view the data on the mobile directly from its touch screen in a human way. Here the error tolerance for the data is based on human error.

[4]. **Logical Acquisition:** In this case, we did a logical
      acquisition. The iOS device connected the USB-
      Lighting cable to the computer; then we connected
      the iPad to the iTunes software, and we got
      specific information about the device as shown in
      Figure 4-4.

Figure 4-4. iTunes Dev status

In our case, logical extraction for Android OS was done mainly using
mobiledit; using this tool while the device is not rooted only extracts
the application without its data. Rooted devices will be described in the
following sections. After a successful acquisition was finished, the Android
file structure was listed as shown in Figure 4-5.

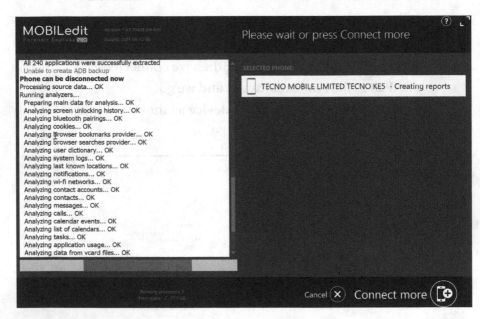

Figure 4-5. *Android file structure*

From our practical case, we can summarize the comparisons between logical backup and device backup; the iOS logical acquisition is fast and compatible with all iOS versions running on Apple devices using iTunes. Also, it gets shared application information but not all data files and databases of the iOS. In device backup, which is bit by bit, the backup will include all file systems with database and SQLite files, and deleted files also will be there. Android devices using ADB backup may get logical backup, since the device is not rooted, but if we have a rooted device, we can get physical backup reaching a low level of the file system with all database files.

[5]. **Analysis:** In this section, we will analyze the data acquired from iOS and Android OS, also comparing the acquisition tools used. The acquisition proceedings were conducted according to the iPad device while it's unlocked, and we used the logical

acquisition because the physical acquisition did not
occur while the iPad was not jailbroken. We moved
over the backup files that iTunes generated from the
device on the preceding path, and then we browsed
the "Manifest.db" database SQLite using the DB
SQLite viewer as shown in Figure 4-11.

[6].   **Verification:** After the acquisition, we did a
verification on the backup file that matches the real
device data by comparing the data in the backup
file with device data. Also, we took the hash value
of the file to make sure that there were no changes
in data. The hash file was taken using PowerShell in
Windows. Figure 4-6 shows the process of calculating
the hash file, also in text representation as SHA256:

00D32E16FE52AE6E69F5448778338344E12FC30F
F46D2FDE4D0C5CC282F29F4F

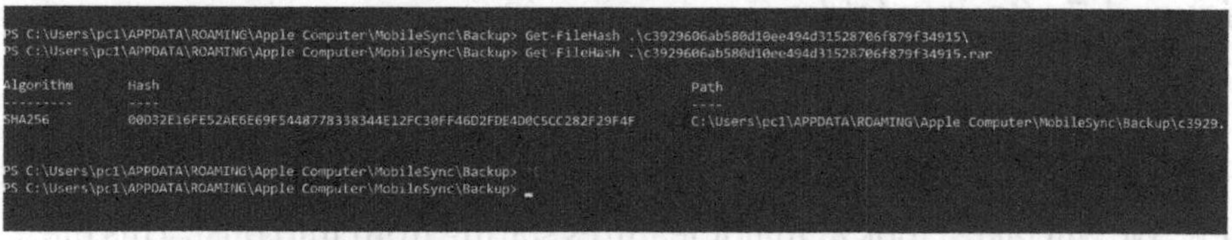

Figure 4-6. *Hash SHA256*

[7].   **Analysis and Findings:** Finally, we had the backup
file for iPad as shown in Figure 4-7. The system
gives a name for the backup as unique identifier
c3929606ab580d10ee494d31528706f879f34915, and
has the following files:

- *info.plist*

- *manifest.plist*

- *status.plist*

- *manifest.db*

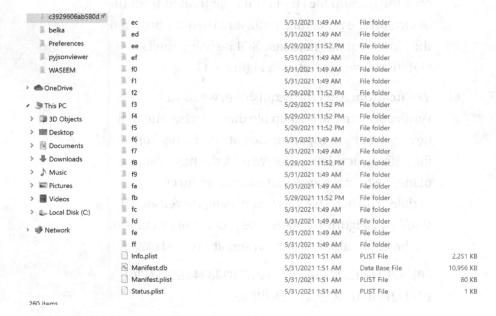

Figure 4-7. *Backup folder*

info.plist:

Inside this folder, as seen in Figure 4-8, is the screenshot for info.plist view. We will take a look at major features staring from info.plist. This file has the following information:

- *Applications:* All applications installed on iPad

- *Build version:* iOS build version: 18D52

- *Device name and display name:* Device owner name: Zain's iPad

- *Globally Unique Identifier (GUID):*
  1FE45D6A5076661CD28000DCC71C30D7

- *Last backup date:* 2021-05-30T22:51:54Z

- *Serial Number:* F9FXK5PYJMVR

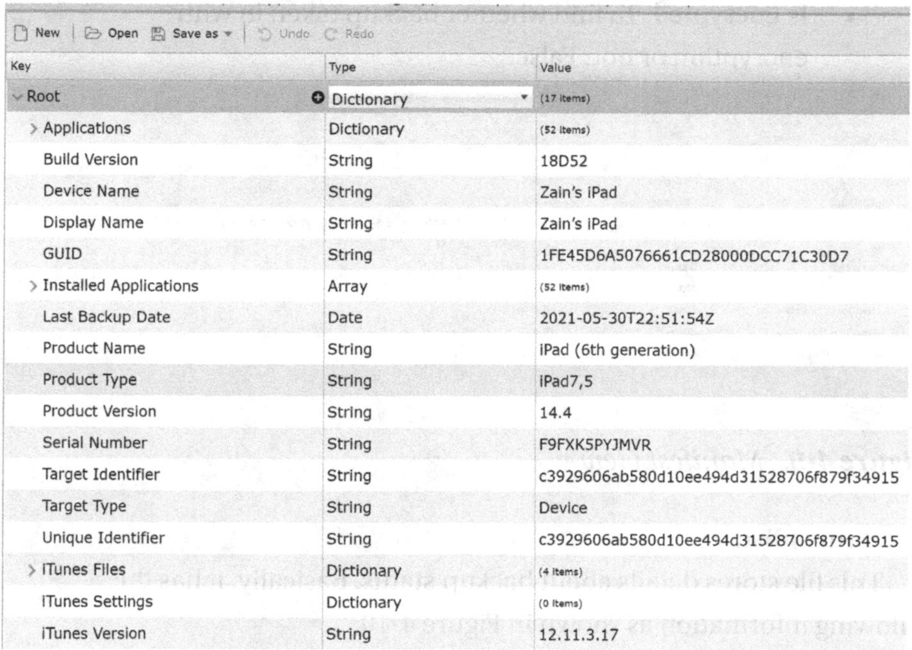

Key	Type	Value
⌄ Root	⊕ Dictionary ▾	(17 items)
› Applications	Dictionary	(52 Items)
Build Version	String	18D52
Device Name	String	Zain's iPad
Display Name	String	Zain's iPad
GUID	String	1FE45D6A5076661CD28000DCC71C30D7
› Installed Applications	Array	(52 Items)
Last Backup Date	Date	2021-05-30T22:51:54Z
Product Name	String	iPad (6th generation)
Product Type	String	iPad7,5
Product Version	String	14.4
Serial Number	String	F9FXK5PYJMVR
Target Identifier	String	c3929606ab580d10ee494d31528706f879f34915
Target Type	String	Device
Unique Identifier	String	c3929606ab580d10ee494d31528706f879f34915
› iTunes Files	Dictionary	(4 Items)
iTunes Settings	Dictionary	(0 Items)
iTunes Version	String	12.11.3.17

Figure 4-8. *info.plist view*

manifest.plist:

This file also describes the content of the backup file as shown in Figure 4-9, including the manifest view and the following information included inside it:

- *Backup keybag*: Key backup

- *Version:* Backup version 10.0

- *Date:* Last backup or updated 2021-05-23T21:38:56

- *WasPasscodeSet*: To find whether a passcode was set or
  was not. NO

- *Lockdown*: Holds iPad details, and other information.

- *Applications*: All third-party applications installed.

- Is Encrypted: To find whether backup taken in with
  encryption or not: False.

Key	Type	Value
C:\Users\pc1\AppData\Roaming\Apple Computer\MobileSync\Backup\c3929606ab580d10ee494d31528706f879f34915\Manifest.plist		
New Open Save as ▾ Undo Redo		
∨ Root	Dictionary	(8 items)
> Applications	Dictionary	(312 items)
BackupKeyBag	Data	<56455253 00000004 00000005 54595045 00000004 00000001 55554944 00000010 11447acc 31ab4...
Date	Date	2021-05-23T21:38:56Z
IsEncrypted	Boolean	False
> Lockdown	Dictionary	(12 items)
SystemDomainsVersion	String	24.0
Version	String	10.0
WasPasscodeSet	Boolean	True

Figure 4-9. *Manifest view*

status.plist:

This file stores details about backup status. Basically, it has the
following information as shown in Figure 4-10.

- *IsFullBackup*: False.

- *UUID:* E79B08BF-FD8E-41F5-9247-7E45474410D5

- *Date:* 2021-05-30T22:51:43Z

- *BackupState:* New

- *SnapshotState:* Has the backup process finished
  successfully: Finished.

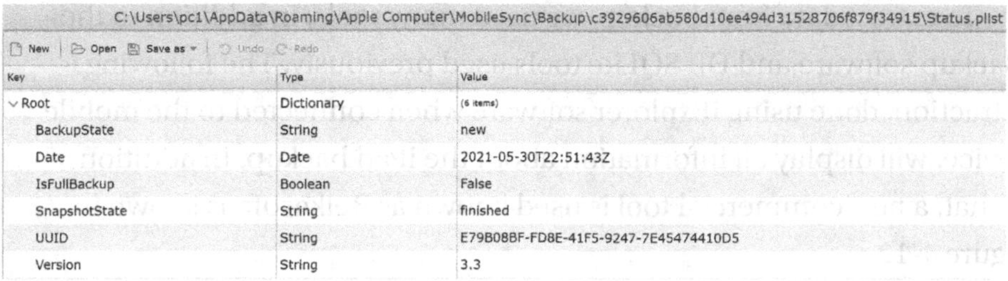

Key	Type	Value
Root	Dictionary	(6 items)
BackupState	String	new
Date	Date	2021-05-30T22:51:43Z
IsFullBackup	Boolean	False
SnapshotState	String	finished
UUID	String	E79B08BF-FD8E-41F5-9247-7E45474410D5
Version	String	3.3

Figure 4-10. *Status.plist view*

manifest.db:

It is an SQLite database that holds a list of all the files and folders extracted from the iPad, showing the table schema and data in the manifest database as shown in Figure 4-11.

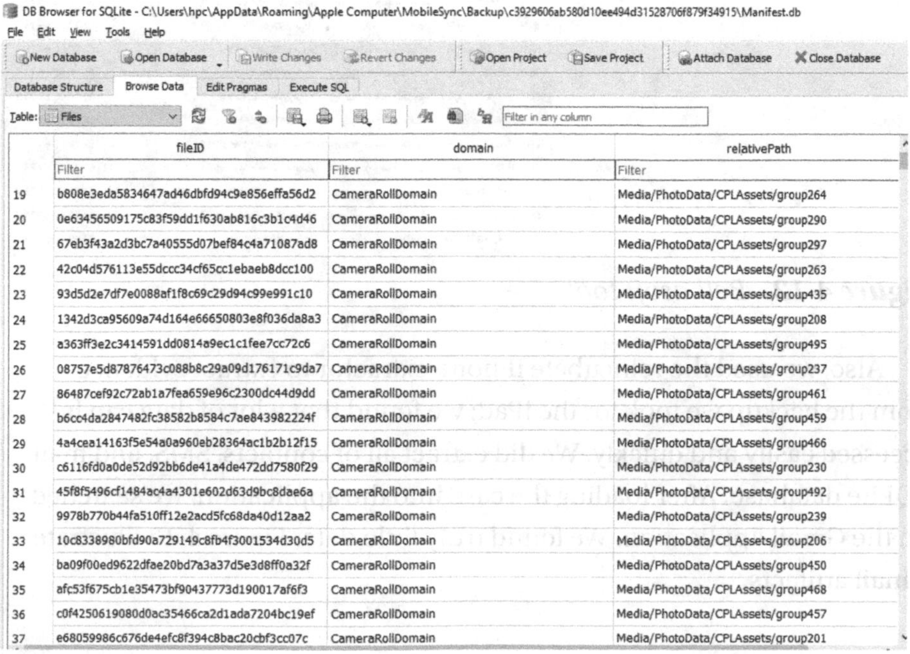

	fileID	domain	relativePath
	Filter	Filter	Filter
19	b808e3eda5834647ad46dbfd94c9e856effa56d2	CameraRollDomain	Media/PhotoData/CPLAssets/group264
20	0e63456509175c83f59dd1f630ab816c3b1c4d46	CameraRollDomain	Media/PhotoData/CPLAssets/group290
21	67eb3f43a2d3bc7a40555d07bef84c4a71087ad8	CameraRollDomain	Media/PhotoData/CPLAssets/group297
22	42c04d576113e55dccc34cf65cc1ebaeb8dcc100	CameraRollDomain	Media/PhotoData/CPLAssets/group263
23	93d5d2e7df7e0088af1f8c69c29d94c99e991c10	CameraRollDomain	Media/PhotoData/CPLAssets/group435
24	1342d3ca95609a74d164e66650803e8f036da8a3	CameraRollDomain	Media/PhotoData/CPLAssets/group208
25	a363ff3e2c3414591dd0814a9ec1c1fee7cc72c6	CameraRollDomain	Media/PhotoData/CPLAssets/group495
26	08757e5d87876473c088b8c29a09d176171c9da7	CameraRollDomain	Media/PhotoData/CPLAssets/group237
27	86487cef92c72ab1a7fea659e96c2300dc44d9dd	CameraRollDomain	Media/PhotoData/CPLAssets/group461
28	b6cc4da2847482fc38582b8584c7ae843982224f	CameraRollDomain	Media/PhotoData/CPLAssets/group459
29	4a4cea14163f5e54a0a960eb28364ac1b2b12f15	CameraRollDomain	Media/PhotoData/CPLAssets/group466
30	c6116fd0a0de52d92bb6de41a4de472dd7580f29	CameraRollDomain	Media/PhotoData/CPLAssets/group230
31	45f8f5496cf1484ac4a4301e602d63d9bc8dae6a	CameraRollDomain	Media/PhotoData/CPLAssets/group492
32	9978b770b44fa510ff12e2acd5fc68da40d12aa2	CameraRollDomain	Media/PhotoData/CPLAssets/group239
33	10c8338980bfd90a729149c8fb4f3001534d30d5	CameraRollDomain	Media/PhotoData/CPLAssets/group206
34	ba09f00ed9622dfae20bd7a3a37d5e3d8ff0a32f	CameraRollDomain	Media/PhotoData/CPLAssets/group450
35	afc53f675cb1e35473bf90437773d190017af6f3	CameraRollDomain	Media/PhotoData/CPLAssets/group468
36	c0f4250619080d0ac35466ca2d1ada7204bc19ef	CameraRollDomain	Media/PhotoData/CPLAssets/group457
37	e68059986c676de4efc8f394c8bac20cbf3cc07c	CameraRollDomain	Media/PhotoData/CPLAssets/group201

Figure 4-11. *Manifest data view*

To extract data from backup, we used many tools, in addition to the
iBackup software and DB SQLite tools used previously. The following
extraction, done using iExplorer software when connected to the mobile
device, will display all information about the iPad backup. In addition
to that, a new commercial tool is used known as Belkasoft as shown in
Figure 4-12.

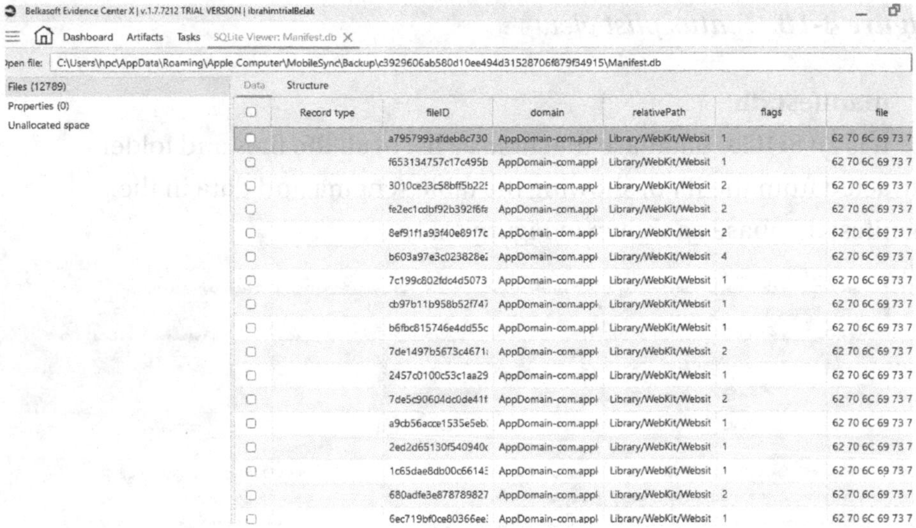

Figure 4-12. *Belkasoft tool*

Also, we used the reincubate iPhone extractor to extract evidence
from the backup we took for the iPad; we found that a lot of data can be
accessed easily and quickly. We did extract all of contacts, SMS, and mail
SQLite database. After loading the case into the application, we searched
on the Gmail application. We found truly little data. Figure 4-13 illustrates
Gmail artifacts.

Figure 4-13. *Gmail artifacts*

Also, we found the contact detail from the same interface; Figure 4-14 shows the data extracted.

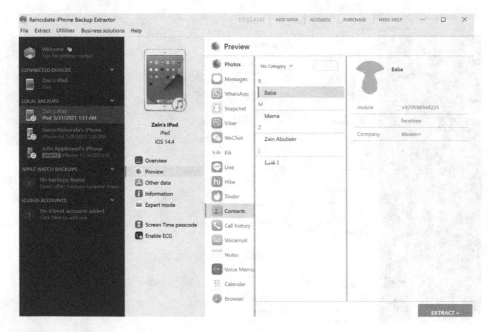

Figure 4-14. *Contact details*

Figure 4-15 shows the SMS extracted from the same software.

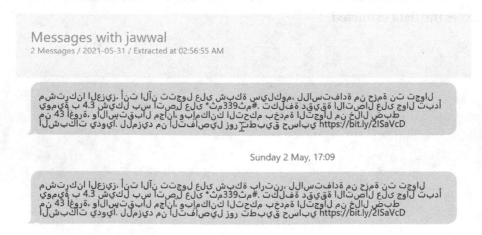

Figure 4-15. *SMS extraction*

130

Using the Belkasoft tools, we found an artifact related to our search topic, which is Gmail artifact. In Figure 4-16 we found messages between two parties as sender and receiver; this data was extracted from a hex dump file analysis.

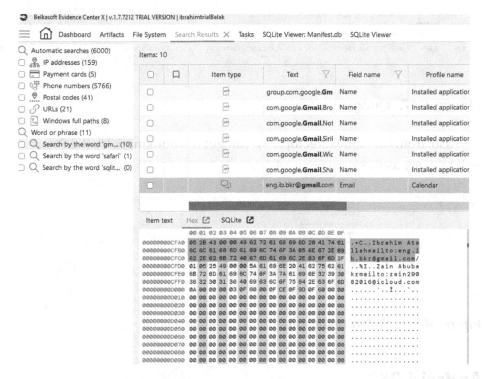

Figure 4-16. *Gmail artifact*

After extracting the backup file using elcomsoft, go to the home domain under the directory path C:\Users\hpc\Desktop\ elcomsoftwaseem\HomeDomain\Library\Safari. We found all directories needed in our investigation. We will look at the following:

> Form home domain/account as shown in
> Figure 4-17, then after performing the following
> command, select * from ZACCOUNTTYPE where
> ZACCOUNTTYPEDESCRIPTION like 'Gmail'.

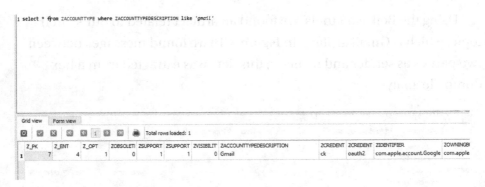

Figure 4-17. *Query result*

Also, from the same directory, we can get the bookmark for the Safari
web browser as shown in Figure 4-18.

	id	special_id	parent	type	title	url
1	0	0	NULL	1	Root	NULL
2	1	1	0	1	BookmarksBar	NULL
3	2	3	0	1	com.apple.ReadingList	
4	3	5	0	1	com.apple.FrequentlyVisitedSites	
5	4	0	1	0	Apple	https://www.apple.com/
6	5	0	2	0	سوار تبحث عن الحروف | ABC Song | sewar Pretend Play Learning Alphabet w/ Toys & Nursery Rhyme ...	https://youtu.be/NKIM0-LJtQw
7	6	0	1	0	Bing	https://www.bing.com/
8	7	0	2	0	سوينا مسبح للجى !!!	https://youtu.be/tVuu8wgdL7M
9	8	0	1	0	Google	https://www.google.com/?client
10	9	0	1	0	Yahoo	https://maktoob.yahoo.com/

Figure 4-18. *Safari bookmark*

Android OS

Our case will use two Android mobile devices (real devices) and one
virtual machine simulator as follows:

1. Tecno Spark 6GO.

2. Xiaomi Mi 8 lite (Figure 4-19 shows the Xaiomi
    mobile information)

3. Nox virtual machine mobile.

Figure 4-19. Xaiomi Mi 8 lite information

Physical extraction can apply only on rooted devices' bit-by-bit copies, including deleted files and nonallocated space of memory; the tool used to dump all data from the mobile is the "dd" command to copy bit-by-bit data, while its rooted mobile is as illustrated in Figure 4-20, which shows the process of physical backup in the shell command then using one of two methods to transfer the file to the Windows machine: either "ADB pull" or the NC command.

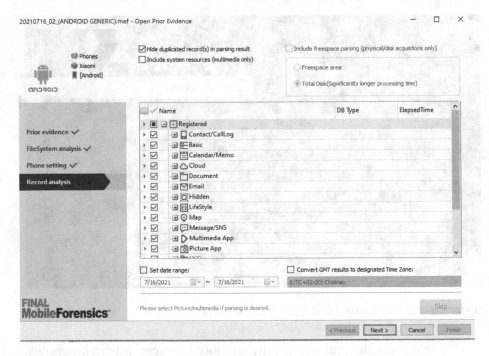

Figure 4-20. *FINALMobile data acquisition*

It is important to know that all acquisition methods will not take
a full backup if the device does not root state. Otherwise, it will be a
logical backup.

The rooting process is driven to get administrative privileges on the
device allowing the investigators to extract data from the application at
the root level. The root shell user called a superuser writes down as #
sign when logged in. We installed a virtual mobile machine on Mi Note 8
successfully after many rooting tries failed on the Chinese one (TECNO
SPART 6 GO) because the CPU architecture did not support the 64-bit
application and virtualizations. However, we did successfully install the
NOX emulator on the Windows computer to go in my experiment. After
doing root configuration on the NOX emulator, finally, we connected to the
shell as shown in Figure 4-21.

```
-r--r--r--  1 root            root            0 2021-07-15 23:26 zor
d2q:/proc # version
/system/bin/sh: version: not found
127|d2q:/proc # cat version
Linux version 4.0.9+ (sam@topaz0) (gcc version 4.8 (GCC) ) #30 SMF
d2q:/proc # cd ..
d2q:/ #
d2q:/ #
```

Figure 4-21. *Root user logged in*

Using Mobiledit and FINALMobile Forensic Software

Again Figure 4-22 shows the acquisition stage using ADB logical backup.
Since the data is found under the path */data/data/com.google.android.gm*,
the directories have only XML files about the emails with no data.

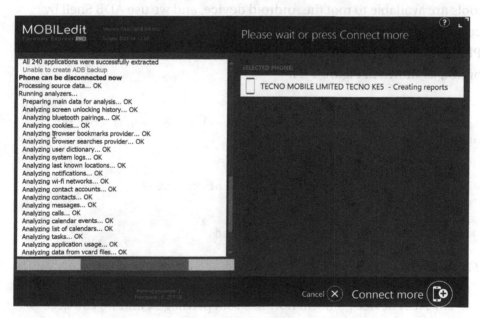

Figure 4-22. *Mobiledit ADB logical backup*

In the FINALMobile software, there was data extracted from the (.emf)
file but it was only cache data, as shown in Figure 4-23.

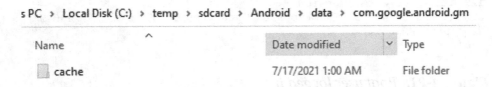

Name		Date modified		Type
cache		7/17/2021 1:00 AM		File folder

s PC › Local Disk (C:) › temp › sdcard › Android › data › com.google.android.gm

Figure 4-23. *FINALMobile software data analysis*

Rooted Device

In this section, we will do our investigation using root privileges; many
tools are available to root the Android device, and we use ADB Shell by
connecting the mobile device through USB cable, then navigating to the
Platform-Tools to view the device information and whether it's connected
or not, as shown in Figure 4-24.

```
::\platform-tools>add decices
 add' is not recognized as an internal or external command,
 perable program or batch file.

::\platform-tools>adb devices
' daemon not running; starting now at tcp:5037
' daemon started successfully
.ist of devices attached
)6094250AD002378          unauthorized
```

Figure 4-24. *ADB device list*

The NOX device platform now has root privileges, and we can access
the device as a superuser as shown in Figure 4-25. Here we connect the
device to the Windows machine using the adb.exe command. We find
the serial for the mobile and we obviously see the # sign, which is root
privileges.

```
-r--r--r--   1 root           root              0 2021-07-15 23:26 zor
d2q:/proc # version
/system/bin/sh: version: not found
127|d2q:/proc # cat version
Linux version 4.0.9+ (sam@topaz0) (gcc version 4.8 (GCC) ) #30 SMF
d2q:/proc # cd ..
d2q:/ #
d2q:/ #
```

Figure 4-25. *Root user logged in*

Using the "ls -l" command, we see the list of all files and directories
inside the Android as shown in Figure 4-26.

```
d2q:/ # ls -l
total 1832
dr-xr-xr-x  18 root   root          0 2021-07-15 23:24 acct
lrwxrwxrwx   1 root   root         50 1970-01-01 03:00 bugreports -> /data/user_de/0/com.andr
drwxrwx---   6 system cache       4096 2021-06-29 06:08 cache
lrwxrwxrwx   1 root   root         13 1970-01-01 03:00 charger -> /sbin/healthd
dr-x------   2 root   root         40 1970-01-01 03:00 config
lrwxrwxrwx   1 root   root         17 1970-01-01 03:00 d -> /sys/kernel/debug
drwxrwx--x  34 system system     4096 2021-06-29 06:08 data
-rw-r--r--   1 root   root        959 1970-01-01 03:00 default.prop
drwxr-xr-x  17 root   root       4100 2021-07-15 23:24 dev
lrwxrwxrwx   1 root   root         11 1970-01-01 03:00 etc -> /system/etc
-rw-r--r--   1 root   root      77090 1970-01-01 03:00 file_contexts.bin
-rw-r-----   1 root   root        396 1970-01-01 03:00 fstab.qcom
-rwxr-x---   1 root   root    1490548 1970-01-01 03:00 init
-rwxr-x---   1 root   root        887 1970-01-01 03:00 init.environ.rc
-rwxr-x---   1 root   root       3688 1970-01-01 03:00 init.qcom.rc
-rwxr-x---   1 root   root      25284 1970-01-01 03:00 init.rc
-rwxr-x---   1 root   root        582 1970-01-01 03:00 init.superuser.rc
-rwxr-x---   1 root   root       9283 1970-01-01 03:00 init.usb.configfs.rc
-rwxr-x---   1 root   root       5716 1970-01-01 03:00 init.usb.rc
-rwxr-x---   1 root   root        411 1970-01-01 03:00 init.zygote32.rc
lrwxrwxrwx   1 root   root         10 2021-07-15 23:24 lib -> system/lib
drwxr-xr-x  11 root   system      240 2021-07-15 23:24 mnt
drwxr-xr-x   2 root   root         40 1970-01-01 03:00 oem
dr-xr-xr-x 144 root   root          0 2021-07-15 23:24 proc
-rw-r--r--   1 root   root       4741 1970-01-01 03:00 property_contexts
drwx------   2 root   root         40 2021-04-21 10:50 root
drwxr-x---   2 root   root        140 1970-01-01 03:00 sbin
lrwxrwxrwx   1 root   root         21 1970-01-01 03:00 sdcard -> /storage/self/primary
-rw-r--r--   1 root   root        758 1970-01-01 03:00 seapp_contexts
-rw-r--r--   1 root   root         70 1970-01-01 03:00 selinux_version
-rw-r--r--   1 root   root     178142 1970-01-01 03:00 sepolicy
-rw-r--r--   1 root   root      11160 1970-01-01 03:00 service_contexts
drwxr-xr-x   4 root   root         80 2021-07-15 23:24 storage
dr-xr-xr-x  12 root   root          0 2021-07-15 23:24 sys
drwxr-xr-x  15 root   root       4096 1970-01-01 03:00 system
-rw-r--r--   1 root   root         38 1970-01-01 03:00 ueventd.qcom.rc
-rw-r--r--   1 root   root       4703 1970-01-01 03:00 ueventd.rc
lrwxrwxrwx   1 root   root         14 1970-01-01 03:00 vendor -> /system/vendor
d2q:/ #
```

Figure 4-26. *List of directories*

To navigate the desired data, we must go under the path *data/data/ com.google.android.gm as* shown in Figure 4-27, which includes the database of the Gmail email application.

```
2|d2q:/ # cd data/data/com.google.android.gm
d2q:/data/data/com.google.android.gm # pwd
/data/data/com.google.android.gm
d2q:/data/data/com.google.android.gm # ▄
```

Figure 4-27. *Gmail database*

Getting the database dump using shell command is the easiest way for us, and the second easiest is moving the database outside the mobile device using the commands in Table 4-2 and as shown in Figure 4-28.

```
d2q:/data/data/com.google.android.gm # mv new.tar /sdcard/
d2q:/data/data/com.google.android.gm # cd /sdcard/
d2q:/sdcard # ls
Alarms    Apps  Download  Music         Pictures  Ringtones  tmp.image   waseem.tar
Android   DCIM  Movies    Notifications Podcasts  new.tar    tmp1.image
d2q:/sdcard # exit

C:\platform-tools>adb pull /sdcard  c:\temp\
/sdcard/: 40 files pulled, 0 skipped. 34.0 MB/s (154206707 bytes in 4.321s)

C:\platform-tools>▄
```

Figure 4-28. *Database files pull process*

By using Linux command, the extracted data is obtained easily rather than the next one using GUI of SQLite, because the encrypted file is not manipulated in GUI but it is easy to decode it in Linux scripting shell as shown in Table 4-2.

Table 4-2. *List of Commands Used*

Tar -cvf new.tar /database/	Compress database directory to new.tar
Mv new.tar /sdcard	Moving archived file to sdcard in order to pull it to our machine
Adb pull /sdcard/new.tar c:\temp	Copy new.tar to temp directory in C drive

Under the path of the data file for Gmail, which is /data/data/com.
google.android.gm/databases, listing all files in this directory as in
Figure 4-29.

```
d2q:/data/data/com.google.android.gm/databases # ls -l
total 4448
-rw-rw----  1 u0_a44 u0_a44 2417664 2021-07-17 01:40 1_threads.notifications.db
-rw-------  1 u0_a44 u0_a44    8720 2021-07-15 11:30 1_threads.notifications.db-journal
-rw-rw----  1 u0_a44 u0_a44  315392 2021-07-15 11:28 EmailProvider.db
-rw-------  1 u0_a44 u0_a44    8720 2021-07-15 11:28 EmailProvider.db-journal
-rw-rw----  1 u0_a44 u0_a44   32768 2021-07-15 11:28 EmailProviderBody.db
-rw-------  1 u0_a44 u0_a44    8720 2021-07-15 11:28 EmailProviderBody.db-journal
-rw-rw----  1 u0_a44 u0_a44   20480 2021-07-16 20:01 accounts.notifications.db
-rw-------  1 u0_a44 u0_a44   12824 2021-07-16 20:01 accounts.notifications.db-journal
-rw-------  1 u0_a44 u0_a44  389120 2021-07-17 02:38 bigTopDataDB.808030098
-rw-------  1 u0_a44 u0_a44   32768 2021-07-17 02:42 bigTopDataDB.808030098-shm
-rw-------  1 u0_a44 u0_a44  524288 2021-07-17 02:42 bigTopDataDB.808030098-wal
-rw-rw----  1 u0_a44 u0_a44   24576 2021-07-16 20:01 crash_reports
-rw-------  1 u0_a44 u0_a44   12824 2021-07-16 20:01 crash_reports-journal
-rw-rw----  1 u0_a44 u0_a44    4096 2021-07-16 10:39 downloader.db
-rw-------  1 u0_a44 u0_a44   32768 2021-07-16 10:41 downloader.db-shm
-rw-------  1 u0_a44 u0_a44   74192 2021-07-16 10:41 downloader.db-wal
-rw-rw----  1 u0_a44 u0_a44    4096 2021-07-16 10:39 metadata.808030098.db
-rw-------  1 u0_a44 u0_a44   32768 2021-07-17 02:33 metadata.808030098.db-shm
-rw-------  1 u0_a44 u0_a44  185432 2021-07-17 02:33 metadata.808030098.db-wal
-rw-rw----  1 u0_a44 u0_a44    4096 2021-07-17 11:30 peopleCache_a0598944225@gmail.com_com.google_11.db
-rw-------  1 u0_a44 u0_a44   32768 2021-07-17 01:52 peopleCache_a0598944225@gmail.com_com.google_11.db-shm
-rw-------  1 u0_a44 u0_a44  300792 2021-07-17 01:52 peopleCache_a0598944225@gmail.com_com.google_11.db-wal
drwx------  3 u0_a44 u0_a44    4096 2021-07-15 11:30 shared_data
-rw-rw----  1 u0_a44 u0_a44   20480 2021-07-16 20:06 suggestions.db
-rw-------  1 u0_a44 u0_a44    8720 2021-07-16 20:06 suggestions.db-journal
drwx------  3 u0_a44 u0_a44    4096 2021-07-15 11:43 user_accounts
```

Figure 4-29. *Gmail database files*

We found that a file with extension (.db) is easy to browse its content
either by command or by GUI as described in later sections. For example, if
we want to browse the data inside accounts.notifications.db, the following
command is used as in Figure 4-30.

```
d2q:/data/data/com.google.android.gm/databases # sqlite3 accounts.notifications.db
SQLite version 3.9.2 2017-07-21 07:45:23
Enter ".help" for usage hints.
sqlite> .tables
accounts          android_metadata
sqlite> .quit
d2q:/data/data/com.google.android.gm/databases # sqlite3 accounts.notifications.db
SQLite version 3.9.2 2017-07-21 07:45:23
Enter ".help" for usage hints.
sqlite> .tables
accounts          android_metadata
sqlite> select * from accounts;
1|a0598944225@gmail.com|11812245057095078101011|0|0|1|1626454876931|-1853296347|1626337812193112
sqlite>
```

Figure 4-30. *Data analysis in Linux command*

And this could be opened on SQLite software. But when trying to open a Write Ahead Log (WAL) file, this could not be opened in GUI as SQLite because this software did not support the extension of this file.

What we did to open the file and extract the messaging from the file itself. We used Linux shell command "cat" concatenated with "grep" as (cat * | grep test); here the term "test" is used for analysis and how the file is written inside. After deep analysis of the result of the preceding command. Finally, we found all things we were searching for, and the following are some hints that help investigators to read the data shown in Figure 4-31.

- Line starting with (↔thread-a) means it is a sent message and has subject and body.

- Line starting with (sg-a) means sender email address.

- Line starting with (∟thread-f) means it is an inbox message and has subject and body.

- Line starting with (deleted email) means it is a deleted email and found in a trash folder.

- Line starting with (▲thread-a:) means it is a draft message.

- Attachment and time creations found in the next section.

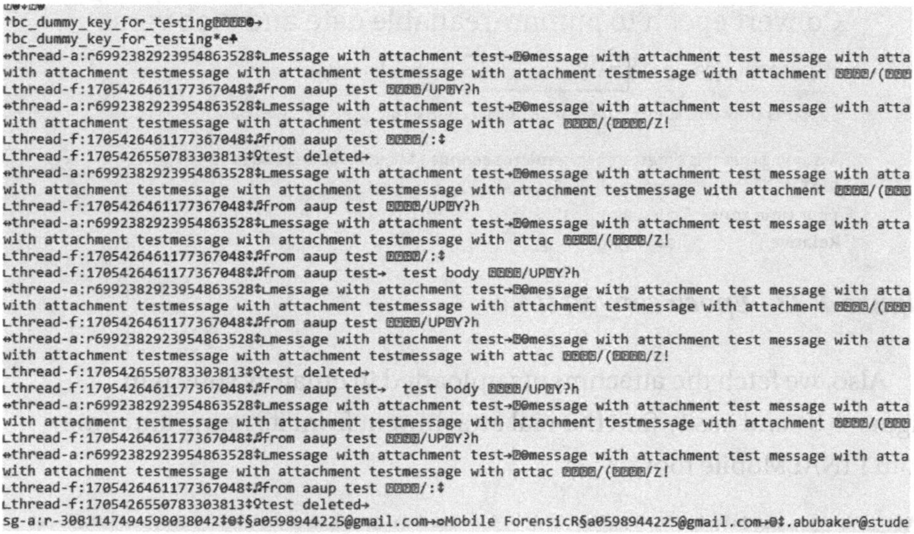

```
ↆbc_dummy_key_for_testing▨▨▨▨➊→
ↆbc_dummy_key_for_testing*e◆
↔thread-a:r6992382923954863528‡Lmessage with attachment test→▨▨message with attachment test message with atta
with attachment testmessage with attachment testmessage with attachment testmessage with attachment ▨▨▨▨/(▨▨▨
Lthread-f:1705426461177367048‡♫from aaup test ▨▨▨▨/UP☺Y?h
↔thread-a:r6992382923954863528‡Lmessage with attachment test→▨▨message with attachment test message with atta
with attachment testmessage with attachment testmessage with attac ▨▨▨▨/(▨▨▨/Z!
Lthread-f:1705426461177367048‡♫from aaup test ▨▨▨▨/:‡
Lthread-f:1705426550783303813‡♀test deleted→
↔thread-a:r6992382923954863528‡Lmessage with attachment test→▨▨message with attachment test message with atta
with attachment testmessage with attachment testmessage with attachment testmessage with attachment ▨▨▨▨/(▨▨▨
Lthread-f:1705426461177367048‡♫from aaup test ▨▨▨▨/UP☺Y?h
↔thread-a:r6992382923954863528‡Lmessage with attachment test→▨▨message with attachment test message with atta
with attachment testmessage with attachment testmessage with attac ▨▨▨▨/(▨▨▨/Z!
Lthread-f:1705426461177367048‡♫from aaup test→ test body ▨▨▨▨/UP☺Y?h
↔thread-a:r6992382923954863528‡Lmessage with attachment test→▨▨message with attachment test message with atta
with attachment testmessage with attachment testmessage with attachment testmessage with attachment ▨▨▨▨/(▨▨▨
Lthread-f:1705426461177367048‡♫from aaup test ▨▨▨▨/UP☺Y?h
↔thread-a:r6992382923954863528‡Lmessage with attachment test→▨▨message with attachment test message with atta
with attachment testmessage with attachment testmessage with attac ▨▨▨▨/(▨▨▨/Z!
Lthread-f:1705426550783303813‡♀test deleted→
Lthread-f:1705426461177367048‡♫from aaup test→ test body ▨▨▨▨/UP☺Y?h
↔thread-a:r6992382923954863528‡Lmessage with attachment test→▨▨message with attachment test message with atta
with attachment testmessage with attachment testmessage with attachment testmessage with attachment ▨▨▨▨/(▨▨▨
Lthread-f:1705426461177367048‡♫from aaup test ▨▨▨▨/UP☺Y?h
↔thread-a:r6992382923954863528‡Lmessage with attachment test→▨▨message with attachment test message with atta
with attachment testmessage with attachment testmessage with attac ▨▨▨▨/(▨▨▨/Z!
Lthread-f:1705426461177367048‡♫from aaup test ▨▨▨▨/:‡
Lthread-f:1705426550783303813‡♀test deleted→
sg-a:r-30811474945980038042‡◊‡§a0598944225@gmail.com→◊Mobile ForensicR§a0598944225@gmail.com→◊‡.abubaker@stude
```

Figure 4-31. WAL file content

SQLite Viewer

In Figure 4-32, we see a pulled directory that contains all data base files; the figure also shows the associated account, which is a0598944225@gmail.com.

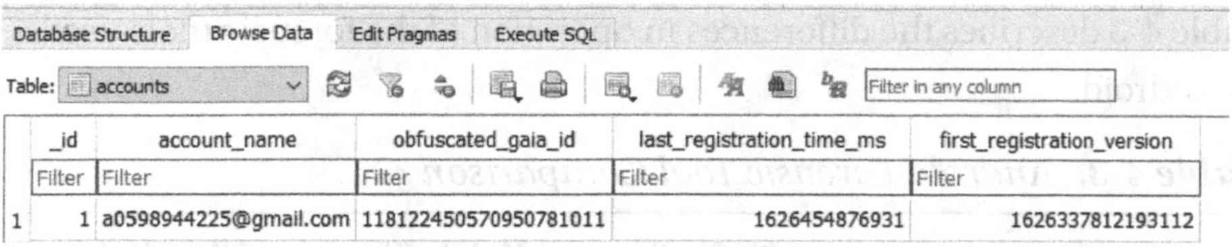

	_id	account_name	obfuscated_gaia_id	last_registration_time_ms	first_registration_version
	Filter	Filter	Filter	Filter	Filter
1	1	a0598944225@gmail.com	118122450570950781011	1626454876931	1626337812193112

Figure 4-32. SQLite viewer Gmail account table

In addition to that, we decode the time of the first_registration_version from epoch time to human-readable time to see when this account is created. The time equal to 1626337812193112 is shown in Figure 4-33.

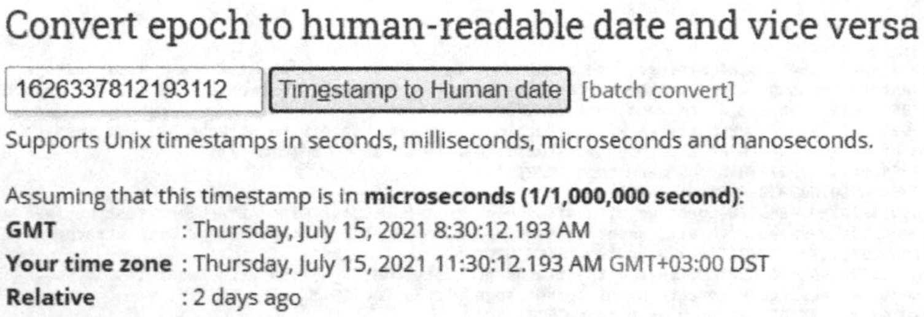

Convert epoch to human-readable date and vice versa

| 1626337812193112 | Timestamp to Human date | [batch convert]

Supports Unix timestamps in seconds, milliseconds, microseconds and nanoseconds.

Assuming that this timestamp is in **microseconds (1/1,000,000 second)**:
GMT   : Thursday, July 15, 2021 8:30:12.193 AM
Your time zone : Thursday, July 15, 2021 11:30:12.193 AM GMT+03:00 DST
Relative   : 2 days ago

Figure 4-33. *Epoch convert time*

Also, we fetch the attachments uploaded in email as shown in
Figure 4-34 and easily find the real attachment from its name and time
from FINALMobile tool.

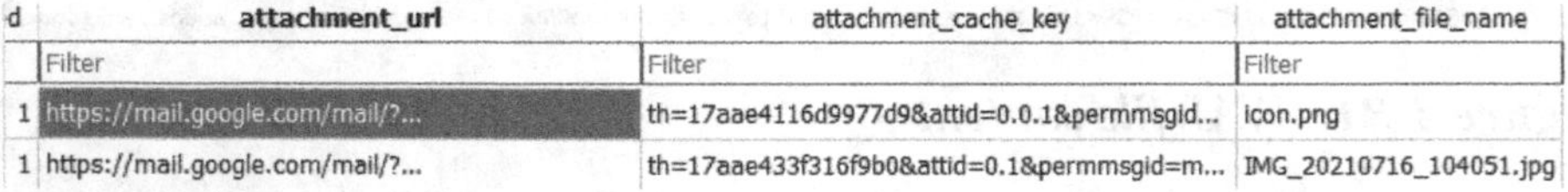

d	attachment_url	attachment_cache_key	attachment_file_name
	Filter	Filter	Filter
1	https://mail.google.com/mail/?...	th=17aae4116d9977d9&attid=0.0.1&permmsgid...	icon.png
1	https://mail.google.com/mail/?...	th=17aae433f316f9b0&attid=0.1&permmsgid=m...	IMG_20210716_104051.jpg

Figure 4-34. *Attachment details*

Forensic Tools Comparisons

Table 4-3 describes the differences in operation of the forensic tools used
in Android.

Table 4-3. *Android Forensic Tool Comparison*

	ADB Shell	**Mobiledit**	**FINALMobile**
Acquisition via connected USB ADB	Yes	Yes	Yes
Gmail data files	Yes	(NO) Only XML	(NO) Meta data
Gmail data file from backup	No	(Yes) Only XML	(Yes) Meta data
SQLite database	SQLite3 built in	No	Yes

Mobile Forensics for Google Drive

Cloud computing is a form of Internet-based computing that allows computers and other devices to access shared information-processing resources and data on demand. Because of the rapid technological evolution related to mobile devices and cloud computing, users could access their resources from any place and at any time. Nowadays, the use of cloud storage media is very popular among Internet users, especially with the Google Drive cloud storage media on smartphones. Google Drive is a file storage and sharing platform that provides storing and synchronizing many types of users' files, which can be accessed via their Google accounts. Google Drive applications can be installed on Apple and Android smartphones, so viewing, editing, uploading, sharing, and synchronizing documents are available on these devices.

This section's case is an exercise in analyzing evidence by applying a mobile forensic method on an Android smartphone, on which the Google Drive application is already installed. To analyze the evidence, a crime situation has been created in which the user saves a photo of drugs on the smartphone's Google Drive. Many forensic software programs were used to acquire the Google Drive data. Firstly, the Belkasoft Evidence center was used but it gives an error "Operation completed with errors" and not all the data required could be opened. Another one is the Mobiledit Forensic Express; the data was acquired but hashed.

Evidence collection is the first step in securing evidence discovered by police or investigators is preservation. In this case, the prosecutor received proof from the owner in the form of a Xiaomi Redmi Note 8 Pro smartphone with the operating system Android 9.0 Pie, 4GB RAM, and the Google Drive application installed on it. The isolation process is required to avoid changing data on the smartphone by triggering the Airplane mode feature. This feature is allowed to disable all data access that might compromise the smartphone's data integrity. This procedure is followed

in order to ensure data integrity. Data integrity is achieved by imaging files
from the physical evidence using Mobiledit Forensic Express. The phone
image was created but hashed.

```
Name=Drive
Package=com.google.android.apps.docs
Version=2.21.141.02.40
IsSystem=2
AppSize=60370344
DataSize=0
CacheSize=0
FirstInstallTime=20081231T160000Z
LastUpdateTime=20210421T120020Z
InstallerPackageName=com.android.vending
PackageUid=10120
```

Figure 4-35. *Google Drive description*

According to Android architecture, the Google Drive app is in the
system app layer where the system application and the user applications
are found. The Google Drive used in our case was the standard application:
version 2.18, as described in Figure 4-35.

Rooting is a term used in mobile forensics that refers to granting the
mobile user an access to their devices to perform activities that are not
allowed normally. In the selected case, when acquiring the unrooted
device, a restricted scope of data was acquired, but in case of rooting,
the data folder could be accessed and more evidence was collected. The
owner of the app (email address) was shown, and the deleted data was also
displayed in the summary report as shown in Figure 4-36.

The Structure of Files (3855 files total, 4 deleted)

Filename		Size	Created	Modified	Accessed
Files/					
Files/My Drive/					2017-11-14 13:27:27
New Doc 1.pdf		1.99 MB	2016-09-25 21:41:05	2016-10-06 14:08:55	2017-12-22 05:19:34
File	https://drive.google.com/file/d/0B69B5YEpc7y7a05WNXp0aXZRbWVaNXJWY1ILUExxT0RDTV9n/view?usp=drivesdk				
Owner	shadiajayousi@gmail.com				
Last Modifier	Shadia Jayousi				
Deleted	Yes				

Figure 4-36. *Deleted data*

A Samsung mobile device with root access was used with the following specifications: model: G7102 Galaxy Grand 2 (SM-G7102), IMEI: 359907052716647, SN: 271644, Android version: 4.4.2, built-in memory: 8 GB. it was rooted using Odin 3.31 as shown in Figure 4-37.

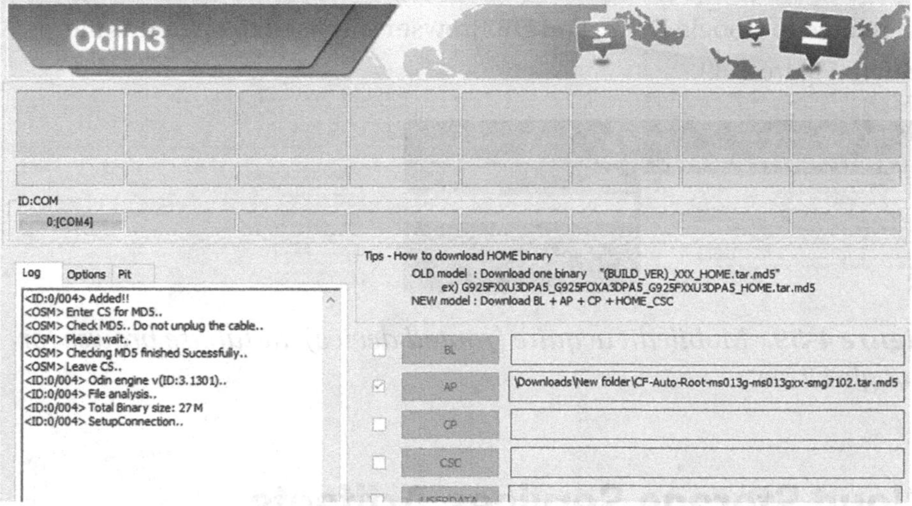

Figure 4-37. *Odin for rooting*

ADB commands were used for displaying the connected device, and ADB was used to back up the data. Then, the image was converted to a .tar file using the Java -jar command, and the image was copied to a local workstation, as shown in Figure 4-38.

```
C:\platform-tools>adb backup -shared -all
WARNING: adb backup is deprecated and may be removed in a future release
Now unlock your device and confirm the backup operation...

C:\platform-tools>bin\java -jar abe.jar unpack C:\platform-tools\backup.ab backup.tar

C:\platform-tools>_

C:\platform-tools>adb.exe pull  /data/data/com.drive.android/databases C:\temp
adb: error: remote object '/data/data/com.drive.android/databases' does not exist

C:\platform-tools>
```

Figure 4-38. *Backup from device to workstation*

Belkasoft was used to acquire the device but it gives "operation completed with errors"; Mobiledit Forensic Express was used to acquire evidence from this device, and it gave a detailed report about the mobile data including all the content of Google Drive like contacts, photos, and files. According to database files, there was a database file in the backup file related to Google Drive, and DB Browser was used to open this file, as seen in Figure 4-39.

Figure 4-39. *Mobiledit acquire (rooted device), database browse for Google Drive*

Cloud Storage Services Artifacts

Analysis of the logical excerpt of the iPhone locates file names related to the identified Google Drive account in the "History.plist" file, and the information was also reported in the .XRY "Web-History.txt" file. As evidence was stored on the iPhone, it was confiscated by IO Jones. The username and filenames for the accessed files are included in the information on an Apple iPhone that identifies the use of Google Drive. Conducting a study on physical extracts of data from an iPhone and comparing them to information from a logical extract would be linked [8]. Each application uses specific methods to manage the cloud data: in the following we introduce how each app manages the data in the mobile device.

- **Amazon S3**: By running Amazon's S3 on an iPhone, a
  plist file and an SQLite database file will be generated.
  The plist file includes the user's name, access key ID,
  and secret access key. These are used for accessing
  Amazon S3 on an iPhone [7].

- **Dropbox**: By running Dropbox on an iPhone, a plist file
  and two SQLite database files will be generated. The
  plist file includes an email address for login, and the
  first login time using that iPhone [7].

- **Evernote**: By running Evernote on an iPhone, many
  types of files will be generated such as applog.txt,
  which is a text file that reports the history of the use of
  Evernote [7].

- **iGoogDocs**: By running iGoogDocs on an iPhone,
  a plist file and an HTML file will be generated. The
  plist file includes a value for auto-login that can be
  "true" or "false." If the auto-login is "true," the plist file
  contains user account information, including even the
  password. In Google Docs for the iPhone, it is possible
  to create text files. They are stored in a folder named
  "Local Files." The contents of the files are in an HTML
  file [7].

Summary

Gmail is the only email that has come with default Android application in
the last couple of years, and it is used to create accounts and define private
(non-Gmail) accounts on it, which makes it easy for the users to handle
their emails via Android mobiles.

147

Nowadays, the data forensic since is used for white and black purposes; we as students at Arab American University achieved the goal of the mobile forensics course, which is how to do successful mobile forensics in order to extract data from mobiles. My experiment shows that there is no way to extract Gmail data by logical acquisition nor by manuals unless you have an authorized access, and the only way to bring the application data from the device is if physical acquisitions are there. But physical acquisition will not be valid without root permission on Android devices or jailbreak on iOS.

Recently, iOS devices have been able to extract data information about the account and sender receiver subject of the email, but no data is given about the email body itself because of the nonjailbreak device; that is why we did not access superuser privileges.

The Android version had no vulnerability to do root easily, and the developers had hardened their codes to be increasingly robust and secure. In our experiment on both devices, Xiaomi Mi 8 lite and Techno Spark with Android 10 QKQ the rooting failed, but we succeeded to root on virtual mobile Galaxy Note 10 successfully.

Lastly, we got all the information in Gmail including accounts, creation date of accounts, sent email, inbox, draft, and deleted files.

References

[1]. J. Starkey, "Google Drive," *The Charleston Advisor,*
      p. 4, 2013.

[2]. D. M. Rathod, "Google Drive Forensics," *csjournals,*
      vol. 8, no. 2, p. 6, 2017.

[3].   2018. *Law by Decree No. 10 of 2018 on Cybercrime.*
[eBook] Available at: `<https://security-`
`legislation.ps/sites/default/files/law/`
`Law%20by%20Decree%20No.%2010%20of%202018%20`
`on%20Cybercrime.pdf>` [Accessed 21 April 2021].

[4].   R. Tamma, O. Skulkin, H. Mahalik and
S. Bommisetty, *Practical Mobile Forensics*, 2020.

[5].   A. Yudhana, R. Umar and A. Ahmadi, "Digital
Forensics," *Scientific Journal of Informatics,* vol. 6,
p. 10, 2019.

[6].   C.-T. Huang, H.-J. Ko, Z.-W. Zhuang, P.-C. Shih and
S.-J. WANG, "Mobile Forensics for Cloud Storage
Service on iOS Systems," *IEICE,* vol. 1, p. 5, 2018.

[7].   M. Faheem, M.-T. Kechadi and N.-A. Le-Khac, "The
State of the Art Forensic Techniques in Mobile
Cloud Environment: A".

[8].   H. Chung, J. Park and S. Lee, "Digital Forensic
Investigation of Cloud Storage Services," p. 20, 2018.

[9].   DarrenQuick, B. Martini and R. Choo, "Google
Drive: Forensic of Cloud Storage Data Remnants," in
Cloud Storage Forensics, Syngress, 2013, p. 95

[10].   Y.-T. Chang, K.-C. Teng, Y.-C. Tso and S.-J. Wang,
"Jailbroken iPhone Forensics for the Investigations
and Controversy to Digital Evidence," *Journal of
Computers,* vol. 26, p.15, 2015.

CHAPTER 5

Forensic Analysis of Telegram Messenger on iOS and Android Smartphones Case Study

Mobile digital forensics science is developing on a daily basis, and every day there is a new tool introduced and a new challenge as well. This chapter is to get hands-on with all available forensics tools, in order to identify the benefits of using each tool, practice them to get results faster, and be able to assess in each situation which is the most suitable tool to use in order to get accurate results in a relatively short time. In this chapter, we used two images for the evidence in order to assess the ability of different tools to extract the results and be able to build a strong case when it comes to Telegram Messenger investigations on iOS devices.

© Mohammed Moreb 2022
M. Moreb, *Practical Forensic Analysis of Artifacts on iOS and Android Devices*,
https://doi.org/10.1007/978-1-4842-8026-3_5

This chapter consists of three experiments that perform evidence acquisition, examination, and analysis along with a discussion of admissible evidence for a digital investigation case against the Telegram Messenger application running on an iOS device and an Android device, and a Telegram desktop application running under Windows OS. The focus is on digital forensics against mobile devices that run iOS and Android OS.

In this chapter, we will cover the following topics:

- Digital Forensics Process Steps

- Telegram App History

- Ethical and Legal Compliance

- Methodology and Experiment Setup

- iOS Device Acquisition

- Android Device Acquisition

- iOS Evidence Analysis Using FINALMobile

- Evidence Analysis Results

Digital Forensics Process Steps for Telegram

Short message services (SMS) are the most commonly used communication means. With the evolution of technology, the messaging services over time became instant messaging (IM) services and allowed the exchange multimedia in different formats rather than just sending a text message. You can now send voice, images, videos, and all documents with different extensions and formats. Nowadays, there are a lot of IMs available all over the world, like WhatsApp, Telegram, Snapchat, iMessage, LINE, and Viber. Most of these services provide a variety of interfaces to use the service itself, including but not limited to mobile applications for different operating systems like Android and iOS, a Web interface that is accessible via internet browsers, and desktop applications that run on different desktop operating systems.

Despite the value presented by the IMs, normal people are still concerned about the privacy of their data while they are stored on their devices, transmitted over the network, and received by other parties. Other types of people consider this as the following question: "Can police detect me if I did something illegal using this IM service?" And from a digital forensics point of view, a digital examiner might think about "How can I get and analyze digital evidence from this service?"

This practical case focuses on the Telegram IM service using its desktop application interface from a digital forensics point of view. The paper investigates the file structure of the Telegram desktop app in terms of data storage on the computer, mobile device file hierarchy, data encryption, and possible ways to analyze the evidence and extract the stored data on the operating system. Telegram IM has a million active subscribers; most of those subscribers are from the Middle East, Central and Southeast Asia, and Latin America [4]. And a more recent study shows that by 2020, Telegram had over 200 million active users monthly [5]. With this high number of users, the probability of using the service in illegal and terrorist actions is high. Since Telegram claims it provides ultrasecurity due to end-to-end encryption, this will encourage illegal actions.

Telegram App History

Telegram was founded in 2013 by the brothers Nikolai and Pavel Durov, who created VK, the best-known Russian social network [8]. It was originally located in Russia, then it got banned in Russia due to a court decision related to an encryption dispute [9]. From Russia, Telegram moved through several locations from Berlin to London and is now located in Dubai [10]. Over the years, Telegram evolved to include more features including but not limited to:

[1]. Channels

[2]. Groups

[3]. Secret Chats

[4]. Stickers

[5]. Audio and Video Calls

[6]. Share Location and Live Location

[7]. Bots

[8]. People Nearby and Groups Nearby

Many researchers conducted a digital investigation against mobile applications, web interfaces, and desktop applications of IM service clients. In 2016, Satrya, Gandeva, and Bayu analyzed the Telegram Android app; the researchers were able to extract data from the application and the Android file system. They were able to explore the cached files, contact information, multimedia, and the data base as shown in Figure 5-1, and they concluded that the acquired data from mobile can be used as digital evidences in cybercriminal cases [14].

/data/app/	/sdcard/Telegram	/data/data/.org.telegram.messenger
APK File	**Telegram Files**	**Cache Database (cache4.db)**
(dex/java file)	1. Telegram Audio	1. User activities
	2. Telegram Documents	2. Contact information
	3. Telegram Images	3. Messages Exchange
	4. Telegram Video	4. Sharing location/files
		5. Delete chat

Figure 5-1. *Telegram Android file system*

In 2018, Gregorio, Alarcos, and Gardel researched forensic analysis of
Telegram in desktop on Mac OS and explained the problem of Telegram
encrypted file headers "0x54444624" ("TDF$" in ASCII), as shown in
Figure 5-2. The researchers stated that there is no straightforward way
to extract data from the acquired device image by analyzing the content
of the encrypted files, but they were able to extract data by running the
acquired device image into a virtual machine and running the Telegram
app and connecting it to the cloud, or by live investigation on the suspect
machine, highlighting that the investigators need to consider the chain of
custody [15].

```
00000000  54 44 46 24 3f 46 0f 00  00 00 00 20 e4 f1 0f e4  |TDF$?F..... ....|
00000010  e3 12 b3 44 5e 27 f5 4e  e6 79 45 6b 16 e6 b6 95  |...D^'.N.yEk....|
00000020  88 97 fe 63 2f a9 37 31  0c 8a b3 e5 00 00 02 c0  |...c/.71........|
00000030  b2 c6 b6 4c 3e e1 27 9a  d5 8f 5c 66 75 fa 1f 0e  |...L>.'...\fu...|
00000040  38 e2 be 8a 3e e9 36 27  6e 13 fa 0c c6 70 15 7c  |8...>.6'n....p.||
00000050  7f a3 82 a0 83 67 b1 94  55 29 40 d7 e5 fc 9c 8e  |.....g..U)@.....|
00000060  3f 7a 8d 0a 1f ff cb b5  22 d8 be 07 96 4f bf df  |?z......"....O..|
00000070  27 43 7e f6 db 16 ff fc  4d ba 0d 5b 8b b6 f8 f4  |'C~.....M..[....|
00000080  88 d8 13 9f 4e 62 49 76  e4 38 d8 0c b1 32 ab 7e  |....NbIv.8...2.~|
00000090  d7 33 3b 41 a1 f2 fb ac  71 bd 60 55 21 9a 75 fd  |.3;A....q.`U!.u.|
```

Figure 5-2. *Telegram files header*

Ethical and Legal Compliance

In 2019, Borodin, Veynberg, Pisarev, and Litvishko researched artifact
simulation for Viber and Telegram IMs in the Windows operating system;
the researchers were able to extract useful artifacts from registry keys
related to the Telegram installation date, file structure, and database.
The files of the application were listed under the following directory:
"/AppData/Roaming/Telegram Desktop/". The database was stored in
encrypted file format and they weren't able to access the content of the
files. Another useful finding was that they can locate the downloaded
documents and media from the Telegram IM desktop app under the

directory of "User Name/Downloads/Telegram Desktop/" without any encryption, just straightforward access [16].

- The researcher confirms that all the actions done during this investigation, starting from fake account setup and ending with evidence acquisition and analysis, are done for learning purposes, that no messages are sent to anyone else except the created accounts for the experiment, and that none of the findings of this research will be used in facilitating criminal activities in any manner.

- The researcher declares that all materials used in creating the research data do not contain any offensive or threatening words, copyrighted media, violent content, or sexual content, and that any word that was used in the context of the research, such as extortion, is only an indication to preserve the context of the research and does not reflect the actual content of the message. The investigation of this case study falls under the local law by decree.

Methodology and Experiment Setup

Our practical case methodology of this chapter aims to set up two Telegram accounts as two parties of communication and send different messages to generate some research data, and then to do evidence acquisition, analysis, and reporting according to NIST recommendations.

A.   Telegram Accounts Setup

The researcher uses the temporary mobile number +1 (940) 666-1798** to create the first Telegram account. The researcher pretends to be a user who sends extortion messages to other users, as well as creating a group chat, and sending different types of messages supported by Telegrams like text messages, voice recordings, images, and video recordings. The second Telegram account is created using the temporary mobile number +1 (940) 448-7279**, which is the second part of communication.

The research uses the first Telegram account as the extortionist and the second Telegram account as the victim who got extorted. After the creation of Telegram accounts, the researcher installed Telegram from the App Store on iOS that is running iOS v14.4.2 and installed the Telegram from Play Store on Android devices running Android v11. After the installation of the application on both devices, the researcher logged in using the extortionist account on both devices to generate the research evidence. To perform the investigation, the researcher built an investigation machine that is capable of performing the needed evidence acquisition, evidence processing, and reporting for both the required hardware and software/ tool set that is capable of doing required tasks. The next section describes in detail the investigation workstation built by the researcher.

B.   Investigation Workstation Specifications

For the purpose of evidence acquisition, analysis, and reporting, the following hardware platform is set up with the following hardware and software specifications:

- **CPU** - *Intel Core i5 10400f 2.90 GHz*

- **RAM** - *16 GB DIMM 2666 MHz*

- **Storage** - *256 GB M.2 SSD*

- **Page File** - *Enabled*

- **Operating System** - *Windows 10 Pro Version 1909*

- **File System** - *NTFS*

- **User Account** - *Microsoft Account*

157

- **Acquisition and Analysis Software** - *Belkasoft Evidence Center*, Version 9.9 Build 4662 x64 [18]

- **Acquisition and Analysis Software**- *FINALMobile Forensics user version*, Version 2020.04.22 [19]

- **Acquisition and Analysis Software** - *Magnet AXIOM*, Version 4.6.0.21968 [20]

- **Analysis Software** - *Elcomsoft Phone Viewer*, Version 5.20 Build 37270 [21]

- **Acquisition Software** - *AccessData FTK IMager*, Version 4.5.0.3 [22]

- **Investigation Software** - *Autopsy Digital Forensics*, Version 4.16.0 [23]

- **Investigation Software** - *Registry Viewer*, Version 1.8.0.5 [24]

- **Virtualization Software** - *VMware Workstation Pro*, Version 16.1.0 Build 117198959 (x64) [25]

- **Utility Software** - *iDeviceInfo*, Version 1.3.17 [26]

- **Utility Software** - *Rufus*, Version 3.14 [27]

iOS Device Acquisition

After the preparation of the experimental evidence, the researcher starts the evidence acquisition process using different techniques depending on the evidence type and OS. The following subsections show the details of the evidence and the acquisition process conducted for each evidence.

The first acquired evidence is an Apple iPhone 6s Model (A1688) running iOS version 14.4.2 with an iCloud account connected to the device. Touch ID is set up and a six-digit screen unlock PIN is associated

with the device. The researcher used iDeviceInfo Script [26] to extract
all the possible details of the devices after connecting them to the
investigation machine. Note that for some reason, the scripts read the
device type to be iPhone 8. Figure 5-3 shows a portion of the device details
obtained using the script.

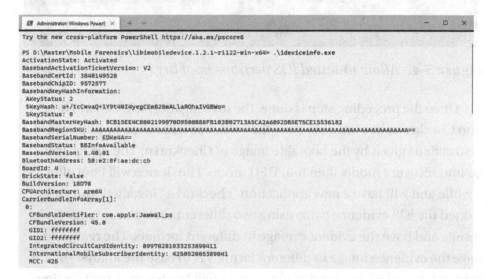

Figure 5-3. *iPhone 6s evidence details using iDeviceInfo*

The purpose of this investigation is to acquire a full disk image using
the "Full File System" option; the researcher performed a jailbreak
operation for the acquired mobile device using Checkra1n software [28].
The case created a live boot USB flash drive for Checkra1n using Rufus
[27] to perform a jailbreak operation on the acquired device. Since the iOS
version of the acquired device is not officially tested and supported by the
developers of the software, the researcher selected to "allow the untested
iOS versions" boot argument in the operation as shown in Figure 5-4; this
is a mandatory step to have this operation be successful.

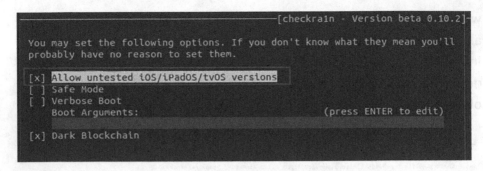

Figure 5-4. *Allow untested iOS versions boot args*

Once the preceding step is done, the investigation workstation booted into Checkra1n live image to have the evidence jailbroken by following the instructions given by the bootable image of Checkra1n. The device will go into recovery mode, then into DFU mode. The device will boot after a while and will have a new application "checkra1n" installed. Our case cloned the iOS evidence twice using two different tools to compare the results and have the evidence image in different formats. The reason to have the evidence image in different formats is to ease the analysis of the evidence based on the needed purpose, as will be shown in next section when analyzing the evidence.

Acquisition Using Belkasoft

Belkasoft is an integrated evidence center that is able to perform acquisition for a wide set of evidence including but not limited to storage media, RAM, mobile devices, and clouds, Belkasoft can show, categorize, and carve artifacts from multiple data sources. The reason behind selecting Belkasoft for acquisition is the generated evidence image after the acquisition is done. Our case is interested in having a full image of the acquired evidence, which is achievable due to having jailbreak enabled on the mobile device. This will allow Belkasoft to create an evidence image

file with the ".tar" extension; this file can be easily handled with a mobile-
specific tool as shown in the next section. Table 5-1 provides the details of
the acquired iPhone mobile evidence image.

Table 5-1. *Acquired iPhone Mobile Details Extracted by FINALMobile*

Dump Image Information	
File Name	20210506 A1688.mef
File Size	9.6GB (10,353,855,818 Bytes)
MD5 Hash Value	9CDB3089FB1010EDF15359F824BBC637
Verified MD5 Hash Value	9CDB3089FB1010EDF15359F824BBC637

Acquisition Using FINALMobile

There are two reasons behind selecting FINALMobile for acquisition in this
case. First, FINALMobile has a strong reporting tool that generates a well-
detailed report and reflects all important information about the acquired
evidence, which is very important to have your case admissible. Second,
it's not always able to open tar files generated by Belkasoft. Table 5-2 shows
the acquired iPhone mobile device details extracted by FINALMobile.

Table 5-2. *Acquired iPhone Mobile
Details Extracted by FINALMobile*

Phone Information	
Phone Model	A1688
Product Name	iPhone 6S
Platform	Apple
Type of Dump	MEF2
Vendor	Apple

Android Device Acquisition

The second set of acquired evidence is from an Android device with model
Ulefone Note 9P running Android 10. The device contains a Gmail account
that is activated and used as a Play Store account as well. To gain the most
benefits from the experiment, the research uses an Android rooted version
[29], which is the equivalent to jailbreak in iOS devices.

Rooting is the process of granting privileged control (known as root
access) over certain Android subsystems to users of the Android mobile
operating system. Because Android is built on a modified version of the
Linux kernel, rooting an Android device grants administrative (superuser)
permissions in the same way as rooting a Linux or other Unix-like
operating system like FreeBSD or macOS does [29]. In order to perform
rooting for the device before being simulated as evidence, the researcher
installed custom recovery into the operating system to gain root access.
Installing custom recovery for an Android operating system can be done
using different methodologies depending on Android version and device
manufacturer. Two common custom recoveries can be used to root an
Android device. The first one is ClockworkMod (CWM) [30], and the
second one is Team Win Recovery Project (TWRP) [31]. Both recoveries
and/or any other custom recoveries allow the user to enable the root
access permission, which results in having the mobile device user able to
completely control the operating system at all levels.

Rooting Ulefone Note 9P Android Device

The device used in the experiment can't be rooted directly using TWRP
or CWM custom recoveries. To achieve root access, the researcher used
unofficial TWRP recovery and then flashed the related programs into the
Android OS to have root access. The following paragraphs explain the
methodology of rooting the device, which has a Mediatek process MT6762
Helio P22 (12 nm).

We installed the following programs and recovery images to root the device. *Magisk V21.4* will provide root access to the applications [32].

1. *vbmeta.img* and *recovery.img* for installing the custom recovery image for the Android and replacing the stock version of the recovery and bootloader.

2. *Orange Red State State Disabler* and *No Verity Opt Encrypt* to avoid bootlock and bypass the Device Mapper Variety (Dm-verity) security mechanisms, which minimize the rate of rootkits that can run on the device and prevent device compromising.

3. *Android SDK Platform Tools* [33] to provide the ability to execute commands through terminal/ command prompt, using *ADB* and *fastboot* commands to reboot the device into recovery mode and install applications using *ADB install* command.

4. *SP Flashtool v5.1924* [34] will be used to flash the custom recovery image into the operating system to replace the stock recovery image and bootloader.

5. Ulefone Note 9P stock firmware *GQ3092SH1_HC_ M629_Ulefone_EEA_20200701_V12.tar.gz,* which will be used to extract the scatter file of the operating system and provided to SP Flash Tool to flash the custom recovery image.

To boot into recovery mode, first, you need to connect the mobile device into the investigation workstation and enable the USB debugging option from the developer options of the mobile settings as introduced in chapter 3. USB debugging allows sending commands from the investigation workstation to the connected mobile device over the USB cable.

1. The first thing to do is to unlock the bootloader
   to be able to flash a new bootloader and recovery
   image. Since the device ships by default with a
   locked bootloader, this means we can't flash a new
   bootloader or modify system partitions [35]. To boot
   into recovery mode, run the command *adb reboot
   recovery*

2. Once the mobile device is rebooted, select the
   FastBoot option from the recovery menu by
   navigating using the volume down button and
   power button to perform the selection.

3. After seeing Fastboot screen on the mobile, execute
   the following command to unlock the OEM
   bootloader *fastboot flashing unlock*

4. After the OEM bootloader is unlocked, we need to
   flash vbmeta.img, recovery.img, and erase userdata
   to adapt with the new partition structure. To do this,
   we execute the following commands in order:

   a. Flash vbmeta.img: *fastboot flash vbmeta vbmeta.img*

   b. Flash recovery.img: f*astboot flash recovery recovery . im*g

   c. Erase user data: *fastboot erase userdata*

   d. Boot into custom recovery: *fastboot boot recovery . img*

Once the steps are done, extract the content of the stock ROM and
locate the scatter file; for the mobile device used in the experiment, the
file name is MT6765_Android scatter.txt. The scatter file is a .txt file that
is used to describe loads of regions in an Android device that is running
on MediaTek's ARM architecture. Figure 5-5 shows a portion of the file
internals.

```
 4  #
 5  ################################################################################################
 6  - general: MTK_PLATFORM_CFG
 7    info:
 8      - config_version: V1.1.2
 9        platform: MT6765
10        project: k62v1_64_bsp
11        storage: EMMC
12        boot_channel: MSDC_0
13        block_size: 0x20000
14  ################################################################################################
15  #
16  #  Layout Setting
17  #
18  ################################################################################################
19  - partition_index: SYS0
20    partition_name: preloader
21    file_name: preloader_k62v1_64_bsp.bin
22    is_download: true
23    type: SV5_BL_BIN
24    linear_start_addr: 0x0
25    physical_start_addr: 0x0
26    partition_size: 0x40000
27    region: EMMC_BOOT1_BOOT2
28    storage: HW_STORAGE_EMMC
29    boundary_check: true
30    is_reserved: false
31    operation_type: BOOTLOADERS
```

Figure 5-5. *MediaTek scatter file*

5. Using SP Flash Tool, we provide the scatter file
    as an input to the tool and specify the location of
    the recovery.img by double-clicking the recovery
    option, ensuring that the only selected option is
    recovery, as shown in Figure 5-6.

165

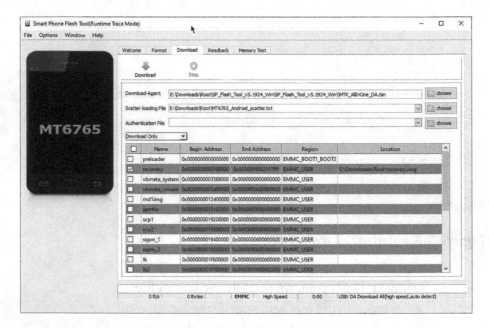

Figure 5-6. *Recovery flashing options – SP Flash Tool*

6. Turn off the mobile, click the download button
    shown in Figure 5-7, and then connect the mobile
    to the investigation workstation using a USB cable.
    SP Flash Tool will detect the mobile and replace the
    boot partition with the recovery.img file content.

7. Connect the device to the workstation and copy the
    Magisk, No verity opt encrypt, orange State Disabler
    files into the mobile internal storage or SD card and
    reboot into recovery again.

8. Once the device is booted into recovery, use the
    option install to flash the files in order Magisk, no
    verity opt encrypt, and finally orange State Disabler.

Once the process is done, the operating system is
rooted and the new bootloader is able to bypass
the device mapper variety security as shown in
Figure 5-7.

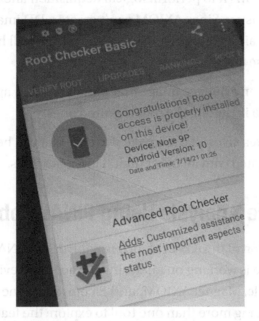

Figure 5-7. *Root verification after flashing process*

Acquisition Using FINALMobile

After rooting the device, the researcher used FINALMobile to perform
acquisition for the connected evidence. During the acquisition process,
FINALMobile wasn't able to detect that the device was rooted and tried to
perform its way of rooting the device. This will be discussed in the analysis
section. We used the Android backup option to generate an image with
MEF format to be fully compatible with FINALMobile parsing tools. Even it
wasn't able to gain the benefit of dealing with rooted devices.

Acquisition Using Magnet AXIOM

We acquired the data using Magnet AXIOM to generate a tar image for the device since it can gain the benefit of having root privilege, as shown in Figure 5-6. This allows it to perform logical acquisition and gain an image with the TAR extension. Since AXIOM can't create a DD image for the acquired device, gaining a logical image of the mobile will be more than enough in this case for two reasons.

- Creates an evidence image that has all the files, apps, and data including the root required ones.

- Generates an evidence image with .tar that can be investigated with all other digital forensics tools.

iOS Evidence Analysis Using FINALMobile

After the acquisition of the iOS evidence is done using FINALMobile and Belkasoft, our case is working on analyzing the acquired evidence images using FINALMobile, Magnet AXIOM, and Elcomsoft Phone Viewer. The analysis is done using more than one tool to explore the features that each tool provides for Telegram artifacts and the ease of use for this purpose. In the next sections, we explain the analysis and processing done using the three tools mentioned in the preceding paragraph.

We used FINALMobile to import the evidence image that was created before using the same software. During the case setup, the researcher selected a list of artifacts that are parsed by the tool like contacts, messages, emails, multimedia, and so on. Figure 5-8 shows the selected options for the added evidence image to include them in the evidence processing.

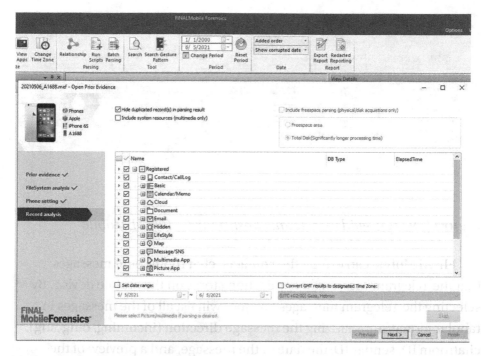

Figure 5-8. *Evidence parsing options using FINALMobile*

After the evidence image parsing is done, the FINALMobile dashboard lists the extracted artifacts in tabs format and shows the categories of the artifacts in the workspace explorer with the ability to change the categories to be based on the app or the category. Figure 5-9 shows the dashboard of the loaded evidence details.

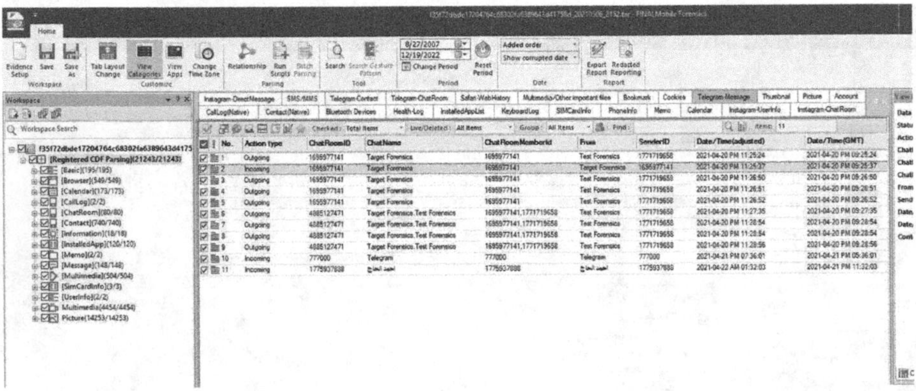

Figure 5-9. *iOS evidence details dashboard – FINALMobile*

FINALMobile can extract the contacts, chat rooms, and messages
that the Telegram Messenger application stores on the mobile device. By
selecting the Telegram messages, the tool will list all of the messages in a
tabular format summarizing the message direction (incoming, outgoing),
chatroom ID, sender ID, the date of the message, and a preview of the
message content as shown in Figure 5-10. To get more details about the
sender of a certain message, we copy the SenderId value for that message
and by exploring the Telegram Contact tab, we can find the details of the
sender. As shown in Figure 5-10, where the research used the sender ID
"1771719658" and by checking the Telegram contacts, all of the available
details are retrieved.

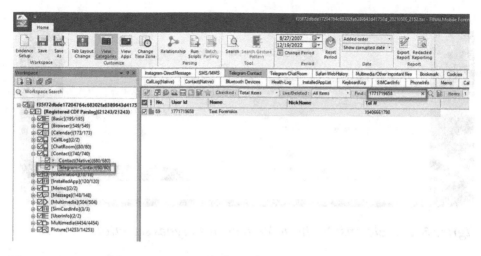

Figure 5-10. *Telegram contact details on iOS evidence- FINALMobile*

iOS Evidence Analysis Using Elcomsoft Phone Viewer

For our practical case, we used Elcomsoft Phone Viewer as a quick tool
to preview the obtained image without too many artifact extraction
techniques, since it's able to open the evidence image in a relatively short
time compared to the deep forensics tools. Elcomost Phone Viewer can
read iOS images with file extension tar, so the research will be using the
acquired evidence image using Belkasoft as a data source for the tool. After
selecting the data source (iOS device image), the tool will ask for the data
types to be processed from the selected image, as shown in Figure 5-5.
And once the processing is done, the tool will show a dashboard with the
acquired device name, serial number, phone number, and so on, and the
available artifacts will be processed from the provided data, source as
shown in Figure 5-11.

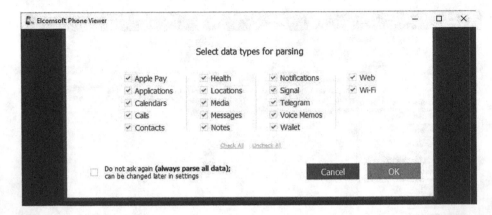

Figure 5-11. *Elcomsoft Phone Viewer data types selection*

After evidence loading and processing is done, the researcher selects
Telegram from the dashboard to start exploring the messages and
contracts connected with the application. The tool shows the details of
the Telegram account that is activated and used on the acquired mobile as
evidence. Figure 5-12 shows the details of the user account.

Figure 5-12. *Telegram account details exported by Elcomsoft*

The tool will categorize the available information that got extracted from the evidence and related to Telegram based on their types, where the investigator can select to navigate to the message sender, for example by clicking the name of the sender. Figure 5-13 shows the extracted messages from the application with hyperlinks to navigate between the tabs using the connections between the messages, senders, and attachments. The tool provides a complete section to explore the attachments, where the investigator can preview the attachments of the messages and find the related path of the attachment to extract it as a separate file aside from other messages. Note that not all of the attachments can be previewed, as will be discussed in the next section.

Figure 5-13. *Telegram message details exported by Elcomsoft*

iOS Evidence Analysis Using Magnet AXIOM

Magnet AXIOM is a very strong forensics tool that can acquire and analyze
evidence from different sources like computers, mobile, cloud, and so on.
The research uses Magnet AXIOM for analysis purposes only. The reason
for using the tool for analysis is to use the same data source that is acquired
from the evidence and perform the comparison using different tools. The
research uses the evidence image that is acquired by Belkasoft as a data
source for Magnet AXIOM in order to perform the analysis since Magnet
AXIOM accepts image files with tar extensions. After providing the evidence
image as a data source to the tool, the researcher selects to process all
possible artifacts that AXIOM can detect and export from the evidence, as
shown in Figure 5-14. Even this process will take a long time, but it will result
in having all the artifacts extracted and organized in a relevant way.

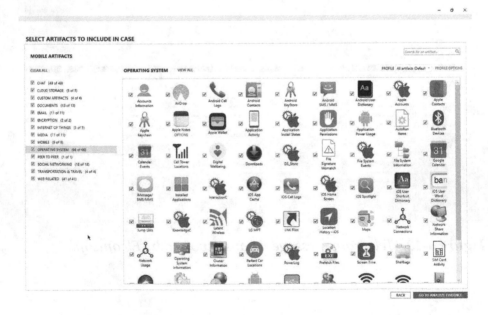

Figure 5-14. *AXIOM artifact selection for iOS evidence image*

After the evidence processing is done, the AXIOM dashboard will
be displayed and show the exported artifacts categorized based on
their relevant category. The investigator can navigate to certain artifact
categories by clicking the name of the desired category or by navigating
the artifacts section and expanding the desired artifact, as shown in
Figure 5-15.

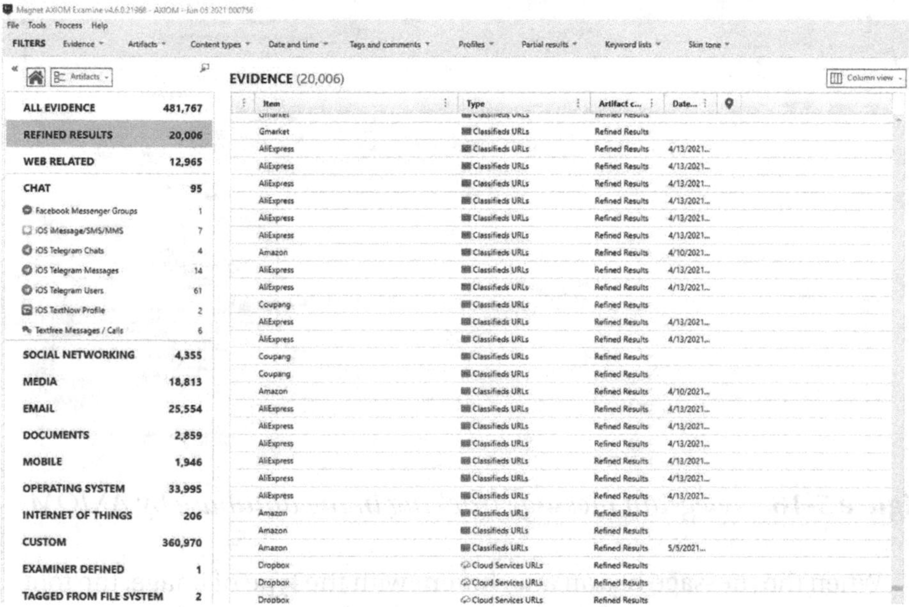

Figure 5-15.   *AXIOM artifacts page for the processed iOS evidence*

The research selects the "iOS Telegram Messages" artifact from the
"CHAT" artifact category. Then the tool displays the messages in a tabular
format with all details related to the message like the sender name,
sender ID, recipient name, recipient ID, message body, date, attachments
thumbnail, message direction (sent, received), message status (read,
unread), and so on. Also, it provides a preview of the attachment. The
advantage of using Magnet AXIOM is that it provides the source of the
extracted message/attachment from the database and shows tracking

for messages in the database records. And in case the message has an attachment, it shows the path of the attachment in the file system with hyperlinks to navigate to the exact file in the acquired evidence image, as shown in Figure 5-16.

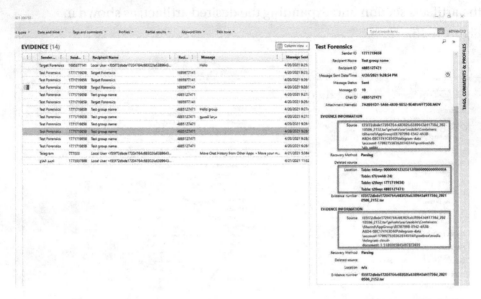

Figure 5-16. *Telegram message tracking in the database by AXIOM*

When the message has an attachment with the type of image, the tool will show preview for the attached image upon selecting the message, as shown in Figure 5-17.

Figure 5-17. *Telegram message attachment preview by AXIOM*

When the attachment type is not an image, note that there is no
straight way to detect this, unlike Elcomsoft Phone Viewer. The tool is still
able to preview the attachment by clicking the source link for the selected
message, the file system view of the tool will be displayed, and the desired
file will be selected, as shown in Figure 5-18. The tool has an integrated
viewer, so it's able to play videos and audio recordings.

Figure 5-18. *Telegram message attachment preview in the file system by AXIOM*

Android Evidence Analysis

After the acquisition of the Android evidence is done using FINALMobile and Magnet AXIOM, the research will work on analyzing the acquired evidence images using FINALMobile, Magnet AXIOM, and Belkasoft Evidence Center. The analysis is done using more than one tool to explore the features that each tool provides for Telegram artifacts and the ease of use for this purpose. These sections discuss analysis, and processing was done using the three tools introduced and used in our practical case.

Android Evidence Analysis Using FINALMobile

The forensics investigator used FINALMobile to open the image created by the tool itself with MEF format. Investigator selected all the artifacts to be processed. The second processing using the image acquires the Magnet AXIOM with the AR extension. The reason for using FINALMobile for those two extensions is to compare what FINALMobile can gain by itself and how

it's able to behave with the TAR extension files once they are provided by
another tool. The processing for the two provided images in FINALMobile
is the same in terms of selecting the source evidence and the device
specifications. For the acquired evidence, there is no clear category for the
mobile, so the researcher selected Android – Other, and then selected all
possible artifacts, parsing options for both images, as shown in Figure 5-19.

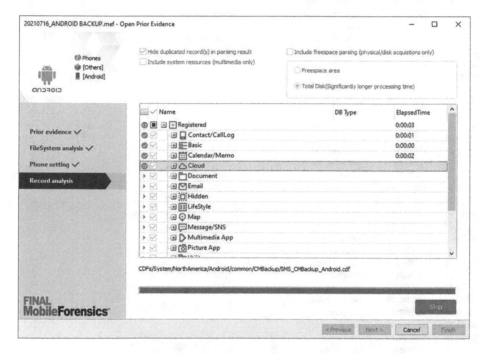

Figure 5-19. *Android image parsing options – FINALMobile*

The analysis of the two given images with MEF and TAR format
resulted in the same Telegram-related artifacts. The tools were able to
extract the Telegram contacts stored on the acquired image as shown in
Figure 5-19, and by using File Explorer of the tool and navigating to the
Telegram file directory, the tool can display all the multimedia stored on
the device under the directory *Media01/sdcard/Telegram.* That was used
by Telegram, as shown in Figure 5-20.

☑	!	No.	User Id	Name	NickName
☑	≣	1	777000	telegram	
☑	≣	2	54357387	elias abu lail	
☑	≣	3	135642408	oksana katrych	oksy10
☑	≣	4	143280593	ahmad khamis	
☑	≣	5	357017584	ayman	arh922
☑	≣	6	371089654	mohammad hilal	mhshilal
☑	≣	7	485324584	ahmad hammoudi	hammoudi00
☑	≣	8	722250167	ammar dawabsheh	ammaro1234
☑	≣	9	741515140	sameh elnabaway	
☑	≣	10	758347436	mohammed metwaly	nouralhayah4cp
☑	≣	11	894774985	tareq issa	
☑	≣	12	928874617	ibrahim shawahni	ibrahimshawahni
☑	≣	13	944734968	khabab shawahni	khabab10
☑	≣	14	975273066	imad tabib	
☑	≣	15	996420017	tamer zorba	
☑	≣	16	1086163529	malik motan	
☑	≣	17	1121538929	mohammed noman	
☑	≣	18	1134897584	ibrahim khalil	
☑	≣	19	1140858705	mohammad salameh	
☑	≣	20	1193695864	khaleel musleh	
☑	≣	21	1230704671	khabab shawahni	
☑	≣	22	1235218927	safa nasser eldin	
☑	≣	23	1253587680	ammar shaar	ammarshaar
☑	≣	24	1289455196	yousef odeh	
☑	≣	25	1332946783	abdaala howari	
☑	≣	26	1380492555	furrera	
☑	≣	27	1409742343	walaa abdul aziz	walaa0987
☑	≣	28	1453789221	mauricio poot	
☑	≣	29	1496972119	rashed abed alhamed	
☑	≣	30	1574040248	motasem shtayeh	
☑	≣	31	1578007022	bodor farra	
☑	≣	32	1608106208	omar zeidan	
☑	≣	33	1618342440	mohammad zetawi	
☑	≣	34	1695977141	target forensics	
☑	≣	35	1765911349	zaer qaroush	
☑	≣	36	1766426680	ateeq ateeq	
☑	≣	37	1771719658	test forensics	

Figure 5-20. *Android Telegram contacts parsing – FINALMobile*

Even the database of the Telegram application was pulled from the
acquired evidence and included in both images; the FINALMobile wasn't
able to recognize or parse the messages stored in the DB as it was able to
do that when conducting iOS analysis; see Figure 5-21.

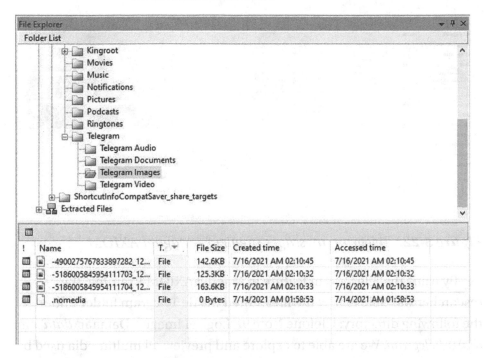

Figure 5-21. *Android Telegram multimedia parsing – FINALMobile*

Android Evidence Analysis Using Magnet AXIOM

Once the Magnet AXIOM Process is completed with processing, and
parsing the provided evidence image as a data source, the researcher
used Magnet AXIOM Examine to explore and extract the Telegram-related
artifacts. The tool was able to extract Telegram contacts, Telegram chats,
and Telegram messages relying on the cache4.db file, but the tool wasn't
able to preview the content of the sent and received messages, as shown in
Figure 5-22.

Figure 5-22. *Telegram messages preview – Magnet AXIOM*

By using the File System feature in Magnet AXIOM Examine, the researcher was able to find the files stored inside Telegram folder under the following directory: Ulefone Note 9P Logical Image – Data.tar*data**media*\\0*Telegram*. We are able to explore and preview all multimedia used by Telegram within AXIOM Examine without the need for exporting the file and viewing it using the external viewer, as shown in Figure 5-23.

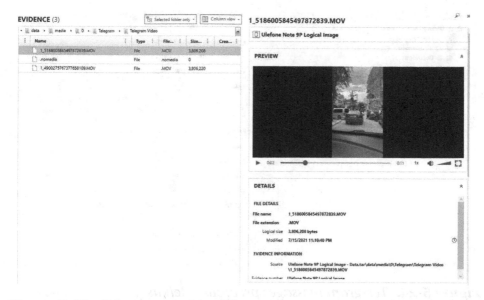

Figure 5-23. *Telegram multimedia preview – Magnet AXIOM*

Android Evidence Analysis Using Belkasoft Evidence Center

We used Belkasoft Evidence Center to process the acquired evidence image using Magnet AXIOM Process with the TAR extension format. Belkasoft started working on processing the provided evidence image with TAR extension and carved its content against the selected artifacts to present the extracted artifacts. After the processing of the evidence is done using the selected artifacts, the tool was able to recognize and extract a decent amount of the messages found inside the Telegram account, but it wasn't able to determine if the messages were sent or received. Additionally, it wasn't able to determine the chats of the Telegram; it just parsed the content of the messages with having the same message displayed more than once, as shown in Figure 5-24.

183

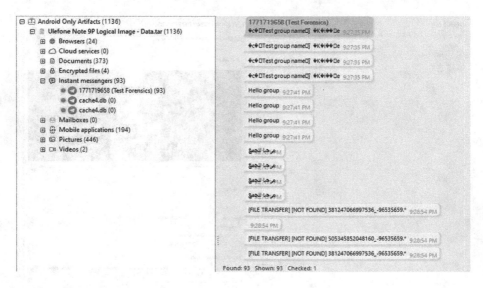

Figure 5-24. *Telegram messages preview – Belkasoft*

The tool wasn't able to detect the Telegram contacts stored on the
mobile device; even when it previewed the messages, the contact name
was displayed, but there was no clear parsing for the Telegram contacts as
AXIOM and FINALMobile did. Using File System explorer, the researcher
was able to find all the multimedia stored on the evidence image and
generated by Telegram through navigating to the following directory
inside the evidence image file: "image: \1*vol 0**data**media*\0*Telegram*".
The tool wasn't able to perform previews for the found multimedia
images, audio, and video. And to preview the content of the found file, the
researcher has to export the file from the evidence image and view it using
an external viewer, while when comparing with another tool like AXIOM
Examine, the tool provides multimedia preview without the need to use
external software.

Evidence Analysis Results

iOS Evidence Analysis Results

Our practical case built a real-life scenario case study that goes against
the Telegram Messenger application on mobile devices that run iOS and
Android. And went through the digital forensics process recommended
by NIST to acquire, process, analyze, and report the seized evidence. We
presented the acquisition and analysis techniques using different forensics
tools and performed a comparison between the used tools. During the
analysis phase, the researcher can find all the data that was simulated
in the experiment setup, including text messages, voice recordings,
images, and video recordings, since the case follows the methodology of
investigating a full disk image of the acquired iOS mobile phone. If the
investigator can acquire a full disk image, then extracting evidence related
to Telegram is relatively easy using the same tools and methodology used
in this research.

As shown in the Analysis section, each tool provides a set of features
that satisfy the purpose of the investigation depending on the investigator's
needs and allowed time. For example, if the investigator doesn't have
enough time to wait for the tool to carve all the images, extract very
detailed artifacts, and build connections with the carved artifacts, then
using Elcomsoft Phone Viewer satisfies the need to investigate Telegram.

Android Evidence Analysis Results

The research simulated real-life usage of Telegram on Android in a case
study that used a rooted mobile device to be free of any restrictions
that might arise during the acquisition process. It's true that not all of
the Android devices that act as digital evidence will be rooted, but the
purposes of the research are to be able to extract the most significant
amount of Telegram-related artifacts when it comes to Telegram digital

forensics on Android devices. Following the methodology recommended by NIST to seize, acquire, and analyze the digital evidence, the research presented the acquisition and analysis techniques using different forensics tools and performed a comparison between the used tools.

During the analysis phase using different digital forensics tools, the researcher can find most of the data that was simulated in the experiment setup including text messages, voice recordings, images, and video recording. The purpose of the research was to acquire a full disk image of the acquired Android mobile phone. And the research was even able to achieve this purpose, and get DD images for all of the partitions on the mobile device, but none of the used tools in the experiment were able to recognize any content of the acquired DD image, which resulted in creating a logical acquisition for all of the data that resides on the Android mobile, including the data that requires root access, since the device was rooted before starting the experiment.

As shown in the Analysis section, each tool provides a set of features that satisfy the purpose of the investigation depending on the investigator's needs and allowed time. For example, if the investigator is interested in extracting the Telegram contacts only, then using FINALMobile will be the shortest path as it processes the evidence image in a shorter time than other tools used in the experiment. If the investigator is interested in reading the content of the text messages without putting in too much effort into understanding the database structure of Telegram and writing the related queries, then using Belkasoft satisfies the purpose, since it gives a decent insight into the text messages contained in all encoding.

Summary

Mobile digital forensics science is developing on a daily basis, and every day there is a new tool introduced and a new challenge as well. The purpose of doing this practical case and many other types of research is to get hands-on with all available forensics tools, in order to identify the benefits of using each tool, practice them to get results faster, and learning to assess for each situation which is the most suitable tool use in order to get accurate results in a relatively short time. For iOS digital forensics, the researchers used two images for the evidence in order to assess the ability of different tools to extract the results and be able to build a strong case when it comes to Telegram Messenger investigation on iOS devices.

As discussed in this practical case, there are many tools for each operating system, and they can be used interchangeably in most cases. But it's up to the investigator to know which tool to use. The following paragraphs summarize the research experiment that was conducted against jailbroken iOS devices and a rooted Android device. When it comes to end-to-end acquisition, processing, and analysis of iOS devices, the research recommends using Magnet AXIOM as the most helpful tool, since it generates an evidence image that is usable by other forensics tools. Also, in terms of processing, it has the ability to extract all the artifacts and preview them within the tool itself without the need for external viewers for multimedia or understanding the schema of the Telegram database and writing your queries to get the artifacts. In case you already have an iOS evidence image and you are looking for artifacts in a short time, the research recommends using Elcomsoft, as it can process the evidence image in a short time and present the findings in a user-friendly format and connect all the found artifacts related to Telegram.

When it comes to the digital forensics of Telegram from an acquired Android device, the story is a little bit difficult. Based on the experiment done, if you have a rooted Android device, the research recommends using Magnet AXIOM to acquire the evidence, since it can generate a logical image with .tar extension usable by all forensics tools.

If the investigator is interested in getting the Telegram contacts' full
list of details including first name, last name, Telegram username, mobile
number, and any other details, then AXIOM is a good tool in satisfying the
purpose. Also, if there is an interest in viewing the multimedia without
using external tools, AXIOM is a recommended choice as well.

But if the investigator is interested in getting to preview and read the
messages sent and received by the Telegram application on the acquired
device or performing an image search based on the image category in case
the acquired evidence image contains a long list of multimedia generated
by Telegram, then the research recommends using Belkasoft Evidence
Center for this purpose. Even it is not able to recognize Telegram contact
and show the same message more than once, but when previewing the
messages, the contact party's name (either sender or receiver) will be
displayed, and you don't need to worry about extracting the Telegram
database and writing your queries to get the content of the messages.

Also, when considering a case where the evidence image contains
a lot of multimedia and the investigator is interested in searching the
multimedia looking for a specific category of images, then Belkasoft is a
good choice as well, since it provides a strong picture analysis tool that
retrieves all the pictures found on the evidence image and matches the
selected picture category.

References

[1]. L. E. Daniel and L. E. Daniel, "Chapter 3 - Digital
      Forensics: The Subdisciplines," in *Digital Forensics
      for Legal Professionals*, L. E. Daniel and L. E. Daniel,
      Eds. Boston: Syngress, 2012, pp. 17–23. [Online].
      Available: https://www.sciencedirect.com/
      science/article/pii/B9781597496438000031

[2]. K. Kent, S. Chevalier, T. Grance, and H. Dang, "Guide
to Integrating Forensic Techniques into Incident
Response," *The National Institute of Standards and
Technology*, 2006.

[3]. T. Dennis, "Digital Forensics Isn't Magic! —
Digital14," 2020. [Online]. Available: `https://
www.digital14.com/insights/blogs/
posts/2020/10/07/digital-forensics-
isn-t-magic!`

[4]. J. Menn and Y. Torbati, "Iran Hackers Reveal
Identities of 15m Telegram Messaging Accounts,"
2016. [Online]. Available: `https://www.
middleeasteye.net/news/iran-hackers-reveal-
identities-15m-telegram-messaging-accounts`

[5]. H. Long, "Telegram Review: NOT as Private and
Secure as You Think," 2020. [Online]. Available:
`https://restoreprivacy.com/secure-encrypted-
messaging-apps/telegram`

[6]. A. Shehabat, T. Mitew, and Y. Alzoubi, "Encrypted
Jihad: Investigating the Role of Telegram App in
Lone Wolf Attacks in the West," *Journal of Strategic
Security*, vol. 10, no. 3, pp. 27–53, 2017.

[7]. Theertharaja, "The Rise of Cybercrime on Telegram
and Discord and the Need for Continuous
Monitoring," 2020. [Online]. Available: `https://
cloudsek.com/the-rise-of-cybercrime-on-
telegram-and-discord-and-the-need-for-
continuous-monitoring/`

[8]. C. Shu, "Meet Telegram, a Secure Messaging App from the Founders of VK, Russia's Largest Social Network," 2013. [Online]. Available: https://techcrunch.com/2013/10/27/meet-telegram-a-secure-messaging-app-from-the-founders-of-vk-russias-largest-social-network/

[9]. J. Stubbs and A. Ostroukh, "Russia to Ban Telegram Messenger over Encryption Dispute," 2018. [Online]. Available: https://www.reuters.com/article/us-russia-telegram-block/russian-court-bans-access-to-telegram-messenger-idUSKBN1HK1OB

[10]. Telegram, "Telegram FAQ." [Online]. Available: https://telegram.org/faq

[11]. R. KILPATRICK, "China Blocks Telegram Messenger, Blamed for Aiding Human Rights Lawyers," 2015. [Online]. Available: https://hongkongfp.com/2015/07/13/china-blocks-telegram-messenger-blamed-for-aiding-human-rights-lawyers/

[12]. P. Mozur and A. Stevenson, "Chinese Cyberattack Hits Telegram, App Used by Hong Kong Protesters," 2019. [Online]. Available: https://www.nytimes.com/2019/06/13/world/asia/hong-kong-telegram-protests.html

[13]. S. Ravikumar, "Reddit, Telegram among Websites Blocked in India: Internet Groups," 2019. [Online]. Available: https://in.reuters.com/article/us-india-internet/reddit-telegram-among-websites-blocked-in-india-internet-groups-idINKCN1RF14D

[14]. G. B. Satrya, P. T. Daely, and M. A. Nugroho, "Digital
Forensic Analysis of Telegram Messenger on
Android Devices," *Proceedings of 2016 International
Conference on Information and Communication
Technology and Systems, ICTS 2016*, no. June 2018,
pp. 1–7, 2017.

[15]. J. Gregorio, B. Alarcos, and A. Gardel, "Forensic
Analysis of Telegram Messenger Desktop on
MacOS," *International Journal of Research in
Engineering and Science (IJRES)*, vol. 6, no. 8,
pp. 39–48, 2018.

[16]. Borodin, R. Veynberg, D. Pisarev, and O. Litvishko,
"Simulation of Artefact Detection in Viber and
Telegram Instant Messengers in Windows Operating
Systems," *Business Informatics*, vol. 13, no. 4, pp. 39–
48, 2019.

[17]. President of the Palestinian National Authority,
"Decree-Law No. 10 of 2018 Regarding Cybercrime,"
May 2018. [Online]. Available: https://security-
legislation.ps/ar/node/100107

[18]. Belkasoft®, "Belkasoft Evidence Center," 2021.
[Online]. Available: https://belkasoft.com/

[19]. Finaldata, "FINALMobile," 2021. [Online]. Available:
https://finaldata.com/mobile/

[20]. Magnet Forensics, "Magnet AXIOM," 2020. [Online].
Available: https://www.magnetforensics.com/
products/magnet-axiom/

[21]. Elcomsoft, "Elcomsoft Phone Viewer," 2021.
     [Online]. Available: `https://www.elcomsoft.com/epv.html`

[22]. "AccessData FTK Imager," 2020. [Online]. Available:
     `https://accessdata.com/products-services/forensic-toolkit-ftk/ftkimager`

[23]. "Autopsy Digital Forensics," 2020. [Online].
     Available: `https: //www.autopsy.com/`

[24]. "Registry Viewer®," 2014. [Online]. Available:
     `https://accessdata.com/product-download/registry-viewer-1-8-0-5`

[25]. "Vmware Workstation Pro," 2020. [Online].
     Available: `https://www.vmware.com/products/workstation-pro.html`

[26]. F. Carlier, "iDeviceInfo," 2021. [Online]. Available:
     `https://github.com/libimobiledevice-win32/imobiledevice-net`

[27]. P. Batard, "Rufus - Create Bootable USB Drives
     the Easy Way," 2021. [Online]. Available: `https://rufus.ie/en/`

[28]. Checkra.in, "Checkr1n," 2021. [Online]. Available:
     `https://checkra.in/releases/`

[29]. "Rooting (Android) - Wikipedia." [Online]. Available:
     `https://en.wikipedia.org/wiki/Rooting`

[30]. CWM, "ClockworkMod." [Online]. Available:
     `https://www.clockworkmod.com/`

[31]. TWRP, "TeamWin - TWRP." [Online]. Available:
     `https://twrp.me/` *BIBLIOGRAPHY*

[32].   Didgeridoohan, "Magisk: The Magic Mask for
Android." [Online]. Available: `https://github.com/`
`topjohnwu/Magisk`

[33].   Google LLC, "SDK Platform Tools Release Notes —
Android Developers." [Online]. Available: `https://`
`developer.android.com/studio/releases/`
`platform-tools`

[34].   Spflashtool.com, "SP Flash Tool - SmartPhone
Flash Tool." [Online]. Available: `https://`
`spflashtool.com/`

[35].   Google LLC, "Locking/Unlocking the Bootloader —
Android Open Source Project." [Online]. Available:
`https://source.android.com/devices/`
`bootloader/`

CHAPTER 6

Detecting Privacy Leaks Utilizing Digital Forensics and Reverse Engineering Methodologies

Most commercial iOS forensics and data acquisition tools will effectively do the job in general, but in cases of data leaks presented, we need to look between the lines to extract all related logs and API communication that occurred inside the mobile system. Thus, in this chapter we will investigate the most recent updated tools and use more and more tools to have better evidence about our case.

In this chapter, we investigated the possibility of detecting data leaks out of mobile applications into the Facebook platform, by using various mobile forensics tools and reverse engineering methodology. With mobile forensics tools, we were able to investigate various important Facebook and other Android applications that might have contributed to privacy leaks, especially the data of the content providers' artifacts, and we were

able to extract the Facebook Android application package (APK). And
with reverse engineering methodology, we were able to decompile the
Facebook (Dalvik code) into its original Java source code and identify
various entry and exit points of data from and into Facebook.

In this chapter, we will cover the following topics:

- Legal Issues Regarding the Local Electronic Crimes Law
  and Mobile Forensics

- Mobile Forensics and Reverse Engineering

- Details of the Reporting Agency and Tools Used in the
  Examination

- Description of Steps Taken During the Examination

- Details of Findings or Issues Identified

- Evidence Recovered During the Examination,
  Including Chat Messages

- Images Captured During the Examination

- Examination and Analysis Information

Local Electronic Crimes Law
and Mobile Forensics

We are living in a world in which mobile devices and their users are
proliferating, where a massive amount of personal private data is being
accessed by mobile applications and with the majority to the social media
applications, like phone GPS, SMS, IMEI, our phone contact list, and more.
The data transmitted and residing on mobile phones becomes a potential
treasure trove to the malicious technology users who can sell data to
advertising companies, analytics companies, competitors' companies, and

even for political and intelligence agencies. Balancing between mobile
privacy and mobile functionality has become a very hot area and emerging
focus for research (Keng, Wee, Jiang, and Balan, 2013)

In alignment with the fact that smartphones' capabilities and
processing efficiencies are the same as personal computers, smartphones
became exposed to the same and greater risks and vulnerabilities as
personal computers. Data stored in smartphones like videos, images,
documents, emails, and short messages might be remotely accessed if the
mobile or smartphone device is connected to the Internet. This reality
poses huge challenges for security professionals in securing mobile and
smartphone devices, as well as detecting and investigating any issues over
such devices. Mobile forensics is a process of collecting digital evidence
where information is retrieved and acquired from the storage of mobile
phones. It all depends on digital evidence extraction from mobile phone
internal memory when there is the ability to access data.

Mobile phones and mobile technologies have witnessed rapid and fast
development recently. There are a huge number of applications that can
run on a mobile and smartphone platform, and more are developed each
day. Taking into account the variety of vendors of the smartphone, mobile
applications, and networking protocols, the forensic analysis tasks on
mobile phones are the biggest challenge. Many software tools are available
to acquire, retrieve, and analyze extracted data from smartphones. Every
tool has many advantages and disadvantages. These tools are extremely
important for smartphones forensics to extract and analyze digital
evidence that might be used in a legal case.

The importance and sensitivity of this chapter come from the core
problem that it aims to investigate in depth. The core problem is with the
massive volume of data leaks from mobile devices and various artifacts
into the Facebook platform for pure marketing, advertising, orientations,
and other malicious purposes. The leaks themselves, especially without
proper permissions of the device's users, are considered a breach of
individuals' privacy, as well as a significant violation of many data

privacy regulations and laws all over the world (GDPR, HIPAA, etc.)
(Wongwiwatchai, Pongkham, and Sripanidkulchai, 2020a). This chapter
will help lawmakers and law enforcement agencies to trace and investigate
similar data leak issues and improve the preservation of individuals'
privacy. The purpose of this practical case study and all generated
reports throughout the investigation of mobile devices is to investigate
the possibility of detecting data leaks from mobile devices into third-
party applications installed on the same device by using various mobile
forensics tools.

Local law such as the Palestinian Cybercrime Law by Decree No.
(10) 2018, ("Presidential Decree," 2018) was issued by the President of
the Palestinian Authority on 29 April 2018, through a presidential decree
entitled the "Electronic Crimes Law." The following provisions and issues
posed in the Palestinian Electronic Crimes Law are important regarding
any forensics case concerning digital evidence investigations:

- Admissibility of the Digital Evidence: The summary of
  the Palestinian Electronic Crimes Law provisions
  governing legal admissibility of the evidence is:

  "Any evidence resulting from any information
  technology means, information system, information
  network, website or electronic data may not be
  excluded because of the nature of the evidence."
  Article No. 37. ("Presidential Decree," 2018)

- Legal Authority to Forensic Examination Request: The
  summary of the Palestinian Electronic Crimes Law
  provisions governing legal authority of the examination
  request is:

"The office of the public prosecutor or the person
appointed by the judicial inspectors may inspect
people, places and anything else related to information
technology relevant to the crime." Article No. 32 (1 – 5).
("Presidential Decree," 2018)

– Seizure and Acquisition of the Evidence: The summary
of the Palestinian Electronic Crimes Law provisions
governing legal seizure and acquisition of the evidence is:

"The prosecutor has the permission to seize and retain
the entire information system and to make use of any
IT tools that would help to uncover the truth." Article
No. 33 (1 – 6). ("Presidential Decree," 2018)

Mobile Forensics and Reverse Engineering

In this section, we will discuss prior and related work in three major areas:
private data leaks over mobile applications, Facebook as an advertising
platform, and reverse engineering of Android applications. in addition, we
will discuss sensitive information transmissions in mobile applications.

Android Mobile Forensics and Private Data Leaks

We have noticed many research studies investigating the causes of
private data leaks over mobile working toward conducting leak-cause
analysis of data. The researchers correlate the actual leaks to the user
actions. The data leaking attitude of an application stays in stable status
with respect to time; a similar data leaking attitude is expected to be
observed repeatedly if an extra and adequate amount of application logs

is analyzed (Ávila, Khoury, Khoury, and Petrillo, 2021). Thus, we are able
to extract and understand log patterns and reveal the actual causes of
data leaking behavior. Several researchers have carried out significant
studies on mobile forensics of private data leaks; the research of Keng,
J. C. J. observed a high-volume ratio of leaky applications. "Out of the
226 applications studied, 121 applications are not leaking private data
(nonleaking apps). Among the 105 apps (46.5%) leaking privacy data,
64 apps (28.3%) were found to leak private data due to user actions on
application widgets. We notice that an application can leak data in various
ways: (1) User-Triggered Leaks (identified by association rules), (2) Start-
Up or One-Time Leaks, and (3) Periodic Leaks" (Keng et al., 2013). In
the first step, the researchers instrumented the mobile system to log and
collect user traces with "Taint- Droid" as their tools for detecting data
leaks. In the second step, the researchers conducted extensive testing of
selected samples of mobile applications to collect the logs and trace the
leaks. Finally, the researchers performed various analyses to produce and
detect the causal relations among the user actions and data leaks. Other
corresponding research on detecting and mitigating privacy leaks over iOS
mobile platforms was conducted by Agarwal, Y. and Hall; the researchers
observed a high volume of inappropriate application access to user data.
"We observe that 48.4% of the total applications access the identifier, 13.2%
access location, 6.2% access contacts and 1.6% access the music library.
Next, we find that a large number of users actively make privacy decisions:
44,260 users make 10-100 decisions while 16,729 users make 100-363
decisions" (Agarwal and Hall, 2012).

Facebook as Mobile Application Advertising Platform

Commercial advertising over online platforms is the basic source of funds
for mobile application developers, as well as playing a vital role in the
growth of the international economy. This situation comes along with

major individuals' privacy and data protection concerns. Advertisers
keep working very hard toward acquiring extensive corresponding
information about their audience to have the ability to present them with
advertisements appropriate for their interests. In other words, this might
be called "behavioral advertising." And due to the current technological
innovations on the online world and social media platforms such as
Facebook and Instagram, it becomes very possible to create profiles of
Internet users and depend on such profiles for designing powerful tools to
control preferences to commercial companies that offer online behavioral
advertising services.

Several researchers have carried out significant studies on the fact
that Facebook is using personal private data for advertising and marketing
purposes. Special research conducted by Marcello M. Mariani investigated
how the Italian regional destination management organizations (DMOs)
strategically employed the Facebook platform to promote and market
their destinations, as well as improving the current metrics for capturing
user engagement. The investigations were carried out based on a big data
analysis approach through extracting the data from the regional DMOs'
Facebook pages, in addition to semistructured face-to-face interviews
conducted with DMO regional managers. The findings of the study
indicated that "the way Facebook is tactically and strategically employed
varies significantly across Italian regional DMOs. Visual content (namely
photos) and moderately long posts have a statistically significant positive
impact on DMOs' Facebook engagement, whereas high post frequency,
and early daily timing (in the morning) of posts have a negative impact on
engagement. Last but not least, the study shows that most of the regional
DMOs (except for Trentino, Tuscany, and Sicily) deploy Facebook with
a top-down approach, allowing for little spontaneous user generated
content (UGC)" (Mariani, Di Felice, and Mura, 2016).

Reverse Engineering of Android Applications

The main goal for analyzing source code and reverse engineering for
Android applications is to provide inclusive understanding of the inner
functionality of applications running over mobile Android platform
(Wongwiwatchai, Pongkham, and Sripanidkulchai, 2020b), and to reveal
additional information on how data are being transferred and moved
through application components and objects into and out of applications
(Tiwari, 2020). The investigations on different methodologies and tools for
reverse engineering of Android applications carried out by Zhang, Baggili,
and Breitinger concluded that there are several methods that can be used
to decompile the precompiled Java code (Dalvik bytecode) into Java source
code readable by application reviewers and developers, due to the fact
that all applications running over the Android platform are programmed
in Java language. One of the most well-known tools is dex2jar, that tool can
convert Dalvik bytecode into Java source code (.jar, .class) (Zhang, Baggili,
and Breitinger, 2017).

Sensitive Information Transmissions in Mobile Applications

While mobile apps often need to transmit sensitive information out to
support various functionalities, they may also abuse the privilege by
leaking the data to unauthorized third parties. This makes us question
if the given transmission is required to fulfill the app functionality (Fu
et al., 2020). "To date, various methods have been proposed to detect and
isolate the third-party libraries that may incur privacy threats. However,
they either rely on the namespace or the program structure. thus, suffering
from the evasion attacks such as obfuscation and call graph manipulation,
or counting on the deep cooperation of developers, which ignores a great

deal of intentional data leakage driven by under-the-table income. More
importantly, all of them are designed to handle the misbehavior from
isolated ad libraries, and they do not apply to malicious transmissions
embedded in the core app logic" (Fu et al., 2020).

The investigator team was able to "automatically detect privacy-
sharing transmissions and determine their purposes by utilizing the
fact that mobile users rely on a visible app interface to perceive the
functionality of the app in a certain context. The characterizations of
nonfunctional network traffic are then summarized to provide network-
level protection. Researchers were not only reducing the false alarms
caused by traditional taint analysis but also captured the sensitive
transmissions missed by the widely used taint analysis system Taint Droid.
Evaluation using 2125 sharing flows collected from more than a thousand
running instances, shows that our approach achieves about 94% accuracy
in detecting nonfunctional transmissions" (Fu et al., 2020).

Data Acquisition Comparison: iOS Devices Image and iOS Backups

Acquire Data from an iOS Device

Logical acquisition captures a part of the data that is accessible to the
mobile user; in other words, what is available in an iTunes backup. This
implies that we are not able to retrieve any of the deleted files, but this can
be done instead using SQLite databases that can navigate the unallocated
space so that we will be able to recover the majority of the deleted records,
including but not limited to SMS, chats, Internet history, and so on.
Logical acquisition is considered the simplest way to acquire data for the
unlocked devices, since this method uses the built-in backup mechanism.
The majority of tools and data acquisition methods designed for logical
acquisition of iOS devices will not succeed and will fail if the device screen

is locked. Even if a physical image were captured, there is little to no need for conducting a logical acquisition. Indeed, not all data can be parsed in a physical image, which is why we have access to a logical image, which generates readable data; this will assist you effectively in mining deep into the physical image looking for artifacts that are able to support your forensic investigation. Logical acquisition is considered the fastest, the easiest, and the cheapest way to get access to the data stored over the iOS device. There are a variety of tools, ranging from commercial paid to free, that can capture mobile devices' logical images. Most of such tools require that acquiring devices are unlocked, or should have the ability to access the plist files through the host investigation's machine.

File system acquisition: We are not able to extract the encryption keys needed to decrypt the device's physical image, so conducting the physical acquisition is useless. However, there is file system acquisition to rescue us. Unfortunately, in most cases, it requires the iOS device to be jailbroken.

Acquire Data from an iOS Backup

The physical acquisitions and extraction of the iOS devices offer the majority of the data in an investigation process; it will be found as a rich area of information within iOS backups has been extracted. iOS mobile device holders have many alternatives to backing up the data available on their devices. Mobile holders choose to back up data to the PCs, using iTunes applications, or over the Apple cloud storage SaaS known as iCloud.

Every time an iPhone is synced with a PC or to iCloud, it generates a backup file by copying the user-selected files to extract from the device. Users can choose and select what they need to include in the backup files, although some backup files may be more significant and related to the case than others. Besides, the user of mobile can do backup to be extracted on both PC and iCloud; this implies that the data extracted from each area may not be similar to the other one. This case most likely happens due to the size constraints of iClouds.

The mobile users might simply back up contacts and images to iCloud; another user might conduct a complete backup of the entire device data to their PC. As mentioned previously, the physical acquisition of mobile data offers the best access to all the data located over the iOS device; thus, backups may be the only available source of digital evidence in many cases. Table 6-1 provides a comprehensive comparison between the iOS device image and iOS backup data extraction methods.

Table 6-1. *Comparison between the iOS Device Image and Backup Image Data Extraction Methods*

Comparison Criteria	Acquire from an iOS Device	Acquire data From iOS Backups
Acquisition types	• Physical acquisition (full) • Logical acquisition (user data) • File system acquisition (+ Stru.) • Acquisition via jailbreaking	• iTunes backups • iCloud backups
Acquisition tools	• Magnet AXIOM • FINALMobile • Libimobiledevice • Belkasoft acquisition tool	• iTunes backups • iBackup Viewer • iExplorer • UFED physical analyzer
Capture capabilities	• Recovers deleted files using SQLite databases and tools	• Recovers deleted files using extracted backup
Acquiring device status	• Will not work for the newest locked device	• Will work for locked devices
Performance	• Fast, easy, cheap (logical)	• Fast, easy, cheap

(*continued*)

Table 6-1. (*continued*)

Comparison Criteria	Acquire from an iOS Device	Acquire data From iOS Backups
Constraints	• New devices need to be jailbroken (file system acq.) • No prior work needed	• No need to be jailbroken • Works on newest devices • Previously synced with the device
Mobile user role	• Cannot control what is contained in a logical image	• Determines what contained in the backup
Data location	• Mobile device	• iCloud backups • Computers
Volume of information	• Full device information	• User information stored in backup

Data Acquisition Comparison: Android Devices Image and ADB Backups

Understanding Android Data Extraction Techniques

Data reset on an Android MD might be an important part of the civil, criminal, or organizational internal investigations conducted as part of corporate internal issues. During the process of dealing with digital investigations for Android MD, the forensic examiners need to be aware of the issues critically and need due diligence and special attention during conducting the forensic process; this might include, but is not limited to, what type of data might be extracted through the investigation process. It is recommended and considered the best choice to extract all possible data

from MD immediately once the investigator can do so. As we explained
in Chapter 3, the data extraction techniques for Android MD might be
classified into three main categories:

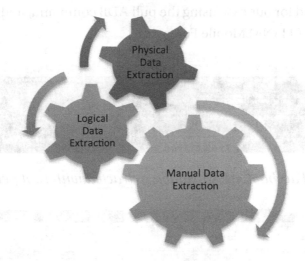

The Manual Data Extraction: This method of data extraction required
the investigators to utilize a normal MD interface to access the content
presented in the device memory. The investigator will walk through
the device manually by accessing different applications' menus to view
and observe any information details like the call logs, the text messages,
and the instant message chats. The contents of every interested screen
needs to be captured by taking a snapshot of pictures, and then it might
be presented as legal digital evidence. The main obstacle to utilizing
this examination type is that we are only able to investigate files that are
accessible through the Android system (in User Interface mode).

The Logical Data Extraction: The logical data extraction method
can extract data presented on the MD by directly interacting with the
mobile OS to have access to the file system. This method is very significant
because it provides various valuable data, works on the majority of devices,
and is easy to use. Logical extraction of data does not require root access

to the devices in general, but having root access to MD would significantly impact the amount and the kind of data that might be extracted even through logical techniques. Figure 6-1 illustrates an example of logical extraction used for our case using the pull ADB command, and Figure 6-2 shows the use of FINALMobile Forensics.

Figure 6-1. *Facebook APK artifacts extracted with root permissions*

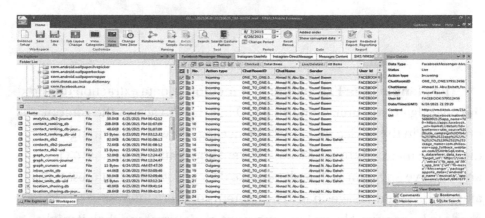

Figure 6-2. *Facebook application artifacts extracted using FINALMobile*

The Physical Data Extraction: The physical extraction of data refers to the process of obtaining an exact bit-by-bit image of a device (Tamma, Skulkin, Mahalik, and Bommisetty, 2020). It is important to understand the reality that a "bit-by-bit" image file will never be the same as copying

and pasting the available contents of an MD. If we try to copy and paste
specific contents of an MD, this process will copy only the available and
presented files, like "visible files, hidden files, and system-related files."
This technique is considered to produce a logical image; any deleted files
and any other files that are inaccessible will not be copied using the copy
command. While in some cases, the deleted files might be recovered based
on certain circumstances and utilizing certain techniques, the physical
extraction of data is typically an exact copy to the MD's memory and will
include more valuable information, like the memory slack space and the
memory unallocated space. Figure 6-3 illustrates an example of physical
data extraction, and a comparison of three data acquisition techniques is
given in Table 6-2.

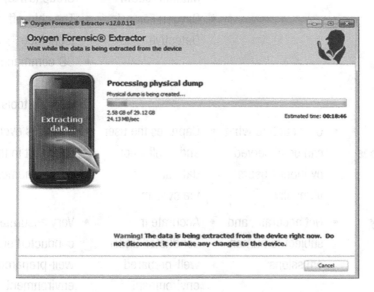

Figure 6-3. *Physical extraction of the mobile data using Oxygen
Forensic Detective*

Table 6-2. Data Acquisition Comparison: Manual, Logical, and Physical Data Extraction

Comparison Criteria	Manual Extraction	Logical Extraction	Physical Extraction
Extracted data	• Access only the content presented in the device memory for the user	• Access user data and file system	• Full access to data
Acquisition tools	• MD interface	• FINALMobile • Magnet AXIOM • Oxygen Forensic Detective	• Joint Test Action Group (JTAG) • The chip-off technique • DD command (ADB) • Various forensic tools
Capture capabilities	• Only capture what can be observed by mobile users manually	• Captures the user and application data and the file system	• Captures every single bit in the device memory
Accuracy	• Not accurate, and subject to human omissions	• Accurate if conducted under well-prepared environment	• Very accurate if conducted under well-prepared environment
Device permission	• Regular Android user permission	• Regular Android user permission (more data for rooted devices)	• Only available for rooted devices

(continued)

Table 6-2. (*continued*)

Comparison Criteria	Manual Extraction	Logical Extraction	Physical Extraction
Deleted file recovery	• Not possible	• Not possible	• Possible in certain circumstances
Security constraints	• Need to know pass code	• Need to know pass code (possible bypass)	• Need to know pass code (possible bypass)
Technical level	• Very high level	• High level	• Low level (machine level)
Time constraints	• Time-consuming (slowest)	• Good extraction time (the quickest)	• Good extraction time
Database direct access	• Not allowed	• Allowed	• Allowed

Detailed Description of Steps Taken During Examination

The following are details of the tools used during the examination to build our forensic environments for examining the data from the Android device:

1. **Tested Device Information:** Samsung Galaxy A10 (SM-A105F/DS): with Android Version 10.0 installed.

2. **Tested Applications:** Facebook application, built-in and other third-party applications installed on the device.

3. **Testing Environment:** A bit-by-bit image (physical image) for the device memory and file system has been acquired to be analyzed using various forensics platforms and appropriate tools: logical data extraction and the file system acquisition.

4. **Digital Forensics and Data Acquisition Tools for Both Device Rooting and Data Extraction:**

   - Android Studio IDE 201.7199119. Platform tools including Android Debug Bridge (ADB).

   - Odin3 v3.12.3. (Samsung's official firmware flashing software) tool.

   - FINALMobile forensics 2020.04.20 tool.

   - Magnet AXIOM forensics tool.

   - Oxygen Forensic Detective 12.0.0.151 tool.

5. **Reverse Engineering Tools Used to Decompile Dalvik Code into Java code:**

   - Dex2jar 2.0. tools (Android application decompiler).

   - GD-GUI-1.6.6. tools (Java programming language decompiler).

Data Acquisition and Extraction

For the purpose of this research, and to be able to investigate the most important artifacts on mobile devices and Facebook applications, we first rooted the Android device (using Odin3) and then located and extracted Facebook application–generated artifacts on the Android file system under

(/data/data) directory (such as app databases, app settings, app files, app
images, app cache) using (ADB), as illustrated in Figure 6-4, Figure 6-5,
and Figure 6-6.

Figure 6-4. *Facebook database artifacts located and extracted with
root permissions*

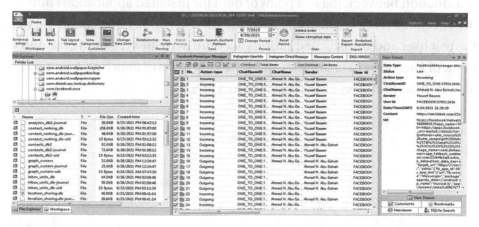

Figure 6-5. *Facebook files artifacts located and extracted with root
permissions*

Figure 6-6. *Facebook application artifacts extracted FINALMobile
forensics*

With root permission on the Android device, we extracted the
Facebook Application Package File (APK) artifacts generated on the
Android file system under the (/data/app/com.facebook.katana-
unIIK4MRZYqhhbj3LV0-IA==/base.apk) directory (base.apk), as
illustrated in Figure 6-7.

Figure 6-7. *Facebook application package file (APK) artifacts
extracted with root permissions*

Facebook Information File Investigations (Account Artifacts)

In order to investigate the various activities regarding sharing of
information between the exit point of data for installed applications into
the Facebook platform, we requested the full Facebook information file for
the test user and investigated various account activities regarding the entry
point of Facebook data artifacts and potential leaks of data (i.e., location
access, IP address), as illustrated in Figure 6-8.

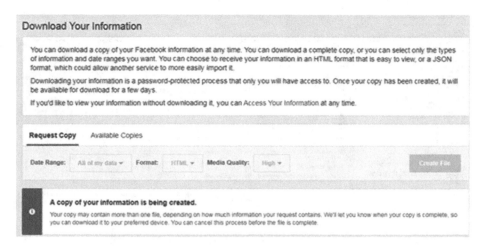

Figure 6-8. *Facebook information file request screen*

Analysis of Facebook Source Code with Reverse Engineering

In order to investigate and analyze the Facebook source code and to reveal evidence on data leaks into its internal components, we deployed reverse engineering techniques to extract (Dalvik code files) located within the Facebook Application Package File (APK) into the Java source. First, we extracted the APK file of Facebook from the application directory of the mobile into a forensic workstation using (Pull Command). Second, we unzipped the file to extract the corresponding (Dalvik code files) named (classes.dex), with a total of 12 Dalvik code files. Third, we used Android applications decompile tools (Dex2jar 2.0.) to decompile the Dalvik code files into a readable Java source code. Finally, we were able to view and investigate the actual Java classes of the Facebook application using the Java programming language decompiler (GD-GUI-1.6.6.); the output of this step illustrated in Figure 6-9.

215

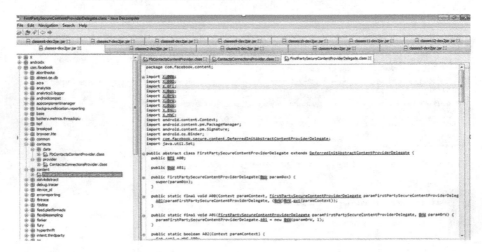

Figure 6-9. *Facebook Java classes*

Case Analysis and Major Findings

Next to the Android device artifact extraction, and in parallel to Facebook
information file acquisition. **First,** we manually explored and analyzed the
majority of Facebook applications and Facebook information file artifacts.
We were able to investigate various important Facebook application
artifacts that store or acquire personal data of mobile users. Such artifacts
include Location Information, Bluetooth Connections and Call Logs,
Communication Information, as well as Facebook user artifacts such as
Facebook contacts, Facebook messages, Facebook posts, and Facebook
news feed. Figures 6-10 to 6-13 present information stored in such artifacts.

```
com. facebook. katana
LE scans (started/stopped)          : 131 / 131
Scan time in ms (min/max/avg/total): 0 / 634 / 522 / 68428
Total number of results             : 536
Last 5 scans                        :
    06-10 21:37:32.562 - 06-10 21:37:33.101 (539ms) Cb Leg 100% 0/4 results 9(126)
    06-10 21:38:32.101 - 06-10 21:38:32.726 (625ms) Cb Leg 100% 0/0 results 9(127)
    06-10 21:48:06.805 - 06-10 21:48:07.317 (512ms) Cb Leg 100% 0/6 results 9(128)
    06-10 21:49:36.819 - 06-10 21:49:37.328 (509ms) Cb Leg 100% 0/1 results 9(129)
    06-10 21:51:06.742 - 06-10 21:51:07.249 (507ms) Cb Leg 100% 0/3 results 9(130)
```

Figure 6-10. *Facebook scanning Bluetooth connections to retrieve
caller information*

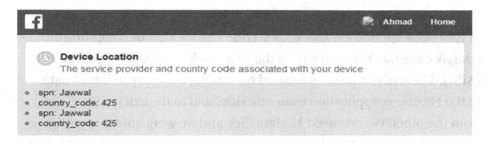

Figure 6-11. *Facebook sample location information passed from mobile device*

Figure 6-12. *Sample mobile device information passed into Facebook*

Figure 6-13. *Sample Facebook contact information artifacts*

217

Second, we manually explored, reviewed, and analyzed the majority of Facebook application Java source code classes after decompiling the (Dalvik code files) located within the Facebook Application Package File (APK). The analysis process focused on finding the entry points of data to the Facebook application from one side, and to the exit points of data from the other. We reviewed 12 class files and we were able to investigate various classes responsible for sharing and transferring data from and into Facebook applications. These included such points as Fileprovider.class, Phone Id, Location Information, and Bookmark Information. Figures 6-14 to 6-16 present data points of exchanges written in such Java classes.

All extracted data have been analyzed, including samples illustrated in the preceding work, considered as supporting evidence to our experimental results. Our artifact analysis process showed that the Facebook application is listening to various data sources and artifacts presented on mobile device. Such artifact include but are not limited to Location Information, Bluetooth Connections and Call Logs, Communication Information, and leaking it to commercial parties with or without explicit permissions from the user. The process of review and analysis of the majority of Facebook application Java source code classes showed that Facebook is collecting and leaking various data from mobile devices throughout programmable functions within the design of general Java classes structure (contents provider information, device ID information, etc.). Our case was investigated using both iOS and Android devices, but with more concentration on Android devices. We conclude that the security of new iOS devices is more reliable and harder to bypass, especially for new devices when compared to Android due to the complex design of iOS security measures.

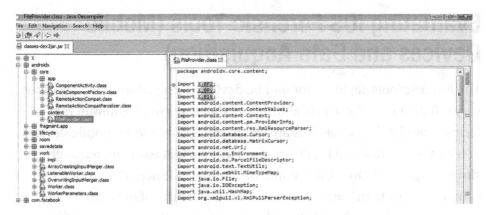

Figure 6-14. *Sample class (contents provider information entry point
into Facebook)*

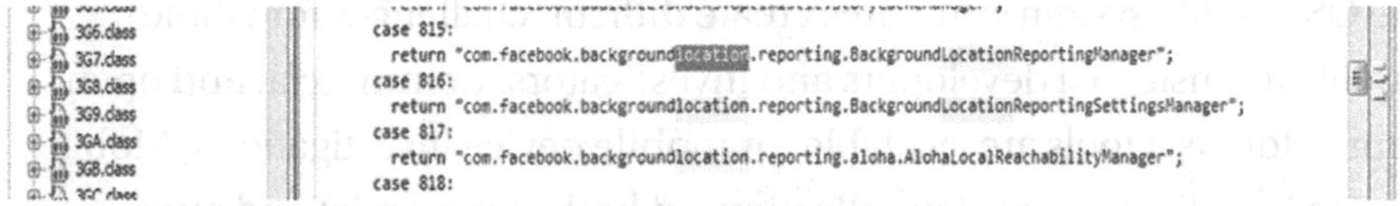

Figure 6-15. *Sample class (device location information entry point
into Facebook)*

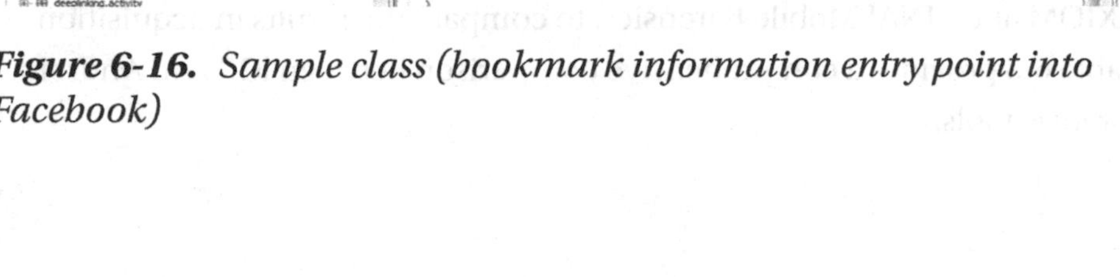

Figure 6-16. *Sample class (bookmark information entry point into
Facebook)*

Evaluating iOS Forensic Tools (Mobile Devices and Data Acquisition)

The forensic tools deployed for mobile device investigations are considered very different from those available to investigate personal computers in terms of availability. While PCs are extremely different from mobile devices in terms of software and hardware, their functionalities are increasingly similar in general. On the one hand, most mobile device OS are open source (like Android), but on the other hand, features of the phone's OS are typically private. Closed OS makes interpreting their associated file system and structure very complex. Several mobile devices with the same OS may also differ widely in their implementation. These differences in the OS and file system structures create difficult challenges for whole mobile forensic tool developers and investigators. Commercial and open source forensic tools are available for mobile device investigations. Mobile device investigators employ collections of both commercial and open source tools for their toolkit. Very tight and short product release cycles are the natural norms for mobile device investigations; this requires the continuous updating of the tools the manufacturer provides to investigators seeking a forensic solution. Older mobile models might be out of date but nevertheless might stay in use for several years after the initial release. Mobile device models that are introduced into one national market might also be used in different areas by exchanging the mobile cellular carrier with that one from another carrier area. In our case, we use two tools, Magnet AXIOM and FINALMobile Forensics, to compare the results in acquisition. Table 6-3 provides a comprehensive comparison between iOS and Android forensic tools.

Table 6-3. *Evaluating iOS and Android Forensic Tools*

Functionality	Magnet AXIOM		FINALMobile Forensics	
	iOS	Android	iOS	Android
Logical imaging	Supported (no, root)	Supported (no, root)	Supported (no, root)	Supported (no, root)
Physical image	Need jailbreak	Need root	Need jailbreak	Need root
SQLite support	Supported	Supported	Supported	Supported
Hash-comparison	✓	✓	✓	✓
Retrieves deleted files	Included through SQLite databases	Included through SQLite databases	✓	✓
Imaging	Included (acquirer)	✓	✓	✓
Mounting of container files	✓	Not included	✓	Not included
File system support	✓	✓	✓	✓
Email analysis	Not included	✓	Not included	✓
Internet traces (browser, messenger)	Included (limited)	Included (limited)	✓	✓
Viewing of pictures	Included (thumbnails)	Included (full view)	Included (full view)	Included (full view)

(*continued*)

Table 6-3. (*continued*)

Functionality	Magnet AXIOM		FINALMobile Forensics	
	iOS	Android	iOS	Android
Native view of file contents	✓	✓	✓	✓
Bookmarking/ tagging	✓	✓	✓	✓
Reporting	✓	✓	✓	✓
Support for investigator analysis	✓	✓	✓	✓
Categorization	✓	✓	✓	✓
Filter	✓	✓	✓	✓

As a result, we conclude that most commercial iOS and Android forensic and data acquisition tools will effectively do the job in general, since the majority of mobile forensics tools can work on both types of devices and extract the data. But in cases of data leaks like those presented in this research, we need to look between the lines to extract all related logs and API communication that occurred inside the Android system. Thus, we need to investigate the most recently updated tools and use more and more tools to have better evidence about our case. The final result of the research will be presented in later chapters.

Summary

In this chapter, we deployed two methods inherited from prior related research with significant tuning for each one. First, we employed digital forensics tools as log and monitoring tools to trace applications activities, in addition to the reverse engineering methodologies to trace and reveal information flow through Android applications. Second, we critically analyzed the user information data acquired from Facebook records. Our method is based on a practical experiment conducted on testing mobile devices and forensics workstations. The experiment will test all possible logs and trace the user's activity using mobile forensics tools to look for any data leak instances, as well as analysis for Facebook records. To test our methodology and research approach, as well as to verify the data leaks into the Facebook platform, our experiment was divided into four phases: data acquisition and extraction, Facebook information and log file investigations, analysis of Facebook source code with reverse engineering, and case analysis.

As shown from our experiment results, we conclude that Facebook is collecting, storing, and processing various types of mobile user private information with or without the prior and explicit permission of users. We support such conclusions through critical analysis of various Facebook and mobile device artifacts, as well as analyzing Facebook application Java source code classes. Future researchers should look in more detail at the process of reverse engineering for detecting data leaks to reveal more pieces of Java code responsible for collecting and leaking mobile users' private data into Facebook applications.

We recommend adopting an enforcing mechanism for detecting data leaks over mobile applications that allows users to easily be able to detect the leaking applications over their devices as well as allowing law enforcement agencies and legal entities to be able to monitor any privacy violations. A mechanism should be based on the developments of mobile applications that look into the most important artifacts presented on mobile applications as well as checking all data traffic for the application's exit and entry point of data.

References

[1]. Agarwal, Y., & Hall, M. (2012). Protect My Privacy:
      Detecting and Mitigating Privacy Leaks on iOS
      Devices Using Crowdsourcing Categories and
      Subject Descriptors, *Proceeding of the 11th Annual
      International Conference on Mobile Systems,
      Applications, and Services*, 6(September), 97–109.

[2]. Ávila, R., Khoury, R., Khoury, R., & Petrillo, F. (2021).
      Use of Security Logs for Data Leak Detection:
      A Systematic Literature Review. *Security and
      Communication Networks*, 2021(4). https://doi.
      org/10.1155/2021/6615899

[3]. Fu, H., Hu, P., Zheng, Z., Das, A. K., Pathak, P. H., Gu,
      T., & Zhu, S. (2020). Towards Automatic Detection
      of Nonfunctional Sensitive Transmissions in
      Mobile Applications, *IEEE Transactions on Mobile
      Computing*, 20(10), 3066–3080. https://doi.
      org/10.1109/TMC.2020.2992253

[4]. Keng, J. C. J., Wee, T. K., Jiang, L., & Balan,
      R. K. (2013). The Case for Mobile Forensics of
      Private Data Leaks: Towards Large-Scale User-
      Oriented Privacy Protection. *Proceedings of the
      4th Asia-Pacific Workshop on Systems, APSys 2013*.
      https://doi.org/10.1145/2500727.2500733

[5]. Mariani, M. M., Di Felice, M., & Mura, M. (2016).
      Facebook as a Destination Marketing Tool:
      Evidence from Italian Regional Destination
      Management Organizations. *Tourism Management*,
      54, 321–343. https://doi.org/10.1016/j.
      tourman.2015.12.008

[6].   Presidential Decree. (2018).

[7].   Tamma, R., Skulkin, O., Mahalik, H., & Bommisetty,
S. (2020). *Practical Mobile Forensics* (Fourth Ed.).
Copyright © 2020 Packt Publishing.

[8].   Tiwari, P. K. (2020). Study and Assessment of
Reverse Engineering Tool, (May), 297–300.

[9].   Wongwiwatchai, N., Pongkham, P., &
Sripanidkulchai, K. (2020a). Comprehensive
Detection of Vulnerable Personal Information
Leaks in Android Applications. *IEEE INFOCOM
2020 - IEEE Conference on Computer
Communications Workshops, INFOCOM WKSHPS
2020*, 121–126. https://doi.org/10.1109/
INFOCOMWKSHPS50562.2020.9163043

[10].   Wongwiwatchai, N., Pongkham, P., &
Sripanidkulchai, K. (2020b). Detecting Personally
Identifiable Information Transmission in Android
Applications Using Light-weight Static Analysis.
Computers and Security, 99. https://doi.
org/10.1016/j.cose.2020.102011

[11].   Zhang, X., Baggili, I., & Breitinger, F. (2017).
Breaking into the Vault: Privacy, Security and
Forensic Analysis of Android Vault Applications.
Computers and Security, 70, 516–531. https://doi.
org/10.1016/j.cose.2017.07.011

CHAPTER 7

Impact of Device Jailbreaking or Rooting on User Data Integrity in Mobile Forensics

Digital devices have become very important in most people's lives in this world, so the usage of these devices for sure will leave traces that can solve the mystery of crimes. A forensic analyst has one goal, which is to get as much data from a device as possible. However, this goal can only be achieved when applying physical image acquisition from the device, which can reach 100% copy. There are many forensic tools that are used in forensic science, and these tools are concerned to handle all forensic process activities. Digital forensics is categorized into three types: The first is manual, meaning opening a personal computer, removing storage, and so on. Another method is to acquire a physical bit-by-bit image. The third method is logical data imaging, by extracting the logical structure of the disk.

© Mohammed Moreb 2022
M. Moreb, *Practical Forensic Analysis of Artifacts on iOS and Android Devices*,
https://doi.org/10.1007/978-1-4842-8026-3_7

In this chapter, we will cover the following topics:

- User Data Integrity in Mobile Forensics
- Jailbreaking's Effect on iOS
- Calc Data Integrity before Jailbreaking
- Calc Data Integrity after Jailbreaking
- Data Extraction from Android
- Android Rooting
- Summary

User Data Integrity in Mobile Forensics

Recently, the use of mobile phone applications has exponentially increased, and this has enabled them to be used widely in cybercrimes against people and society. The increase of mobile device usage, and the expected number in the coming years until 2026, are illustrated in Figure 7-1.

This chapter focuses on the effect of iOS jailbreaking and Android rooting on the security of user data and the devices themselves. This will contain the acquisition techniques and user data, which is considered as the main player in cybercrime investigation processes. Various tools were used in the experiments and proofs, such as SQLite, Magnet AXIOM, Belkasoft, and Autopsy, as well as other supporting tools that helped in this process, like HASH CALC to calculate hash values, and FTK imager to acquire images. Results showed that both rooting and jailbreaking have a serious effect on mobile data security, especially on confidentiality and user access privileges, in addition to creating vulnerability to malicious scripts and attacks.

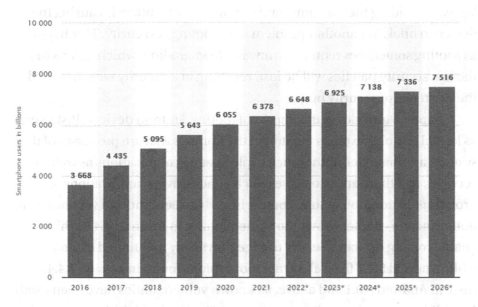

Figure 7-1. *Number of mobile users (2021-2026)*

Much research has focused on rooting and jailbreaking for both iOS
and Android devices, their effect on data file and security issues, and the
impact of jailbreaking on the iOS device. Other topics of investigation
include the impact of rooting on Android devices and other negatives
that may result from this operation such as warranty voiding, bricking,
data leakage, unauthorized access to sensitive information, and enabling
the download and installation of additional applications, themes, and
extensions that the manufacturers have are not allowed on the official
platform.

Rooting has benefits and disadvantages [6]. One of the most
desired benefits is to remove bloatware, which consists of unnecessary
applications that consume device resources, causing delay and other
problems in the device; another benefit is to grant root access to the device
to enable the user to apply high-privilege processes like configurations
on CPU, RAM, and so on. In addition, this benefit can be considered a
disadvantage. Rooting also has other disadvantages: one of the most

229

known is voiding the warranty, and another disadvantage is causing the device to brick. Yet another problem with rooting is security. This happens as rooting sometimes requires firmware downgrading, which means that the last security patches will be lost, resulting in a security weakness and the existence of security bugs.

Chapter 3 introduces the impact of rooting Android devices. Risks such as kernel exploits, exploits that target the libraries that are processes of the system, are illustrated. Other such exploits attack applications as well as services, and there are also those which attack drivers, applications, and programs. In addition to that, comparisons between Android versions were done, and the chapter shows the vulnerabilities in Android 4.4.4 which enable rooting devices to easily use the previously mentioned exploits, while Android 5.1.1 fixed all kernel root exploits found in version 4.4.4. Also, in Android 6.0.1 and above, all known vulnerabilities have been fixed. In addition to that, according to apps statistics, Android devices are used widely throughout the world. Figure 7-2 shows that around 70% of mobile users have Android devices, which outperforms iOS [2].

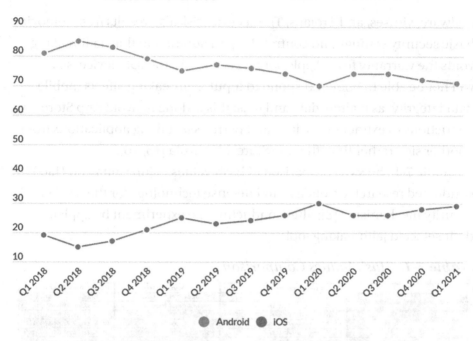

Figure 7-2. *Android vs iOS global market share (%)*

Users tend to jailbreak their iOS devices: we introduce in Chapter 2
about how jailbreaking uses vulnerabilities in the kernel in order to apply
and privilege escalation and remove controls and restrictions in order to
install and apply unauthorized applications, while authorized applications
are approved from Apple [11]. To be authorized, apps are subjected to an
approval cycle executed by Apple; they are tested and checked to ensure
that Apple controls are maintained and applied on developed applications
[12]; such controls include integrity, reliability, and security. Jailbreaking
is a privilege escalation technique that has a lot of disadvantages that
affect iPhone devices: the most important issues are security, warranty,
and bricking [13]. Since jailbreaking escalates users' privileges by allowing
users to get root access, the device falls into a high security risk status;
therefore, jailbreaking enables installing unauthorized third-party
applications that are untrusted and may contain malicious software like

231

malware, viruses, and Trojans. The security risk also results from removing
basic security settings and controls [14]. In addition to that, jailbreaking
voids the warranty from Apple, and it also breaks the iOS device, so it
will not be able to boot or respond to input. Jailbreaking affects mobile
data integrity, as it alters data and files; this is done to avoid App Store
restrictions to extract more data, and permits installing applications from
another side rather than the App Store, like Cydia [15, 16].

Table 7-1 shows a comparison of hash values. Sijun Chua and Hao Wu
conducted research on offense and defense technology for the iOS kernel
security mechanism [18]; after conducting the experiment by applying
their selected jailbreaking tools.

Table 7-1. *Hash Values Comparison*

File	Baseline vs Jailbreak	Jailbreak vs Restore	Restore vs Baseline
AddressBook.sqlitedb	FS & Logical Match	FS & Logical Mismatch	FS & Logical Mismatch
AddressBookImages.sqlitedb	FS & Logical Match	FS & Logical Match	FS & Logical Match
Bookmarks.db	FS Match & Logical Mismatch	FS & Logical Mismatch	FS & Logical Mismatch
Calendar.sqlitedb	FS & Logical Mismatch	FS & Logical Mismatch	FS & Logical Mismatch
Extras.db	FS & Logical Match	FS & Logical Mismatch	FS & Logical Mismatch
call_history.db	FS & Logical Match	FS & Logical Mismatch	FS & Logical Mismatch
cache_encryptedA.db	FS Mismatch	FS & Logical Mismatch	FS & Logical Mismatch
consolidated.db	FS & Logical Match	FS & Logical Mismatch	FS & Logical Mismatch
Cache.db	FS Match	Not Recovered in Restore	Not Recovered in Restore
notes.idx	FS & Logical Match	FS & Logical Mismatch	FS & Logical Mismatch
notes.sqlite	FS & Logical Match	FS & Logical Mismatch	FS & Logical Mismatch
Photos.sqlite	FS & Logical Match	FS & Logical Mismatch	FS & Logical Mismatch
sms.db	FS & Logical Mismatch	FS & Logical Mismatch	FS & Logical Mismatch
voicemail.db	FS & Logical Mismatch	FS & Logical Mismatch	FS Match & Logical Mismatch

FS = Filesystem acquisition; Logical = Logical acquisition

After applying the experiment by applying their own jailbreaking
programs [16], they achieved the results shown in Table 7-2, which
presents the changes that occurred after jailbreaking, as the device came
under attack on the kernel level.

Table 7-2. *Changes Occurring after Jailbreaking [17]*

Tools' Name/iOS version	Before Jailbreak			After Jailbreak		
	iOS Kernel Security Mechnasim Integrity Detection	sensitive kernel APIs Detection	Test result	iOS Kernel Security Mechnasim Integrity Detection	sensitive kernel APIs Detection	Test result
Exploit and root/ iOS9.2.1	No abnormality	find	High-risk APP	Discovery of abnormality	find	under attack
Pangu9.1	No abnormality	find	High-risk APP	Discovery of abnormality	find	under attack
Pangu9.3	No abnormality	find	High-risk APP	Discovery of abnormality	find	under attack
Qwerty 9.x remote jailbreak	No abnormality	No abnormality	secure	Discovery of abnormality	No abnormality	under attack

Data integrity on iOS: Despite the importance of this issue related
to data modification in jailbreaking iDevices, there are few studies that
demonstrate this and verify the extent to which a jailbreak modifies data,
whether it is system data or user data. Some previous investigations on this
issue provide clarity: for example, in 2015 [20] and in 2019 [21], research
showed that this procedure will not change the iPhone's internal digital
evidence. But with the development of new versions of the iOS operating
system and jailbreak tools, we need to keep up with checking this, in terms
of updates to analyze the jailbreak process, what is actually being done by
the jailbreak code in the device, and the data that is already modified that
may raise concerns and questions about data integrity.

The boot process sequence as shown in Figure 7-3 starts when an
iPhone is turned on; it will start with reading system startup code (boot
ROM), where the CPU can only read from this area. After that, the boot
ROM will encrypt the low-level bootloader (LLB) startup stage containing
the root certificate of the boot integrity test. The next step will be detection
on the iOS kernel based on the command code on iBoot; after that, it can
run an application, and then, the system is ready for use [22].

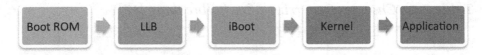

Figure 7-3. *iOS boot process for iPhone*

In our practical case, we applied the mobile forensics process that is described in Chapter 1, which includes four stages, to get evidence to be included in the witness report to be admitted by the court. This process is divided as follows:

[1].   In the seizure stage, there should be a search order (warrant), which should be issued from an expert and responsible person, that contains clear details about the case, and what should be seized. We assumed that we received the order including all details about the case and what should be exactly examined in the mobile of the suspect.

[2].   In the acquisition stage, logical acquisition was used; the logical structure of the content of memory can be extracted, and the backup was stored in external storage media and protected from any unexpected conditions, like theft or damage. Once the acquisition stage was completed, a report was prepared including information about image information like time, date, size, hash values, and so on, as well as investigator information (name).

[3].   In the analysis stage, the investigator uses the information from the acquisition report, which includes images from the device, to start analyzing the case. First of all, the investigator will check the integrity of the files.

[4].   In the reporting stage, the analyst prepares a report about
this case, which includes information about the reporter,
documents of all evidence found, and the time sequence.

Jailbreaking's Effect on iOS
Calc Data Integrity before Jailbreaking

Data acquisition is one of the steps of the mobile forensics investigation
process (Al-Dhaqm, Razak, Ikuesan, Kebande, & Siddique, 2020). The data
acquisition process varies depending on the device manufacturer and the
operating system and could be a challenging process for some vendors like
Apple; therefore, iOS jailbreak might be required based on the extent of the
data that needs to be extracted (Aenurahman Ali, Dwi Wahyu Cahyani, &
Musthofa Jadied, 2019).

Logical acquisition is the process of acquiring the files stored on
the iPhone file system to the forensic investigation machine; it only
acquires the files that are stored on the iPhone, and no deleted data will
be recovered in this type of acquisition. The advantage of this type of
acquisition is the speed and easiness of retrieval of the required artifacts
and evidence (Cheema, Iqbal, & Ali, 2014). Plenty of tools can be used for
that type of acquisition like Belkasoft Evidence Center, FINALMobile, and
Magnet AXIOM, and many others.

The logical acquisition can be done by

1.   Acquiring data from the iPhone, which requires the devices
to be unlocked to proceed with this type of acquisition.

2.   Otherwise acquiring data from iTunes backup, by
browsing the SQLite databases and the plist files
in the backup, which may allow recovery of some

deleted records of the data using some Python
script like (sqliteparse.py), which can be used to
carve them from the hex dumps. In addition to this,
a string dump of the database file can also reveal
deletion. Another tool that can be used is (Undark),
but the issue with this tool is that it retrieves all
records whether deleted or undeleted.

It is worth mentioning that this method is sometimes challenging if the
iTunes backup encryption is enabled; the solution for such a scenario is to
use a tool to decrypt the backup such as Elcomsoft Phone Breaker.

Physical acquisition involves obtaining a bit-by-bit copy of the entire
iPhone storage. It provides the forensic investigator with a complete copy
of all of the iPhone's stored data (Cheema et al., 2014). The physical image
of the device allows the examiner to view additional items like deleted
items in unallocated space (forensic analysis on iOS devices). However, it
requires the iOS device to be jailbroken to conduct this type of acquisition.
In our case, to know the impact of jailbreaking on user data integrity, we
start with the seizure of an iPhone 7, proceeding as follows:

The first part of the experiment:

1. Conducting logical acquisition of the mobile data.

2. Examining the results and extracting some evidence.

3. Generating hash values of the extracted evidence
   and keeping a record of these values.

The second part of the experiment:

4. Applying jailbreak for the iPhone.

5. Conducting physical acquisition for the
   whole mobile.

6. Generating hash values of the extracted evidence
   and keeping a record of these values.

Finally, we compare the hash values of the acquired evidence from each
part to confirm whether it is getting affected after jailbreaking the iPhone.

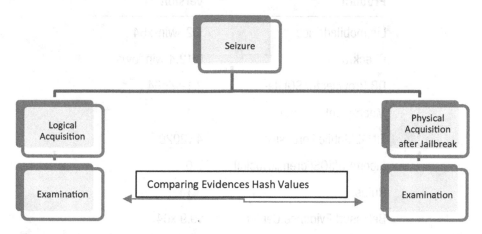

Figure 7-4. *Experiment flow*

Data acquisition details are as shown in Table 7-3, from an iOS device
using iTunes to get a backup image from the device. Therefore, iTunes
connected to the iPhone 7, and iTunes recognized the device and viewed
the information related to it as shown in Table 7-4.

Table 7-3. *Information about the Acquisition*

Investigator name	Bashar Jabr
Tools used	iTunes, Axiom process, Belk soft, 3uTools, Hash Calc
File name	Perfect's iPhone_20210615_131551.bak
Size	3.09 MB (3,243,921 bytes)
Date created	15 June 2021, 01:15:51 PM

Once we clicked the backup process of acquiring the image from
the iPhone, it started and the backup copy was stored on the PC in the
workstation. Table 7-3 lists the main software and tools used in our case.

Table 7-4. *Software Used in the Experiment*

Product	Version
Libimobiledevice	1.2 -win-x64
Checkra1n	0.12.4 windows
DB.Browser.for.SQLite-	3.1-win64
MacroplantiExplorer	4.4
FINALMobile Forensics	4.v2020
ElcomSoftiOSForensicToolkit	7.0
Rufus	3.14
Belkasoft.Evidence.Center	v9.9.x64
MOBILedit	10.1

The values for the zipped file for the backup folder are calculated in addition to files contained in this folder, like DB1, DB2, Info, Manifest B, Manifest PLIST, and Status, using MD5 algorithm, which will be used in the analysis stage for comparisons, as described in Table 7-5.

Table 7-5. *Hash Value for Backup before Jailbreaking*

File name	Name	Hash Value
Zipped folder	32a02511a35d69b9e6fae92acdaa5d1c7d26932e	23a15940e6a6dac31e198821a93e26f8
Info PLIST file	Info	46639a3af936e065011cb568d7e68006
Manifest database file	Manifest	47917872be52861114d01d9317fbc148
Manifest PLIST file	Manifest	5d82da1c43cbe822a46ab183024a4041
Status PLIST file	Status	cc3763ad04961da44a316794f20bb730

Details for extracted data from internal files, image files, and media files before jailbreak are listed in the following:

Internal files

Internal Files (49 files)

Filename	Size	Created	Modified	Accessed
/	0 B	2021-06-05 20:19:03	2021-06-05 20:19:03	
com.apple.itunes.lock_sync			2021-06-13 21:38:54	
/Books/	0 B	2020-09-23 18:22:11		
Books.plist.lock		2020-09-23 22:12:46	2020-09-23 22:12:46	
Backup-Books.plist	216 B	2020-09-23 22:12:46	2020-09-23 22:12:46	
Books.plist	216 B	2020-09-23 22:12:46	2020-09-23 22:12:46	

Image Files

Filename	Size	Created	Modified	Accessed
07f66010d295c1e5b85495db46eb09569.png	1.63 KB	2021-03-23 11:47:10	2021-03-23 11:47:10	2021-03-23 11:47:11
09e31231050a88c50c3eb00dd8f03c0.png	1.38 KB	2021-03-23 11:47:12	2021-03-23 11:47:12	2021-03-23 11:47:12
0b259720ebc0b68c7bfa7f479da54c99.png	654 B	2021-03-23 11:47:11	2021-03-23 11:47:11	2021-03-23 11:47:11
0ba45cdebce44f53f4452ab686bf4423.png	1.43 KB	2021-03-23 11:47:11	2021-03-23 11:47:11	2021-03-23 11:47:11
0f5ca35f9d0a3b34f6d11426602f6c2baf.png	699 B	2021-03-23 11:47:12	2021-03-23 11:47:12	2021-03-23 11:47:12
0fe3fed31dea32705d4867b90712be83.png	719 B	2021-03-23 11:47:12	2021-03-23 11:47:12	2021-03-23 11:47:12
15c7d42f9d76bb0c446ce3a2e2bea2cb.png	1.71 KB	2021-03-23 11:47:12	2021-03-23 11:47:12	2021-03-23 11:47:12
15d0b020659c27254ee5caabf9d42f07.png	1.49 KB	2021-03-23 11:47:12	2021-03-23 11:47:12	2021-03-23 11:47:12
1f12cd1d50c8badcd4bd6f67a70669baa47.png	1.34 KB	2021-03-23 11:47:11	2021-03-23 11:47:11	2021-03-23 11:47:11

Media Files

Filename	Size	Created	Modified	Accessed
/Apple_Backup/CameraRoll/Domain/backup/Media/PhotoData/CPLAssets/		2020-09-23 22:31:20	2020-10-09 01:38:36	2020-10-09 01:38:36
/Apple_Backup/CameraRoll/Domain/backup/Media/PhotoData/CPLAssets/group101/		2020-09-24 10:09:34	2020-09-24 10:10:18	2021-06-06 12:14:56
7C608E2C-4E36-4DE0-BE0A-32A0697724FC.JPG	70.8 KB	2020-10-09 01:38:21	2020-10-09 01:38:33	2021-06-06 12:13:25
D06F2D7D-E85D-41F6-9A02-761A2E1B5CC0.PNG	1.45 MB	2020-09-23 22:34:47	2020-10-09 01:51:17	2020-10-09 01:51:17
/Apple_Backup/CameraRoll/Domain/backup/Media/PhotoData/CPLAssets/group102/		2020-10-09 01:44:44	2020-10-09 01:44:58	2021-06-06 12:13:26
8C032599-8A80-4BD7-87E5-5384712D55C5.HEIC	1.46 MB	2020-10-09 01:50:44	2020-10-09 01:51:15	2020-10-09 01:51:15
8C032599-8A80-4BD7-87E5-5384712D55C5.MOV	1.72 MB			

239

Calc Data Integrity after Jailbreaking

In our case we used Cydia from `https://www.Apphacks.co/Cydia`. As a
first step, we needed to install open it from the home screen, which means
that the iPhone is already jailbroken. Now the device is jailbroken, and the
next step is to calc the hash value and compare with previous value as seen
in Table 7-5. After getting a new backup from iTunes, hash values were
recalculated as shown in Table 7-6.

Table 7-6. *Hash Values after Jailbreaking*

File name	Name	Hash Value
Zipped folder	32a02511a35d69b9e6fae92acdaa5d1c7d26932e	239bcbfc24b1fcb7e2d9158b95115490
Info PLIST file	Info	e63f9c08719cacbdf877e34b3c5d22bf
Manifest database file	Manifest	facedfbf038bb5830f5ad0984ed1465b
Manifest PLIST file	Manifest	e12d54e69236e9efe5e7da9acf45433d
Status PLIST file	Status	35f21971e69e9271eaaf73e18d5b96a6

Details for extracted data from internal files, image files, and media
files after jailbreak are listed in the following:

Internal files

Internal Files (49 files)

Filename	Size	Created	Modified	Accessed
com.apple.itunes.lock_sync	0 B	2021-06-05 20:19:03	2021-06-05 20:19:03	
/Books/		2020-09-23 18:20:11	2021-06-13 21:38:54	
Books.plist.lock	0 B	2020-09-23 22:12:46	2020-09-23 22:12:46	
Backup-Books.plist	216 B	2020-09-23 22:12:46	2020-09-23 22:12:46	
Books.plist	216 B	2020-09-23 22:12:46	2020-09-23 22:12:46	

Image Files

Filename	Size	Created	Modified	Accessed
0765601d29fcc1a5b85495ch46cb09569.png	1.63 KB	2021-03-23 11:47:10	2021-03-23 11:47:10	2021-03-23 11:47:10
09e31231050a88c50c3ebc0dd8ff03a0.png	1.38 KB	2021-03-23 11:47:12	2021-03-23 11:47:12	2021-03-23 11:47:12
0b42970ebc0b68c7bfa74794ed4ca99.png	654 B	2021-03-23 11:47:11	2021-03-23 11:47:11	2021-03-23 11:47:11
0b345ccfebce44f6366452888bf4423.png	1.43 KB	2021-03-23 11:47:11	2021-03-23 11:47:11	2021-03-23 11:47:11
05ca359b9b3f4f681f42660f46c2baf.png	699 B	2021-03-23 11:47:12	2021-03-23 11:47:12	2021-03-23 11:47:12
0fe3fecf14ea32709548671b90712be83.png	719 B	2021-03-23 11:47:12	2021-03-23 11:47:12	2021-03-23 11:47:12
15c2c42f3df68b0c446ce3a2e2bea2cb.png	1.71 KB	2021-03-23 11:47:12	2021-03-23 11:47:12	2021-03-23 11:47:12
1540b020659c27254e54caab9c4207f.png	1.49 KB	2021-03-23 11:47:12	2021-03-23 11:47:12	2021-03-23 11:47:12
1f17cc1d6bcdbadd48cf67a70669baa47.png	1.34 KB	2021-03-23 11:47:11	2021-03-23 11:47:11	2021-03-23 11:47:11

Media Files

Filename	Size	Created	Modified	Accessed
/Apple Backup/CameraRollDomain/backup/Media/PhotoData/CPLAssets/				
/Apple Backup/CameraRollDomain/backup/Media/PhotoData/CPLAssets/group101/				
7C808E2C-4E36-40B8-BE0A-32A0697724FC.JPG	70.8 KB	2020-09-23 22:31:20	2020-10-09 01:38:36	2020-10-09 01:38:36
D00F2D7D-EB50-41F6-9A02-761A2E1B5CC0.PNG	1.46 MB	2020-09-24 10:09:34	2020-09-24 10:10:18	2021-06-06 12:14:56
/Apple Backup/CameraRollDomain/backup/Media/PhotoData/CPLAssets/group102/		2020-10-09 01:38:21	2020-10-09 01:38:23	2021-06-06 12:13:25
8C032599-BABf-4BD7-87E5-538471205SCS.HEIC	1.46 MB	2020-09-23 22:23:47	2020-10-09 01:51:17	2020-10-09 01:51:17
8C032599-BABf-4BD7-87E5-538471205SCS.MOV	1.72 MB	2020-10-09 01:44:44	2020-10-09 01:44:58	2021-06-06 12:13:26
		2020-10-09 01:50:44	2020-10-09 01:51:15	2021-06-05 18:25:02

Comparison for Data Integrity Using Hash Value before and after Jailbreaking

As illustrated in Table 7-7, the hash values of the mentioned files and folder were changed, which means that the mobile data was affected by jailbreaking and also that the integrity was affected.

Table 7-7. *Comparison of Hash Values*

File name	Name	Hash Value Before Jailbreaking	Hash Value After Jailbreaking
Zipped folder	32a02511a35d69b9e6fae92acdaa5d1c7d26932e	23a15940e6a6dac31e198821a93e26f8	239bcbfc24b1fcb7e2d9158b95115490
Info PLIST file	Info	46639a3af936e065011cb568d7e68006	e63f9c08719cacbdf877e34b3c5d22bf
Manifest database file	Manifest	47917872bc52861114d01d9317fbc148	facedfbf038bb5830f5ad0984ed1465b
Manifest PLIST file	Manifest	5d82da1c43cbc822a46ab183024a4041	e12d54e69236e9efe5e7da9acf45433d
Status PLIST file	Status	cc3763ad04961da44a316794f20bb730	35f21971e69e9271eaaf73e18d5b96a6

Another result noticed is that by installing Cydia, the security controls were changed, as it is doable to install any application; never mind if it is trusted or not trusted, which decreases the level of security.

In a comparison between iTunes backup and logical acquisition using Belkasoft, it was found that iTunes backup uses current and in new versions of data, so it uses incremental backup. Therefore, once the device is synced with iTunes it creates complete backup, but it applies backup only on changed or modified data. This means that deleted files and unallocated space will not be included in the new copy of backup, so it updates the current one instead of creating new copy every time backup is executed. However, in Belkasoft, every time acquisition is executed it creates a new copy of image, and it contains deleted files and unallocated space; the deleted file can be retrieved and viewed, which will be useful in comparison between images. Another difference is that iTunes can make logical backup, but physical acquisition couldn't be implemented, which creates a bit-by-bit copy of the data, while Belkasoft can do so, and create both logical and physical acquisition, but for physical acquisition it requires jailbreaking the device as shown in Figure 7-5.

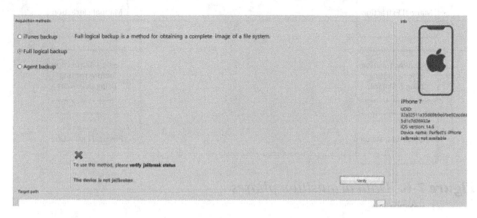

Figure 7-5. *Belkasoft requires jailbreaking when creating physical backup*

In jailbreaking, we found that Cydia was installed on the device, which means that any application, even it's malicious, will be downloaded; this will affect the security controls on a device, as well as data integrity. Compare the results for hash values before and after the jailbreaking.

Data Acquisition from Android Device

This stage contains three phases; each phase is divided into three steps as shown in Figure 7-6:

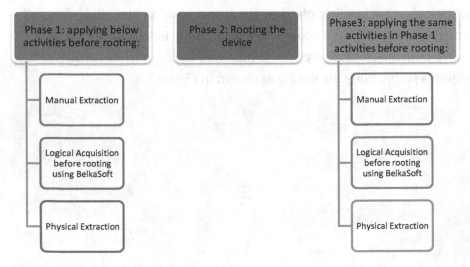

Figure 7-6. *Data acquisition phases*

Data Extraction

The manual data extraction technique involves manual browsing of data, files, folders, and all other needed information, and capturing all the evidence associated with the investigated case. The following is a sample of data captured manually from the tested device: Figure 7-7 shows the list of folders.

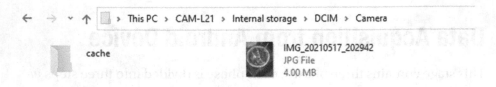

Figure 7-7. *Browsing data folders*

Before taking backup or acquisition, mobile should be turned into
Airplane mode, by following steps: Go to **Settings ➤ Airplane ➤ Turn on**.
Also turn Bluetooth on. Wi-fi should be turned off. In the acquisition
phase, we produced information about two experiments in iOS and
Android. Table 7-8 shows information for HUAWEI CAM-L21 about
this stage for these two cases, including examiner information, tools
used in this stage, dates and times, image information, name, size, and
hash values.

Table 7-8. *Information about the Acquisition*

Investigator name	Bashar Jabr
Tools used	Belk soft, 3uTools, HASH CALC, FTK imager, Wondershare TunesGo
Filename	HUAWEI CAM-L21_20210716_174404.bak
Size	688 MB (721,888,569 bytes)
Date created	16 July 2021, 04:50:52 PM

Data extraction was done using many tools to explore the capabilities
and the functionality of each to determine which one is most suitable for
our experiment. The most suitable one for our experiment is Mobiledit, as
it is easier to use and provides hash values for the extracted files that will
be used to make a comparison of acquired files before and after jailbreak.

Logical data extraction deals with files and folders; therefore it focuses
on extracting data from a file system. As a result of logical extraction, we
will browse file structures containing files and folders. We tried several
tools for data logical extraction like Belkasoft and ftk imager, and all of
them failed until we succeeded using Wondershare TunesGo. Figure 7-8
shows the main screen for Wondershare, which we used in extracting the
logical image from the acquired device.

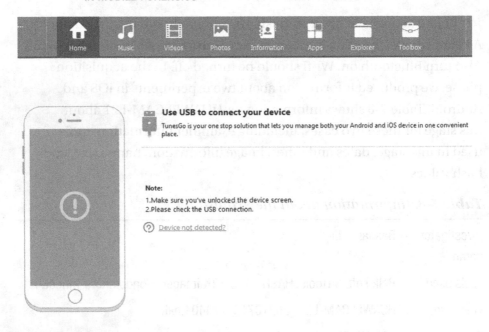

Figure 7-8. *Wondershare*

Then, using HASH CALC tools, we calculated the hash value for the logical disk image file with file name HUAWEI CAM-L21_20210716_165035. bak and a file size of 688 MB (721,474,708 bytes). We used the HASH CALC tool to calculate the hash value in the MD5 algorithm, in addition to the hash value of the file, as illustrated in the Table 7-9.

Table 7-9. *Information about the Backup Image File*

File size	688 MB (721,888,569 bytes)
File name	HUAWEI CAM-L21_20210716_174404.bak
Created date & time	16 July 2021, 04:50:52 PM
Hash value (MD5)	7bf2c25efbd3d493fe42264049e3ef4c
Hash value (SHA1)	0195aaf872e94ad46a20a122e0f2f366be88a1d8

Logical backup succeeded for all data in the mobile except app data, which required the device to be rooted. This shows that backup of applications requires rooting, and this is an indication that the device is not rooted. For that, physical acquisition requires rooting; this will be illustrated in the next sections.

When we tried to extract physical images from the mobile, we used several tools to achieve this task, but unfortunately, we couldn't. As proof, physical data extraction requires rooting for the device, since physical extraction needs a super root user to enable execution of this task. Bypassing screen lock techniques and gaining root access can be done by deleting Gesture.key, which is a hash file that contains the pattern lock on a device, and passcode. This can be done by executing the following command on adb.exe shell.

cd /data/system rm gesture.key

First, we tried to delete the Gesture.key file but we did not succeed because the device is not rooted. Then we applied the following steps:

1. Installing ADB from the Internet.

2. Connecting the mobile to the forensic computer that Windows 10 used in the experiment.

3. From CMD command, entering the platform tools folder, which contains adb.exe.

4. Reaching the folder where ADB is stored. See Figure 7-13.

Other Unlock Techniques

- In rare cases, some unusual techniques can be used to unlock a device. A smudge attack is one technique that can be used on touchscreen devices. This is based on following the smudges from the user's fingers on the screen.

- Different techniques can make use of the forgot password option or forgot pattern. This can be useful if the associated Google account can be accessed. This option can be triggered after several failed unlock attempts. A reset link will be sent to Gmail to create a new code or pattern on the device.

- In very rare cases, some users use third-party applications to lock the device. Simply reboot the device in safe mode then disable or uninstall the app. Reboot in normal mode and the device will boot without the lock.

- In cases where the device was previously connected to a computer in debugging mode with the authorization prompt accepted for that computer, the trust keys are stored on the computer. These keys can be located under the username folder in windows inside the .android folder for that user. The files are adbkey and adbkey.pub. The files are copied from the targeted computer to the forensic lab computer to bypass the ADB authentication process.

- This method depends on the availability of the Google account associated with the device. The idea is to reset the lock code on the device from the related Google account on device manager from https://www.google.com/android/devicemanager. This can be done from the Lock section: set a new code to lock the device. Then, the device can be unlocked using the new code.

- The final approach to be followed by experts in
  extremely rare cases is the JTAG technique. This
  involves physical soldering and chip-off from specific
  circuits on the device. This is a very advanced
  technique that requires extensive training and research
  on the target device's technical structure.

Several attempts have been made to root the phone, using tools like
Wondershare, Dr fone, MobiKin Doctor, ADM, KingRoot, and Vroot, as
well as several trials to root the device using mobile apps, but all of these
attempts were unsuccessful for Android.

Data Extraction Using Belkasoft and AXIOM

From the current practical case, Belkasoft is classified as the best tool
for mobile forensics. It extracts more files and artifacts than AXIOM: 700
types of artifacts are supported and can be extracted, which is larger than
Magnet AXIOM, which supports 500 types of artifacts [34]. Also, logical and
file system acquisition is doable in Belkasoft, in addition to jailbreaking.
Another difference is that Belkasoft enables editing SQLscripts, as SQLite
viewer is embedded inside the tool, and yet other very important feature
that it can generate both encrypted or unencrypted iTunes backup.
Belkasoft can also integrate with other forensic tools, as well as extracting
many types of reports like XML, PDF, and Excel. Magnet AXIOM supports
SQLite viewer, but for viewing only, not editing and writing SQL statement
scripts. Another important feature in Belkasoft is that unallocated files
can be discovered, since the database contains a field "Is Deleted"; if it is
"Yes," this means the file is deleted, while "No" means that it is not deleted.
Figure 7-9 shows the field "Is Deleted":

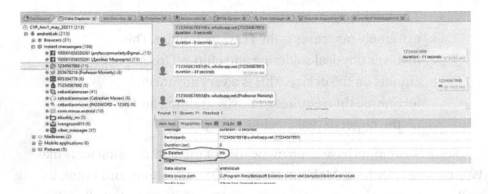

Figure 7-9. *"Is Deleted" field in Belkasoft SQLite*

The best and most valuable feature of Magnet AXIOM is that it enables start extraction and processing on the fly, so there is no need to wait until the acquisition process is complete to start the analysis process. Belkasoft does not support this feature. In addition, it can create cases shared with other third-party applications to import reports and data from it. Like Belkasoft logical and physical extraction, encrypted and unencrypted backups can be performed in Magnet AXIOM.

From our case, and after comparing a set of tools for data acquisition, we can summarize that ADB tools can back up the device data using a command line, and are used for debugging, app installation, and transfer files from mobile. Also, there are several commercial tools that can achieve similar tasks. One main disadvantage of ADB backup we found is that it can't back up all applications stored in a device, while other applications cannot parse all applications in a device, so there is no commercial tool that can support all devices. In addition to that, other applications like Belkasoft and ftk imager have simpler interfaces.

Android Rooting

1. First, use the TunesGo Wondershare tool to get a
    backup before rooting and then root. As shown in
    Figure 7-10, then you can try rooting the mobile
    using this tool and may succeed or not; it depends
    on the device model and Android version. If it fails,
    you can go to the next step.

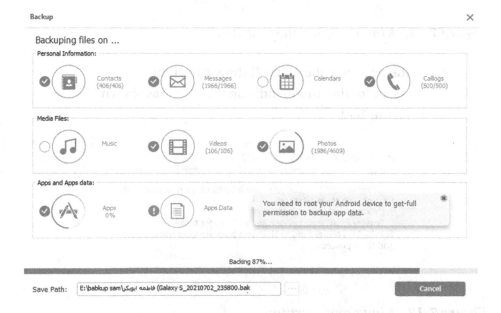

Figure 7-10. *TunesGo Wondershare backup*

2. Using the Kingo root tool, try to take root for the
    device as shown in Figure 7-11.

Figure 7-11. Kingo rooting: the first step

3. In the next step, the tool will show a warning
    message for the user to indicate the effects as shown
    in Figure 7-12.

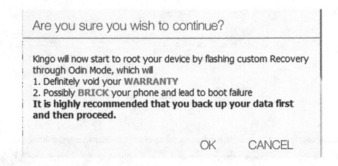

Figure 7-12. Kingo root warning

The investigator should indicate the problems that may happen after
taking root. It may break the warranty, brick the mobile phone, and then
the boot may fail. The user must be sure before making root for the device,
and it is highly recommended to make a backup (step 1) before rooting,
carefully as we did before. If users are sure, they must press ok to start
rooting.

4. The rooting is done successfully, as shown in Figure 7-13.

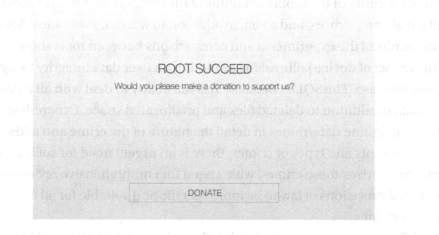

Figure 7-13. Kingo root successfully rooting

This figure shows that the rooting process is done successfully and the
device now is rooted; another case is described in detail to root the Huawei
device in Chapter 13. Now, we can do physical acquisition and reach more
file systems in the mobile device, as we will use in next chapters.

Summary

In this chapter, we have discussed mobile data extraction techniques, and
experiments were applied on these methods. Successful data extraction
was accomplished on two of them, and physically we did not succeed,
because of the need for rooting, which couldn't be accomplished.

Rooting also has disadvantages: one of the most important of them
is warranty voidance, as well as security, in addition to the acquisition,
Android architecture has been illustrated, which contains five layers:
application layer, Android framework, native libraries, Android runtime,
HAL layer, and Linux kernel.

Findings proved that the jailbreaking of the iPhone has a serious effect on the security of the mobile, in terms of the integrity of data and threats like malware, viruses, and so on, in addition to warranty voidance. Also, the results of the experiments and comparisons between tools show the impact of device jailbreaking or rooting on user data integrity using practical case. The SQLite database has the ability to deal with all types of data, in addition to deleted files and unallocated space. Cybercrime law in Palestine determines in detail the nature of the crime and adds new concepts and types of crimes; there is an urgent need for such a law that categorizes these crimes, with a need for comprehensive review and updated provisions of law to be more specific and suitable for all digital forensic types.

When comparing the hash values for extracted data after and before jailbreak, it was found that the hash values are the same, and hence data integrity is not affected by jailbreaking an iPhone device, so investigators can use the jailbreaking technique to acquire data for suspected iPhone devices that allow a deeper level of data acquisition that can be used to support the case.

References

[1].   [Online]. Available: https://www.statista.com/statistics/330695/number-of-smartphone-users-worldwide/.

[2].   [Online]. Available: https://www.businessofapps.com/data/android-statistics/.

[3].   *"The Legal Framework of Cybercrime in Palestine,"* *Arab Law Q.*, 2021, doi: 10.1163/15730255-bja10076. [Art].

[4]. L. &. V. A. Casati, "The Dangers of Rooting: Data Leakage Detection in Android Applications," *hindawi,* 2018.

[5]. L. &. V. A. Casati, "The Dangers of Rooting: Data Leakage Detection in Android Applications. Mobile Information Systems," *hindawi,* 2018.

[6]. N. N. J. &. G. B. Rahimi, "Android Security and Its Rooting—A Possible Improvement of Its Security Architecture. Journal of Information Security," *scirp. org,* 2019.

[7]. C. Odongo, "Enhanced Forensic Framework for Rooted Mobile Phones and the Impact on User Data Integrity–A Case of Android Smartphones (Doctoral dissertation, United States International University-Africa)." *http://erepo.usiu.ac.ke/,* 2018.

[8]. H. Yan, "Methods for Avoiding Rooting in Android System," diva-portal, 2017.

[9]. Negi, C., Mishra, P., Chaudhary, P., and Vardhan, H. (2021). A review and Case Study on android malware: Threat model, attacks, techniques and tools. *Journal of Cyber Security and Mobility.* https://doi.org/10.13052/jcsm2245-1439.1018.

[10]. Sihag, V., Vardhan, M. and Singh, "A Survey of Android Application and Malware Hardening," *Computer Science Review,* 39, 100365, 2021.

[11]. G. D. M. X. Q. &. W. H. C. Zhou, "Detection Model for Potential Channel of iOS".

[12].   K. Karhu, Gustafsson, E. B. H. R. and &. S. C. O.,
         "Four Tactics for Implementing a Balanced Digital
         Platform Strategy," 2020.

[13].   R. V. Gaika, "The Pros and Cons of Jail-Breaking iOS
         Devices".

[14].   A. H. M. R. K. &. W. Kellner, "False Sense of Security:
         A Study on the Effectivity of Jailbreak Detection in
         Banking Apps." In *2019 IEEE European Symposium
         on Security and Privacy, IEEE,* 2019, June.

[15].   J. Bays and U. Karabiyik, "Forensic Analysis of
         Third Party Location Applications in Android
         and iOS," *IEEE INFOCOM 2019 - IEEE Conference
         on Computer Communications Workshops
         (INFOCOM WKSHPS)*, 2019, pp. 1-6.

[16].   Barros, A., Almeida, R., Melo, T., and Frade,
         M. (2022). Forensic analysis of the Bumble Dating
         App for Android. Forensic Sciences, 2(1), 201–221.
         https://doi.org/10.3390/forensicsci2010016.

[17].   Hamilton, "Artifact Integrity in Forensic Acquisitions
         of iPhones Using Jailbreak," 2019.

[18].   S. Chu & H. Wu, "Research on Offense and Defense
         Technology for iOS Kernel Security Mechanism," in
         AIP Conference Proceedings, 2018.

[19].   D. R. S. P. Parmar, "Logical Acquisition of iPhone
         without Jail Breaking," *IJSRST, 2018*. [Art].

[20].   A. Aenurahman Ali, N. Dwi Wahyu Cahyani, and
         E. Musthofa Jadied, "Digital Forensic Analysis
         on iDevice: Jailbreak iOS 12.1.1 as a Case Study,"
         Indones. J. Comput., 2019.

[21]. A. Aenurahman Ali, N. Dwi Wahyu Cahyani, and
E. Musthofa Jadied, "Digital Forensic Analysis
on iDevice: Jailbreak iOS 12.1.1 as a Case Study,"
Indones. J. Comput., 2019. [Art].

[22]. "Apple, "Code-Signing," Apple, [Online]. Available:
https://developer.apple.com/support/code-
signing/.

[23]. R. Tamma, O. Skulkin, H. Mahalik, and
S. Bommisetty, *Practical Mobile Forensics Fourth
Edition,* p. 47, 2020.

[24]. B. Iqbal, A. Iqbal, and H. Al Obaidli, "A Novel
Method of iDevice (iPhone, iPad, iPod) Forensics
without Jailbreaking," 2012, doi: 10.1109/
INNOVATIONS.2012.6207740."

[25]. N. N. J. &. G. B. (. A. S. a. I. R. P. I. o. I. S. A. J. o. I. S. 1.
9.-1. Reference: Rahimi.

[26]. [Online]. Available: Ext filesystem4 (slideshare.net).

[27]. [Online]. Available: http://www.linux-kongress.
org/2009/slides/ext4+btrfs_jan_kara.pdf.

[28]. [Online]. Available: HUAWEI Y6II CAM-L21
Specification - IMEI.info.

[29]. [Online]. Available: https://www.imei.info/
phonedatabase/huawei-y6ii-cam-l21/#basic.

[30]. A. i. 7. -. 1. -. B. (. (. +. G. M. |. eBay. [Online].

[31]. R. Tamma, O. Skulkin, H. Mahalik and
S. Bommisetty, *Practical Mobile Forensics Fourth
Edition,* 2020.

[32]. Karhu, K., Gustafsson, R., Eaton, B., Henfridsson,
       O., and Sørensen, C. (2020). Four Tactics for
       Implementing a Balanced Digital Platform Strategy.
       MIS Quarterly Executive, 19(2), 105-120. `https://`
       `doi.org/10.17705/2msqe.00027`

[33]. P. M. F. (unep.org). [Online].

[34]. K. G. R. E. B. H. O. &. S. C. Karhu, "Four Tactics
       for Implementing a Balanced Digital Platform
       Strategy." 2020.

[35]. A. H. M. R. K. &. W. Kellner, "False Sense of Security:
       A Study on the Effectivity of Jailbreak Detection in
       Banking Apps." In *2019 IEEE European Symposium
       on Security and Privacy, IEEE,* 2019, June.

[36]. S. u. 2. |. Statista, "Statista," [Online].

[37]. [Online]. Available: `https://www.imei.info/`
       `phonedatabase/huawei-y6ii-cam-l21/#basic.`

[38]. [Online]. Available: `http://www.linux-`
       `kongress.org.`

[39]. [Online]. Available: HUAWEI Y6II CAM-L21
       Specification - IMEI.info.

[40]. [Online]. Available: imei.info/phonedatabase/
       huawei-y6ii-cam-l21/#basic.

[41]. "`https://en.wikipedia.org/wiki/Rooting_`
       `(Android)`," [Online].

[42]. [Online]. Available: `https://pre-uneplive.`
       `unep.org/redesign/media/assets/images/`
       `Practical%20Mobile%20Forensics.pdf.`

CHAPTER 8

The Impact of Cryptocurrency Mining on Mobile Devices

In this chapter, we will work on measuring the impact of mining digital coins by mobile on the main resources of the phone, by means of experiments conducted on iOS devices and Android devices. The experiments were conducted within four scenarios, which are as follows: A. Measuring the impact of cryptocurrency mining on the main resources of the phone when the mining program is running in the foreground of the system while keeping the phone screen active. B. Measuring the impact of cryptocurrency mining on mobile resources when the mining program is running in the foreground of the system and keeping the screen idle. C. Measuring the impact of cryptocurrency mining on the main resources of the mobile while the mining program is running in the background and keeping the mobile screen active. D. Measuring the impact of cryptocurrency mining on the main sources of the mobile while the mining program is running in the background and keeping the mobile screen in the login mode. This is to determine the effects resulting

© Mohammed Moreb 2022
M. Moreb, *Practical Forensic Analysis of Artifacts on iOS and Android Devices*,
https://doi.org/10.1007/978-1-4842-8026-3_8

from the mining process on mobile resources, such as high CPU usage, high temperature, battery power consumption, and high temperature, in addition to the increase in RAM consumption, clarifying the results for each experiment, which are reflected in the mobile performance and functions. In addition, a fair use policy must be provided, and the experiments could suggest one. For both iOS and Android devices, the results will help to control and analyze the programs installed on the mobile to ensure that the user does not fall victim to malicious programs that use the mobile resources in the mining process and consume them without the knowledge or consent of the user.

In this chapter, we will cover the following topics:

- Introduction to Cryptocurrency Mining

- Measurement and Work Mechanism

- Tools, Programs, And applications Used in Cryptocurrency Mining

- Experiment and Analogy by iOS

- Experiment and Analogy by Android

- Results and Analysis

Introduction to Cryptocurrency Mining

Information technology played an important role in the economic sector when it presented itself as a solution to the global financial crisis of 2008 and established a free, transparent, and uncontrolled economy, which was embodied in blockchain technology. Blockchain technology relies on storing data in the form of blocks distributed on millions of devices around the world and working to complete financial transactions without an intermediary and with full transparency [1]. A person calling himself "Satoshi Nakamoto" announced the creation of a digital currency called

Bitcoin as an application of the blockchain system. The tremendous jumps that took place in the price of digital currencies made them an important sector for investors to invest in, whether in trading or in mining; this made many miners turn to illegally mining digital currencies and using the devices of others without permission or knowledge, in a process called cryptojacking. Cryptocurrency mining relies primarily on the CPU and the graphics card. In 2011, mining methods used through the browser were called Coinhive, as this technology relies on JavaScript, which provided a fertile environment for illegal miners by cryptojacking visitors' devices to mine digital currencies [2]. The large number of mobiles in use and their spread among a great number of people gave us major motivation to conduct a study to measure the effects of cryptocurrency mining on mobile devices. In this experiment, we will use the Pi network software to mine and test on iOS system mobile (iPhone 6s) and Android system mobile (LG g5, Samsung Galaxy A8 Plus). This experiment depends on the following four scenarios, which we will apply to the mentioned devices:

- Measuring the impact of running a mining Pi Network application in the foreground while the screen is the inactive mode.

- Measuring the impact of running a mining Pi Network app in the foreground while the screen is idle.

- Measuring the impact of running the Pi Network mining application in the background while the screen is the inactive mode.

- Measuring the impact of running the Pi Network mining application in the background while the screen is idle.

Local laws such as those in Palestine suffer, as is the case for most of the laws in the world, from a weakness in defining cybercrime and all its aspects, as it is a rapidly spreading, developing, and transcontinental crime. The Palestinian law, an amendment to the Telecommunications

Law No. 3 of 1996, broadly criminalizes cryptojacking, that is, the mining of digital currencies on other people's devices without permission or knowledge, and this is inferred from Palestinian Law No. 10 of 2018 regarding cybercrime, where Article 20 stipulates the following: "Whoever violates a right of intellectual, literary or industrial property in accordance with the legislation in force, through the electronic network or any means of information technology, punishable by imprisonment for a period not exceeding six months, or by a fine of no less than five hundred Jordanian dinars and not more than one thousand Jordanian dinars, or what equivalent in the legally circulated currency, or with both penalties." Likewise, Article 26 stipulates that "Whoever possesses, for the purpose of use, a device, program, or any prepared electronic data, password, or tram? It is permissible to enter, present, produce, distribute, import, export, or promote it, for the purpose of committing any of the crimes stipulated in this law by decision, punishable by imprisonment for a period not exceeding five years, and a fine of not less than three thousand Jordanian dinars, and not exceeding five thousand Jordanian dinars or its equivalent in the legally circulated currency." This study measures the impact of digital currency mining on mobile devices to determine the extent of its impact on the programmatic and physical side of the mobile.

Mobile phones have brought about a new concept of data and big data so that the trend has become toward independent prediction [4]. This role that mobile phones play in our daily life has made them a target for digital currency mining, as in 2011 the trend toward a new service for mining digital currencies via the browser called Coinhive [2] was promoted as an alternative to ads, as 72% of the 228 million Android device users expressed their acceptance of using their mobile phones for mining as an alternative to ads. The mining process takes place by exploiting the resources of miners' devices to solve complex calculations in exchange for giving them a reward in digital currencies to motivate them to continue, and this affects the basic resources of the device such as reducing battery life and affecting the performance of other applications. The terms of the mobile mining process require a phone connection to the Internet and a battery charge of greater than 15% [5]. After the emergence of digital currency mining operations via the browser and mobile phones, a bad phenomenon appeared called cryptojacking, whereby the owners of websites or applications put digital currency mining codes in their sites or applications or through ads so that they could exploit the devices of visitors and users without their knowledge. In 2017, checkpoint considered mining through the Coinhive browser as being the largest percentage of global threat indicators for its ability to affect a large proportion of global institutions [2], as some studies revealed that mining in certain cases led to an 11-fold battery consumption from normal consumption [8]. This would raise mining costs and deplete the main equipment resources. To prevent the depletion of the device's main resources from the mining process, it has been suggested to incorporate mining programs into games or other programs, and this would reduce battery consumption, as the process of mining digital currencies takes place when using the application and not in the traditional way by opening the browser only for the sake of mining. This would organize the mining process to reduce users' inconvenience from consuming the resources of their devices and achieve a fair distribution for the owners of applications that use mining as an alternative to advertisements as a source of income [5]. To prevent cryptojacking attacks, it has been suggested to develop a system-wide solution that warns users of the existence of a certain activity that is consuming the resources of their devices significantly in order to detect mining operations on their devices without their consent [6], and suggest the use of ad-blocking tools such as uBlock Origin and antimining tools such as NoCoin [2]. However, it is sometimes difficult to detect this through energy analysis measurements because the algorithms differ from one another in terms of the hash rate of digital currencies [7].

Since the topic of the research revolves around measuring the impact of cryptocurrency mining on the resources of mobile devices, in Chapter 1 to Chapter 3 we introduced the architecture of iOS and Android operating systems; this will focus our work in this chapter on measuring the impact of cryptocurrency mining on mobile resources, which are concentrated in the fourth layer, hardware abstraction.

Measure of Cryptocurrency Mining

To measure the impact of cryptocurrency mining on mobile devices, we chose the Pi Network application, and the reason for this is the great use of this application. As of this report, it has been downloaded on Google Play over 10 million times, as shown in Figure 8-1.

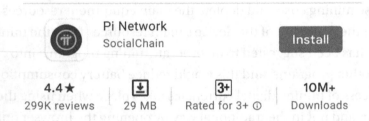

Figure 8-1. *Number of downloads of Pi Network on Google Play*

The tests were conducted on the devices on which the study was conducted with more than one scenario. The duration of each experiment is 10 minutes, and the experiments are as follows:

- Measuring the impact of the mining process when running the mining app on the front of the phone while keeping the screen active.

- Measuring the effect when keeping the mining app on the front and the screen idle.

- Measuring the effect when running the application in the background and keeping the screen in the active mode and then measuring when running.

- Measuring the effect when running the application in the background and keeping the screen in an idle mode.

Tools, Programs, and Applications Used in Cryptocurrency Mining

To achieve an accurate measurement, many applications and auxiliary programs have been used in order to contribute to taking different readings of the phone's resources, which are as follows. See Table 8-1.

Table 8-1. *Tools, Programs, and Applications That Were Used in the Experiments*

App/Program Name	Details
Belkasoft	Mobile forensics
DB Browser (SQLite)	A tool to read databases for mobile
3uTools	Get device information
AccuBattery app	Used to measure battery consumption for Android
CPU Monitor app	Measure CPU and RAM consumption
iCelsius	Used to measure battery consumption for iOS
Lirum Device Info Lite	Used to measure CPU & RAM consumption for iOS
AccuBattery	Measure battery of Android device
CPU Monitor	Measure CPU and RAM for Android devices

    A.   **iPhone 6S:**

This phone works on the iOS system version 13.3.1 and 16 GB storage, 2 GB RAM, processor Apple A9, and battery capacity 1715mAh, as shown in Figure 8-2.

Figure 8-2. *Mobile details from 3uTools*

B.   **Samsung A8 plus:**

This phone works on the Android system version 9, 3500 mAh battery, 64 GB storage, 4 GB RAM, and an eight-core processor.

C.   **LG G5:**

This phone works on the Android system version 8, 1520 mAh battery, 4 GB RAM, 25.23 GB memory, and a quad-core processor.

Experiment and Analogy by iPhone 6s

1. Measuring the impact of running the Pi Network mining application on the front of the iPhone 6s mobile while the screen is inactive is described in Table 8-2.

Table 8-2. *While the Screen Is Inactive*

	Ram free space	Battery %	Memory free space	CPU core 1	CPU core 2
Before	3.51%	52%	2.95 GB	31%	**36%**
After	9.26%	46%	2.75 GB	81%	**76%**

In our case, the use of RAM increased from 3.51% to 9.26%, the charge level in the battery decreased by 6%, and there was a decrease in memory by 20 MB, the use of CPU core1 increased from 31% to 81%, and the percentage of CPU core2 usage increased from 36% to 76%.

2. Measuring the impact of running the Pi Network mining application on the front of the mobile while the screen is in idle mode:

Figure 8-3 shows the result for the same case to measure the effects while running the application on the front of the phone while the screen is idle. The RAM usage decreased from 1.47% to 3.07%, the battery charge decreased by 1%, the storage memory decreased from 2.74 GB to 2.73 GB, the use of CPU core1 increased by 18%, and the use of CPU core2 increased by 16%.

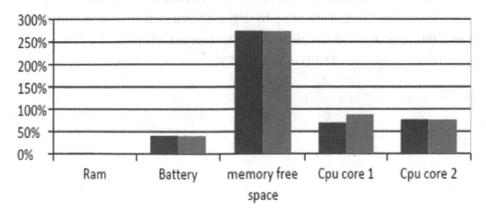

Figure 8-3. *iPhone 6s - while the screen is in idle mode*

3. Measuring the impact of running a mining Pi Network application in the background while the screen is inactive mode:

Table 8-3 shows the results for measuring the impact of running the Pi Network mining application on iPhone 6s in the background while the screen is the inactive mode. The greatest impact was on CPU core1, where consumption increased from 68% to 92%, then consumption in CPU core2 increased from 69% to 82%, then the battery charge level decreased by 8%, RAM consumption increased by 0.28%, and main memory decreased by 0.02%.

Table 8-3. *While Pi app. running on the background*

	Ram free space	Battery %	Memory free space	CPU core 1	CPU core 2
Before	1.70%	31%	17.07%	68%	69%
After	1.42%	23%	17.05%	92%	82%

4. Measuring the impact of running the Pi Network mining application in the background of the iPhone while the screen is idle.

In this experiment, there was an increase in the use of RAM by 13.25%, a decrease in the level of charging by 3%, a decrease in storage memory from 2.89 GB to 2.73 GB, an increase in the use of CPU core1 by 27%, and an increase in the use of CPU core2 by 27%.

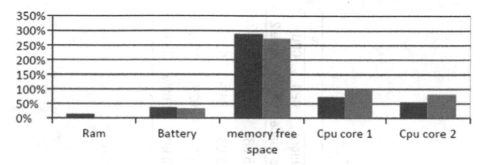

Figure 8-4. *While the screen is in idle mode*

In the result, we note that the greatest impact of the process of mining cryptocurrencies on the iPhone was in the first experience when running the program in the foreground while keeping the screen activated and that the greatest impact on the device resources that were measured occurred on the CPU, then on the battery, then on RAM, and then on the main memory. This would lead to the consumption of the main resources of the mobile, which would slow it down in carrying out the rest of its tasks and then lead to its long-term damage. See Table 8-4 and Table 8-5.

Table 8-4. Experiment on an iPhone 6s Device

Before						After					
Exp.	Ram free space	Battery %	Memory free space	CPU core 1	CPU core 2	Ram free space	Battery %	Memory free space	CPU core 1	CPU core 2	
1	3.51%	52%	2.95 GB	31%	36%	9.26%	46%	2.75 GB	81%	76%	
2	1.74%	41%	2.74 GB	70%	77%	3.07%	40%	2.73 GB	88%	93%	
3	1.70%	31%	2.4GB	86%	89%	1.42%	23%	2.3 GB	92%	82%	
4	14.40%	37%	2.89 GB	73%	55%	1.15%	34%	2.73 GB	100%	82%	

Table 8-5. *Result of the Experiment on iPhone 6s Device*

Exp.	Ram free space	Battery %	Memory free space	CPU core 1	CPU core 2
1	5.75% +	−6%	−0.02GB	+ 50%	+40%
2	+1.6%	−1%	−0.01GB	+ 18%	+16%
3	−0.28	−8%	−0.1 GB	+6%	−7%
4	−13.25%	−3%	−0.16 GB	+27%	+27%

We used the digital investigation program Belkasoft to search for files or remnants of the use of the cryptocurrency mining program (Pi Network), and then we checked the database version on the program DB Browser (SQLite) as shown in Figure 8-5. The result was that no trace was stored on the device. But this could be done using the Coinhive technique, which is a technology that appeared in 2011 and that works by data mining through browsing. The user application acts as a display interface for a browser through which mining operations are performed by exploiting the device's resources.

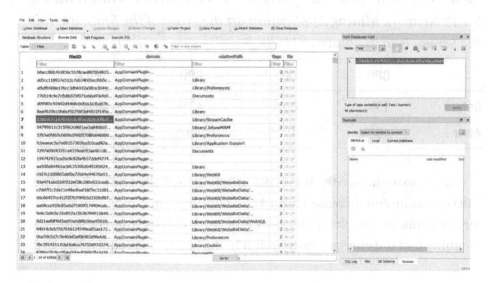

Figure 8-5. *DB Browser (SQLite)*

Experiment and Analogy by LG g5 Mobile

1. Measuring the impact of running the Pi Network mining application on the front of the mobile while the screen is the inactive mode for LG g5 is described in Table 8-6, and the effects on CPU frequency are shown in Table 8-7.

Table 8-6. *Effects of Pi Network Mining While the Screen Is in the Inactive Mode*

	RAM free space	CPU Frequency	Battery %	Memory free space	Battery life	CPU temperature	Battery temperature
Before	1.79 GB	43.75%	85%	21.6 GB	20 h 9 m	41 °C	36 °C
After	1.32 GB	100%	77%	21.4 GB	18 h	46 °C	37.2 °C

Table 8-7. *Measuring the Effects on CPU Frequency While Running the Pi Network Mining Application on the Front of the Mobile While the Screen Is in the Inactive Mode*

	CPU 1	CPU 2	CPU 3	CPU 4
Before	19%	60%	48%	**48%**
After	100%	100%	100%	**100%**

In this experiment, the RAM consumption increased by 0.47 GB; the CPU consumption increased from 43.75% to 100%, meaning that the increase was 56.25%; the battery power level decreased from 85% to 77%, meaning that the energy consumption in the battery was equivalent to 8%;

the storage of the main memory is 0.2 GB; the battery usage life decreased from 20 hours and 9 minutes to 18 hours, meaning that the percentage of decrease in the battery usage time was 2 hours and 9 minutes; the CPU temperature increased by 5 degrees Celsius, from 41 degrees Celsius to 46 degrees Celsius; and the battery temperature increased from 36 degrees Celsius to 37.2 degrees Celsius, meaning the increase was 1.2 degrees Celsius. See Figure 8-6.

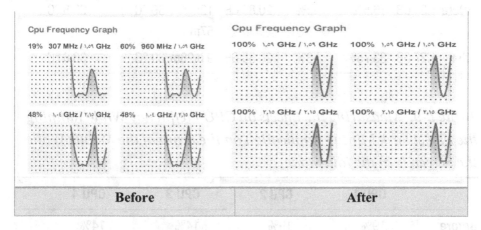

Figure 8-6. *Measuring the Effects on CPU Frequency before and after install Pi App*

2. The impact of running the Pi Network mining application on the front of the mobile while the screen is in the idle mode is described in Table 8-8, and the effect while the screen is in inactive mode is described in Table 8-9.

Table 8-8. *Measuring the Impact of Mining via the Pi Network Mining Application on the Front of the Mobile While the Screen Is in the Idle Mode*

	Ram free space	CPU Frequency	Battery %	Memory free space	Battery life	CPU temperature	Battery temperature
Before	1.34 GB	16.5%	55%	20.83 GB	12h 57m	36 °C	26.8 °C
After	1.27 GB	83.75%	53%	20.83 GB	9 h 28m	39 °C	30.6 °C

Table 8-9. *Measuring the Effects on CPU Frequency While Running the Pi Network Mining Application on the Front of the Mobile While the Screen Is in the idle Mode*

	CPU 1	CPU 2	CPU 3	CPU 4
Before	19%	19%	14%	**14%**
After	87%	87%	61%	**100%**

In this experiment, when the mining program was running at the forefront of the system and the screen was in a sleep state, it was noted that the RAM consumption increased by 0.07 GB, where the free space in RAM before the experiment was carried out was 1.34 GB and after the experiment was executed it became 1.27 GB. The CPU usage rate increased from 16.5% to 83.75%. The percentage of energy in the battery decreased from 55% to 53%, that is, by 2%. There was no change in the size used for the main memory and the rest of the free space, as it is 20.83 GB. The estimated life of the battery usage decreased from 12 hours and 57 minutes to 9 hours and 28 minutes, that is, an average 3 hours and 29 minutes.

The CPU temperature increased by 3 °C (from 36 °C to 39 °C), and the battery temperature increased from 26.8 °C to 30.6 °C (a rise of 3.8 °C). See Figure 8-7.

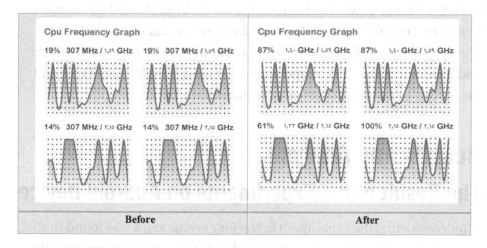

Figure 8-7. *Frequency of CPU before and after*

When conducting an experiment with the Pi Network cryptocurrency mining program in the background of the system with the screen remaining active, it was noted that the consumption of RAM increased from 1.37 GB to 1.17 GB, meaning that the RAM usage increased by 0.2%; the CPU usage increased from 16.5% to 88%; the power level decreased in the battery from 46% to 41%, meaning the decrease was by 5%; and the main memory usage increased by 0.01%. The battery usage life decreased from 10 hours and 20 minutes to 6 hours and 18 minutes; the CPU temperature increased at a rate of 8 °C, where the rise was from 38 °C to 46 °C; and the battery's temperature dropped from 34.8 °C to 34.6 °C, meaning that the decrease was by 0.2 °C.

In our case, we ran the cryptocurrency mining program in the background of the system and kept the screen in sleep mode. This led to an increase in RAM usage by 0.16 GB, a CPU usage increase from 59.75% to 70%, a battery power level decrease from 38% to 36%, and no change in free space (the free memory in the main memory remained at 20.84 GB). The battery usage life decreased from 12 hours and 18 minutes to 9 hours and 19 minutes, the CPU temperature increased from 39 °C to 41 °C, and the battery temperature decreased from 34 °C to 30 °C.

Results and Analysis
The Result of the Experiments on Android Device

After conducting the experiment in the four scenarios, it was found that the greatest effect on the LG g5 mobile due to the mining process was the effect on the CPU in terms of frequency and temperature rise; this was followed by the decrease in the charging level, then the decrease in battery life, then the effect of increased RAM usage, and then the effect on the main memory. See Table 8-10.

Table 8-10. *Result of Four Scenarios on an LG g5*

Ram free space	CPU Frequency	Battery %	Memory free space	Battery life	CPU temperature	Battery temperature
1.79 GB	43.75%	85%	21.6 GB	20 h 9 m	41 °C	36 °C
1.34 GB	16.5%	55%	20.83 GB	12h 57m	36 °C	26.8 °C
1.37 GB	16.5%	46%	20.83 GB	10 h 20m	38 °C	34.8 °C
1.32 GB	59.75%	38%	20.84 GB	12 h 18 m	39 °C	34 °C
1.32 GB	100%	77%	21.4 GB	18 h	46 °C	37.2 °C
1.27 GB	83.75%	53%	20.83 GB	9 h 28m	39 °C	30.6 °C
1.17 GB	88%	41%	20.82 GB	6 h 18 m	46 °C	34.6 °C
1.16 GB	70%	36%	20.84 GB	9h 19m	41 °C	30.8
+ 0.47 GB	+ 56.25%	**−8%**	−0.2 GB	−2h 9m	+5 °C	+ 1.2 °C
+ 0.07 GB	+ 67.25	**−2%**	**00**	−3h 29m	+ 3 °C	+ 3.8 °C
+ 0.2 GB	+ 71.5%	−5%	−0.01 GB	−4h −2m	+ 8 °C	−0.2 °C
+ 0.16 GB	+ 10.3%	−2%	**00**	−3 h 1m	+2 °C	−3.2 °C

After obtaining the results of the experiments for the four scenarios on the Samsung Galaxy A8 Plus mobile-only, it was noticed that the device's resources were most affected by the cryptocurrency mining process in the first place, in terms of usage and high temperature. The next most prominent effect was in terms of low battery charging and also battery life. Finally, the main memory was affected and RAM usage was increased.

Summary

The results of the preceding experiments that were acquired on iOS and Android devices showed that the greatest impact was primarily on the CPU in terms of an increase in its use, high temperatures, a decrease in the battery charge level, a decrease in the life of use and an increase in its temperature, and then the increase in memory usage. The greatest impact falls on the important and main resources in the mobile, such as the CPU, battery, random memory, and main memory. This could cause damage to the device on the remote level or slow down the implementation of the tasks assigned to it because the main resources are occupied with the mining process.

We suggest that there be a fair use system activated in mobile operating systems, which depends on analyzing the software that is installed on the mobile, monitoring its behavior in the use of the main resources of the mobile, and notifying the user to solve their use exceeding the reasonable limit and leaving the option to complete its work or stop it from working. This will help combat malicious programs that exploit users' devices in the mining process without their knowing [10], thus combatting cryptolocker attacks.

References

[1].   Zibin Zheng, Shaoan Xie, Hongning Dai, Xiangping Chen, and Huaimin Wang, "An Overview of Blockchain Technology," *IEEE*, p. 8, 2017.

[2].   J. Rauchberger et al., "The Other Side of the Coin: A Framework for Detecting and Analyzing Web-Based Cryptocurrency Mining Campaigns," ACM Int. Conf. Proceeding Ser., 2018, doi: 10.1145/3230833.3230869.

[3]. J. Rauchberger et al., "The Other Side of the Coin: A Framework for Detecting and Analyzing Web Based Cryptocurrency Mining Campaigns," ACM Int. Conf. Proceeding Ser., 2018, doi: 10.1145/3230833.3230869.

[4]. M. Musolesi, "Big Mobile Data Mining: Good or Evil?," *IEEE*, 2014.

[5]. Sinh Huynh, Kenny Tsu Wei Choo, Rajesh Krishna Balan, and Youngki Lee. 2019. CryptoCurrency Mining on Mobile as an Alternative Monetization Approach. In Proceedings of the 20th International Workshop on Mobile Computing Systems and Applications (HotMobile '19). Association for Computing Machinery, New York, NY, USA, 51–56. DOI:https://doi.org/10.1145/3301293.3302372.

[6]. "Cryptocurrency Mining: A Mobile Device Perspective," 2018 16th Annu. Conf. Privacy, Secur. Trust. PST 2018, pp. 1–5, 2018, doi: 10.1109/PST.2018.8514199.

[7]. S. Sankaran, N. Pramod, and K. Achuthan, "Energy and Performance Comparison of Cryptocurrency Mining for Embedded Devices," *IEEE*, pp. 0–4, 2019.

[8]. Gronli, T. M. et al. (2014) "Mobile Application Platform Heterogeneity: Android vs Windows Phone vs iOS vs Firefox OS," *Proceedings - International Conference on Advanced Information Networking and Applications, AINA*, pp. 635–641. doi: 10.1109/AINA.2014.78.

[9].   Brähler, S. (2010) "Analysis of the Android
Architecture," *Os. Ibds. Kit. Edu*, p. 52. Available at:
http://os.ibds.kit.edu/downloads/sa_2010_
braehler-stefan_android-architecture.pdf.

[10].   Brähler, S. (2010) "Analysis of the Android
Architecture," *Os. Ibds. Kit. Edu*, p. 52. Available at:
http://os.ibds.kit.edu/downloads/sa_2010_
braehler-stefan_android-architecture.pdf.

CHAPTER 9

Mobile Forensic Investigation for WhatsApp

Due to the rapid development in smartphones and their applications resulting from the development of technology and communication, and due to their ease of mobility, cost, and energy consumption, smartphones have replaced computers in many uses. The WhatsApp (WA) application is considered to be the largest messaging application around the world and an important source of information; recently they added a new algorithm that works on end-to-end encryption features, which creates a major challenge for forensic investigators and analysts. This chapter explains how to extract the encryption key from WA, encrypt databases, and extract valuable artifacts that are presented and stored in the Android and iOS systems, as a way to present and analyze artifacts extracted from the latest version of WA to discover traces of new and valuable evidence and artifacts to help investigators and forensic analysts in the investigation. This means using many tools, devices, and types of software for portable devices specializing in digital forensics; many tools used in this chapter were used on a free-trial basis.

© Mohammed Moreb 2022
M. Moreb, *Practical Forensic Analysis of Artifacts on iOS and Android Devices*,
https://doi.org/10.1007/978-1-4842-8026-3_9

In this chapter, we will cover the following topics:

- WA Architecture

- WA Experiment

- Tools Used in the Examination Process for iOS

- Tools Used in the Acquisition Process for Android

- iOS Analysis Stage

- Android Analysis Stage

- Examination on a Backup Taken by iTunes

- Examination on a Backup Taken from the Connected Device

- Forensic Tools Comparison

WA Architecture

After the rapid and exponential development in communication technology and the Internet, also accelerated development in smartphones and their data connectivity like 3G and 4G. Social networking and instant messaging (IM) companies developed their mobile applications. The mobile forensic method divides the investigation process into four stages: seizure, acquisition, analysis, and reporting. Here, the mobile forensic process was used in an investigation over iOS and Android smartphones, where a digital crime was assumed to be committed through WA. First, during the seizure stage, the smartphones were identified, preserved, documented, secured, and disconnected from all types of networks. The acquisition stage was completed by the phone's imaging process and the hash value (MD5) was calculated. The analysis stage was completed by accessing chat details and logs, call logs, and multimedia to determine the evidence. The investigation process was carried out according to a legal framework and approved procedures that regulate the process by monitoring its stages to ensure that evidence is protected from alteration or destruction, and to ensure that the witness's report is admissible in court. Finally, the investigation process and evidence were reported. In conclusion, WA forensic artifacts could be analyzed and discovered successfully using the mobile forensic process.

WA is a popular IM application in smartphones. WA allows users to exchange text messages, images, video files, audio files, document files, pdf files, and many others. WA allows users to create user groups to send messages and files to all group members. WA also allows the user to control personal profile information such as name, profile photo, and information about the user [8]. WA messaging is done in end-to-end encryption, and therefore no man-in-the-middle can read messages between two WA users [9]. WA stores its data in the mobile phone's internal memory. WA automatically connects to the phone contacts database, detects the contacts that use the WA application, and adds them to its database. The WA application also includes a procedure named "com.whatsapp", which is a procedure for operating the external media management service and the messaging service that runs in the background, as this procedure works when turning on the smartphone [10]. WA used the SQLite database "ChatStorage.sqlit" to save messages that were exchanged between users and other information from the user activities on WA [11].

Among the many IM applications on smartphones, WA has become the most popular IM application [2]. According to a statistic made by Statista in October 2020 for the most popular and widespread IM application based on the number of active users per month [3], WA is the most used by 2 billion active users, followed by Facebook Messenger (1.3 billion), WeChat (1.206 billion), QQ (648 million), Snapchat (433 million), and Telegram (400 million active users).

Cybercrime is increasing exponentially and in various ways and for different purposes, including personal fund gain, commercial competition, theft of intellectual property, personal theft, bullying, harassment, money laundering, terrorism, and so on. It's always necessary to legally deal with cybercrimes, investigate them, and prosecute cybercriminals [4]. As well, there must be specialized laws to define the tools and types of cybercrime. Therefore, specialized law enforcement agencies must be founded to investigate and present it to the judiciary. Additionally, the penal laws must be developed to address this type of crime [5].

Most countries around the world are issuing cybercrime laws. Specialized law enforcement agencies are also being founded to investigate this type of crime [6]. The state of Palestine, like many other countries, has issued a cybercrime law by Decree No. 10 of 2018. This law defines activities, tools, and terminology related to cybercrime, and determines the law enforcement agencies that are responsible for the investigation and prosecution of cybercrime and the penalties for these crimes [7].

There are many different tools that support acquisition data in the WA application, and the main goal of using these tools is to access the data stored in the protected logic of the mobile device to obtain WA data. The way these tools work depends on two methods—namely, rooting the Android device and going back to the previous version of the WA application—and the use of these two methods is completely related to obtaining the data from the WA application and understanding the method on which the structure of the WA application depends. This section will discuss the WA application, and then the main mechanisms used to obtain data and items from the WA application will be clarified. The WA application is an application that works on IM and is free of charge, as it allows users to receive and send messages—whether text, images, audio or video clips, and many other files—in a very easy way, as this application is available for all operating systems around the world such as Windows, Android, and iOS. Often, we think about how messages are transmitted from phones through the receiving servers, without thinking about the invisible mechanism that may take place in the phones. In fact, when the sender presses the send button and directly sends the message, it is stored inside a file and this file is stored in turn inside both devices: the sender and the receiver. Figure 9-1 explains the process of sending and encrypting the sent message and transferring it to the WA server and then sending it to the receiver, decoding it, and displaying it to the user.

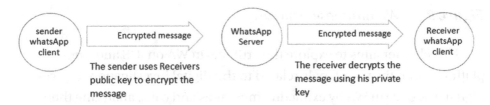

Figure 9-1. *WA transmission*

Usually, forensic investigators are interested in locating the places where messages are stored, so they can obtain them and then run them according to WA policy, so all sent and received messages are stored in the servers of the WA application temporarily. WA servers contain a large amount of evidence usually stored in servers for a very short time. In addition, investigators need to refer to the owner company directly and adhere to the company's privacy policy to retrieve any evidence in their servers, and that is a very difficult procedure. Here comes the importance of investigating the sender's and receiver's devices because the sent and received messages are kept in mobile devices, so that WA users store many artifacts of high value as proof for the investigation, as the files that are saved are the message log and the database. For all conversations and correspondences (sent and received), The *WA database structure* (Figure 9-2) describes the database structures stored in the internal memory of the mobile device in a hierarchical manner, which includes three levels: the first level contains the main WA data hall, the second level contains the subdatabases, and the third level, located at the bottom level of the hierarchy, shows the other subfiles.

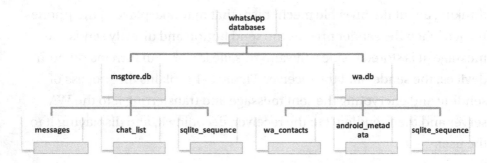

Figure 9-2. *WA database structure*

This chapter aims to explore the artifacts in WA on iOS and Android platforms and the use of tools related to the digital investigation to access digital evidence in WA by extracting messages and calls, analyzing them, and linking them in a chronological sequence to reach the digital evidence of the case.

Old versions of WA used the SQLite database "msgstore.db" to save messages that were exchanged between users; this database was unencrypted. Because unencrypting the database led to easy access to the details of the messages stored in it, to bypass this problem and to achieve better protection for users' privacy, an encryption mechanism was developed for the WA database on the Android platform using an advanced encryption algorithm (AES) with an encryption key (192-bit length). As a result, the database name has changed to msgstore.db.crypt, msgstore.db.crypt5, msgstore.db.crypt7, and msgstore.db.crypt8. In recent versions of WA, the AES algorithm was used with a 256-bit key and the database became msgstore.db.crypt12 [10].

Research studies mostly deal with forensic methodologies on various mobile applications, such as forensic analysis of contact lists, SMS messages, and social media. Some researchers have compared several analysis tools by applying them to the analysis of processes for obtaining WA messages and files on Android platforms. Other researchers determined different artifacts on Android platforms generated by WA such as contacts database, messages database, and the database encryption key (Shidek, Cahyani, and Wardana, 2020). Another study focused on the decryption of WA encrypted databases. The researcher used five different tools to achieve the study's goals; these tools are WA key, db extractor, WA viewer, WA extract, SQLite spy, and Android backup extractor. Some of these tools are written in python code, so a python compiler is also needed in their experiment [12]. A comparison study between two forensic tools for examining iPhone devices was also done [13]. The study showed a comparison between Elcomsoft iOS forensic toolkit and Oxygen 2012 in terms of the ability of these tools to examine nonjailbreak and jailbreak iPhones [13]. This study focused on mobile forensic investigation in WA on iOS and Android platforms using a variety of digital forensic tools.

WA Experiment

To achieve the aim of our case, a forensic examination was conducted on Android and iOS smartphones. An assumed scenario was used to simulate the case to implement the mobile forensic stages, then analyze the evidence extracted from WA, and finally, write a mobile forensic analysis report.

The assumed scenario is that a public sector employee in the Public Services Office seeks to request a bribe from a citizen to complete the processing of the citizen's documents via WA messages. While bribery is one of the corruption crimes in the public sector, the anticorruption commission is the specialized entity to address this type of crime according to local laws in your country. Furthermore, the mobile device is a digital tool used to facilitate this type of traditional crime [7].

The scenario depicts the suspect blackmailing the victim through text messages and voice calls via WA. The investigator shall follow the mobile forensic process in dealing with evidence to seize, secure, and preserve it from any changes. The evidence data is then extracted from the evidence image to explore the conversations, voice calls, and images that occurred between the suspect and the victim via WA. In this scenario, the smartphone is in an active state and can be powered on. In the simulation process, the mobile forensic process, which is explained in Chapter 1, is as shown in Figure 9-3. All steps were taken to obtain valid and admissible evidence to be presented in a witness report that can be submitted to the court to decide the case.

Figure 9-3. *Mobile forensic process*

In the seizure stage, a reasonable and specific search warrant from a legal authority such as the Public Prosecution must be issued. The digital evidence must be determined in the search warrant. Seizures are done by law enforcement personnel trained in the digital evidence seizure process or experts in digital investigation accompanied by judicial officials to ensure that digital evidence is protected and preserved. At this stage, the adopted procedures in the seizure process must be adhered to, and the laws related to privacy and the rights of individuals must be observed. Judicial seizure officers work at this stage to secure the crime scene and document it in writing and photography. The seized devices are also documented in the seizure report, where the name of the owner, the make, the model, the serial number, IMEI, and any other information distinguishing the seized device are documented, in addition to photographing the seizures. Work is being done to preserve the seized devices in their original condition. In addition to disconnecting the communication signals from the devices, all wireless networks must be disconnected to prevent any alteration or destruction of the digital evidence.

The data processing and verification of the evidence are then carried out on backup and imaging data on the smartphone using forensic tools. In this study, the FINALMobile forensic tool was used to implement the data imaging process. This process is carried out in the acquisition stage.

In the data acquisition process, a logical acquisition from a seized smartphone was used, where a backup of the data was taken from the internal memory. The backup data image was saved in the storage media to protect it and perform an analysis process later. When this process is completed, the acquisition process information is saved and documented in a report. This information includes investigator information, acquiring time and information, and image information, which includes a file name, file size, and the MD5 hash value for the file.

The investigator used the image taken in the previous stage to perform the analysis process to obtain more evidence related to the crime. Evidence is collected and verified by exploring and reading the conversations stored in the WA database. Before beginning the analysis stage, the investigator checks the integrity of the evidence image by recalculating the image hash value (MD5) and comparing it with a hash value calculated in the acquisition process.

After the analysis stage, the results and data obtained from all stages of the investigation will be reported. The report contains information about the investigator and an introduction to the crime. The report includes documentation of all the evidence that was reached, including the documentation of the chronology of the events that were collected. The conduct of all operations must be within the law and the approved procedures for the report to be admissible to the court, based on the legal jurisdiction of the Anti-Corruption Commission to receive complaints of suspicion of corruption and investigate them based on the law by decree No. 7 of 2010 to combat corruption. In addition to the adopted procedures in the seizure and investigation processes, actions started in the assumed scenario are as follows:

[1]. According to the complaint from the victim to the Palestinian Anticorruption Commission, the investigation department issued a search warrant from the anticorruption prosecution against the suspect based on the law by decree no. 7 of 2010 on anticorruption and the law by decree no. 10 of 2018 on cybercrime.

[2]. The judicial officers in the investigation department have requested technical assistance from digital investigation experts to participate in the implementation of the digital evidence seizure process based on the law by decree no. 10 of 2018 on cybercrime.

Seizure Stage

This stage was conducted based on the search warrant issued by the anticorruption prosecution based on article no. 32 (paragraphs 1 and 2) in the law by decree no. 10 of 2018 on cybercrime. During the seizing process, the following information was documented on a seizure report based on article no. 32 (paragraph 3) and article no. 33 (paragraph 6):

1. **The reporting agency:** Anticorruption commission/ Digital Forensic Department.

2. **Case identifier:** Investigative Case No: 20/2021. (Assumption); Digital Forensic Case No.: 7/2021. (Assumption)

3. **Forensic investigator:** Job ID NO.: 00046. **Name** Shadi Zakarneh.

4. **Identity of the submitter:** Anticorruption commission/Investigation Department.

5. **Date of the evidence receipt:** 20/04/2021.

6. **Details of the seized devices:** All details related to the seized iPhone are described in Table 9-1 and the details for the seized Android device are described in Table 9-2.

Table 9-1. *The Seized iPhone Device Details*

Device category	Smartphone
The owner	The mobile is owned individually by XYZ
Make	Apple iPhone 11
Model no.	MWM42HB/A
Serial no.	F4GZW027N73H
IMEI	356562105937766
MEID	35656210593776
ICCID	8997028122332690670683
iOS version	14.4.2
Internal storage	128 GB
External storage	No
SIM carrier	Jawwal
Passcode	The mobile passcode is: 989429 "Provided by the suspect"
Front color	Black, See Appendix 1
Back color	Yellow, See Appendix 1
Power state	Power ON
Battery charge percentage	79%

During the seizing process, the suspected devices were powered on and left on. Also, the devices were converted to airplane mode. The wireless communication was disconnected. A Faraday bag is used to ensure that all the radio signals are disconnected. These measures were taken due to the necessity of protecting the digital evidence based on article no. 33 (paragraph 5) in the law by decree no. 10 of 2018 on cybercrime (local laws). The main tools used in the seizure process include a digital camera for photography, a Faraday bag used to ensure signals are disconnected, and handwriting documentation for the documentation process.

Table 9-2. *The Seized Android Device Details*

Device category	Smartphone
The owner	The mobile is owned individually by YYYY
Make	Samsung
Model No.	Galaxy J6 SM-J600F
Serial No.	RF8KA38324A
IMEI	356423092355498
Android version	Android 10 with Knox version 3.5
Internal storage	32 GB
External storage	No
SIM carrier	Jawwal
Passcode	12345 provided by the suspect
Front color	Black
Back color	Black
Power state	Power ON
Battery charge percentage	95%
Mobile external case	No Damages, No Scratches
Device Photographs	See Appendix 4

Chain of custody documentation: While the seized device was documented. The device is labeled with the owner's name, investigative case no., digital forensic case no., and receipt date. Then the device is preserved in a protected area until the next stage of the examination. This information is also recorded in the digital forensic lab record with the name of the digital forensic examiner.

Acquisition Stage

The process of forensic investigation of mobile devices is not very different from that for laptops, but some of the tools that are used in mobile forensics are somewhat different, as most mobile operating systems are closed, so it becomes difficult to understand the file system and the structure of phones. Many open source Android tools used in digital forensics are available for users, both for purchase and for free, to allow you to begin data extraction, backup operations, and so on.

This stage takes place according to the direct access warrant from the anti-corruption prosecution based on article no. 32 (paragraph 4) in the law by decree no. 10 of 2018 on cybercrime. In the data acquisition process from the seized iPhone device, the iTunes backup tool and Belkasoft forensic tool will be used. While the mobile is unlocked, the iTunes backup acquisition will be used. An iPhone USB cable will be used for connecting the mobile device to the forensic workstation. Alsom in the acquisition for the Android seized device, the ADBs backup command-line tools, the Belkasoft forensic tool, the MOBILedit tool, and the FINALMobile forensic tool will be used. A Samsung mini-USB cable will be used for connecting the mobile device to the forensic workstation. Besides, storage media will be used to store the acquired evidence image. The goal of the examination and the data needed for the investigation must be identified beforehand, and the documentation information for this stage includes the following:

The examiner's name and information.

The suspect device details

The tools used in the process.

Date and time of the process.

The duration of the process.

The name of the image file.

Size of the image file.

The hash value of the generated image.

Due to the access warrant issued by the public prosecution (based on the law by decree no. 10 of 2018 on article no. 32 paragraph 4), the acquisition stage was conducted. When the device was unlocked, logical acquisition was used.

Tools Used in the Examination Process for iOS

This stage was conducted using different forensic tools: in the beginning, iTunes software for backing up the device, and then other tools were used for evidence acquisition from iTunes backup. Enigma Recovery Software, DB Browser for SQLite, and iBackup Viewer.

iTunes Backup for iOS

Obtaining data from devices (iOS) can be achieved either through a backup copy or by making a physical copy. Obtaining data and analysis from backup is done the same way, but it is possible that backup copies do not give us enough data required, specifically for deleted messages, pictures, and other things. Therefore, it is preferable to take data through the physical copy, but the seriousness of this case in Apple devices is that it needs a jailbreak, and this may sabotage many things in the mobile and take it out of the protection and security system. The iTunes software is used to make a backup for the iPhone device.

1.   When iTunes connected to the suspected device and the iPhone information was viewed, the automatic synchronization was disabled, the backup was determined to be on this computer, and the encrypted local backup was disabled to get an unencrypted backup as shown in Figure 9-4.

Figure 9-4. *iTunes backup settings*

2.   In the final process, the backup started and created in the default folder in Windows 10 as follows:

– Backup folder path:

(C:\Users\ExamplePath\AppData\Roaming\ Apple Computer\MobileSync\Backup).

– The folder name was 00008030-000338D2149A802E. Because the suspected device is a new device, the backup folder name length was 24 ASCII characters.

– Backup size: 36.03 GB.

The full backup is the stored name of the archive chosen, which can be redesigned so that the file system is from a complete copy to a new volume, where it can be returned in many cases in case of data loss or other problems. One of the disadvantages of this copy technique is that it is very slow in the copying process and requires a large amount of memory, as its strategy is to repeat and update files all the time, so the other copy will have less and smaller space, but the recovery process may need longer than normal.

iOS Acquisition Using Enigma Recovery Software

This software is used to make a backup from the iPhone device or explore the iTunes backup, and from Enigma Recovery by selecting "view my saved scan," the examiner can select the saved backup and explore the evidence as shown in Figure 9-5.

Figure 9-5. *Engima Recovery saved scan explore*

iOS Acquisition Using DB Browser for SQLite

SQLite is now used in a wide range of applications and products. It's
included in Apple's Mac OS X operating system as part of the CoreData
application framework. It's also found in Apple's Aperture holography
software, as well as the Safari web browser, Mail.app email client, and
RSS manager. SQLite is a database that serves Sun's Solaris platform's
service management facility, which debuted with Solaris 10, and is a key
component of its self-healing predictive technology. The Mozilla Project's
mozStorage contains SQLite. For Firefox, Thunderbird, and Sunbird, the
API C++/JavaScript layer will serve as the backbone for storing personal
information. SQLite was included in the PHP 5 library. It's also included
in the Trolltech Qt C++ application framework, which is the foundation
for the popular KDE window manager and a slew of other products. On

embedded platforms, SQLite is extremely common. Richard Heep had a lot to do with SQLite. This tool is used to explore SQLite databases recovered from mobile devices. By this tool, the manifest.db database from iTunes backup was explored. The operations in it are very easy and simple and there are no additional consequences. It is are customized and designed in an easy and fast way in transportation and its use is open source, as shown in Figure 9-6.

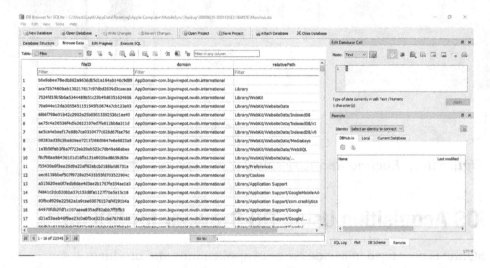

Figure 9-6. *Browsing data from SQLite (iOS)*

Next, we introduce the Android WA artifacts in the permanent storage memory without expanding to the volatile random memory, since in this chapter experiments were conducted on a Xiaomi mobile. An application stores the data of the user in a database (SQLite) called msgstore.db. After making the backup, we will find the following files:

- / sdcard/WhatsApp/Databases

- / sdcard/WhatsApp/media

- / sdcard/WhatsApp/Backups

☐ msgstore.db.crypt12	7/1/2021 08:15 ص	CRYPT12 File	291,031 KB
☐ msgstore-2021-06-30.1.db.crypt12	6/29/2021 02:02 ص	CRYPT12 File	288,804 KB
☐ msgstore-2021-07-01.1.db.crypt12	7/1/2021 02:02 ص	CRYPT12 File	290,994 KB

Figure 9-7. *WA database*

After we were able to get WA database files from the Android backup without rooting the device as shown in Figure 9-7, in this section of the study we will start the decryption procedures (msgtore.db) so that we can get the artifacts.

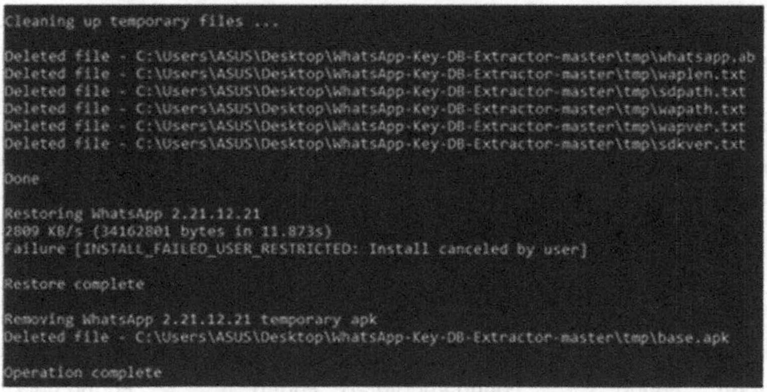

Figure 9-8. *Extracting database*

We used WA Key/DB Extractor from GitHub for extracting and retrieving msgstore and to decrypt and display WA databases (see Figure 9-8). After we were able to get the key of the database (msgstore. db) we needed to decrypt the database with the same key through the WA viewer tool, and then we opened it to be able to view the contents through the same tool as shown in Figure 9-9.

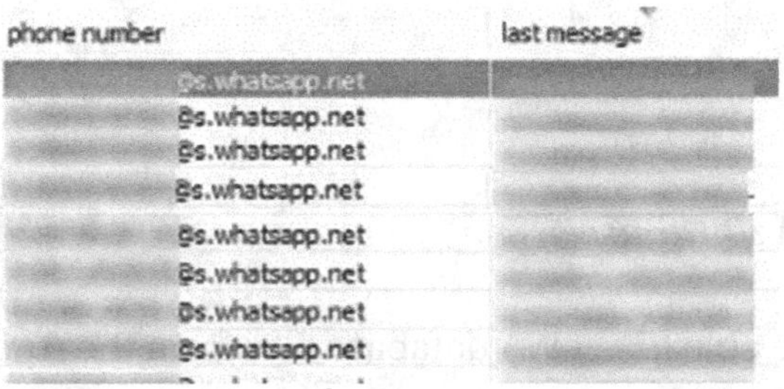

Figure 9-9. *Open WA database*

From the preceding, we can summarize our findings and results of the artifacts by making a direct comparison between the methods as described in Table 9-3.

Table 9-3. *Comparison of Artifacts of WA Discovered by Different Tools*

	iOS		Android	
	Internal storage & no rooting	SDcard & No rooting & WhatCrypt	Internal storage & no rooting	SDcard & No rooting & WhatCrypt
Msgstore.db	Found encrypted	Found encrypted	Found encrypted	Found encrypted
Wa.db	Not found	Not found	Found	Found
Phone number	Found	Found	Found	Found
Messages	Found	Found	Found	Found
Media files	Found	Found	Found	FOUND
Contact card	Found	Found	Found	Found
Deleted messages	Not found	Not found	Not found	Not found
Deleted media	Not found	Not found	Not found	Not found

iOS Acquisition Using iBackup Viewer Pro

This tool can explore iTunes local backup and explore and view the backup data as shown in Figure 9-10.

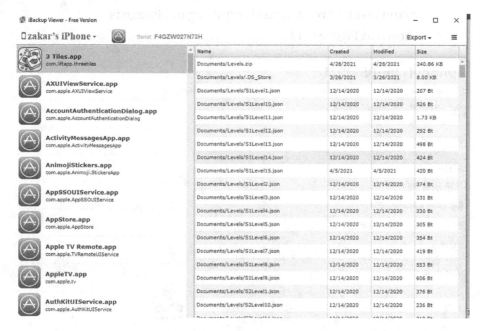

Figure 9-10.   *iBackup Viewer exploring data for app store*

iOS Acquisition Using Belkasoft Evidence Center

In this forensic tool, the acquisition can be directly conducted by making a backup for the smartphone using logical or physical acquisition. The acquisition here was conducted by opening a mobile image that was created by iTunes software in the local computer.

1. In the Belkasoft evidence center, the new case was created, and then the mobile image was chosen to load the iTunes backup folder. The data and applications that need to be searched are selected as the result of reading and acquiring the image is shown in Figure 9-11.

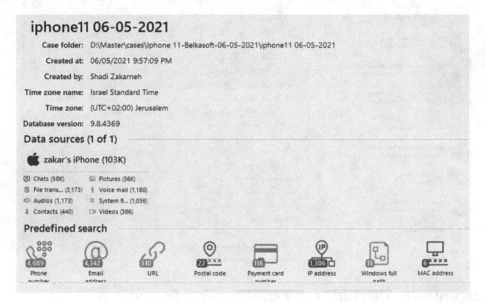

Figure 9-11. *Belkasoft backup reading and acquiring results*

Tools Used in the Acquisition Process for Android

Before the logical acquisition, the developer options and USB debugging were enabled.

Android Acquisition Using ADB Command-Line Tools

The acquisition process started from the backup of the mobile using ADB command-line tools. Then opening and acquiring the backup files was performed using the Belkasoft evidence center and FINALMobile forensic. The following steps will describe the acquisition process in detail:

1. The examiner identified the suspect's device and reviewed the details with the details recorded during the seizure stage.

2. ADB command-line tool was used to back up the device as shown in Figure 9-12.

```
C:\platform-tools>adb.exe devices
List of devices attached
52002fbe4a4995e1          device


C:\platform-tools>adb backup -shared -all
WARNING: adb backup is deprecated and may be removed in a future release
Now unlock your device and confirm the backup operation...
```

Figure 9-12. ADB command lines to back up Android devices

3. After the backup process is completed, the resulting backup.ab file is converted to a backup.tar file to be used with forensic software tools as shown in Figure 9-13.

```
C:\platform-tools>java -jar abe.jar unpack backup.ab backup.tar
C:\platform-tools>
```

Figure 9-13. Convert backup.ab file to backup.tar file

Android Acquisition Using Belkasoft

The acquisition process started from the backup of the mobile using the Belkasoft evidence center after the case was created. The following steps will describe the acquisition process in detail:

1. The data source was added to the created case by selecting the mobile data source and Android mobile type as shown in Figure 9-21.

2. Then Belkasoft connected to the device and presented the device type, manufacturer, and model as shown in Figure 9-14.

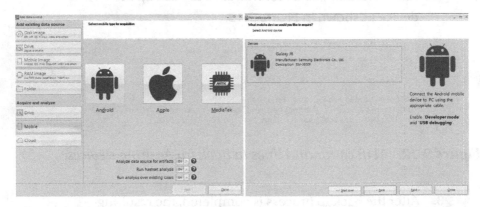

Figure 9-14. *Select data source connect with the device*

3. Then ADB backup was created; after the backup process was completed, the investigator selected the data type to be analyzed. Now the acquired data is ready for the analysis stage.

Android Acquisition Using FINALMobile Forensic Software

The acquisition process was started for the Android mobile by using FINALMobile forensic after the category of the device as a smartphone and the type of the operating system, which is Android. The following steps will describe the acquisition process in detail:

1. The model of the mobile device is selected.

2. The logical acquisition method using Samsung backup protocol is selected as shown in Figure 9-15.

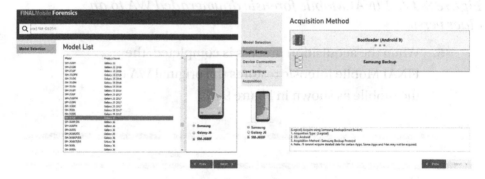

Figure 9-15. *Acquisition method in FINALMobile forensic*

3. In the preparation for ADB backup, the FINALMobile forensic selects the apps to downgrade due to database encryption in order to decrypt the SQLite database as shown in Figure 9-16.

Figure 9-16. *Selecting apps to downgrade in FINALMobile forensic*

305

4. During the acquisition process, the FINALMobile
    forensic downgraded WA from version 2.21.12.21 to
    version 2.11.414 to decrypt the WA SQLite database
    and back it up as shown in Figure 9-17.

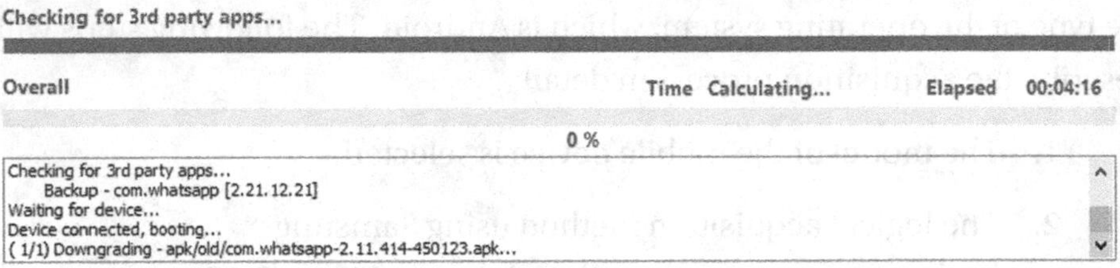

Figure 9-17. *FINALMobile forensic downgraded WA to an
older version*

5. When the acquisition process is completed, the
    FINALMobile forensic restores the original WA to
    the mobile as shown in Figure 9-18.

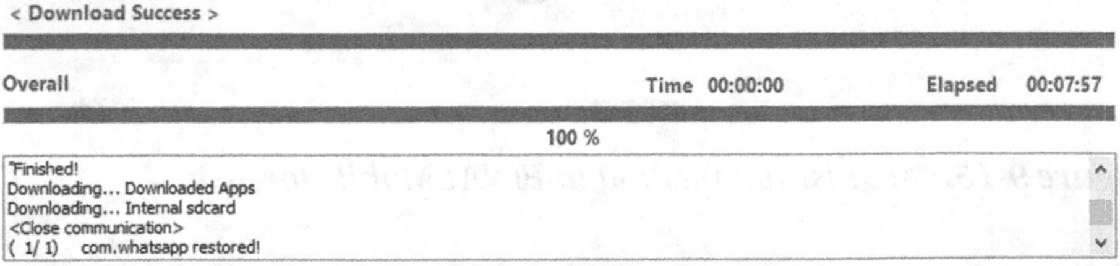

Figure 9-18. *FINALMobile forensic restoring the original WA version*

Android Acquisition Using MOBILedit

The acquisition process started after connecting the mobile to the forensic
workstation, then MOBILedit software connected to the mobile and
discovered information such as manufacturer, model number, phone time,
and software version, as shown in Figure 9-19.

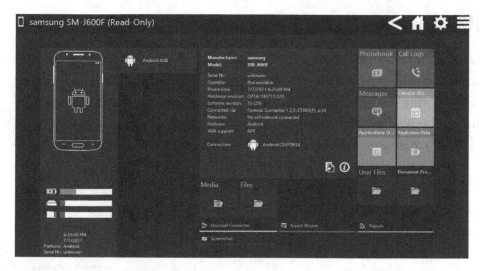

Figure 9-19. *Logical acquisition using MOBILEdit forensic*

WA Analysis Tools for iOS

The analysis process succeeded as the evidence was found by reviewing
WA chats and calls, as well as reviewing audio files, video files, and photos
exchanged through the WA application. Using the iBackup Viewer, the
applications list in the manifest.plist files was explored. By this tool, the WA
version was determined to be 2.21.72.1 as shown in Figure 9-20.

Key	Type	Value
∨ net.whatsapp.WhatsApp	Dictionary	(4 items)
CFBundleIdentifier	String	net.whatsapp.WhatsApp
CFBundleVersion	String	2.21.72.1
ContainerContentClass	String	Data/Application
Path	String	/var/containers/Bundle/Application/E4D3B5FD-5082-4CAA-904D-A0948100B863/\

iBackup Viewer - Free Version

C:\Users\zakar\AppData\Roaming\Apple Computer\MobileSync\Backup\00008030-000338D2149A802E\Manifest.plist

New   Open   Save as ▾   Undo   Redo

Figure 9-20. *WA version from Manifest.plist file*

iOS Analysis Using Belkasoft

Using Belkasoft evidence center, the acquired case opened and the dashboard information for the case was viewed as shown in Figure 9-11. By exploring the files and folder using the file system viewer in Belkasoft, under the WA folder ("\AppDomainGroup-group.net.whatsapp.WhatsApp. shared") there were files and folders for WA as shown in Figure 9-21.

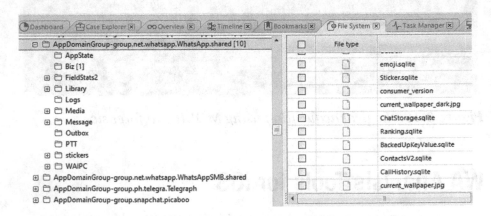

Figure 9-21. *WA folders and database files*

The non-empty folders inside the WA folder are described in detail in Table 9-4.

Table 9-4. *Subfolder Descriptions under the WA Folder*

Folder Name	Details
Biz	This includes SQLite database "Biz.sqlite"; this database includes information and business account profiles.
Library\ preferences	This folder includes a plist file with the name "group.net.whatsapp. WhatsApp.shared.plist"; this file includes information about the WA account such as full user name, user current status, own device ID, and own jabber ID, which is the same as account ID shown in Figure 9-34.
Media\profile	This folder contains images and thumb files for the profile pictures for the friends of this account.
Message\ media	This folder contains subfolders with the names of the ID accounts of the friend's users; under these subfolders the multimedia is exchanged between the user and the friends such as images, videos, and audio messages.
Stickers	Contains sticker images.
WAIPC	Includes extensions for notification service and other services.

The files contained in the WA folder include the WA SQLite databases as follows:

1. Emoji.sqlite: contains WA emoji information.

2. Stickers.sqlite: contains WA sticker information.

3. ChateStorage.sqlite: contains tables for information and contents of chats between the user and friends in the table "ZWAMESSAGE" and all information about groups and group members in the tables "ZWAGROUPINFO", "ZWAGROUPMEMBER", and "ZWAGROUPMEMBERCHANGE" as shown in Figure 9-22.

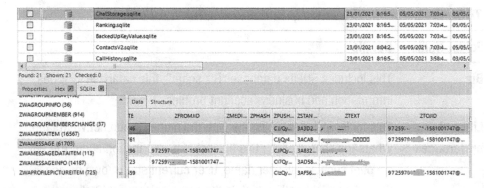

Figure 9-22. *ChatStorage.sqlite database contents*

4. ContactsV2.sqlite: contains information about the friend's users like the WA account and their status text as shown in Figure 9-23.

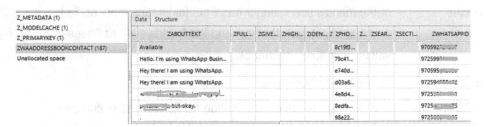

Figure 9-23. *ContactsV2.sqlite database contents*

5. Callhistory.sqlite: contains the WA call logs as shown in Figure 9-24.

Figure 9-24. *CallHistory.sqlite database contents*

Another way to view WA chats is by using the Belkasoft evidence center, in the case explorer and under the instant messengers, and the investigator can browse WA messages from the case explorer.

iOS Analysis Using Magnet AXIOM Examine

Using Magnet AXIOM Examine, the acquired case is opened, along with the dashboard information for the case; then investigators can start exploring the artifacts, which are classified into various categories. While the examination in this study related to the investigation on WA, WA chats can be examined from the chat category in the artifacts as shown in Figure 9-25.

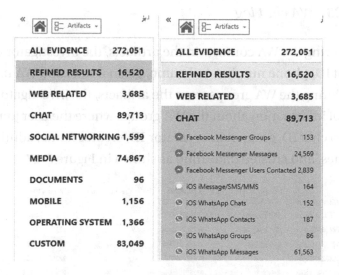

Figure 9-25. *Magnet AXIOM Examine & WA chat artifact classification*

In the artifacts module in Magnet AXIOM Examine, the software explores WA chat logs, WA contacts, WA groups, and WA messages as shown in Figure 9-25. The investigator can browse WA chat logs, which show individuals' names, group names, the chat ID, the last message sent or received, and the last message date and time as shown in Figure 9-26.

Individual Chat...	Group Chat Name	Chat ID	Last Message	Last Message Date/Time
N███████		97259█████		05/05/2021 6:32:15 PM
█████		97259█████@status	████████الصو	03/05/2021 9:01:38 PM
●███		9725█████	███████████...	28/04/2021 9:34:12 PM
████		97259█		05/05/2021 11:59:48 AM
████		97259█████@status		
████████		9725█	████████████..	29/04/2021 10:08:38 AM
+972████████		972569██████	█████	03/05/2021 9:06:33 AM

Figure 9-26. *WA chat log*

By exploring the WA contacts in the artifacts, the investigator can show the account ID, phone number, full name, given name, and WA user IDs, and by exploring the WA groups from the artifacts, the investigator can show a lot of information about the WA groups where the user joined such as the group chat ID, group name, creator ID, creator name, admin IDs, admin names, and created date/time as shown in Figure 9-27.

Group Chat ID	Group Name	Creator ID	Creator Name	Admin IDs	Admin Name
97█████████████████us	●████████)	9██████████		9█████████919	
972598██████████████0@g.us	██●███	972598██████		97259█████████	
97259█████████-1579217616@g.us	●███████P	97259█████		9725█████████	
97259█████████-1591294985@g.us	███████	9725█████████	████	97█████████	████
97259█████5-1587580292@g.us	.	97259██████	█████	9725██████	███
97259952█████-1584009194@g.us	████████████	97259██████		9720█████████	
97259█████1587465963@g.us	●████████..	97259990█████	●●●████	96279█████	●●●████
97259█████████-1564524445@g.us	████████████	9725█████████	█████	97██████████8, 972...	████

Figure 9-27. *WA chat groups*

By exploring the WA messages from the artifacts, the investigator can view the list of the chats, and by selecting any row of these logs as shown in Figure 9-27, the investigator can show the details of the chat in the preview pane as shown in Figure 9-28.

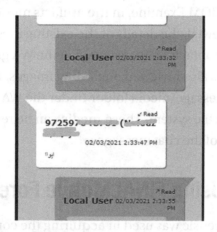

Figure 9-28. *WA chat details in the preview pane*

You can also use the file system for the investigation and exploring the WA folder, using WA SQLite databases as shown in Figure 9-29.

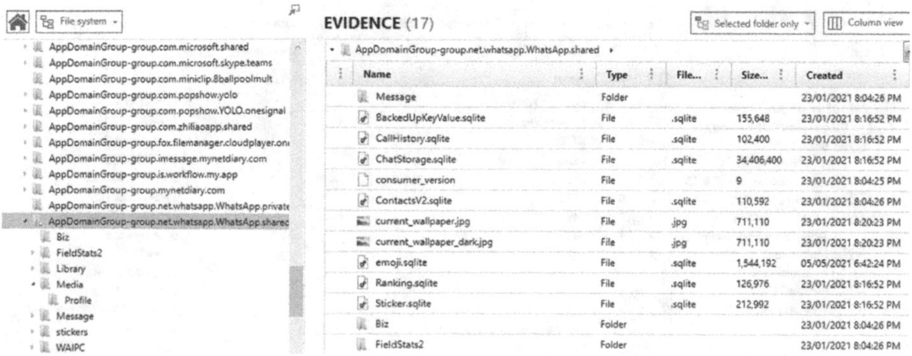

Figure 9-29. *WA folder in the file system*

313

As in the Belkasoft evidence center, the investigator can explore the files and folders under the WA folder and show and export the media files that are exchanged between the user and their friends. But for SQLite databases, the investigator needs a third-party tool to explore the contents.

Using Magnet AXIOM Examine, in the artifacts module, the message lists on WA were reviewed, the details of the existing messages were read, and in addition, WA contacts were reviewed in the WA groups list. The exchanged media was also reviewed, including images, files, and audio messages from the message\media folder under the WA folder using the examination on a file system. These media can be reviewed when exploring the details of the chat messages.

iOS Analysis Using FINALMobile Forensic

The FINALMobile forensic was used in acquiring the connected mobile phone, and also in acquiring the iTunes backup on the local storage. By using the two methods, the results were insufficient to conduct an investigation regarding WA, as using this tool the files for WA did not appear, as shown in Figure 9-30.

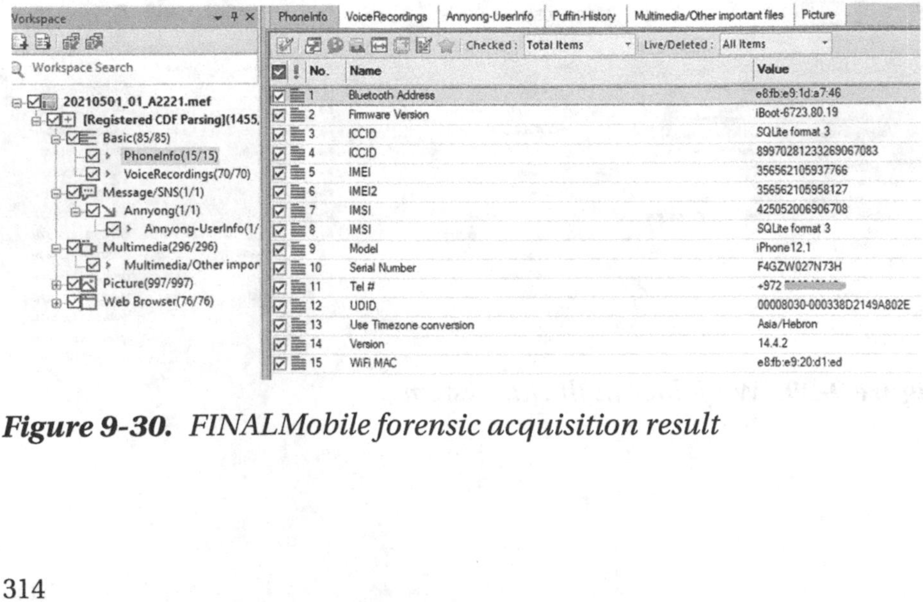

Figure 9-30. *FINALMobile forensic acquisition result*

iOS Analysis Using Enigma Recovery Tool

While the Enigma Recovery tool has the ability to back up data from the iPhone device directly or from the iTunes backup, the tool used here performed the backup of the data from the connected device directly. With the selected option, the investigator must choose what to recover from the connected device. After the backup process is completed, the investigator can open the backup by selecting the saved scan. The investigator can browse the WA chats by selecting WA and then select an account from the list to view the chat message details as shown in Figure 9-31.

Figure 9-31. *WA chat details in Enigma Recovery tool*

Using the Enigma Recovery tool, the message lists on WA were reviewed; the details of the existing messages were read.

iOS Analysis Using iBackup Viewer Tool

By using iBackup Viewer, the investigator can open the iTunes backup as shown in Figure 9-32 and explore the artifacts using this tool. The investigator can open the WA icon to view the WA messages as shown in Figure 9-32.

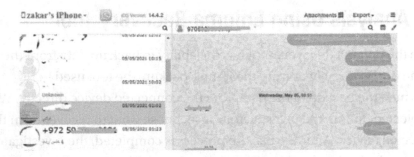

Figure 9-32. WA message details in iBackup Viewer

WA Analysis Tools for Android

The analysis stage was conducted with the different acquisition methods and using different forensic tools such as Belkasoft evidence center, MOBILedit forensic, and FINALMobile forensic tools. The analysis of the backup file taken by the ADB command-line tool didn't have any files or data related to WA because the acquired device is unrooted. This was clarified by analyzing the backup file on the Belkasoft evidence center, as well as in the FINALMobile forensic as shown previously.

Analysis using the Belkasoft evidence center stage was conducted on data acquired using the Belkasoft evidence center. While the investigation aims to search for the digital evidence in the WA application, there are no files related to WA through the analysis and exploring of the file system collected through the Belkasoft software in the acquisition stage as shown in Figure 9-33.

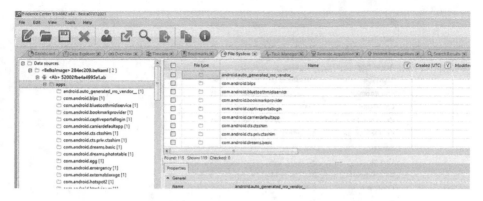

Figure 9-33. *Forensic investigation using Belkasoft evidence center*

We tried to analyze using the image acquired by MOBILedit forensic; the WA folders and database files can be viewed. The SQLite DB for WA is encrypted by the AES encryption algorithm, as shown in Figure 9-34, so the content data cannot be viewed and presented.

File Name	Size
msgstore-2021-07-07.1.db.crypt14	122.11 KB
msgstore.db.crypt14	121.50 KB

Figure 9-34. *WA database files viewed in MOBILedit*

Using FINALMobile forensic on the analysis stage to acquire the image, the digital evidence was collected, analyzed, and documented, and the WA account information was retrieved. The message lists on WA were reviewed, and the details of the existing messages were viewed, along with deleted messages, including both texts and attachments, as shown in Figure 9-35.

Figure 9-35. *Details of a deleted WA message in FINALMobile forensic*

Forensic Tools Comparison on iOS Platform

Different tools were used for the acquisition and analysis of iPhone 11 for investigating WA messages. A backup using iTunes was taken and used for the examination and analysis using Belkasoft evidence center, Magnet AXIOM Examine, FINALMobile forensic, Enigma Recovery, and iBackup Viewer. In the acquisition phase, not all of these tools support the acquisition from the connected device directly. The other tool supports the acquisition from the connected device using iTunes backup or logical backup, while the logical backup needs to jailbreak the device to conduct the process. The assumed case in this study is about a cybercrime committed via WA application, and the analysis using these tools focuses on WA data and files. It was clear that there are differences between all of these tools in the examination process and in the way to view and present the evidence from WA.

318

Examination on a Backup Taken by iTunes

Using the Belkasoft evidence center, the WA databases and files were examined and reviewed by exploring the file system. The database contents include message details, contacts information, groups, and other information opened and reviewed by a built-in SQLite viewer in Belkasoft. The SQLite viewer views the data and structure for the databases as database tables. The other contents of the chats, like media, are viewed from the folders in the file system.

Using Magnet AXIOM Examine, the WA folders, files, and database are reviewed from the file system. In addition, the valuable data for WA is viewed from the artifacts easily and classified for a quick examination. The Magnet AXIOM viewed the contents of the WA database and the contents of the chat messages viewed in a user interface similar to the WA interface. Using a FINALMobile forensic, the tool can't view the needed data from WA for the investigation. Using Enigma Recovery and WA viewer, the data is viewed as you see in the WA application.

Examination on a Backup Taken from the Connected iPhone Device

The tools used to back up the connected device are Belkasoft evidence center, Magnet AXIOM Examine, FINALMobile forensic tool, and Enigma Recovery. The backup option used is the iTunes Backup because the device needs to be jailbroken for the logical backup to be conducted.

With the Belkasoft evidence center, while the device is backed up using the iTunes backup option, the result in the examination is the same as when acquiring the iTunes software backup from the local storage. With Magnet AXIOM Examine, the iTunes backup option was selected but the process failed on the high-storage device, while the software needed more hardware resources on the forensic workstation. The FINALMobile forensic succeeded in backing up the connected devices but basic data was collected, without the needed data from WA files and databases. With the Enigma Recovery tool, a backup from the connected device was taken, and the WA chat messages were reviewed as seen with WA applications like text or media messages. After using the five tools in the experiment, it is clear that there are differences between these tools in the options for the acquisition and in the ways to view WA data and files, as shown in Table 9-5.

Table 9-5. *Forensic Tool Comparison on iOS Platform*

	Belkasoft	Magnet AXIOM	FINALMobile Forensic	Enigma Recovery	iBackup Viewer
Acquisition from iTunes software backup	Yes	Yes	Yes	Yes	Yes
Acquisition from the connected device using iTunes option	Yes	Yes	Yes	Yes	No
Acquisition using logical backup	Yes, but needs to jailbreak the device	Yes, but needs to jailbreak the device	Yes, but needs to jailbreak the device	No	No

(continued)

Table 9-5. (*continued*)

	Belkasoft	Magnet AXIOM	FINALMobile Forensic	Enigma Recovery	iBackup Viewer
WA data and files	Data and files viewed and the database contents reviewed. The results are the same from iTunes software backup and the connected device backup	Data and files viewed and the database contents were also reviewed	Not successful	Chat messages only reviewed	Chat messages only reviewed
SQLite database for WA and other apps	Viewing SQLite database data in SQLite Viewer viewing live and deleted data, and flag the deleted rows with deleted column	Viewing SQLite database data in SQLite Viewer viewing live and deleted data, and flag the deleted rows with deleted column	Viewing the data not successful	View all the data including deleted data and flag the deleted with red color and recycle bin icon	View the live data only

According to the comparison as shown in Table 9-5, and due to the investigation on WA on the iOS platform, the valuable artifacts and evidence can be extracted using Belkasoft evidence center and Magnet AXIOM Examine. This does not mean that these two programs are the best in mobile digital investigation, but regarding the assumed case in this study, the best results were taken from these two programs.

Forensic Tools Comparison on Android Platform

Different tools were used for the acquisition and analysis of Samsung Galaxy J6 with Android 10 and Knox security features for investigating WA messages. The acquisition stage was conducted using ADB command-line tools, and the analysis on the resulting backup file was conducted using Belkasoft evidence center and FINALMobile forensic. Another acquisition process was conducted using forensic tools such as Belkasoft evidence center, MOBILedit, and FINALMobile forensic. The acquired backup using ADB command-line tool was not useful for the assumed case study as the investigation on WA, because during the analysis stage the investigator found there is no data or files related to WA in the backup file due to the inaccessible storage location for WA on the unrooted device.

The acquisition of the Android device was conducted using the ADB backup option with the choice of backup with the shared storage. At the analysis stage using the Belkasoft evidence center, the investigator found there are no folders, files, or data related to the WA. The acquisition stage was conducted using ADB logical backup. After the acquisition was completed, the file system was explored to view the WA folders and data. WA SQLite database files are viewed as encrypted files with the name msgstore.db.crypt14. Therefore, the database cannot be opened and explored using any SQLite DB viewer. The subfolders under the WA folder were viewed. Images, videos, and documents sent and received by

WA were saved in subfolders under the WA folder (com.one plus the WA version was downgraded to the older and unencrypted version during the acquisition stage. Therefore, the WA database was decrypted and the messages and their details were viewed. The existing and deleted messages are viewed with a status (Deleted) for the deleted messages and live for the existing messages. By exploring the file system, the WA folder and its subfolders are viewed; the SQLite database for the messages can be exported and viewed using SQLite database viewer. Also, all subfolders contain media files, and documents sent and received via WA are viewed and can be exported. After using the five tools in the experiment, there are differences between these tools in the options for the acquisition on Android devices, and in the way of viewing WA data and files as shown in Table 9-6.

Table 9-6. *Forensic Tools Comparison on Android Platform*

	Belkasoft	**MOBILedit**	**FINALMobile Forensic**
Acquisition from ADB command-line backup	Yes	No	Yes
Acquisition from the connected device ADB backup option	Yes	Yes	Yes
WA files and folders from ADB command-line tools backup	No WA files or folders viewed	--	No WA files or folders viewed

(continued)

Table 9-6. (*continued*)

	Belkasoft	MOBILedit	FINALMobile Forensic
WA files and folders from the forensic software backup	No WA files or folders viewed	WA folder and subfolders, files are viewed	WA folder and subfolders, files are viewed
SQLite database for WA and other apps	There is a SQLite viewer in Belkasoft, but unencrypted databases only can be viewed. WA database not found in the backup to view it due to the encryption and because WA was not acquired in the backup	WA database files viewed in the system file as encrypted with the extension .db. crypt14. They can be exported but cannot be viewed with any SQLite viewer	While the WA downgraded in the acquisition stage, the WA database was decrypted and viewed using the internal SQLite viewer and can be exported and viewed with any external SQLite DB viewer

While the Android version on the mobile device is Android 10 with Knox security, the root process failed. The challenge in rooting a device that has Android 10 is that in this version of Android, the ramdisk doesn't include the root file system. The root file system is merged along with the system, which makes it complex to root. Also with the Knox security feature, any unofficial image or custom ROM prevented flashing or installation on the device. So, the root cannot be conducted. Different operating systems are released for mobile devices, tablets, and other smart devices such as Android, iOS, and HarmonyOS. There are many differences between these operating systems, as shown in Table 9-7.

Table 9-7. *Comparison of Operating Systems*

OS Feature	Android OS	iOS	HarmonyOS
Type of mobiles and devices support	Touchscreen mobile like Samsung, oneplus, Nokia, etc., TV, watch	iPhones, iPad, iWatch, etc.	Huawei and Honor phones, watches, fitness bands, and other IoT devices
Architecture	Layered architecture	Layered architecture	Layered architecture
File system types	FAT32, Ext3, and Ext4, exFAT, or NTFS	APFS and HFS+	F2FS and Ext4
Security	Android uses the concept of user-authentication-gated cryptographic keys, which requires cryptographic key storage and service provider and user authenticators	iOS and iPadOS devices use a file encryption methodology called data protection, whereas the data on an Intel-based Mac is protected with a volume encryption technology called FileVault.	HarmonyOS's microkernel design; we will see that this network system makes use of formal methods of verification. This allows the users to reshape the security of their primary systems and scale their frameworks from the ground up, over a Trusted Execution Environment (TEE).
Kernel	A modified version of the Linux kernel	ARM variant of Darwin, derived from BSD, a UNIX-like kernel	Microkernel.

Summary

WA is the most popular application for IM, where people can exchange text messages, audio files, video files, and documents. This research has focused on forensic investigation of WA on the iOS and Android platforms. The NIST digital forensic method is used in the research. The Belkasoft evidence center, FINALMobile forensic, MOBILedit, Magnet AXIOM, and other tools are used in the examination and analysis stages. The iTunes software was used to back up the seized iPhone and ADB logical backup was used to back up the seized Android mobile. In the analysis stage, the messages, photos, audio files, videos, and contacts are viewed and analyzed to determine the evidence related to the assumed crime. Another tool used for the acquisition and the examination is to show the differences and capabilities between these tools in the examination process and the results of extracting the digital evidence from WA on iOS and Android platforms. While jailbreak is needed for iOS or root for Android to conduct the file system acquisition, not all iOS versions can jailbreak, and not all Android versions can be rooted. Due to the comparison between the forensic tools used on iOS and Android platforms, FINALMobile forensic can downgrade the WA version to an older one with an unencrypted database, so all the data viewed and the deleted chats are recovered. To protect users, the operating system must enable features to prevent downgrading WA to keep and protect user privacy.

References

[1].   R. Umar, I. Riadi, and G. M. Zamroni, "Mobile
       Forensic Tools Evaluation for Digital Crime
       Investigation," *Int. J. Adv. Sci. Eng. Inf. Technol.*, vol.
       8, no. 3, pp. 949–955, 2018.

[2].   Ubaidillah *et al.*, "Analysis WhatsApp Forensic and Visualization in Android Smartphone with Support Vector Machine (SVM) Method," *J. Phys. Conf. Ser.*, vol. 1196, no. 1, 2019.

[3].   J. Clement, "Most Popular Global Mobile Messaging Apps 2020," *Statista*, 2020.

[4].   I. Abdulai Sawaneh, "Examining the Effects and Challenges of Cybercrime and Cyber Security Within the Cyberspace of Sierra Leone," *Int. J. Intell. Inf. Syst.*, vol. 7, no. 3, p. 23, 2018.

[5].   FBI's Internet Crime Complaint Center, "2019 Internet Crime Report," *2019 Internet Crime Rep.*, pp. 1–28, 2019.

[6].   A. Shahbazi, "Technological Developments in Cyberspace and Commission of the Crimes in International Law and Iran," *J. Leg. Ethical Regul. Issues*, vol. 22, no. 4, pp. 1–12, 2019.

[7].   PNA, "Law by Decree No. 10 of 2018 on Cybercrime," no. 10. pp. 1–15, 2018.

[8].   S. Udenze and B. Oshionebo, "Investigating 'WhatsApp' for Collaborative Learning among Undergraduates," *Etkileşim*, vol. 3, no. 5, pp. 24–50, 2020.

[9].   H. Shidek, N. Cahyani, and A. A. Wardana, "WhatsApp Chat Visualizer: A Visualization of WhatsApp Messenger's Artifact Using the Timeline Method," *Int. J. Inf. Commun. Technol.*, vol. 6, no. 1, p. 1, 2020.

[10]. J. K. Alhassan, B. Abubakar, M. Olalere,
M. Abdulhamid, and S. Ahmad, "Forensic
Acquisition of Data from a Crypt 12 Encrypted
Database of Whatsapp," *2nd Int. Eng. Conf.,*
October, 2017.

[11]. R. Gyorödi, D. Zmaranda, V. Georgian, and
C. Gyorödi, "A Comparative Study between
Applications Developed for Android and iOS," *Int.
J. Adv. Comput. Sci. Appl.,* vol. 8, no. 11, 2017.

[12]. G. L. Jhala KY, "WhatsApp Forensics: Decryption
of Encrypted WhatsApp Databases on Non Rooted
Android Devices," *J. Inf. Technol. Softw. Eng.,* vol. 5,
no. 2, pp. 2–5, 2015.

[13]. T. Höne, K. Kröger, S. Luttenberger, and
R. Creutzburg, "iPhone Examination with Modern
Forensic Software Tools," *Mob. Multimedia/
Image Process. Secur. Appl. 2012,* vol. 8406, May,
p. 84060R, 2012.

[14]. PNA, "Anticorruption Law by Decree No. (7) 2010,"
PNA, no. 7. pp. 1–9, 2010.

CHAPTER 10

Cloud Computing Forensics: Dropbox Case Study

This chapter describes how to use Android and iOS mobiles in data acquisition and in finding results. This analysis and study of new versions of the Dropbox app with different versions of Android OS and iOS will increase knowledge about cloud storage forensics artifacts. In addition, it will help investigators to use it in investigations when criminal activity has taken place on it.

In this chapter, we will cover the following topics:

- Forensic Artifacts in Cloud Storage

- Cloud Computing Forensics

- Android Logical and Physical Acquisition Tools

- iOS Logical Acquisition Using Tools

- Results and Analysis

- Cloud Forensic Challenges

- Summary

© Mohammed Moreb 2022
M. Moreb, *Practical Forensic Analysis of Artifacts on iOS and Android Devices*,
https://doi.org/10.1007/978-1-4842-8026-3_10

Forensic Artifacts in Cloud Storage

Recently, with the high usage of the Internet and technology and with high dependence on users on cyberspace to save their data and to do more activities through the Internet, the usage of cloud computing has become more valuable. According to T. Sree and S. Bhanu, "cloud computing provides a set of services such as storage, memory, applications, CPU and network bandwidth to the users by renting out physical machines at an hourly basis or by dynamically allocating virtual machine (VM) instances and software services" [1]. Cloud computing lets companies and users pay only for services that they use. So, it can avoid the high costs and complexity of owning and maintaining its own IT infrastructure [3]. There are several cloud storage services, such as Google Drive, Dropbox, AWS, and so on. From another side, cloud computing has become an important source for traditional and digital crimes. So, cloud computing, due to its importance and its high usage and especially because of the cloud storage services and data that are stored on them, has become an important focus of attention from criminals, and this in turn requires investigators to work hard to do forensics and find the evidence and artifacts for these cloud computing services when crimes happened on them.

The use of cloud storage media, particularly Google Drive cloud storage on smartphones, is highly widespread nowadays. The growing number of people who use Google Drive as a storage medium does not rule out the probability that it will be used to store criminal material, and use it for malicious activities, and so on. In this project, mobile forensic for Google Drive is applied on Android smartphones, Xiaomi, and Samsung devices to acquire Google Drive data in case of rooting and unrooting, to see the difference between the two approaches. Manual, logical and physical extraction is explained, also many forensic tools were used for acquiring the evidence like the MOBILedit Forensic Express, Magnet AXIOM, etc., Moreover an iPhone s6 backup folder was analyzed by the use of many forensic tools explained in the experiment section.

So, in this practical case, we will illustrate the cloud computer procedures artifacts, and especially on cloud storage forensics artifacts on mobiles, and will take Dropbox accounts on Android and iOS mobiles as a case study. Will indicates that using different tools, OS and procedures can find different artifacts and also differences in data that can be acquired. In addition, we will explain which forensic tool is better for our job.

From the law side, the international and local laws criminalize cybercrimes and illegal data acquisition. Palestinian laws indicate that each person who possesses, presents, produces, distributes, imports, exports, or promotes a device for the purpose of use, or a program or any ready-made electronic data, a password, or access codes for the purposes of perpetrating any of the crimes provided in Palestinian laws will be punished. Also, it indicates that the public prosecution or the officers tasked with judicial duties, whom it delegates, shall be entitled to search persons, places, and means of information technology with relevance to the crime. The search warrant must be reasoned and specific. Such searches can seize devices, tools, or means relating to the crime, and the officers vested with judicial duties are entitled to deal with devices, tools, means, electronic data or information, traffic data, data relating to communication traffic or users, or relevant subscriber information with relevance to cybercrime, and then must compile a report on the seized items and present the same to the public prosecution to take necessary measures. The evidence, including information technology, information systems, information networks, electronic websites, or electronic data and information, shall be deemed to be prosecution evidence. In addition, the judge of the Court of Conciliation shall be entitled to permit the Attorney General or Assistant Attorney General to conduct surveillance of, record, and deal with communications and electronic conversations to search for the evidence relating to a crime or misdemeanor [2].

In this and from the practical side, we will use a laptop and mobile devices to find the artifacts on the Dropbox cloud storage mobile app after activities such as installation, creating a new account, signing in with a created account, uploading, sharing photos and documents, and deleting some data and trying to recover it. We will use different forensics tools to find the results and evidence in this experiment and check if there are differences in acquired data. We will use mobile Samsung Galaxy S5 and iPhone 5S as different OS devices in these case studies.

According to M. Alkhanafseh et al., "cloud forensics can be defined as an application of digital forensics in cloud computing environments" [2]. It's defined as a subset of network forensics. Many have researched digital forensics for cloud storage [4] and taken a Dropbox artifact analysis on mobiles as a case study. They have focused on Android mobiles of two types: Android Lollipop and Android Nougat (OPPO A37 smartphone and Samsung A7 smartphone, respectively). They have studied the data artifacts when the user accesses the Dropbox app from mobile and do some activities on it such as app installation, creating files, uploading pictures or documents, deleting data, and so on, and then find the changes and data modified. The researchers were concerned about changing directories and databases after each activity in order to find artifacts that can be used if any criminal activities occur on the Dropbox app.

In doing their research about cloud storage forensics and especially for Dropbox on Windows 8, authors aim to find the data remnants of cloud storage activity, they illustrate in this research the identification of data remnants of user activities according to Dropbox analysis on Windows 8. The researchers [5] performed their experiment through an installed Dropbox app on Windows 8 that was installed on a VMware machine, because it is quick to set up and easy to reconfigure. The experiment was done by downloading two different interface apps on the same windows, namely, the desktop app and the metro app interface, and finding the major difference in its artifacts.

The authors in [6] investigate potential forensic artifacts in cloud storage application, focusing on Dropbox in the Linux operating system, and they illustrate more data recovery from Dropbox after deletion.

They use Linux OS because when creating an account on Dropbox, it is automatically synced with the Linux machine, and after the deletion activity from the Dropbox account it is also deleted from the machine and it is easy to recover it by using one of the recovery tools for Linux. For more details, they viewed a Linux tool called PhotoRec it used in the recovery of data but explained that data only gets recovered in encrypted form only, and the same can only be viewed by downloading as documents. Also used is a Testdisk tool for recovery; it is the most common tool used in Linux for recovery as well. So this tool and analysis can help investigators to identify the potential forensics artifacts.

T. Z. Khairallah [7] investigates cloud drive forensic artifacts to identify the forensic artifacts from the cloud storage app on Windows 10 64-bit operating system, taking Google Drive as a case study. In the experiment, I used VMware using Oracle VM VirtualBox and downloaded a Google Drive app to use it, and focused on deleted data from it. As a result of this experiment, it was found that the artifacts of cloud drive activity can be found on local files on local machines. It also explained that username, the cache files, and log activity can help to find the deleted file and recover it. From another side, it was explained that the artifacts on Windows 10 are matched to Windows 7 but with a small difference on some important artifacts that earlier researchers missed, such as (cloud_graph.db, Global. db, log files, and the registry, OpenAuth IDs). Also, the most important artifact is the registry ShellIconOverlayIdentifiers, which Google Drive uses for file icons while processing its state (synced, syncing, error), focusing on the important point that using VM when finding forensic images helps to access the cloud storage for the user.

Mobile forensics of cloud storage services for iOS systems [8] focused on Google Drive on iOS platforms, as it is the most popular cloud storage service. Also, researchers represented the data remnants that can be found and also explained how investigators can deal with content and show it, especially if the content can't be recovered in different scenarios. In their experiment, they used the iPad Air 2 running iOS version 9.3.2, and they used a desktop running Windows 10 with UFED Physical Analyzer version 5.4.6.7. They used iTunes to take a backup from mobile and then used the UFED Physical Analyzer to extract iTunes backup and then import it to iTools to examine the iTunes backup. They found that the best way for finding good artifacts is to return to mobile devices, because they always have a huge amount of data that may be helpful for investigators. In addition, they found which files are easier to recover, and also found that the thumbnails are the most useful because they have a lot of data remnants and artifacts that help in investigations. On the other hand, there is very little research done about the cloud on iOS devices, and this is an area that requires more research.

Dropbox cloud storage services provide a free 2GB of storage, and then the user can move to a purchase account with more storage capacity and higher-level available features. It allows users to share photos, documents, and files, make backups, sync data, and also can still store data and files online. New technologies, devices, and services that are provided everywhere make access to all accounts easy. Dropbox can be accessed through a web page or from apps installed on PCs, mobiles, or tablets. So, storing important data for users on Dropbox accounts means the data is still available online, and high usage of digital devices and especially mobiles increases the criminal activity possibilities that may happen on these accounts. The study of cloud storage becomes very important to identify the evidence and artifacts on it, and especially on Dropbox as a case study to help the investigator to find artifacts and evidence. To see if any criminal activity happened there that can be used in investigations, we will use the Magnet AXIOM forensics program to find forensics artifacts.

Cloud Computing Forensics

Cloud computing can be divided according to the service model into three types: the first is Infrastructure as a Service (IaaS), the second is Platform as a Service (PaaS), and the third is Software as a Service (SaaS). When talking about cloud storage services, it is defined as an IaaS because it provides storage space for users to save and synchronize their documents, photos, and files, which can be accessed through a web browser or by installing its application on laptops, PCs, mobiles, and tablets [3].

According to Steve Jobs, "I do not need a hard disk in my computer if I can get to the server faster.... Carrying around these nonconnected computers is byzantine by comparison" [4]. This indicates the importance of cloud computing in our world and how cloud computing can provide good services and make a big change in our digital world. In cloud computing forensics, the evidence sources that can be used to do investigations can be server-side forensics and client-side forensics. In server-side forensics, investigators can find evidence and artifacts from server logs, application logs, database logs, and user authentication logs; the main problem and restrictions investigators can face on this side are the inaccessibility of data and the unknown location for the data. In client-side forensics, investigators can find evidence and artifacts from log files, database files, traces in the registry, user accounts, and synchronization logs. In addition, the client-side artifacts represent the important side for artifacts and evidence, and these client-side artifacts store the most important personal data, which can help in investigations [4].

The cloud forensic process flow can be explained in four steps: identification, evidence collection, examination and analysis, and then presentation and reporting. These steps show how to do forensics for cloud computing crimes. The diagram that explains the process flow of the cloud forensics is shown in Chapter 1. These steps can be clarified: in the first step, identification, the investigator needs to check if a crime has happened or not. In the second step, evidence collection, the

335

investigator needs to identify the evidence according to its model type of cloud services, which can be SaaS, IaaS, or PaaS. Different model types need to monitor different things; SaaS models can identify the evidence by monitoring the VM information of each user through accessing the log file like access log, error log, authentication log, application log, and so on. In the IaaS model, this involves monitoring the system-level logs, firewalls, network packets, storage logs, backups, raw virtual machine files, unencrypted RAM snapshots, and so on. In the PaaS model, monitoring is via an application-specific log and is accessed through API, operating system exceptions, and so on. The third step is examination and analysis; the investigators need to analyze the evidence and artifacts to reach a reasoned conclusion. The last step is presentation and reporting, which means that after finding artifacts and evidence and the conclusion, then the investigator needs to represent their findings in an organized report [1].

According to the importance of Dropbox and the important data that is stored on it, I will experiment to identify the forensics artifacts of the Dropbox cloud storage account using different forensics tools and using Android OS and iOS. In addition, I will use Android mobiles in the experiment as a different evidence source for the cloud storage account to analyze and identify forensics artifacts for each process. I will need to create an account on Dropbox and install a Dropbox app on mobile, which is Samsung Galaxy S5 (Android version: 5.0 Lollipop) in this experiment and iPhone 5s. Then, I will upload and share photos and documents on it to identify the forensics artifacts after these activities using different forensic tools to acquire data from evidence source: Dropbox mobile app in this experiment, along with forensic tools like Magnet AXIOM Examine, MOBILedit Forensic Express, FINALMobile, and others to show all artifacts that may be found.

In this chapter, we will use a laptop and mobile devices to find the artifacts on the Dropbox cloud storage mobile app after some activities such as installation, creating a new account, signing in with a created account, and uploading and sharing photos and documents. At first, we will install the Dropbox app on mobile Samsung G900 Galaxy S5 (SM-G900H), sign in with a created account, upload photos and documents on it, and then connect the mobile to the laptop using a USB cable after enabling the debugging mode and airplane mode on mobile. After that, we will use a set of forensic tools like AXIOM forensics software MOBILedit, FINALMobile, ADB shell, and DB Browser for SQLite to acquire data and find the differences in artifacts when using different evidence sources with same account and mobile using different forensics tools and evidence sources. We will apply the same case on Android and iPhone mobile devices and do acquisition and find the different artifacts that can be acquired. The IMEI website [10] shows more details; using the IMEI website, we will indicate more information about the device in this experiment. By using this unique IMEI number, you may get to know such data as the network and country from which your device originally comes, warranty information, date of purchase, carrier information, system version, device specification, and more detailed information as shown in Figure 10-1, which indicates a set of features for used mobile device type, size, SIM card, and internal and external memory. This information about devices helps the investigator do their work correctly and more easily. Every single point makes the investigation go in a good way.

Basic information	Parameters	Comments	Other
Device type:		Smartphone	
Design:		Classic	
Released:		2014 г.	
SIM card size:		Micro Sim	
GSM:		✔ 850 900 1800 1900	
HSDPA:		✔ 850 900 1900 2100 HSPA+	
LTE:		✔ LTE-FDD: 1800, 2100, 2600 ✔ LTE-TDD: 1900, 2300, 2500, 2600	
Dimensions (H/L/W):		142 x 72.5 x 8.1 mm, vol. 83 cm³	
Display:		SUPER AMOLED Color (16M) 1080x1920 px (5.1") 432ppi	
Protection LCD:		Corning Gorilla Glass 3	
Touch screen:		✔	
Weight:		146 g	
Time GSM (talk/stand-by):		21 / 390 hrs. (16.3d)	
Battery:		Li-Ion 2800 mAh	
Built-in memory:		✔ 32 GB	
Memory card:		✔ microSDXC max. 128 GB	
RAM Memory:		2 GB	
OS:		Android 4.4 KitKat	
Chipset:		Qualcomm Snapdragon 801 MSM8974AC	
CPU #1 Type:		Krait 400	
CPU #1 freq.:		2500.0 MHz (4-core)	
GPU Type:		Qualcomm Adreno 330	

Figure 10-1. *Galaxy S5 device info*

Android Acquisition Tools

Acquisition Using AXIOM Forensic Tool

The first experiment in this research, we will use the mobile option as an evidence source and then acquire data logically.

338

[1]. Connect mobile with a laptop using USB cable, enable debugging mode and stay-awake mode on mobile, disable Wi-Fi, and disconnect the SD card.

[2]. Use the mobile option as an evidence source, then select the mobile operating system.

[3]. Choose the required mobile that wants to acquire the artifacts and evidence from it, which is Samsung Galaxy S5 with model SM-G900H and with OS version 5.0 as examples of our case.

[4]. AXIOM starts acquiring and imaging for data to find the artifacts from the mobile that was selected and then analyzes for evidence.

[5]. The final step is representing all evidence in an artifacts overview after the search finishes. This representation appears in another program related to AXIOM called AXIOM Examine, which indicates all found artifacts ordered in categories with details. In this way, all mobile artifacts are found (around 470,780 artifacts) including contact names and numbers, chats, apps installed on it, and its data, photos, emails, and all contained data as shown in Figure 10-2.

Figure 10-2. *Artifacts overview related to Dropbox from mobile*

AXIOM forensic tool indicates the artifacts that appeared according to Dropbox; it showed the account size, number of items in Dropbox, and also any related objects such as when the app was installed and if someone made a search about it on Google for example. Also it showed the last access date and last modified date. However, it didn't have any content in it; it appeared as encrypted data. According to this study and experiments, it may be due to Dropbox's security terms and conditions.

For more details, I tried using another way to get artifacts from Dropbox cloud storage using the cloud option as an evidence source to check if there any changes made when using different evidence sources for the same cloud account and to check all the data in the same account.

1.   Use Magnet AXIOM forensics software to acquire data and find artifacts from Dropbox cloud storage using the cloud option. In this step, we need to use the cloud option as an evidence source to acquire data from it as an imaging location.

2. The next step is to choose the cloud platform that
    wants to acquire data from it, and in this experiment
    we will choose Dropbox as shown in Figure 10-3.

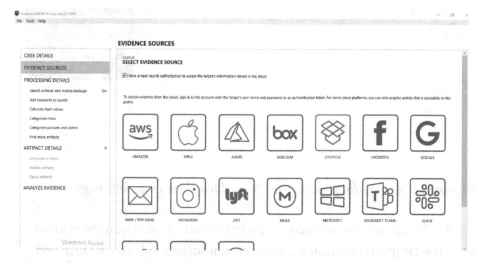

Figure 10-3. *Choose Dropbox from cloud platforms options as an
evidence source*

In this step will appear all cloud platforms that are supported by
AXIOM like Amazon, Azure, Microsoft teams, Dropbox, and others, and
then after that it will be necessary to sign in using the required account.
In this experiment, you will choose Dropbox and then sign in using
the created account and then let AXIOM access files and folders in it to
acquire data.

3. AXIOM asked to trust accessing cloud accounts; it
    will need to access with username and password
    and then do the acquisition step and give the results
    of all artifacts with details divided into categories
    using Magnet AXIOM Examine program as shown in
    Figure 10-4.

Figure 10-4. *Artifacts acquired from Dropbox cloud storage*

AXIOM shows the artifacts that were found when acquiring evidence from the Dropbox cloud storage account; it includes the username and password from this account, identifiers including people who accessed it, all photos, files, and folders uploaded to it, time and date for each activity, and so on.

Acquisition Using MOBILedit Express Tool

In this section, we will use different forensic tools for acquiring data and analyzing it, and we use the MOBILedit express pro tool to do the logical acquisition.

1. In each forensic case we need to put the mobile in airplane mode, turn on debugging mode, enable the stay-awake setting, disable Wi-Fi, and remove the SD card. Then we need to plug the mobile into the PC via USB. Then the mobile will ask for trust in this PC device; we must bypass the mobile lock

technique to make trust to enable the connection with it and see all the data. In our case, we know the passcode, which we type and access the device.

2. In this step, the connected mobile is asked to enable the backup process from it.

3. Then the phone is connected and it appears on the screen with its type.

4. Now choose what we want to do. For our experiment, we will choose application analysis and confirm by clicking Next.

5. In this step, we will see a list of all the applications installed on the mobile phone. Choose the one you want to analyze. This is shown in Figure 10-5.

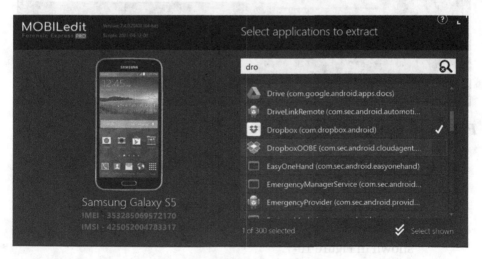

Figure 10-5. *Choose which application we want to extract*

6. In this step, you can choose which output you want
    to have. When analyzing an app for the first time,
    we need to make a backup. By default, it will make
    an XML file with some other folders for analyzed
    data, as shown in Figure 10-6. Then a dialog for
    starting the backup will start. Finally, if the backup
    extraction is completed correctly, the wizard will
    show the message.

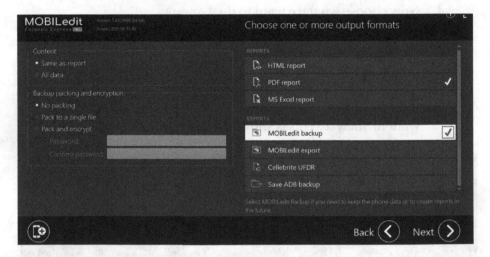

Figure 10-6. *Choose output format*

7. Now you can access the "results folder" as shown in
    the last step. You will find a set of folders for backup
    and analyze data with pathname being the same as
    the name of the application we choose to extract, as
    shown in Figure 10-7.

> Documents > MOBILedit Forensic Express > Samsung Galaxy S5 (2021-05-08 22h56m50s)

Name	Date modified	Type
pdf_files	08-May-21 10:57 PM	File folder
phone_files	08-May-21 10:57 PM	File folder
log_full	08-May-21 10:57 PM	TXT File
log_short	08-May-21 10:57 PM	TXT File
mobiledit_backup	08-May-21 10:57 PM	XML Document
Report	08-May-21 10:57 PM	Adobe Acrobat D...
report_configuration.cfg	08-May-21 10:57 PM	CFG File

Figure 10-7. *Extracted folders*

Here and after accessing these files, we found that all the files are empty and encrypted. According to the tool's documentation, some applications preserve all in their data right here and are pretty easy for similarly processing and analyzing, but different applications may contain all the data. However, they are pretty hard to process similarly because they could be encrypted. Thus, it's far from constant that similar processing can be used from case to case. As a result of our experiment, we found that all files are empty.

Acquisition Using ADB Tool

In this section, we will use the command prompt to make a logical backup from our devices in our case (Galaxy S5) and then extract the backup file. First, we need to install platform tools: SDK, JDK.

1. Connect the mobile to the PC using a USB cable connector and then enable airplane mood and debugging mode. In this step, we must unlock the mobile device to bypass it. In our case, we have the passcode. But we must notice that if the Android mobile is locked we need to unlock it by using different techniques, one of them is using ADB to bypass the screen lock. We need to delete the

gesture.key file, after accessing ADB shell using the command: adb.exe shell > cd /data/system rm gesture. key. This command will work when the device is rooted, and it may not work if it is not rooted. Also, we must check that the USB is connected as a transfer mode and not a charging mode. Open cmd and detect success platform tools and then use ADB to access the shell. Also, check if port 5073 is open and use port 5037 commands.

2. We can now check for connected devices. We must find the connected device to have the ability to access it, as described in Figure 10-8. If the device is connected successfully and we can reach it, it can now access its data.

3. Use the ADB command to take a backup from mobile to reach the entire files and database and find artifacts and evidence. You will do this using the command adb backup -shared -all. As shown in Figure 10-8, we use command adb backup -shared -all. This means we want to take a backup from all files for mobile and also shared ones.

```
Microsoft Windows [Version 10.0.19042.1052]
(c) Microsoft Corporation. All rights reserved.

C:\Users\sajeda>cd c:
C:\Users\sajeda

C:\Users\sajeda>cd/

C:\>cd platform-tools

C:\platform-tools>adb.exe devics
adb.exe: unknown command devics

C:\platform-tools>adb.exe devices
* daemon not running; starting now at tcp:5037
* daemon started successfully
List of devices attached
320859124374513b          device


C:\platform-tools>adb backup -shared -all
WARNING: adb backup is deprecated and may be removed in a future release
Now unlock your device and confirm the backup operation...
```

Figure 10-8. *cmd view for connected devices*

4.   Now when the backup is finished, a backup file will be created as backup.ab file in the platform tools folder.

5.   Now we need to convert this ab file to a .tar file to make this file universal and allow accessing it or opening it using different tools, using adb command line java -jar abe.jar unpack c:\platform-tools\ backup.ab backup.tar to convert a backup file from .ab to .tar as shown in Figure 10-9.

```
C:\platform-tools>adb backup -shared -all
WARNING: adb backup is deprecated and may be removed in a future release
Now unlock your device and confirm the backup operation...

C:\platform-tools>adb backup -shared -all
WARNING: adb backup is deprecated and may be removed in a future release
Now unlock your device and confirm the backup operation...

C:\platform-tools>aaa
'aaa' is not recognized as an internal or external command,
operable program or batch file.

C:\platform-tools>adb.exe devices
List of devices attached
320859124374513b          device


C:\platform-tools>adb backup -shared -all
WARNING: adb backup is deprecated and may be removed in a future release
Now unlock your device and confirm the backup operation...

C:\platform-tools>cd bin

C:\platform-tools\bin>java -jar abe.jar unpack c:\platform-tools\backup.ab backup.tar
Error: could not open `C:\platform-tools\lib\i386\jvm.cfg'

C:\platform-tools\bin>java -jar abe.jar unpack c:\platform-tools\backup.ab backup.tar
```

Figure 10-9. *Convert backup file .ab to .tar*

6. For the final result, we convert the file and have a tar
    file that can be opened via different tools as shown
    in Figure 10-10.

api-ms-win-crt-multibyte-l1-1-0.dll	01-Jul-21 2:26 PM	Application exten...	19 KB
api-ms-win-crt-private-l1-1-0.dll	01-Jul-21 2:26 PM	Application exten...	65 KB
api-ms-win-crt-process-l1-1-0.dll	01-Jul-21 2:26 PM	Application exten...	12 KB
api-ms-win-crt-runtime-l1-1-0.dll	01-Jul-21 2:26 PM	Application exten...	16 KB
api-ms-win-crt-stdio-l1-1-0.dll	01-Jul-21 2:26 PM	Application exten...	17 KB
api-ms-win-crt-string-l1-1-0.dll	01-Jul-21 2:26 PM	Application exten...	18 KB
api-ms-win-crt-time-l1-1-0.dll	01-Jul-21 2:26 PM	Application exten...	14 KB
api-ms-win-crt-utility-l1-1-0.dll	01-Jul-21 2:26 PM	Application exten...	12 KB
awt.dll	01-Jul-21 2:26 PM	Application exten...	1,183 KB
backup	01-Jul-21 3:22 PM	TAR File	4,280,528 KB
bci.dll	01-Jul-21 2:26 PM	Application exten...	18 KB
dcpr.dll	01-Jul-21 2:26 PM	Application exten...	145 KB

Figure 10-10. *Backup tar file*

7. Now we can access this folder, extract it, and take
    the desired file related to a specific case or can open
    all these backup files using forensic tools such as
    FINALMobile or MOBILedit (introduced in the
    previous section).

8. In our case, we search for Dropbox data. When we
    opened the backup folder we found no database
    files and no data with the backup file; after this
    experiment we concluded that investigators can't
    find data files related to the Dropbox app. We only
    found a manifest file of 3KB size. So, from this point,
    we want to do physical acquisition instead of the last
    logical one and find the different artifacts that we
    can find.

In this experiment, we will try to find the desired data from a physical
acquisition from connected mobile. This means we need to take root for
the device to reach system files and find desired artifacts after the rooting
process is done successfully, and the device now is rooted as explained
in Chapter 7. Now, we can make the physical acquisition and reach
more file systems into mobile devices. So, in this chapter and after, these
experiments can find the Dropbox cloud storage mobile app artifacts, and
using different tools and procedures can find different artifacts.

Physical Acquisition Using MOBILedit Tool

This section will use this tool to make a physical acquisition to reach more
file systems and find desired artifacts and evidence for investigations.

1. After connecting the mobile device to the workstation, this tool will recognize the device and let the user start work. From the first step when trying to make acquisition, the tool will check if the device is rooted or not. In our case, it shows a message to indicate that it is rooted as shown in Figure 10-11, that the mobile is rooted. Then you can click OK and start the acquisition.

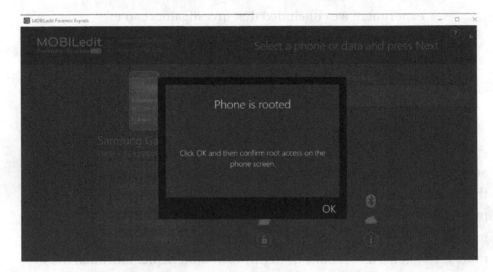

Figure 10-11. *Kingo root successfully rooting*

2. In this step, we will choose full content to acquire all mobile file systems as a physical acquisition process, and we can choose the acquisition type. In our case, we want to make the full content acquisition as we explained before.

3. The acquisition process took around 19 hours to
    finish and procedures can get 17.8 Gb as backup file
    size as a result.

4. For files related to our case "Dropbox", we need to
    access related files as shown in Figure 10-12.

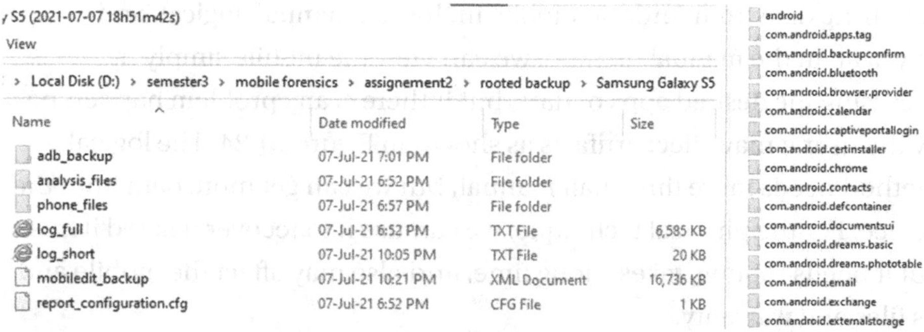

Name	Date modified	Type	Size
adb_backup	07-Jul-21 7:01 PM	File folder	
analysis_files	07-Jul-21 6:52 PM	File folder	
phone_files	07-Jul-21 6:57 PM	File folder	
log_full	07-Jul-21 6:52 PM	TXT File	6,585 KB
log_short	07-Jul-21 10:05 PM	TXT File	20 KB
mobiledit_backup	07-Jul-21 10:21 PM	XML Document	16,736 KB
report_configuration.cfg	07-Jul-21 6:52 PM	CFG File	1 KB

S5 (2021-07-07 18h51m42s)
View
> Local Disk (D:) > semester3 > mobile forensics > assignment2 > rooted backup > Samsung Galaxy S5

android
com.android.apps.tag
com.android.backupconfirm
com.android.bluetooth
com.android.browser.provider
com.android.calendar
com.android.captiveportallogin
com.android.certinstaller
com.android.chrome
com.android.contacts
com.android.defcontainer
com.android.documentsui
com.android.dreams.basic
com.android.dreams.phototable
com.android.email
com.android.exchange
com.android.externalstorage

Figure 10-12. *Backup file details*

We are seeking to examine all files that we can get from full content
backup from a mobile device after making root. But we need to check for
application files to reach Dropbox files; to do this, the investigator can
search for all files related to our case about Dropbox. The backup file
contains only the manifest file with a size of only 3KB and we can't open
any file using SQLite DB browser to view it and show the database files
contained in it. So in this case, we could not have achieved anything from
using physical acquisition and this method can't provide any helpful way
to find new artifacts and evidence. So, as we can see, the rooting process
could not add value in finding new files and their related artifacts about
Dropbox apps. So, we can say that there is no need for rooting in Dropbox
investigations. Also, there may be dangerous changes that the root can
affect on mobile devices including breaking the warranty and allowing
harmful programs to do bad effects on devices.

For Android devices, we can note that if the mobile device is locked we must unlock it using any suitable technique. In addition to the ADB shell technique that we talked about before, there are powerful automated tools to unlock Android devices like XRY and UFED tools and most of them require enabling USB debugging.

As we can see, there are many different tools and methods for acquiring data from Android mobile including manual, logical, and physical. In the manual method, we can view the mobile simply by accessing the desired apps or data, but if there is any problem happening by the user it may affect artifacts as shown in Figure 10-24. The logical method needs more time than manual, but we can get more data from the device. For the physical technique, we can use it to recover deleted items but it needs rooting, takes a long time, and also may affect the mobile and its files and warranty.

This section will use iOS mobile with type iPhone 5s to use it in our experiments and will use different forensic tools for acquiring data and analyzing it and find the required artifacts and then find the differences between them that are related to the Dropbox case. We have a set of forensic tools the digital forensic analyst can use to find artifacts and collect evidence that is needed for investigations.

iOS Logical Acquisition Tools
iOS Logical Acquisition Using iTunes Tool

1. We use iTunes to take a backup from an iOS device as in Figure 10-13, and then we can access the backup files on computer files.

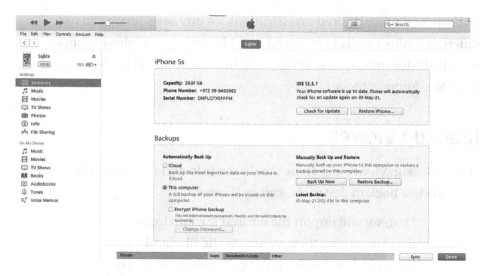

Figure 10-13. *iTunes backup*

The iTunes backup method depends on making a backup from the device and then analyzing it by forensic tools to find the artifacts that will help in investigations. It is by default an unencrypted backup and if wanted it will make it encrypted by using the option "encrypt iPhone backup." Also, we need to prevent automatic synchronization before connecting it with forensic tools.

The backup process will depend on the data size that is stored on the iPhone in the first backup. Then when the backup is done, there is a file called backup stored in the backup folder. This file will have a file name that will consist of a 40-character hexadecimal string related to UDID (Unique Device Identifier), but now it consists of a 24-character string and the name will be represented according to it. The backup includes a copy for all data on the mobile data, emails and passwords, UDID, SIM, serial number, and phone number.

Now, we can work with iTunes backups and make data acquisition from the iOS backup and then analyze backups with iTunes. We can use every file from backup files and open other forensic tools to find all artifacts and make desired investigations for any case. So we can use different forensic tools to view and use this backup and also to check mobile device info such as device-info, libiMobile, iBackup viewer, and iExplorer forensic tools.

iBackup Viewer

Using iBackup viewer can show the device info and internal mobiles files from the last backup that was taken by iTunes.

1. First, we will import the desired backup from the iTunes tool; then we access the files and all content of mobile from the grid view as shown in Figure 10-14.

Figure 10-14.   iTunes backup using iBackup

In this grid view, we can view all content in mobile call contacts, history, web history, call messages, notes, Safari, and websites.

2. In addition to this grid view, we can use the raw files option to view the entire file system as in Figure 10-15; then we can view the device info and all related files in the backup.

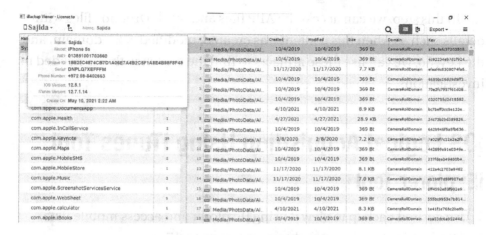

Figure 10-15. *Device info from iBackup viewer*

3.   Now we can access entire files and check about
     ones that are related to Dropbox files as shown in
     Figure 10-16.

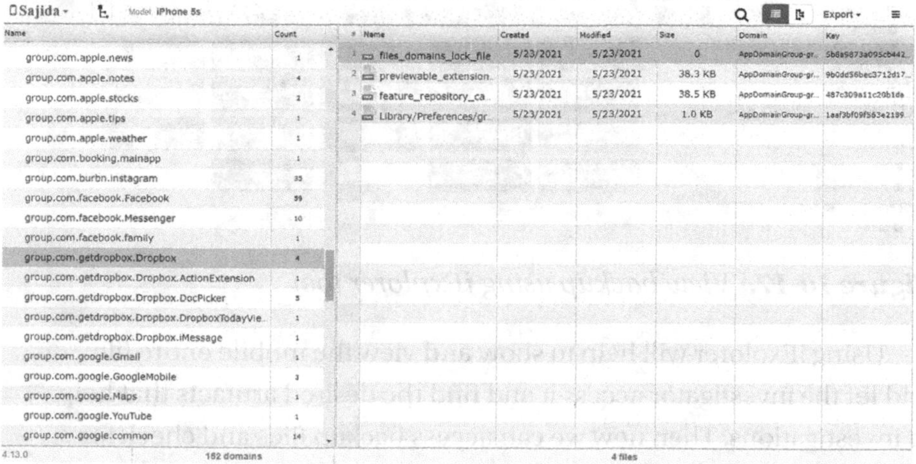

Figure 10-16. *Dropbox info from iBackup viewer*

In this step, we can access the APP files and reach Dropbox files with details such as when this content was created, modified, size, domain, and the key. So, we can use these artifacts to find the evidence that is needed in investigations.

iOS Logical Acquisition Using iTunes Tool iExplorer Tool

1. Use desired backup to view it using iExplorer and access mobile data and find desired evidence as shown in Figure 10-17.

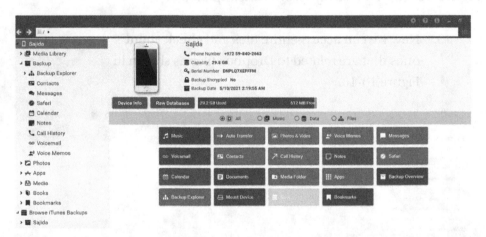

Figure 10-17. *View backup using iExplorer tool*

Using iExplorer will help to show and view the mobile entire file and let the investigator access it and find the desired artifacts that help in investigations. Then now we can access backup files and check for required artifacts to use in investigations. And we can access entire files in backup such as Safari history, calls, contacts, wireless, notes, apps data, photos, music, messages, and so on for our experiment to reach to cloud

356

files and the Dropbox files in particular. Figure 10-18 shows the files that
are related to clouds, such as *cache.db*, which contains Dropbox files and
pictures. We need to export these files from this tool and then we can use it
with another tool such as DB browse to explore the data.

Figure 10-18. *Dropbox cache DB in iExplorer tool*

DB Browser Tool

Now we can use the DB browser to access specific files that we took
from our last backup. We can access the desired file by exporting it from
iExplorer to PC and then can import it into the DB browser for SQLite. This
backup is unencrypted. By default in iTunes backup, four main folders
will appear in the backup file: manifest.plist, status.plist, info.plist, and
manifest.dp. To extract iTunes backup using DB browser, we will need
to export the "manifest.dp" or another .plist or database file into DB
browser and analyze the data. The tables in the dp file will consist of a set
of columns. One of them is the "fileID"; it is a SHA1 hash of the domain
(Secure Hash Algorithm) . In addition, we can export specific files from
backup into the DB browser as needed.

1. We export the cache.db from iExplorer, then import it into the DB browser. As listed in Figure 10-19, using this step we let the user recover the content in each file that is related to Dropbox.

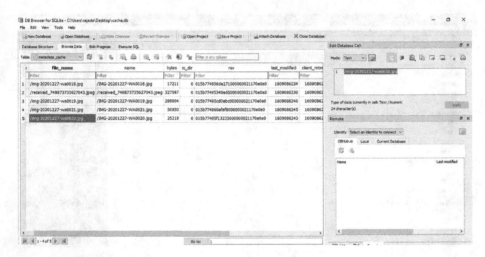

Figure 10-19. *cache.db entire content*

This figure shows all the content in this database file, indicating that there are five jpg images in a table called "metadata_cache". For images, we can use the binary representation and other forms, but we cannot see it as an image view. Also, Figure 10-20 details about images (file content) when it is in a binary representation. We can see its details, but can't when we check for image representation. This means this tool can be used and give helpful results, but we talk about images, so we need a different forensic tool to show it.

Figure 10-20. *Image in binary representation*

In addition, we can make an acquisition from the last iTunes backup by using different forensic tools or can acquire data from live mobile.

AXIOM Forensic Tool

First, we need to acquire data from mobile logically and will connect the mobile device, which is the iPhone 5s in our study. We can use backup files or make a live acquisition from an unencrypted backup.

a. Acquiring cloud evidence source from an unencrypted backup

1. The first step we need to connect the mobile iPhone
    5s with a laptop and enable debugging mode
    and turn on airplane mode. This step represents
    choosing the logical acquiring method to acquire
    data directly from mobile after making trust for the
    laptop workstation. The important point we must
    mention is the passcode for mobile. In many cases,
    the logical acquisition can be performed if the
    phone is unlocked, but depending on the mobile
    model, iOS firmware, and also passcode complexity,
    we can obtain access to the mobile device using a
    brute force attack.

2. We choose the Dropbox app as an evidence source
   in this experiment as shown in Figure 10-21.

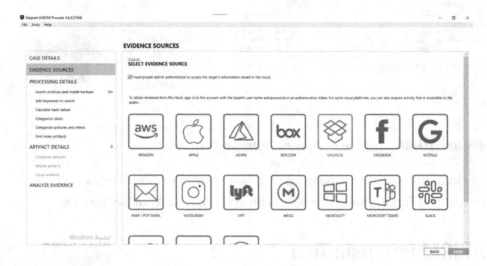

Figure 10-21. *Select evidence source*

3. Now we need to login into the Dropbox user
   account in order to reach all artifacts that we need.
   In these steps you will need to log in to the Dropbox
   app using email and password. Then an email will
   arrive to the email account that we registered.

4. Now will choose the logged-in Dropbox account to
   use in our acquiring method.

5. This step acquiring process starts and there are
   more than 108 possible artifact details from all
   cloud apps. The AXIOM will be acquired from
   Dropbox only.

6. Now we can customize the cloud artifacts and use only
   what you want. In our experiment, these are selected
   as shown in Figure 10-22 to include them in our case.
   Then the program starts extracting and analyzing data.

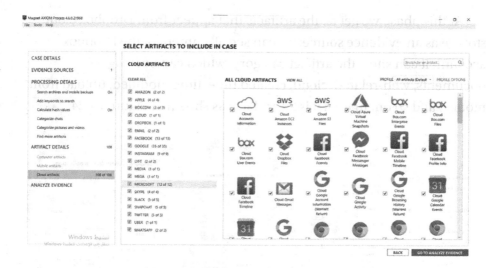

Figure 10-22. *Select artifact sources to include in case*

7. Now all artifacts that the program can reach are
    shown; see Figure 10-23.

Figure 10-23. *All cloud artifacts*

At this phase we get all the artifacts that appear from Dropbox cloud storage as an evidence source; we can see all content of the Dropbox account. It can show the artifact category, which can be images, documents, web-related, cloud, created time, time modified, upload from mobile, and so on. In total it is 29 artifacts as shown in Figure 10-24.

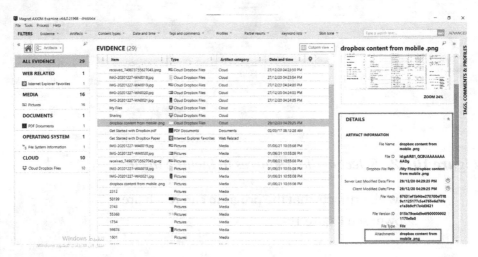

Figure 10-24. *All cloud artifacts details*

Results and Analysis

So, after making three experiments for AXIOM with cloud, we can say that we can reach the app's content, artifacts, and we can retrieve the images and documents clearly, and include detailed info for the files by using the cloud as an evidence source. However, we cannot do this by using only the mobile as an evidence source. Also, AXIOM lets the user access the evidence that was found before the acquiring process was finished. This option is an advantage for the AXIOM tool. On the other hand, it can make a separate acquisition from mobile, cloud, and computer, so we can make acquisitions from these sources. In addition, for each evidence source we can choose the desired app we want to acquire data from. These options make the usage of this tool more flexible and easier; it will find and provide the artifacts and evidence in a short time instead of waiting a long time for finishing all acquiring processes and for a full device.

In iOS mobiles and for Dropbox cases, there is no need for physical because we can get a lot of artifacts by some tools such as Magnet AXIOM logical acquisition.

Depending on different acquisition methods (mainly physical acquisition and logical acquisition), and also by comparing between methods, we can say that physical acquisition can access and find more data generally. In addition, even a backup that is protected by a password contains considerably less info than exists on the device. The device stores monumental amounts of data like system databases (with detailed location data), third-party application data from secure messengers, along with SQLite write-ahead logs (WAL) that will contain deleted data and temporary files, WebKit data, Apple Pay transactions, notifications from all applications, and plenty of different types of vital evidence. It also provides a complete keychain. Conversely, the mobile warranty will be lost and also the mobile may not be able to be returned to factory settings; also, this method needs special tools and it's expensive. But in logical acquisition, it's easy and safe and also very familiar with iTunes. Taking backups from iTunes is the most major process in logical acquisition. But the biggest problem with backups is password protection, and the password must be known to let the user access it and show the data. We need to explain that the protected backups contain more information than the unprotected backups. So, the logical acquisition exceeds just a backup process and it can reach to the device's media and metadata, which may contain data about deleted files, and also it can contain a thumbnail. As an aside, if we grant that one of the pro points for logical acquisition is backup encryption, we will still need the screen passcode to access the device and extract data. Also, not all data can be found.

We indicate the differences between used forensics tools in these iOS experiments. It indicates how each tool can help in this experiment and how it can help in finding artifacts and evidence. Since data recovered must be valid, accurate, and reliable, we can find that using different kinds of mobile phones from different manufacturers will make it difficult to develop a single process or tool to examine all types of phone devices. Every tool will help in a part of the investigation process. In addition, some tools become more professional in viewing the content of the mobile, acquiring and extracting data, examining, printing reports, an so on. So, as investigators, we must choose an appropriate tool for each process. This way will help greatly in investigations and make their results more valid and reliable. On another side, by comparing Android and iOS experimental results and techniques related to security rooting and security and data acquisition tools, we can find that in our experiment there is no need for root for iPhone devices and can access Dropbox data and find many artifacts using some tools. But for Android, all data was encrypted or empty in most tools, so we needed this step to try accessing more system files bit by bit to find desired artifacts. In the Android rooting step, we didn't find any new data related to Dropbox. So we can say there is no need for rooting in Dropbox investigation cases. Despite the security on iOS devices being higher than Android devices, old versions of OS and using suitable tools can be of good help in dealing with mobile and can access more files. Table 10-1 will show a comparison between Android and iOS devices.

According to operating system security for iOS and Android, we can say that the iOS operating system has long been considered the more secure of the two operating systems because Apple's operating system is a closed system. It doesn't release its source code to app developers, and the owners of these devices can't modify the code on their phones themselves. This makes it more difficult for hackers to find vulnerabilities on iOS-powered devices. But Android devices are the opposite, relying on an open source code; that means that the owners of these devices can tinker with their devices' operating systems. Too much tinkering and owners might create a weakness in their devices' security. Then there are manufacturers themselves. If a phone maker puts out a new device with a modification to the Android operating system and there's a vulnerability in that code, hackers will find it. From another side, we want to explain that the forensics tools used these vulnerabilities can collect a large amount of data from devices.

Table 10-1. *A Comparison between Android and iOS Devices*

Tool	Process type	Android	iOS
Magnet AXIOM	Logical acquisition	Find many artifacts	Find many artifacts
MOBILedit	Logical & physical acquisition	All files are empty or encrypted	Not used
FINALMobile	Logical acquisition	Dropbox data is still encrypted	Empty data for cloud
ADB shell	Logical acquisition	Can't find data file related to Dropbox	Not used
Tunesgo wondershare	Logical backup & rooting	Failed (mobile not supported)	No need for rooting
Kingo root	Rooting	Done successfully and easily	No need
iTunes	Logical backup	Not used	Recommended for backups

(continued)

Table 10-1. (*continued*)

Tool	Process type	Android	iOS
iBackup viewer	Backup viewing	Not used	Recommended for checking specific files and showing the backup content. Can reach Dropbox files and export them.
iExplorer	Backup viewing	Not used	Recommended for checking specific files and showing the backup content. Can reach Dropbox files and export them.
BD SQLite	Backup viewing	Can't find DB files and couldn't use this tool	Recommended in access file databases and show contents. Can show the cloud's content and find many artifacts.

Cloud Forensic Challenges

Cloud forensics is one branch of digital forensics that presents several challenges. Digital forensic analysts or examiners encounter obstacles at the stage of evidence acquisition, preservation, and recovery of the evidence. They have the flexibility to spot correct account control among the cloud by clients and to realize access to the specified information in cloud storage. This method unremarkably needs help from cloud service providers. Thanks to the massive volume and remote access of cloud storage, many forensic examiners find it difficult to get an entire image of cloud storage in a forensically sound manner. Validation of images and distinguishing deleted information within the cloud attribute to a particular user remains difficult at this time. Besides, time synchronization of live acquisition is still unclear for cloud services. Additional coaching and knowledge sharing in the field of cloud forensics are important [15].

Summary

After this study, we can say that the Magnet AXIOM tool is the perfect one for Dropbox apps on Android and iOS. In addition, there is no need for rooting and physical acquisition in these cases. This study can increase the knowledge about the Dropbox cloud storage evidence and artifacts and how to analyze and acquire data using different evidence sources and also different forensic tools. On another side, it helps investigators and researchers use these results in their research or investigations. Also, it helps to clarify the impact of Dropbox forensics, which can be added to cloud forensic fields for both Android and iPhone. In addition, another important thing that can be mentioned is that the found artifacts may be changed according to differences in evidence source and devices. So, it can be reported that the analyzed services may find different artifacts according to differences and changes of different features of the devices, OS, and used forensics tools.

Future work can be on new Dropbox app versions and with new and different OS mobile versions using new forensics tools, and also another cloud storage application still can be tested to investigators sent artifacts from different devices and platforms.

References

[1].   T. Sree and S. Bhanu, *Data Collection Techniques for Forensic Investigation in Cloud*. IntechOpen, 2020, p. 3.

[2].   G. Satrya, Digital Forensics Study of a Cloud Storage Client: A Dropbox Artifact Analysis. *CommIT (Communication & Information Technology) Journal* 13(2), 57–66, 2019.

[3].   N. Reddy, Cloud Forensics In: *Practical Cyber Forensics*. Berkeley, CA: Apress, 2019, pp. 244-246.

[4].   Magnet AXIOM, "Magnet AXIOM", Irp-cdn. multiscreensite.com, 2020. [Online]. Available: https://irp-cdn.multiscreensite.com. [Accessed: 15- Dec- 2020].

[5].   forensic.manuals.mobiledit, "How to Make an Application Backup", forensic.manuals.mobiledit. com, [online]. Accessed:https://forensic. manuals.mobiledit.com/MM/How-to-make-an-application-backup.1821474845.html. [Access: 1-May-2021]

[6].   igetintopc, "FINALMobile Forensics 2020", igetintopc.com.[online]. Available:https:// igetintopc.com/finalmobile-forensics-2020-free-download/. [Accessed :1-May-2021].

[7].   C. Huang, H. Ko, and H. Zhuang, *Mobile Forensics for Cloud Storage Service on iOS Systems*, Singapore, IEICE, 2018.

[8].   support.apple, "Identify your iPhone Model",
        igetintopc.com.[online]. Available on https://
        support.apple.com/en-in/HT201296. [Accessed:
        20-May-2021].

[9].   imei.info, apple, "IMEI.INFO: APPLE IPHONE
        5S", [online]https://www.imei.info/
        phonedatabase/12876-apple-iphone-5s/.
        [Accessed: 20.May.2021]

[10].   support.apple, "iTunes 12.10.11 for Windows
        (Windows 64 bit)", www.imei.info.[online].
        Available: https://www.imei.info/
        phonedatabase/12876-apple-iphone-5s/,
        [Accessed: 1-Jun-2021].

[11].   imactools, "Extract Data from iPhone Backups", www.
        imactools.com.[online].available:https://www.
        imactools.com/iphonebackupviewer/.[Accessed:
        1.Jun.2021]

[12].   softexe, "iExplorer", softexe.net [online].
        Available:https://softexe.net/win/hobbies-
        lifestyle/mobile/iexplorer:hega.html,
        [Accessed: 1-Jun.2021].

[13].   sqlitebrowser, "DB Browser for SQLite",
        sqlitebrowser.org,[online]. Available: https://
        sqlitebrowser.org/., [Accessed:1-Jun-2021].

[14].   Q. Do, B. Martini, and K. Choo, *A CloudFocused
        Mobile Forensics Methodology, IEEE Cloud
        Computing,* 2015 IEEE 2325-6095/14/$31.00 ©
        2015 IEEE

CHAPTER 11

Malware Forensics for Volatile and Nonvolatile Memory in Mobile Devices

Day after day, malware and malicious programs are spreading continuously, especially for unprotected mobile devices. Mobile device malware can reside in the nonvolatile memory, or it can hide itself behind some process in the RAM, and so, in the latter case, there is no need for any file in the mobile storage to perform its tasks. Mobile memory forensics tasks can help investigators to extract interesting information from the two types of mobile memory, such as detecting some of resident malware and its related details, which in the same time traditional techniques—like antivirus software—either can detect or cannot.

In this chapter, we will cover the following topics:

- Mobile Malware Forensics

- Smartphone Volatile Memory

- Mobile Device Case Details and Experiment

© Mohammed Moreb 2022
M. Moreb, *Practical Forensic Analysis of Artifacts on iOS and Android Devices*,
https://doi.org/10.1007/978-1-4842-8026-3_11

- Logical Acquisition

- iPhone Physical Acquisition

- Android Physical Acquisition

- iOS Analysis and Results

- Evaluating Extraction Tools and Methods for Android
  and iOS Devices

- Evaluating Android Extraction Techniques for Volatile
  and Nonvolatile Memory

- Summary

Mobile Malware Forensics

Mobile memory can be considered as a basic and important part of
the mobile device, holding user data, photos, applications, and so on.
In general, mobile devices have different types of memory such as SIM
memory, read-only memory, random access memory, internal memory,
and external memory. However, all the previous types of memory can
be categorized as either volatile or nonvolatile memory. Only RAM—the
physical memory—represents the volatile memory of the device, which
will be erased and volatilized when the device is powered off. On the other
hand, all the remaining types can be considered as nonvolatile memory,
which is used to store programs, media, and various data.

Mobile devices with the two types of memory can be considered as a
valuable environment for threats, attacks, and malware. Malware can be
defined as software that can cause harm or destruction for the system, and
affects the effectiveness of device functions or steals some important data.
It can be inserted into the system without user permission or knowledge
[2]. According to McAfee Labs' threat reports, most attacks were launched
by malware in the second quarter of 2020, with 35% of publicly reported

incidents. See Figure 11-1, which also shows how malware spread
enormously in the last quarter of 2019 and the first two quarters of 2020.
The volume of malware threats observed by McAfee Labs averaged 419
threats per minute, an increase of 44 threats per minute (12%) in the
second quarter of 2020 [3].

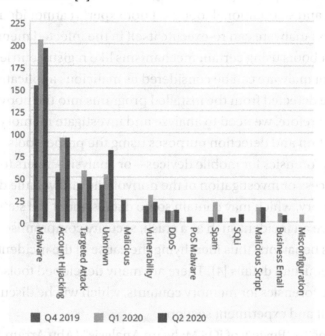

Figure 11-1. *Top 10 attack vectors in the last quarter of 2019, and the
first two quarters of 2020 [3]*

Android operating systems (OS) can be considered as an ideal
environment for malware and threats, due to their system vulnerabilities.
According to Cisco 2014 Annual Security Report, 99% of the malware that
affects mobile devices targeted Android devices in 2013. For iOS devices,
as it can be considered a small UNIX system, the attacker can also find
some way to attack the system. Malware or malicious code in general can
be considered as the most common way to break system security and
access the system contents (Dunham 2009).

As a result, many cybersecurity experts have developed various security tools like antivirus programs that can help in fighting these threats. Unfortunately, these security tools still cannot detect malware and malicious programs written directly into RAM [4]. This type of malware, called RAM fileless malware or memory-resident malware, leaves few signs of infection, and so traditional tools and nonexperts cannot identify it easily. Fileless malware can re-execute itself in the infected memory when the system reboots using certain mechanisms like registry entries [5]. The other types of malware can be considered as malicious applications, which can easily be detected from the installed programs into the nonvolatile memory. Therefore, we need to analyze and investigate memory contents for investigation and detection purposes using the proper tools.

Memory forensics for mobile devices—or analysis—refers to the analysis process or investigation of the nonvolatile and volatile data in mobile memory, which may contain some details about the state of the system before an incident such as a crash, security compromise, attacks, or malicious behaviors, thus identifying the cause of the incident and gaining other useful details [4]. There are many developed tools that can carry mobile forensics for memory contents, which will be discussed in the development and experiment section.

According to "Review of iOS Malware Analysis" (Abu Arram & Moreb, 2021), iOS mobile devices can infected by wide range of malware, which can be categorized into two main groups as follows:

A.   **Malware for Jailbroken Mobiles**: There are different examples of this type such as **iKee**, which can modify the wallpaper and add iOS devices into the botnet, and **APPBuyer**, which can use Apple ID and related passwords to download applications without getting the user's permission.

B. **Malware for Non-Jailbroken Mobiles**: There are
    different examples of this type such as **SpyPhone**,
    which can collect user personal data like photos,
    contacts, locations, and much else; **XcodeGhost,**
    which can collect user privacy and popup windows;
    and **Jekyll,** which can send messages, emails, or
    videos or dial random phone calls.

C. **Malware for both Jailbroken and Non-Jailbroken
    Mobiles**: Such as **YiSpecter,** which can collect the
    device UUID, install applications, and replace some
    applications with others.

According to the previously mentioned points, **the aim** of this project
is to analyze and investigate the mobile volatile and nonvolatile memory
for potential malware. To achieve this, the literature on the state of the
art of mobile device malware and memory analysis will be searched.
Then, Android and iOS devices will be acquired both logically and
physically after rooting or jailbreaking by the proper software, and finally,
the captured device memory image will be analyzed for malware and
suspicious processes.

Smartphone Volatile Memory

In "Review of iOS Malware Analysis" [6], Yixiang and Kang made a quick
revision about iOS versions and how related security methods for it
were developed. See Figure 11-2. Then they talked about iOS jailbreak
definition and how jailbreaking is used to break and minimize the
restrictions by iOS application program (App Store). Also, they mentioned
the different malicious applications—and its important related details
and information—that can infect either jailbroken or non-jailbroken iOS
devices such as XcodeG host, YiSpecter, and so on.

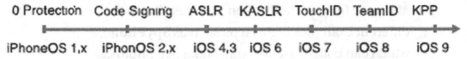

Figure 11-2. *iOS versions and related security methods [6]*

In "Review of Mobile Malware Forensic" (Abu Arram & Moreb, 2021),
the authors discussed mobile devices and GSM technology and its history.
Then they discussed mobile device hardware components such as RAM,
ROM, microprocessors, and so on, and mobile OS iOS and Android
fundamentals and properties. They turned after that to talk about
security threats on mobile devices. They show some software that can be
downloaded from sites containing jailbreak applications and can infect
mobile devices. Also, they named some applications to install Bylock threat
on mobile phones such as Best Free Music, Freezy-Find Music Listen,
and others that try to find some vulnerabilities on the mobile device and
connect to Bylock servers. Then, they defined malware and direct attacks
and their ways to vulnerable the system. They turned after that to talk
from a mobile forensics perspective. They mentioned applications used
for evidence collection, data collection methods—logical, physical, and so
on—phases of mobile forensics and a description for each phase, and the
properties of mobile forensic tools such as Cellebrite and Encase. Finally,
they discussed and analyzed a practical case about an SMS message sent
to a mobile device that contains a malicious file link. In "Survey of Mobile
Malware Analysis, Detection Techniques and Tools" (Gyamfi & Owusu,
2019), the authors discussed the characteristics of malware along with
specific types like Trojan, spyware, and others. Then, they turned to talk
about static and dynamic techniques of malware detection. Then, they
explained the static detection types and their meaning, which are signature-
based detection technique and heuristic detection technique. The same
goes for dynamic detection types, which are anomaly-based detection and
emulation-based detection. Then, they browsed analysis tools for the static
and dynamic techniques such as IDA pro and FileMon, respectively.

Then, they reviewed the limitations of both static and dynamic approaches with their different types. Finally, they discussed the hybrid detection method, which is a blend of both static and dynamic techniques, such as Sandbox Android application.

In "Mobile Devices Forensic Platform for Malware Detection" Suciu et al., 2019 talked about commercial and open source forensic tools such as UFED, DEFT (respectively), and many others along with their features. Then they proposed a platform to analyze malware on mobile devices, which consists of reverse engineering applications, online behavior analysis model, data retrieval agent, forensic tools, and central web platform. In "Smartphone Volatile Memory Acquisition for Security Analysis and Forensics Investigation" (Thing & Chua, 2013), Thing and Chua presented a method for the acquisition and analysis of the volatile memory data from mobile device smartphones. First, they talked about volatile memory acquisition approaches, which are run-mode debugging, stop-mode debugging, and kernel modules. Then they proposed an acquisition approach consisting of two parts, which are a user-side component to load the kernel and initialize the client-side logical channel, and a kernel-side component that plays as a logical device driver to set up the logical channel with the user-side component to support communication during operation. Then, they captured a ROM shadow image and analyzed the hexadecimal content of kernel data, heap, and stacks, which from its malware can be easily detected by a simple search. Then, they explored the kernel mapping memory region where the RAM loaded drivers reside, which is also important for malware analysis. In "Malware Memory Analysis for Non-specialists: Investigating a Publicly Available Memory Image of the Zeus Trojan Horse" [7], Carbone talked about how to analyze a memory image of a malware-infected Windows environment, using a combination of investigation tools like volatility framework plug-ins, data carving utilities, novice analysts, and various antivirus programs. The writer investigated a publicly known memory image infected with the hidden Zeus Trojan horse. At first, they used

Photorec software to perform data carving operations. Then, six antivirus scanners such as Avast and AVG were used to scan the memory image and the carved data files. Only AVG gives positive results for malware existence. After that, they examined the memory dump using various volatility plugins to check processes list, connections, drivers, registry, DLL, printkey, and other plug-ins, to perform a deep analysis for the related details to find the malware.

In "Volatile Memory Based Forensic Artifacts & Analysis" [8], Dave et al. listed the different programs used in capturing RAM image according to OS type. For Windows OS, Belkasoft Live RAM Capturer, ManTech Memory DD, Mandiant Memoryze, WinPmem, and many others can be used. For Linux OS, LiME can be used. For UNIX OS, Mac Memory Reader and OSXPmem can be used. Then, they mentioned the artifacts that can be found from the memory image, such as login information, chats, registry details, ARP cache, network connections, system information, and many others. For analyzing memory parts, they preferred to use wxHexEditor rather than Autopsy or WinHex. They explained in a simple way how to use wxHexEditor to extract some information from a memory image, like username and password for a Gmail account, Facebook credentials, and chat conversations. In "A Review on Fileless Malware Analysis Techniques" [9], Khushali investigates the nature of fileless malware and how antivirus cannot find them. This is because they are written into the memory directly, instead of using a file on the hard drive. Then, she explained the life cycle of a fileless malware attack, which consists of the fileless delivery stage, the fileless persistence stage, and finally the malware execution stage. She moved after that to talk about the previous works in the same field. The most prominent paper she reviewed was "Survey on Malware Analysis Techniques: Static, Dynamic, Hybrid and Memory Analysis" by Sihwail, Omar, and Ariffin (2018). Their paper mentioned the methods of malware detection: the first is signature based, which uses hash files in malware to detect other similar malware, and the other is heuristics based, which analyzes the malware behavior or activities. Khushali also reviewed

"The Growth of Fileless Malware" by Alzuri, Andrade, Escobar, and
Zamora. Their paper talked about fileless malware growth over the years,
and how malware in 2016, 2017, and 2018 tended to be fileless rather than
file-based. Finally, she reviewed "An Approach to Detect Fileless Malware
and Defend Its Evasive Mechanisms" by Sanjay, Rakshith, Akash, and
Hegde. The paper sorted fileless malware categories into RAM resident
malware and script-based malware, which exploits Windows applications
and PowerShell. The last paper browsed malware evasion techniques,
which are malicious documents such as downloaded email attachment,
malicious scripts, malicious code in memory, and living off the land
malware. The last interacts with an installed application on the machine
to attack it, stealing some important information, and launching malicious
software.

Mobile Device Case Details and Experiment

The performed experiment is to investigate the volatile and the
nonvolatile memory of the mobile for potential malware or malicious
applications. The investigated devices are an iPhone 6s and a Redmi Note
8; their properties were mentioned before in the seized devices in case
details section. The PC device used to perform investigation is Lenovo
ThinkPad with

- Windows 10 Pro x64 OS.

- 8 GB RAM.

- AMD A8-7100 Radeon R5 processor, with eight compute cores
  4C + 4G and a frequency of 1.8 GHz.

The experiment has five main stages: mobile backup, logical
acquisition, jailbreaking/rooting, physical acquisition, and analyzing the

acquired device image. We start with backup to create a backup copy of
the mobile device, which includes the local data residing on the mobile
such as call logs, messages, third-party applications, and so on, in order to
avoid any data loss from it during experiment, especially when the device
is jailbroken or rooted. iPhone backup can be accomplished using many
software such as 3uTools, iTunes, and others. Backup files for the device
can be restored to it through previously mentioned backup software. One
of the important points to take into consideration is that backup process,
restore, or analysis cannot be accomplished without an iTunes password
and so it can be considered as a protected operation.

iOS Backup using 3uTools: The backup process can simply be
accomplished by plugging the device to the PC, then pressing the Back
Up Now button from the Backup/Restore section on 3uTools, and finally
submitting the iTunes password. See Figure 11-3.

Figure 11-3. *Backup using 3uTools*

Note   When the iPhone is plugged into the PC, the iPhone pops up
a message asking the user if they want to trust this PC, so the user
should trust to complete the process successfully. Backup using
iTunes is the same as 3uTools; the backup process can simply be
accomplished by plugging the device to the PC and then pressing the
Back Up Now button from the Backups section on iTunes as shown in
Figure 11-4.

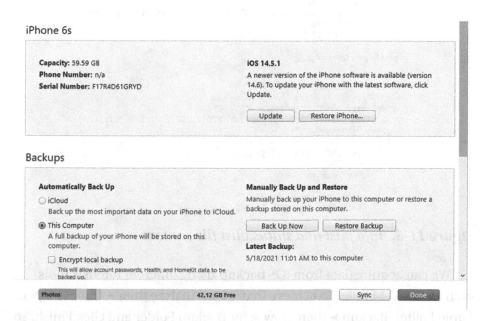

Figure 11-4. Back up using iTunes

The backup folders for both 3uTools and iTunes consist of many files
and folders. The most important file is manifest.db, which is the backup
file that contains backup data. Its content can be viewed using the DB
browser of the SQLite program. The info.plist can be considered from the
important files that contain general information about the iPhone such
as build version, serial number, and so on. See Figure 11-5. Manifest.plist

and status.plist are other important files that have backup operation details such as backup version, list of third-party applications, backup date, and many others.

Figure 11-5. *info.plist and status.plist file content*

We can acquire data from iOS backup using different forensic tools such as FINALMobile. To achieve that, go to Analyze then ➤ Choose Open Apple Folder/Backup ➤ then browse for Backup Folder and click Finish, so the analysis/acquisition from backup will start. See Figure 11-6. When the operation finishes, the iOS will be able to be investigated.

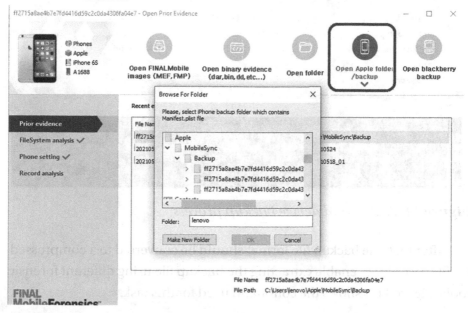

Figure 11-6. *Acquisition from iOS backup*

Android backup aims to create a backup copy of the Android
device that includes the local data residing on the mobile, such as call
logs, messages, third-party applications, and so on, in order to avoid
any data loss from it during experiment, especially when the device is
rooted. Android backup can be accomplished using many software such
as MOBILedit forensics, Android debug bridge (ADB) platform tool,
and others. Backup files for the device can be restored to it through the
previously mentioned backup software. The investigator can make sure of
the privileges that it has by the following: if the output is $, then the user
in normal mode, otherwise -output is #-, and the user has root privileges.
After showing the previous commands, the backup process will be
performed. The investigator can back up the Android device as described
in the previous chapter. When the backup process is finished, then the
backup file will be shown in the same ADB tool directory:platform-tools
directory with .ab extension, as shown in Figure 11-7.

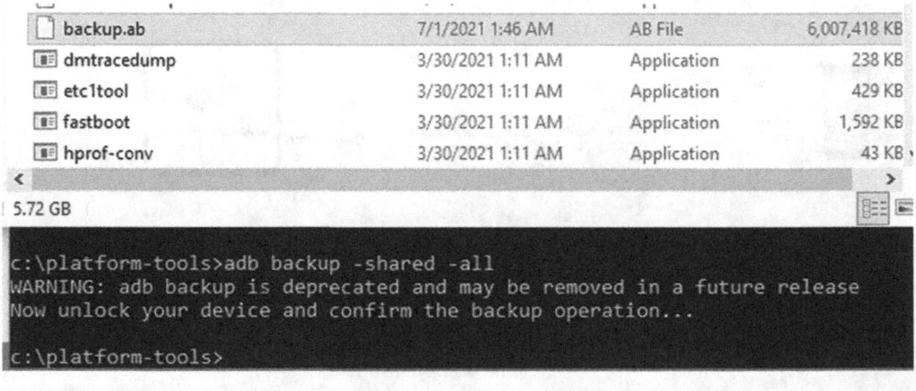

backup.ab	7/1/2021 1:46 AM	AB File	6,007,418 KB
dmtracedump	3/30/2021 1:11 AM	Application	238 KB
etc1tool	3/30/2021 1:11 AM	Application	429 KB
fastboot	3/30/2021 1:11 AM	Application	1,592 KB
hprof-conv	3/30/2021 1:11 AM	Application	43 KB

5.72 GB

```
c:\platform-tools>adb backup -shared -all
WARNING: adb backup is deprecated and may be removed in a future release
Now unlock your device and confirm the backup operation...

c:\platform-tools>
```

Figure 11-7. *Android device backup process*

After that, the backup file format should be converted to a compressed
tar file, in order to enable extracting the backup file using different forensic
tools. Figure 11-8 shows the command used for this task.

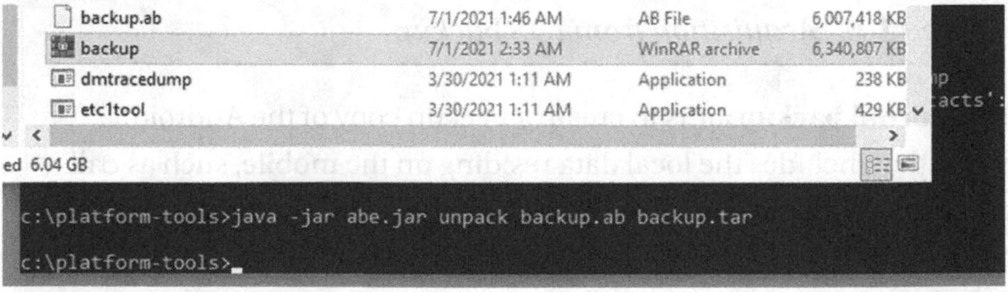

backup.ab	7/1/2021 1:46 AM	AB File	6,007,418 KB
backup	7/1/2021 2:33 AM	WinRAR archive	6,340,807 KB
dmtracedump	3/30/2021 1:11 AM	Application	238 KB
etc1tool	3/30/2021 1:11 AM	Application	429 KB

ed 6.04 GB

```
c:\platform-tools>java -jar abe.jar unpack backup.ab backup.tar

c:\platform-tools>
```

Figure 11-8. *Converting backup file format*

Now, the backup file can be investigated using the DB browser in
addition to extracting any desired file as a standalone file. See Figure 11-9.

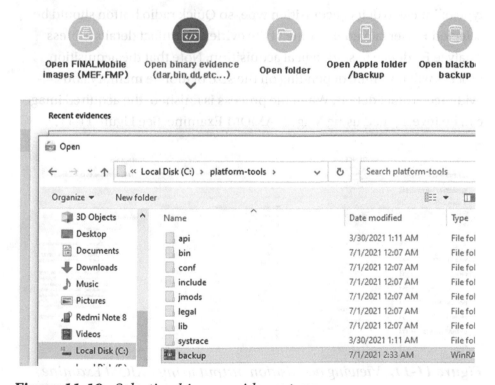

Name	Type	Schema
⌄ ▦ Tables (36)		
› ▦ ACTIVITY_EVENTS		CREATE TABLE ACTIVITY_EVENTS (Id INTEGER PRIMARY KEY AUTO
› ▦ ARTWORK_CACHE		CREATE TABLE ARTWORK_CACHE(RemoteLocation TEXT PRIMARY k
› ▦ CLOUD_QUEUE		CREATE TABLE CLOUD_QUEUE(Id INTEGER PRIMARY KEY, Version IN
› ▦ CLOUD_QUEUE_CONTAINERS		CREATE TABLE CLOUD_QUEUE_CONTAINERS(Id INTEGER PRIMARY I
› ▦ CLOUD_QUEUE_ITEMS		CREATE TABLE CLOUD_QUEUE_ITEMS(Id INTEGER PRIMARY KEY AU
› ▦ DB_PARAMS		CREATE TABLE DB_PARAMS(id INTEGER PRIMARY KEY AUTOINCREM
› ▦ INNERJAM_DISMISSALS		CREATE TABLE INNERJAM_DISMISSALS (Id INTEGER PRIMARY KEY A
› ▦ KEEPON		CREATE TABLE KEEPON(KeepOnId INTEGER PRIMARY KEY AUTOINCF

Figure 11-9. *Investigating backup file content*

Also, the backup for the Android device can be acquired using forensic
tools such as FINALMobile software. Binary evidence type should be
selected in order to recognize backup tar files. See Figure 11-9. After
analyzing the evidence process finished, the investigator can browse
backup file content easily. See Figure 11-10.

Figure 11-10. *Selecting binary evidence type*

Logical Acquisition

Logical acquisition is nearly the same as a backup operation. Moreover,
it retrieved some data related to diagnostic or crash logs, and some of the
shared apps data. Logical acquisition can be performed using commercial
programs like FINALMobile forensic, Magnet AXIOM forensic, and so on,
or by free tools like libimobiledevice software. After performing logical
acquisition, only some nonvolatile memory was retrieved, including the
installed applications. So physical acquisition is primarily needed.

iPhone logical acquisition using Magnet AXIOM process: at first, the
mobile device should be plugged into the PC using USB Cable ➤ choose
create now case ➤ choose case name and case details ➤ select the evidence
source: mobile-iOS ➤ then select acquire evidence, and so the program
will view the available devices that the software can detect ➤ choose the
type of image to detect acquisition type, so Quick radio button should be
selected ➤ user can adjust some of the evidence artifact details ➤ press
Analyze Evidence to start logical acquisition. Note that the acquisition
process will take time depending on the size of mobile memory and
evidence artifact details. When the process is finished, the acquired image
can be investigated using Magnet AXIOM Examine. See Figure 11-11.

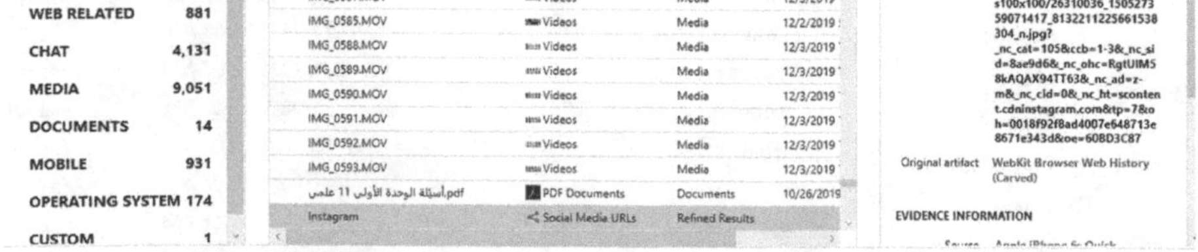

Figure 11-11. *Viewing acquisition output using AXIOM Examine*

Logical acquisition using FINALMobile Forensics is shown in
Figure 11-12: first the mobile device should be plugged into the PC using
USB cable ➤ choose Acquire ➤ smart device from select evidence target
➤ iOS from select platform ➤ then select mobile model from model list,
which is in this case A1688 iPhone S6 ➤ then select the device from the
connected devices list ➤ for logical acquisition select iTunes backup from
acquisition method ➤ then select user information and settings ➤ after
the program will pop up a window to specify iTunes backup parts to be
acquired, and finally the logical acquisition will start. When the process is
finished, the acquired image can be investigated to view different artifacts
by analyzing the image.

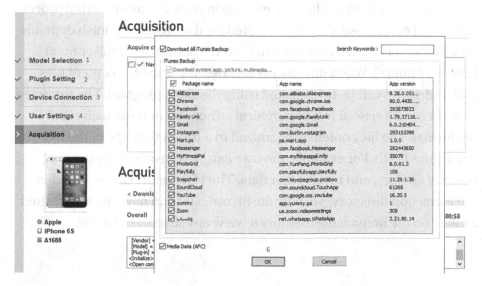

Figure 11-12. *Logical acquisition using FINALMobile acquisition*

If we compare the data retrieved by logical acquisition, that is,
acquisition from iOS device with acquisition from iOS backup using
FINALMobile we can conclude that the logical acquisition is more
detailed and has more artifacts and records than the iOS backup using

the same forensic tool. Compare data retrieved number of records in
Figures 11-14 and 10-15. Note that the iPhone is backed and logically
acquired in the same period, while keeping the device away from any
alteration.

Android logical acquisition using MOBILedit software will be used
and discussed next. At first, the investigator has to choose the content
that needs to be extracted. Specific selection means that the extraction
is limited to some field the investigator chose. On the other hand, full
content will create a full logical copy and complete backup of the Redmi
device, which can be used instead of rooting and physical acquisition
in some cases. The investigator can also make different formats of the
acquired content. After adjusting extraction settings, the acquiring process
will start. For our case, the time required for the process to finish depends
on whether it is for selected content (about 3 hours) or for full content
(about 24 hours). When the process finishes, the acquired content files
and directories can be investigated using the same program. The extracted
content can be viewed in a hierarchical structured manner using PDF
file format. The file content is organized in a tree at the right of the file.
See Figure 11-13. For example, the user can view installed application,
browser cookies, and much other data. The PDF report can be found in
the extraction directory. So, now the investigator can navigate any desired
artifact on the nonvolatile memory to view any suspect behavior.

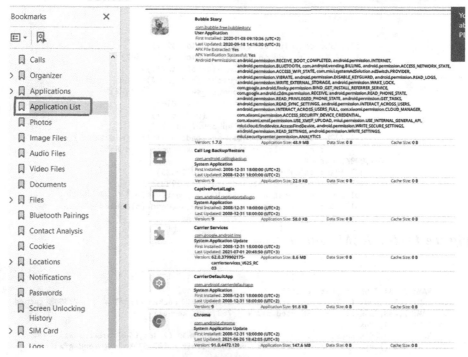

Figure 11-13. *Viewing applications list*

For volatile memory, all the information that relates to RAM such as
running processes and services exists on meminfo.txt. see Figure 11-14
and Figure 11-15.

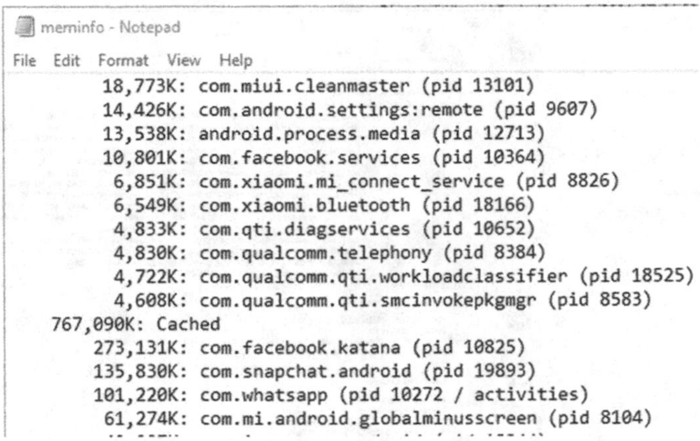

```
📄 meminfo - Notepad
File  Edit  Format  View  Help
        18,773K: com.miui.cleanmaster (pid 13101)
        14,426K: com.android.settings:remote (pid 9607)
        13,538K: android.process.media (pid 12713)
        10,801K: com.facebook.services (pid 10364)
         6,851K: com.xiaomi.mi_connect_service (pid 8826)
         6,549K: com.xiaomi.bluetooth (pid 18166)
         4,833K: com.qti.diagservices (pid 10652)
         4,830K: com.qualcomm.telephony (pid 8384)
         4,722K: com.qualcomm.qti.workloadclassifier (pid 18525)
         4,608K: com.qualcomm.qti.smcinvokepkgmgr (pid 8583)
       767,090K: Cached
       273,131K: com.facebook.katana (pid 10825)
       135,830K: com.snapchat.android (pid 19893)
       101,220K: com.whatsapp (pid 10272 / activities)
        61,274K: com.mi.android.globalminusscreen (pid 8104)
```

Figure 11-14. RAM content

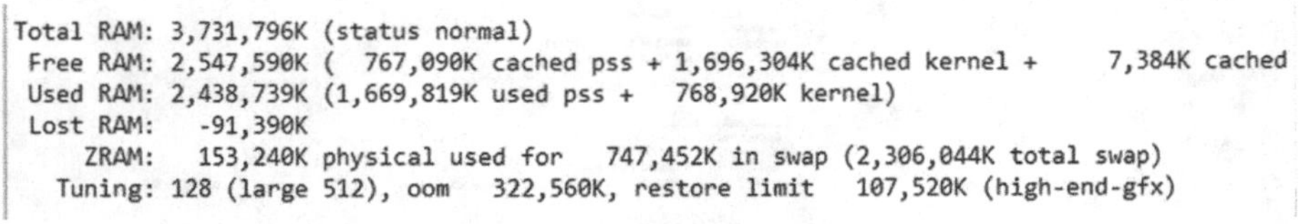

```
Total RAM: 3,731,796K (status normal)
 Free RAM: 2,547,590K (  767,090K cached pss + 1,696,304K cached kernel +     7,384K cached
 Used RAM: 2,438,739K (1,669,819K used pss +   768,920K kernel)
 Lost RAM:   -91,390K
    ZRAM:   153,240K physical used for   747,452K in swap (2,306,044K total swap)
  Tuning: 128 (large 512), oom   322,560K, restore limit   107,520K (high-end-gfx)
```

Figure 11-15. RAM details

iPhone Physical Acquisition

Jailbreaking is the first main prerequisite of the physical acquisition
process. When the device is jailbroken, the evidence mobile device will be
altered, which violates investigation rules, and as the device is rebooted
during jailbreaking, then the RAM content will be erased. However, as
mentioned before, fileless malware can re-execute itself in the infected
memory when the system reboots. The investigator can jailbreak the
iPhone using several methods like jailbreaking with Cydia and 3uTools;
in our case we tried jailbreaking using these tools but it failed, so we
recommend that investigators jailbreak using *Checkra1n* software; it's
the ideal way to jailbreak iOS devices as it's available for all iOS versions
including the newest versions.

Checkra1n is available as a Mac OS first option; we can connect iPhone
to Apple PC and start the analysis phase, but if you use Windows OS,
you can burn Checkra1n on a USB flash drive to make it a Linux-based
bootable drive. Then you can use Chechra1n even with independent
OS. In this practical case, the Rufus-3.13 tool is used to burn the latest
version of Checkra1n on a 32GB USB flash drive and make it bootable. See
Figure 11-16. After papering the USB drive, the iPhone should be plugged
into the PC, then restart the last, and then enter to boot settings and alter
it to boot from the USB drive. After booting, the Checkra1n software will
appear. See Figure 11-16. Then ➤ go to Options and check Allow untested
iOS versions, then follow the instructions to put the iPhone in DFU mode,
and click Start to complete the operation. Finally, the device is jailbroken.

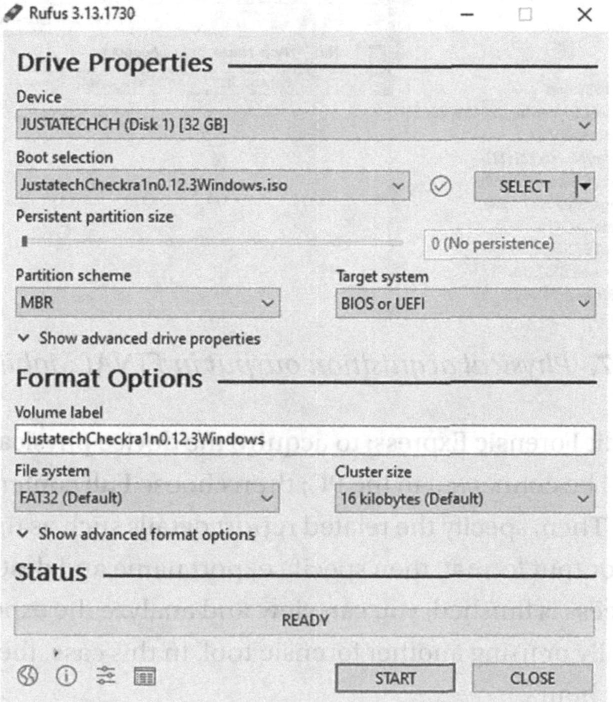

Figure 11-16. Configuring USB drive using Rufus

Magnet AXIOM: the instructions to achieve successful physical acquisition are the same as in the logical acquisition, except when choosing the type of image to detect acquisition type, so Full should be selected. Unfortunately, AXIOM failed to acquire the physical image of the iPhone. It took about 6 hours and no progress happened. So, the experiment is altered to use FINALMobile Forensics.

FINALMobile Forensics: the instructions to achieve successful physical acquisition are the same as in the logical acquisition, except when choosing the acquisition method, so iPhone-full file system-Chechraln should be selected. After the process is finished, you can view your evidence. See Figure 11-17.

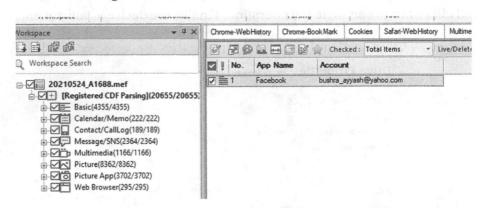

Figure 11-17.   *Physical acquisition output in FINALMobile Forensics*

MOBILedit Forensic Express: to acquire the device physically, the device should be connected to the PC; then choose Full content. See Figure 11-18. Then, specify the related report details such as time zone, then choose output format, then specify export name and destination. After the process is finished, you can view and analyze the exported files either manually or using another forensic tool. In this case, the process took about 13 hours.

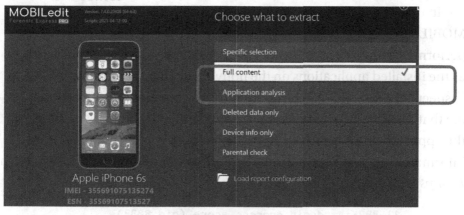

Figure 11-18. *Physical acquisition using MOBILedit software*

Android Physical Acquisition

As mentioned before, rooting is the main prerequisite for physical
extraction. As rooting on the Redmi Android device failed, another
rooted device was brought to extract it physically in order to highlight the
differences between logical and physical acquisition. Figure 11-19 shows
Ulefone properties, which shows that the device is rooted.

Manufacturer	**Ulefone**
Product	**Note 9P**
HW Revision	**QP1A.190711.020**
Platform	**Android**
SW Revision	**10 (29)**
Serial Number	**3092SH1001008091**
IMEI	**352079580160677**
IMEI 2	**352079580160685**
Rooted	**Yes**
SIM Card	**No**

Figure 11-19. *Rooted Ulefone Android device*

In this part of the experiment, the device is connected to the
MOBILedit tool on the workstation, and then a full content extraction is
performed. Now, the investigator can navigate any desired artifact such
as the installed applications on the nonvolatile memory to view any
suspect behavior. This can be done simply by opening the extraction PDF
file that MOBILedit generates and viewing artifact submenus such as
the application list. Figure 11-20 shows in detail volatile memory, RAM
information such as running process, and services found on *meminfo.txt* in
Dumpsys directory.

```
    11,897K: android.process.acore (pid 8033)
    10,539K: android.process.media (pid 7479)
     7,361K: com.android.providers.calendar (pid 7913)
  19,832K: B Services
    10,773K: com.google.android.ims (pid 6712)
     9,059K: com.android.systemmanager:service (pid 7538)
 400,929K: Cached
    96,347K: com.google.android.gms (pid 2081)
    50,316K: com.google.android.apps.youtube.music (pid 8073)
    36,890K: com.google.android.gms.unstable (pid 5340)
    34,738K: com.google.android.youtube (pid 6864)
    29,575K: com.google.android.apps.messaging (pid 6741)
    28,715K: com.google.android.apps.wellbeing (pid 7590)
    21,892K: com.topjohnwu.magisk (pid 7951)
```

```
Total RAM: 3,921,672K (status normal)
 Free RAM: 2,641,745K ( 400,929K cached pss + 2,207,360K cached kernel +    33,456K free)
 Used RAM: 1,482,924K (1,247,612K used pss +   235,312K kernel)
 Lost RAM:    53,692K
    ZRAM:   130,404K physical used for   476,512K in swap (2,156,420K total swap)
  Tuning: 256 (large 512), oom   483,840K, restore limit   161,280K (high-end-gfx)
```

Figure 11-20. *Details about running services on RAM and
RAM details*

As mentioned in Chapter 7, rooting is a prerequisite for physical
extraction. For learning and training purposes, the investigator can install
a virtual machine (VM) on the Android device in order to enable rooting
on this VM. ***Vmos*** is a VM application that runs on the Android devices;

after installing and configuring vmos, it can simply be rooted from the
VM settings, and then the root checker application is installed on vmos to
make sure of root privileges see Figure 11-21.

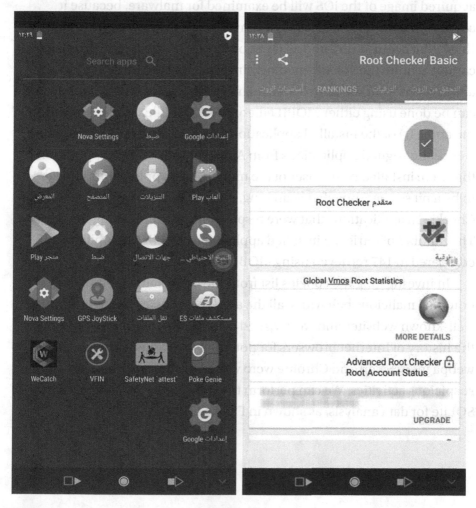

Figure 11-21. *vmos app and vmos settings*

iOS Analysis and Results

After the acquisition step using different programs, only the physical acquired image of the iOS will be examined for malware, because it consists of the whole artifacts that can be found on the mobile phone (bit-by-bit acquisition), and as mentioned before, the logical acquisition cannot acquire the volatile memory. Investigating the installed applications from the nonvolatile memory for potential malicious apps can be done using either MOBILedit or FINALMobile. After reviewing the apple ID of the installed applications, most of the applications found were either signed applications from Apple, or well-known applications that were installed by the user of the mobile. Two applications looked to be a bit strange, but after searching, it found that they were Cydia and Checkra1n applications that were responsible for jailbreaking the device. The number of retrieved installed applications by FINALMobile was 138 compared to 147 retrieved using MOBILedit.

In investigating the cookies list from the nonvolatile memory for potential malicious behaviors, all the available cookies found were for well-known websites and were visited by the user, and in investigating the history of Internet browsers for potential malicious activities, all the webpages in Safari and Chrome were visited by the user and there were no suspicious activities. We can perform the previous investigations using iOS SQLite for data analysis, as shown in Figure 11-22.

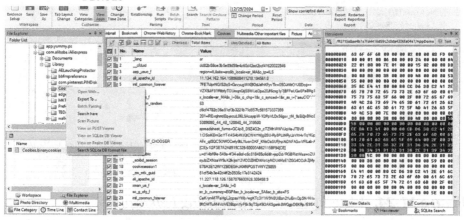

Figure 11-22. *Using iOS SQLite*

It is important to investigate the iOS RAM content from the volatile
memory, as RAM content may contain valuable data that is related to
malware residing on it. For FINALMobile software, it did not retrieve any
data related to RAM, neither in the content viewer, nor in file explorer. For
MOBILedit, it retrieved two files related to the volatile memory. One was
related to device RAM and the other was for Checkra1n application. See
Figure 11-23; the investigator is concerned with the device RAM content.

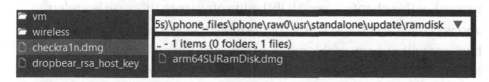

Figure 11-23. *Checkra1n volatile file and mobile RAM file*

To view arm64SURamDisk.dmg, Belkasoft evidence center is used.
After showing its content, it can be recognized that it has only 24 thumbnail
pictures that are related to the mobile system as shown in Figure 11-24. This
is because the iPhone is jailbroken and then physically acquired, and it is
known that the mobile device is rebooted during the jailbreaking process.
It is clear that the mobile device has no residing malware in the RAM.

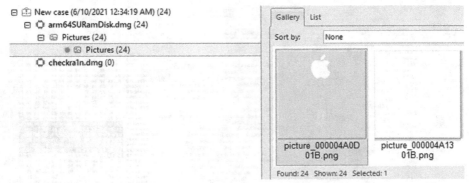

Figure 11-24. *Viewing RAM content using Belkasoft*

Evaluating Extraction Tools and Methods for Android and iOS Devices

For the iOS forensic tools, there is no ideal software for all mobile cases. According to tool properties, features, and capabilities in acquisition and analysis, and according to the existing case and the desired artifacts to be extracted, the investigator should select the forensic tool. Moreover, some cases may need more than one tool to be used in a combined manner as in this case. Table 11-1 summarizes the tools used in this case with their usage. For this chapter case, MOBILedit software in this case is preferred and was the ideal. It was able to perform all types of acquisitions and backups without any problems. In addition to the nonvolatile artifacts, MOBILedit retrieved the artifacts that related to the volatile memory, in contrast to FINALMobile, which did not; also, the number of records and data retrieved were more for the physical acquisition in MOBILedit as shown before. Physical extraction and jailbreaking are needed here to retrieve the volatile artifacts that the logical extraction did not.

Table 11-1. Forensic Tools Usage in This Case

Tool	Acquisition Type	Retrieved artifacts
iTunes, 3uTools	iOS backup	Nonvolatile artifacts such as photos, messages, call history, etc.
FINALMobile Forensics	Logical/physical acquisition	For the two acquisitions modes, nonvolatile artifacts such as photos, messages, call history, etc., in addition to the deleted contents for the physical acquisition. Nonvolatile memory is retrieved.
Elcomsoft toolkit	Logical/physical acquisition/installed agent acquisition	The operation fails for all acquisition types— no data is retrieved.
Belkasoft evidence center	Logical/physical acquisition	The operation fails for all acquisition types— no data is retrieved. Belkasoft is used only to show RAM file content acquired using MOBILedit.
MOBILedit Forensics	Logical/physical acquisition	For the two acquisitions modes, nonvolatile artifacts such as photos, messages, call history, etc., in addition to the deleted contents and volatile memory content—RAM—for the physical acquisition.
Magnet AXIOM	Logical/physical acquisition	Nonvolatile artifacts such as photos, messages, call history, etc. The physical acquisition failed.

For Android analysis and after performing several acquisitions using different extraction types and programs, the results will be discussed, and the extraction techniques will be evaluated. Either logical or physical acquisition can be used because they retrieved the same type of evidence.

Investigating the installed applications from the nonvolatile memory for potential malicious apps will be done using the MOBILedit tool. After reviewing the installed and existing applications, most of the applications found were either signed applications from Android or well-known applications that were installed by the user of the mobile. Logical and physical extraction using MOBILedit retrieved the list of applications. However, adb backup files extracted by the FINALMobile tool couldn't be retrieved. In investigating the cookies list and web search history from the nonvolatile memory for potential malicious behaviors and activities, all the available cookies found were for well-known websites and were visited by the user. In investigating Android RAM content from the volatile memory, the RAM content may contain valuable data that related to malware residing on it, according to an investigation of Android device processes along with their ID, running process, running services, caches, and other valuable information. After reviewing the *meminfo.txt* that exists on the destination *phone_files\phone\applications1\Dumpsys*, no suspicious data or services were founded.

Evaluating Android Extraction Techniques for Volatile and Nonvolatile Memory

If we compared the data retrieved by logical acquisition (acquisition from Redmi device) using MOBILedit with acquisition from Android backup (backup done by adb) using FINALMobile, we can conclude that the logical acquisition is more detailed and has more artifacts and records than acquisition from Android backup (e.g., adb backup does not view applications list). Also, MOBILedit is more user-friendly in viewing and presenting artifacts as shown previously in the PDF backup file. Note that the Android device is backed up and logically acquired in the same period, keeping the device away from any alteration.

It is clear that manual extraction was useless for this case, due to inability to view RAM content and some nonvolatile memory aspects. Also, for this case, related to volatile and nonvolatile memory, no difference was found between logical and physical acquisition using MOBILedit in extracting the desired data that is related to RAM and applications data.

Rooting an Android device in this case is not necessary (i.e., we can use logical rather than physical extraction). Rooting mostly alters the evidence, which violates forensics rules, voids the manufacturer warranty, and makes the device susceptible to various exploits or threats. The method used for bypassing screen lock—Android Device Manager—can be considered as an inefficient method, because it erases the device data, and so there is no data to investigate, and it also alters the evidence, which violates forensics rules.

As for the forensic tools, there is no ideal software for all mobile cases. According to tool properties, features, and capabilities in acquisition and analysis, and according to the existing case and the desired artifacts to be extracted, the investigator should select the forensic tool. Moreover, some cases may need more than one tool to be used in a combined manner as in this case. MOBILedit software in this case was preferred and was the ideal. It was able to perform all types of acquisitions and backups without any problems. In addition to the nonvolatile artifacts, it retrieved the artifacts related to volatile memory, in contrast to FINALMobile, which did not. Also, it presented the acquired artifacts efficiently.

In the Android device, we see no need to recommend either rooting or physical extraction. Logical gives all related artifacts for volatile and nonvolatile. In the iOS device, jailbreaking and physical extraction are needed. Logical cannot extract the volatile memory RAM.

Summary

From this point and after investigating this case, we can conclude that
sometimes we need to investigate and analyze the volatile or nonvolatile
data residing in the mobile memory for some purposes, such as detecting
malware. So, memory analysis or memory forensics for mobile devices
can serve to achieve the desired need. In this project, memory analysis
is performed among several stages and different tools. At the end of the
experiment and until this point of investigation, no malware was found.

There are several approaches used by different investigators in
analyzing mobile memory to detect malware, such as static memory
analysis, dynamic memory analysis, hybrid memory analysis, and
automated systems for detecting mobile malware. This work depends on
different forensic tools to perform backup process, and logical and physical
acquisition, in order to handle malware analysis processes in the volatile
and nonvolatile memory. After finishing the experiment, it was clear
that in an Android device there is no need for either rooting or physical
extraction. Logical gives all related artifacts for volatile and nonvolatile.
On the other hand, in the case of the iOS device, jailbreaking and physical
extraction were needed, as logical could not extract volatile memory.

References

[1].   tutorialsweb.com, "Cellular Phones: Memory and
        Battery Life of Mobile Phones," [Online]. Available:
        `https://www.tutorialsweb.com/Cellular/cell-`
        `phones-2.htm`. [Accessed 25 May 2021].

[2].   Rami Sihwail, Khairuddin Omar, and Khairul Akram
        Zainol Ariffin, "A Survey on Malware Analysis
        Techniques: Static, Dynamic, Hybrid and Memory
        Analysis," *International Journal on Advanced Science*

Engineering and Information Technology, vol. 8,
no. 4-2, p. 1662, 2018.

[3].   Christiaan Beek, Sandeep Chandana, Taylor
       Dunton, Steve Grobman,Rajiv Gupta, Tracy Holden,
       Tim Hux, Kevin McGrath, Douglas McKee, Lee
       Munson, Kaushik Narayan, Joy Olowo, Chanung
       Pak, Chris Palm, Tim Polzer, Sang Ryol Ryu, Raj
       Samani, and Sekhar Sarukkai, "McAfee Labs Threats
       Report," McAfee, San Jose, 2020.

[4].   N. Lord, "What Are Memory Forensics? A Definition
       of Memory Forensics," 2020. [Online]. Available:
       `https://digitalguardian.com/blog/what-are-`
       `memory-forensics-definition-memory-forensics.`
       [Accessed 24 November 2020].

[5].   T. Redscan-team, "Memory Forensics: How to
       Detect and Analyse Memory-Resident Malware,"
       2018. [Online]. Available: `https://www.redscan.`
       `com/news/memory-forensics-how-to-detect-and-`
       `analyse-memory-resident-malware/`. [Accessed 20
       December 2020].

[6].   Z. Yixiang and Z. Kang, "Review of iOS Malware
       Analysis," *IEEE Second International Conference on
       Data Science in Cyberspace,* pp. 63-72, 2016.

[7].   R. Carbone, "Malware Memory Analysis for Non-
       specialists: Investigating a Publicly Available
       Memory Image of the Zeus Trojan Horse," *Defence
       R&D Canada,* 2013.

403

[8].   R, Dave, N. R. Mistry, and M. S. Dahiya, "Volatile
       Memory Based Forensic Artifacts & Analysis,"
       *International Journal for Research in Applied
       Science and Engineering Technology,* vol. 2, no. 1,
       pp. 120-124., 2014.

[9].   V. Khushali, "A Review on Fileless Malware
       Analysis Techniques," *International Journal of
       Engineering Research & Technology,* vol. 9, no. 05,
       pp. 2278-0181, 2020.

[10]. www.theiphonewiki.com, "Jailbreak," [Online].
       Available: https://www.theiphonewiki.com/wiki/
       Jailbreak. [Accessed 20 May 2021].

[11]. O. Afonin and V. Katalov, *Mobile Forensics –
       Advanced Investigative Strategies*, Birmingham:
       Packt Publishing Ltd., 2016.

[12]. R. Tamma, O. Skulkin, H. Mahalik and
       S. Bommisetty, *Practical Mobile Forensics*,
       Birmingham: Packt Publishing Ltd., 2020.

[13]. M. Parahar, "Difference between Volatile Memory
       and Non-Volatile Memory," 2019. [Online].
       Available: https://www.tutorialspoint.com/
       difference-between-volatile-memory-and-non-
       volatile-memory. [Accessed 10 December 2020].

[14]. Lithmee, "Difference Between Volatile and Nonvolatile
       Memory," 2018. [Online]. Available: https://
       pediaa.com/difference-between-volatile-and-
       nonvolatile-memory/. [Accessed 12 December 2020].

[15]. R. Carbone, "Malware Memory Analysis for Non-
       specialists: Investigating Publicly Available Memory
       Images for Prolaco and SpyEye," *Defence R&D
       Canada,* 2013.

[16]. R. Carbone, "Malware Memory Analysis for Non-
       specialists: Investigating Publicly Available Memory
       Image 0zapftis (R2D2)," *Defence R&D Canada,* 2013.

[17]. Vera, "3 Solutions to BSvcProcessor Has Stopped
       Working Error [MiniTool News]," 2020. [Online].
       Available: `https://www.minitool.com/news/`
       `bsvcprocessor-has-stopped-working.html`.
       [Accessed 21 December 2020].

[18]. Jake, "Remove BSvcProcessor.exe: Complete
       Removal Steps," [Online]. Available: `https://www.`
       `exefilesupport.com/remove-bsvcprocessor-`
       `exe-complete-removal-steps`. [Accessed 23
       December 2020].

[19]. file.net, "Bsvcprocessor.exe," [Online]. Available:
       `https://www.file.net/process/bsvcprocessor.`
       `exe.html`. [Accessed 23 December 2020].

[20]. Autopsy-User-Documentation, "Volatility Data Source
       Processor," [Online]. Available: `http://sleuthkit.`
       `org/autopsy/docs/user-docs/4.17.0/volatility_`
       `dsp_page.html`. [Accessed 16 December 2020].

[21]. Speed-Guide, "Port 443 Details," [Online]. Available:
       `https://www.speedguide.net/port.php?port=443`.
       [Accessed 24 December 2020].

[22].   AbuseIPDB, "AbuseIPDB," [Online]. Available:
       https://www.abuseipdb.com/. [Accessed 11 December 2020].

[23].   L. Abu Arram and M. Moreb, "Cyber Security In
       Mobile Apps And User CIA," 2021 International
       Conference on Information Technology (ICIT), 2021,
       pp. 7–12, doi: 10.1109/ICIT52682.2021.9491657.

CHAPTER 12

Mobile Forensic for KeyLogger Artifact

This chapter investigates mobile forensic investigation for the KeyLogger application installed on iOS or Android; it introduces and helps the investigator to discover traces of a spy application case, determine which tools were used to investigate and search for various spy programs, and shows how to report results obtained from the iPhone spy program, which was installed and used for espionage and access to sensitive data.

In this chapter, we will cover the following topics:

- Introduction to Mobile KeyLogger

- Methodology and Case Study Setup

- Mobile Malware and Spyware

- Evidence Recovered during the Examination

- Evidence Recovered Using Magnet ACQUIRE

- Examination and Analysis KeyLogger Result

- Summary

© Mohammed Moreb 2022
M. Moreb, *Practical Forensic Analysis of Artifacts on iOS and Android Devices*,
https://doi.org/10.1007/978-1-4842-8026-3_12

Introduction to Mobile KeyLogger

Currently, applications of technology and communication, including smartphones, are incredibly developed. We chose implementation for a mobile forensic investigation on Android smartphones and iOS smartphones because of their widespread use and user base. Android is the market leader over iOS.

Malware, short for malicious software, is a term that covers viruses, worms, trojans, and other malicious computer programs used by hackers to cause havoc and gain access to sensitive data [1]. Keyloggers are hardware or software tools that record characters and numbers typed on a keyboard and sent to a computer. Keylogging programs, also known as keyloggers, are a type of malware that tracks user input from the keyboard to steal personal and confidential information [11]; methods for detecting mobile malware act as countermeasures to emerging malware [5] as illustrated in Figure 12-1.

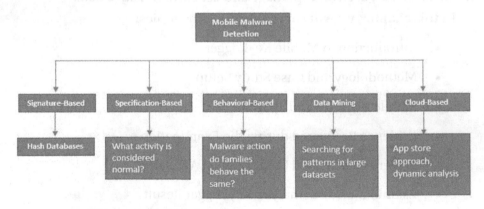

Figure 12-1. *Mobile malware detection classification*

Seizure Phase

For the practical case study in this chapter, we will assume the following details for the reporting agency. The governorate oversees the implementation of laws, regulations, instructions, and orders issued by the President of the National Authority or the Council of Ministers. It is responsible for public security, order and morals, public health, and the protection of public freedoms and the rights of citizens. The governor has the powers of the Minister for the administrative staff of the department. The functions and powers of the director of the governor's office are very sensitive, as the director is responsible for all the activities of the governor and has all the working papers of the governor's office. Therefore, there are many attempts to break into the governor's office cell phone to use sensitive information related to the work of the governor and the governor's office.

The director of the governor's office was on a mission outside the governorate, and was interrupted by Israeli occupation soldiers in a checkpoint and had everything confiscated, including the work cell phone. The director was released after an hour and got everything back. Based on this incident, the director reported the incident to the governor. In that report, the director stated a suspicion of spyware on the cell phone because data usage was unusually high; the phone showed signs of activity in standby mode and performed unexpected reboots, and battery life was deteriorating.

Based on the country's cybercrime law, such as No. 10 from the year 2018 and Article No. 32, the governor issued an administrative decree based on the powers under the applicable laws and presidential decrees, especially Decree No. 22 for the year 2003 on the powers of the governor, and Decrees No. 77 and No. 2021 dated April 20 2021 giving powers to the IT Department, cell phone data was extracted from MI Note 8 Pro Android mobile by the director of the governor's office and analyzed for suspected spying applications. Figure 12-2 shows the details of the device seized for examination including serial number, make, and model.

The mobile was seized by a committee consisting of the governorate's Human Resources, Legal, and Security Departments and handed over by the committee to the Department of Computer and Information Systems to conduct the needed forensics.

Figure 12-2. Device information

Android Acquisition Phase

The forensic workstation image was *re-ghosted* to a computer, and all appropriate security and reliability patches were applied. The workstation used was an Asus I7, 6th generation, containing Windows 10 pro, Belkasoft evidence center 2020, and Microsoft Defender Antivirus. All products were updated remotely via removable media and therefore had never been connected to the Internet; thus they can be judged to be forensically and operationally sound in that they will represent accurately all data they process and display. The image of the computer has been retained for future use and reference should it be required. In this section, we describe the details of the forensic equipment and tools used in the examination related to Android devices as follows:

- **Android Debug Bridge**: adb command-line tool introduced in the previous chapter. We use it in this case for connecting the Android device with the workstation using the command line.

- **APK Analyzer:** After the development process is complete, Android Studio features an APK Analyzer that offers quick insight into the composition of your APK. The APK Analyzer may help you save time troubleshooting issues with DEX files and resources in your app, as well as minimize the size of your APK. It may also be run from the command line using APK Analyzer [3].

- **jadx GUI decompiles an APK**: The Apache 2.0 License governs the use of this program, which is open to the public to decompile an APK. To use jadx with a graphical user interface, run the jadx-gui. bat file (included in the jadx-folder/bin folder) as an administrator. First, you'll get a box where you may select the APK file to decompile [8] See Figure 12-3.

- **FINALMobile**: Used in previous cases, it's a strong software and mobile solution for legal inspectors that gives the most advanced data mining and information extraction capabilities to the legal community. This software can convert raw data into executable and ready files with just a few clicks thanks to its comprehensive knowledge of system files and

411

information patterns. Information on mobile devices is stored in specific formats, and in many circumstances, this information is not totally wiped. For our case, this software may quickly recover deleted (hidden) files, and also it is easy to recover information for future mobile devices because most mobile devices follow the same pattern. The software can evaluate the data by scanning each sector if the file system experiences an error during retrieval. With this software, you can also categorize your data in a variety of ways and export it as Excel or PDF reports [6].

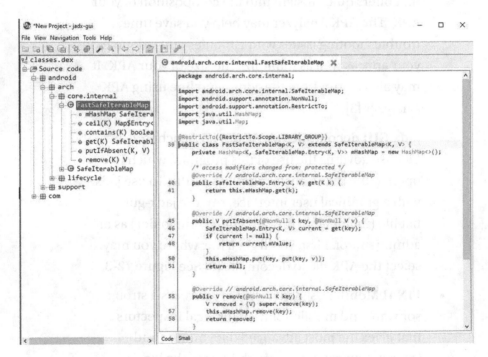

Figure 12-3. Decompile an APK or DEX file using jadx in Windows

- **Magnet AXIOM**: AXIOM gets to the most relevant information quickly because it is built on the idea that artifacts-first forensics is the most efficient way to search and analyze data. Browser history, email, conversations, photographs, location data, videos, documents, and social networks are just a few of the artifacts that are instantly accessible for immediate study. Use Dynamic App Finder to locate relevant artifact data from apps that aren't currently supported, such as chats [10].

Manual Backup via Android Debug Bridge

All details described in Chapter 3 and subsequent chapters are the main steps we use in the current phase of our project. You must enable USB debugging in the device system settings, under Developer options, to use adb with a device connected through USB. The Developer options screen is disabled by default on Android 4.2 and above. Go to Settings ➤ About phone and press Build number seven times to make it visible. Return to the previous screen and scroll down to Developer options.

(a). Navigate to the Settings section menu.

(b). Tap System at the bottom of the page.

(c). Choose "About phone".

(d). Enables Developer options.

Tap the device's Build number seven times until Developer options are enabled.

(e).   Select Developer settings from the System menu by pressing the back button.

(f).   Toggle Developer options on. Toggle on USB debugging by scrolling down, as shown in Figure 12-4.

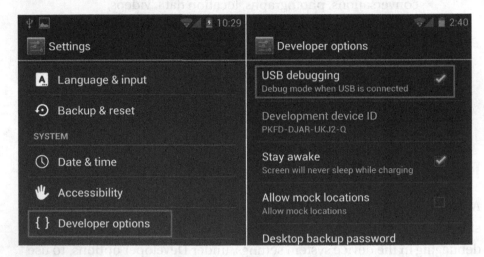

Figure 12-4. *USB debug setting*

The use of ADB is as described previously in many cases. The following are the main steps:

(a).   Download the Android SDK Platform Tools ZIP file.

(b).   The contents of this ZIP file should be extracted to a convenient location such as *C:\platform-tools*.

(c).   Go to the location where the contents of this ZIP file were extracted using Windows Explorer.

(d).   Start a command prompt from the same directory as the ADB binary. Right-click within the folder while holding Shift, then select "Open command window here" from the menu. (Some Windows 10 users may see "PowerShell" rather than "command window.")

(e).   Use a USB cord to connect your phone to your computer. Set the USB mode to "file transfer (MTP)". Some OEMs may or may not need it, but for general compatibility, it's better to just keep it in this state.

(f).   To start the ADB daemon, use the following command in the Command Prompt window: adb devices.

(g).   A popup screen will appear on the phone's screen to accept or refuse USB Debugging access. Naturally, when requested, you should grant USB Debugging access (and tap the always allow check box if you never want to see that prompt again).

(h).   Re-enter the command from step (f) at the end. If everything went well, we should now be able to view the serial number of your device at the command prompt (or the PowerShell window).

(i).   ADB pull data extraction: Logical data extraction operates on a wide range of devices and is simple to use. On a nonrooted device, certain data can be extracted, but root access will unlock the device and give you access to all of the files on it. Using one or more of the previous data, the Android application saves data on the device in one of the following locations:

- Shared preferences: This uses a lightweight XML format to store data in key/value pairs. The shared-pref folder in the application's /data directory is where shared preference files are kept.

- Internal storage: This is where private data is stored in the device's internal memory. Other apps cannot access files stored to the internal storage since they are private.

- External storage: This puts public data on the device's external memory, which often lacks security measures. This information may be found in the /sdcard directory.

- SQLite database: This information may be found in the database */data/data/PackageName/. The.db* file extension is most commonly used.

(j). For ADB backup extraction, the command used for full backup is the following:
`adb backup -shared –all`

- When the command is run, authorizing permission on the device must be acceptable. Then to start a backup, the device's screen must be unlocked. By default, an Android backup file is saved as *.ab* file in the Android SDK's *platform-tools* subdirectory.

- The .ab file is converted to a .tar file, which can then be converted by using Android Backup Extractor [12]. Because this is a Java-based utility, Java must be installed on the workstation before using it, to convert the backup file to .tar file, using the command line `java -jar abe.jar unpack backup.ab backup.tar`, as shown in Figure 12-5.

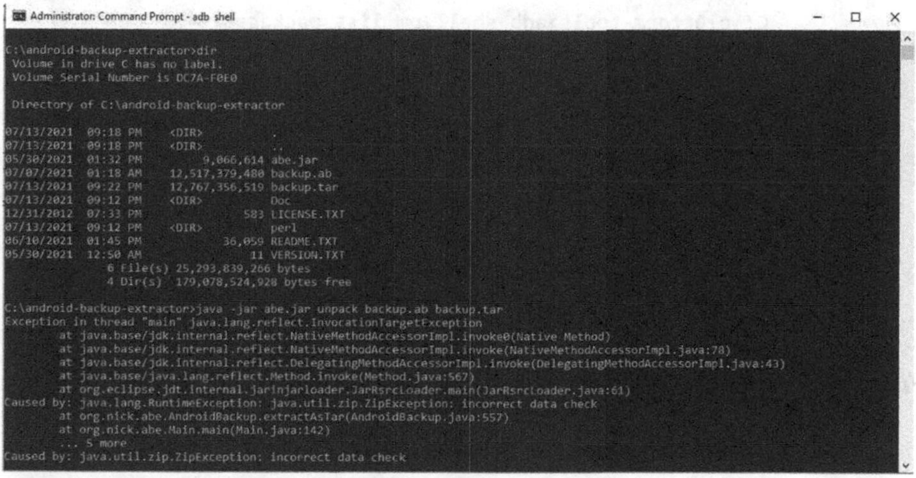

Figure 12-5. *Convert the backup file to .tar file*

Then you can use any archive programs such as WinRAR or 7Zip can read .tar files. By default, the backup file includes two main directories in the archive file, and the ***apps*** folder includes all of the information for the apps included in the backup that is found under */data/data* and shared folder, which includes all data stored on the SD card.

Reverse Engineering for Extracting an APK File

1. We need to access the device's APK files (for nonrooted devices) by identifying the package name of the app command `adb.exe shell pm list packages` as shown in Figure 12-6.

```
C:\platform-tools>adb shell pm list packages
package:com.lge.theme.superbatterysaving
package:com.hy.system.fontserver
package:com.android.LGSetupWizard
package:com.android.cts.priv.ctsshim
package:com.google.android.youtube
package:com.google.android.ext.services
package:com.lge.sizechangable.weather.platform
package:com.android.providers.telephony
package:com.google.android.googlequicksearchbox
package:com.android.providers.calendar
package:com.android.providers.media
package:com.google.android.apps.docs.editors.docs
```

Figure 12-6. *The steps for extracting an APK file*

2. By giving the following command, you can
    determine the complete pathname of the APK file
    for the requested package (Figure 12-7).

```
C:\platform-tools>adb shell pm path  /sdcard/Android/data/com.akxlom.firo
```

Figure 12-7. *Determine the complete pathname of the APK file*

3. Using the APK file from the Android device, transfer
    it to the forensic workstation (Figure 12-8).

```
C:\platform-tools>adb shell pm path   com.akxlom.firo
package:/data/app/com.akxlom.firo-rsOkrCoDP0CD911zYPP__A==/base.apk

C:\platform-tools>adb pull /data/app/com.akxlom.firo-rsOkrCoDP0CD911zYPP__A==/base.apk c:\temp
/data/app/com.akxlom.firo-rsOkrCoDP0CD911zYPP__A==/base.apk:... file pulled, 0 skipped. 12.8 MB/s (2892568 bytes in 0.216s)

C:\platform-tools>
```

Figure 12-8. *Pull the APK file*

4. After obtaining the APK file, start the reverse
    engineering for the Android apps.

    (a). Rename the *APK* extension (base.apk) to *ZIP* (base.zip).

    (b). Extract base.zip file (Figure 12-9).

418

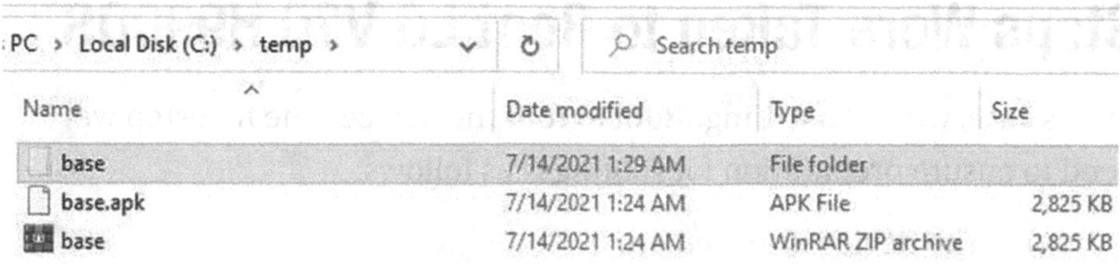

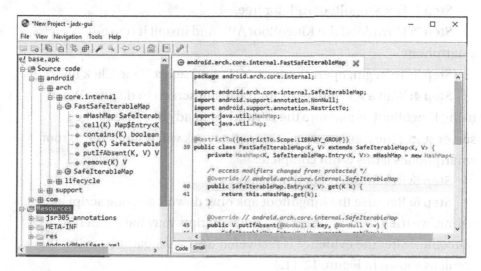

Figure 12-9. *Rename the APK extension and extract APK*

(c). Using the dex2jar tool to convert *classes.dex* into a Java
class file using command line d2jdex2jar.bat classes.
dex dex2jar classes.dex -> classesdex2jar.jar, a new
class, *dex2jar.jar*, is created in the same directory.

(d). Open the JAR file using jadx-GUI to examine the code, and
examine how the app saves data, permissions, and malware
(Figure 12-10).

Figure 12-10. *Open JAR file using jadx-GUI to examine the code*

Steps Were Taken to Root LG V20 H990DS

In this case, we will use KingoRoot to root the device. The first step we need to ensure preparation for rooting is as follows:

(a).   The device is turned on.

(b).   The battery level must be at least 50%.

(c).   Use of the Internet is required (Wi-Fi network suggested).

(d).   Allow applications to be installed from unknown sources.

Unknown Sources (Settings ➤ Security ➤ Unknown Sources)

Steps for Rooting Android using the KingoRoot APK

Step 1: Get KingoRoot APK for free.

Step 2: Download the KingoRoot APK and install it on your smartphone.

Step 3: To begin, open "Kingo ROOT" and select "One Click Root".

Step 4: Wait a few moments for the result screen to display. When using KingoRoot, make sure the network is steady because Kingo's server stores the rooting scripts. KingoRoot apk will not be able to root smartphones if this is not complete.

Step 5: Result: succeeded or failed.

Step 6: Because the KingoRoot apk only downloads one script at a time, we tried it multiple times. Various scripts may have different outcomes; after the evidence is recovered the investigator can view the result as shown in Figure 12-11.

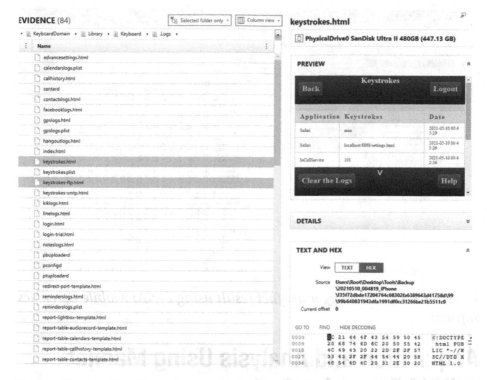

Figure 12-11. *Evidence recovered using Magnet forensic software*

Acquisition and Analysis Using FINALMobile Forensics Software

Step 1: Connect the Android smartphone (LG V20) PC using a USB cable to start the acquisition phase using FINALMobile Forensics software.

Step 2: Open FINALMobile Forensics software to acquire the Android smartphone (LG V20).

Step 3: Start acquisition phase using FINALMobile software.

Step 4: Start the analysis phase using FINALMobile software.

Step 5: Results and artifacts found from the analysis phase are as shown in Figure 12-12.

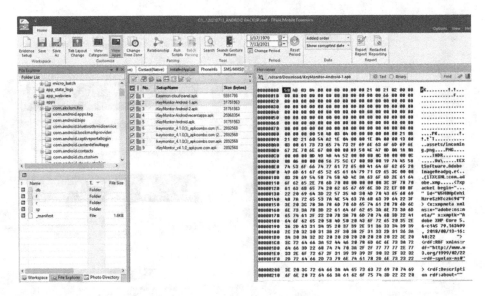

Figure 12-12. *KeyLogger artifact result using FINALMobile Forensics software*

Acquisition and Analysis Using Magnet AXIOM Forensics Software

Step 1: Connect the Android smartphone (LG V20) PC using a USB cable to start the acquisition phase using software forensic (FINALMobile).

Step 2: Open Magnet ACQUIRE (AXIOM Process) Forensics software to acquire the smartphone (LG V20) device and create a new case.

Step 3: Select an evidence source.

Step 4: Acquire evidence.

Step 5: Start analyzing; then the result and findings will be displayed for the user as shown in Figure 12-13.

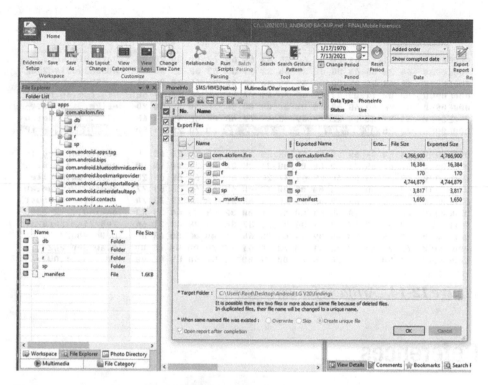

Figure 12-13. *Details of findings or issues identified using FINALMobile Forensics software*

Results and Conclusions

At this point, after the digital forensic investigation, results were obtained from the analysis using various types of digital forensic analysis software; based on the results, it was determined that there was a spy program installed on the Android smartphone (LG V20). Based on these findings, it was recommended that the mobile phone should not be given to anyone to keep private and sensitive data from being lost or exploited by anyone.

For evidence recovered during the examination, searching for patterns and signatures using FINALMobile and ACQUIRE Forensics software was done by the investigator in order to find artifacts for keylogger in the file system application named com.akxlom.firo as shown in Figure 12-14.

423

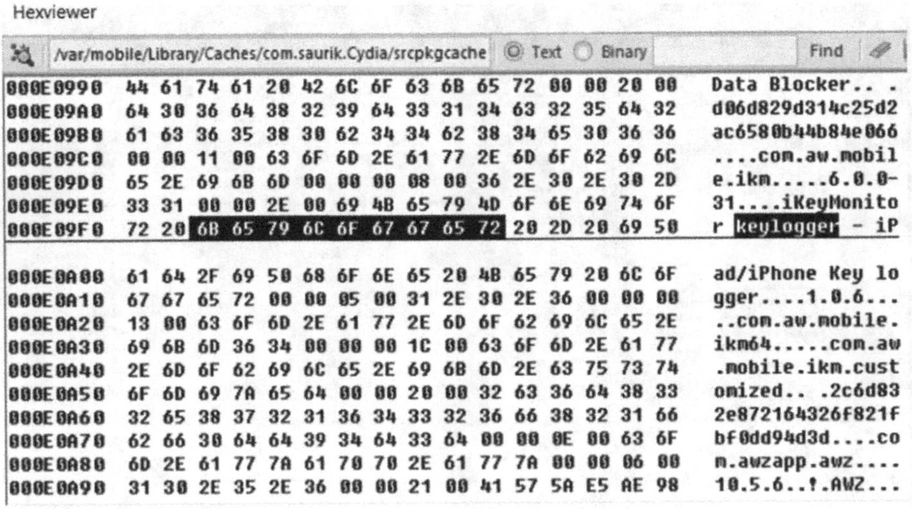

Figure 12-14. *Artifacts for keylogger*

References

[1].   CSO. *Malware Explained*. 2019. URL: https://
        www.csoonline.com/ article/3295877/what-is-
        malware-viruses-worms-trojans-andbeyond.html.

[2].   Kevin Curran et al. "Mobile Phone Forensic
        Analysis". *International Journal of Digital Crime and
        Forensics* 2.3 (2010), pp. 15–27. ISSN: 19416229. DOI:
        https://doi.org/10.4018/jdcf.2010070102.

[3].   Developer.android.com. *Android Debug
        Bridge (adb)*. 2021. URL: https://developer.
        android.com/studio/command-line/
        adb?gclid=CjwKCAjw_o-HBhAsEiwANqYhp_1p_
        NOVXmZolalK2OOr5uXe3KmzLkqUgDLn5myBt7otj
        kUISiROxoC4nMQAvD_BwE&gclsrc=aw.ds (visited
        on 2021).

[4]. Dotnettricks. Understanding Xamarin Android - Build Native Android App. 2021. URL: https:// www.dotnettricks.com/learn/xamarin/ understandingxamarin-android-build-native- android-app.

[5]. Sarah Edwards et al. "The Most Relevant Evidence per Gigabyte". In: Walidumar.my.id. 2022. [online] Available at: https://walidumar.my.id/buku. elektronik/Forensic/BukuElektronik/DFIR%20 Smartphone%20Forensic.pdf [Accessed 26 March 2022].

[6]. Finaldata. *FINALMobile Forensics*. 2021. URL: https://finaldata.com/mobile/.

[7]. Github.com. *dex2jar*. 2021. URL: https://github. com/pxb1988/dex2jar.

[8]. Github.com. *jadx to Decompile an APK GUI*. 2021. URL: https://github.com/skylot/jadx/releases.

[9]. D. Hamdi et al. "Multimedia File Signature Analysis for Smartphone Forensics". In: *Proceedings - 2016 9th International Conference on Developments in eSystems Engineering, DeSE 2016* (2017), pp. 130–137. DOI: https://doi.org/10.1109/DeSE.2016.22.

[10]. Magnetforensics.com. *Magnet AXIOM*. 2021. URL: https://www.magnetforensics.com/products/ magnet-axiom/.

[11]. Priyanka Sahu and Preeti Tuli. "System Monitoring and Security Using Keylogger". In: *IJCSMC* 2.3 (2013), pp. 106–111. URL: `http://d.researchbib.com/f/8nq3q3YzydL3AgLl5wo2OiMT9wpl9jLKOypaZiGJSlL2tlZQRmY1LlFGZlZQRmZwVhpTEz.pdf`.

[12]. Sourceforge.net. *Android Backup Extractor*. 2021. URL: `https://sourceforge.net/projects/adbextractor/`.

[13]. Statcounter. *Mobile Operating System Market Share Worldwide*. 2021. URL: `https://gs.statcounter.com/os-market-share/mobile/worldwide`.

CHAPTER 13

Evidence Identification Methods for Android and iOS Mobile Devices with Facebook Messenger

Facebook Messenger (FBM) is widely used by most mobile users. FBM is used for normal communication in addition to its involvement in criminal cases. Following a scientific mobile forensic analysis approach keeps the evidence admissible. This study follows the NIST mobile forensic process to retrieve data from FBM. The study provides several techniques for device identification, data acquisition, and analysis of FBM data from both Android and iOS devices. Several tools were used for acquisition including Libimobiledevice, iTunes, Belkasoft, AXIOM, and ADB. Additionally, several tools were used for data analysis including AXIOM Examine,

© Mohammed Moreb 2022
M. Moreb, *Practical Forensic Analysis of Artifacts on iOS and Android Devices*,
https://doi.org/10.1007/978-1-4842-8026-3_13

Belkasoft, and DB viewer for SQLite. This study shows that the appropriate
forensic tool for FBM analysis is AXIOM; based on the results of analyzing
encrypted iTunes images for iOS, Belkasoft was better in performance for
analyzing ADB images for Android, while FBM data extraction requires the
device to be rooted.

In this chapter, we will cover the following topics:

- Introduction to FBM Application

- Introduction to Mobile Messenger Application

- Experiment Tools

- Evidence and Scene Security

- Evidence Isolation

- Data Acquisition

- FBM Data Analysis Using Magnet AXIOM Examine

- FBM Data Analysis Using Belkasoft

- FBM Data Analysis Using DB Browser for SQLite

- Recovering Deleted Evidence from SQLite
  Property Lists

- Summary

Introduction to FBM Application

Internet access has dramatically increased during the last two decades;
more than 60% of the global population can access the Internet these
days. Among those who can access the Internet, 92.6% did so via mobile
devices [1]. The availability of Internet services over mobile operators'
networks and services like 5G, 4G, and 3G were essential factors in the
increased Internet access via mobile devices. With the huge growth of

Internet access via mobile devices, messaging had been evolved from only text exchange, which was the main feature of mobile messaging, into voice and video communications, with the ability to exchange pictures and files. This introduced instant messaging as a chatting platform offering real-time text messaging over the Internet, and messaging evolution created an opportunity for competition between several social network platforms to provide smooth and fast messaging apps. The most popular mobile messaging platform is Facebook. As shown in Figure 13-1, the most popular messaging mobile application is WhatsApp followed by FBM; Facebook owns both WhatsApp and FBM.

Facebook has become an important part of all of our lives and has a greater impact on life than other social networking sites, due to its multiple use by all ages and because it brings together a huge number of people. In many cases, the conversation has come to take place on the FBM application. Since it is one of the most effective applications due to its many advantages, it has also had a clear impact on the increase in the rate of electronic crimes.

People spend most of their time on the smartphone; the phone has become an integral part of every person's life, regardless of age or use, and for this reason, cybercrimes of all kinds have increased, including blackmail, impersonation, and spreading lies and rumors, as the smartphone has an effective and clear effect on the social, political, security, international, and economic aspects of life. Smartphones have had a clear role in many countries' coups against their governmental systems, and this is also a reason for the use of social media sites. The average time spent daily by social media platform users has increased in recent years, reaching a total of above 1 hour in 2021.

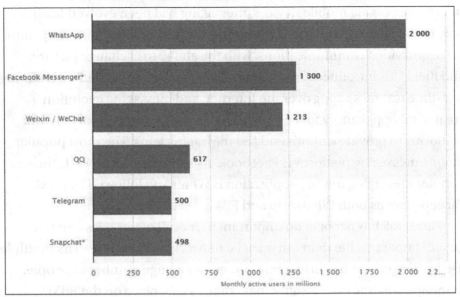

Figure 13-1. *Most popular mobile messenger apps - January 2021-monthly active users [2]*

The use of messaging apps is not limited to normal good usage only; these apps can be used by criminals to contact each other or to perform crimes. FBM is one of the apps that can be used by criminals in digital crimes. The application can be used to plan for several types of crimes such as drug dealing, theft, murder, or terrorism, or to carry out direct crimes through the app such as extortion, harassment, fraud, or others. Using FBM will keep traces that can be used to help investigators in court. The trace or evidence cannot be accepted at court unless it is retrieved based on a specific procedure. Therefore, forensics analysis will be based on mobile forensics principles, which is a branch of digital forensics science.

FBM is a leading social media messaging platform, and it is expected to become more popular with its development and new features. It will be able to chat directly with other messaging platforms; now it involves a lot of customizations and services including money transfer. For this, it

430

is expected to be involved more in crime investigations. For iOS devices, FBM works from the top application layer, through the media layer, to some components in the core services layer. The growing number of artifacts for FBM is related to its continuous development by Facebook.

In this chapter, Android and iOS forensic examination techniques are presented and introduced with mobile operating systems architecture. What is needed to prepare for data extraction from Android and iOS devices is discussed. Data extraction techniques are presented with their different approaches. Data analysis of FBM is presented with details.

Introduction to Mobile Messenger Application

The identification of digital evidence for the FBM app [3] was performed on retrieving evidence from an Android device using Magnet AXIOM and Oxygen Forensics tools. The researchers were able to view the device details and recover the evidence in both tools. They used indexed calculation numbers to get the performance of each forensic tool. Based on NIST method parameters, they found that the AXIOM result is 75% whereas Oxygen got 79%. The researchers used only an Android device. They did not use iOS devices for comparison. Additionally, they used only AXIOM and Oxygen as forensic tools.

In performing mobile forensics on Android-based IMO messenger services using the Digital Forensic Research Workshop (DFRWS) Method [4], researchers followed a three-phase methodology that involves identification, preservation, and collection. They compared data extraction from rooted and unrooted devices with IMO apps installed: MOBILedit, DB Browser for SQLite, FTK Imager, and Belkasoft are used as forensic tools. The result can retrieve all IMO data from the rooted device, but nothing was retrieved from the unrooted one. An experiment was conducted [7] to analyze LINE Messenger on virtual Android machines.

The researchers used a VMware workstation with BlueStacks and LINE Messenger installed on the machines. To extract the data, they suspended the virtual machine and acquired the files related to volatile memory and nonvolatile memory using WinHex, EnCase, and Root Explorer for analyzing the database. Researchers were able to identify the related artifacts and data locations in LINE Messenger.

Instagram forensic [8] analysis was performed on Android virtual devices using Genymotion, DB Browser for SQLite, Android Studio Device File Explorer, and Sqliteparser. The researchers were able to identify and access datastores of the application on /data/data; there was no mention of whether the user device was rooted or not. Similar research was conducted to forensically analyze the TikTok app [9] on Android; researchers separated the identified artifacts into two categories. The first category is accessible without the need of having root privileges within the smartphones, and the secunde category include artifacts are only available within a rooted device.

This practical case methodology is guided by NIST's special publication of guidelines on mobile devices forensics [18] utilizing the mobile forensics process to recover the evidence in forensically sound conditions. As depicted in Figure 13-2 (and as seen in Chapter 9 and Chapter 10), the process has four stages, and each stage has its rules to keep the evidence admissible. The main purpose is to protect the evidence from changes during the process.

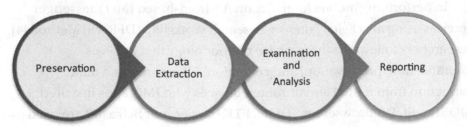

Figure 13-2. *Four stages for Mobile forensics process*

In the next section, we follow the four stages of seizing the device and taking care of its related digital evidence in secure conditions to prevent changes on the data or manipulation of the evidence. Then comes acquisition (i.e., getting evidential information from the device or its related media), and then the examination and analysis stage to search for and reveal hidden or deleted evidence by working on an identical copy of the acquired image in the first phase using different toolkits during the investigation. The last phase we describe in detail is the reporting stage, which depends on the precise records of information taken during the previous stages; all the information and the conclusions made based on the results of the investigation are presented in the report, which is made to the court or the legal parties according to well-understood procedures.

Experiment Tools and Devices

For the experiment in this case study, the following tools and devices were selected: one iOS device, one Android device, and four forensic tools. The following subsections present the details of the devices and tools. The following devices will be used in this experiment as shown in Table 13-1.

Table 13-1. *Experiment Devices*

Device	OS	Model Name	Model Number
Apple iPhone	iOS 14.6	iPhone 6s	A1688
Huawei Mobile	Android	Y3 2017	CRO-U00
HP Laptop	Windows 10	ProBook 640 G1	

The following forensic toolkits will be used in this experiment as shown in Table 13-2.

Table 13-2. *Experiment Forensic Tools*

Tool Name	Version	Note
iTunes	12.11.3.17	Apple app for Windows
Libimobiledevice	18/05/2020	Windows compiled
Belkasoft Evidence Center	9.9	For Windows
Magnet AXIOM Process	4.6	For Windows
Magnet AXIOM Examine	4.6	For Windows
DB Browser for SQLite	3.12.2	For Windows
ABD Android toolkit	1.0.41	For Windows

iOS Device Identification

Device Identification Using Libimobiledevice

Using Libimobiledevice forensic tools, we can show device information and characteristics by connecting to the workstation. This tool is used to identify the device in this experiment. In this case, you can follow these steps to get device identification:

[1]. Using the command idevice_id to learn the UDID of the device, which will help in identifying the device-related iTunes backup. idevice_id.exe -l *Output*: 53e291a4587a7e9572dd729f02c534ca4772c53f

[2]. Using the command ideviceinfo shows a huge number of forensically useful identifications for the device. This includes information other forensic tools cannot show: ideviceinfo.exe

Device Identification Using Belkasoft Evidence Center

Forensic tools can show device information before acquisition to choose which device to image. In Belkasoft, when adding a data source to the case, selecting the device brand will show the connected device info as shown in Figure 13-3. In some cases, if investigators need more details related to iOS such as hardware internal identification details, we recommend using the *Libimobiledevice* tool as described previously.

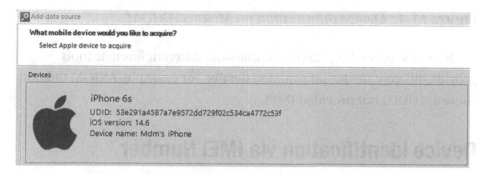

Figure 13-3. Device information in Belkasoft Evidence Center

Device Identification Using Magnet AXIOM

The same can be applied to Magnet AXIOM when adding evidence sources on the AXIOM Process as shown in Figure 13-4.

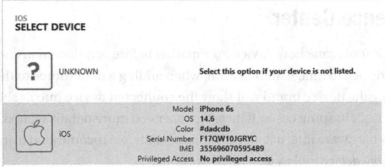

Figure 13-4. Device information on Magnet AXIOM

From the preceding simple comparison, different forensic tools
provide different device information details. For example, AXIOM did not
show the UDID but provided IMEI.

Device Identification via IMEI Number

The International Mobile Equipment Identifier or IMEI number is 15 or 16
digits containing device information. The information includes the device
serial number, the origin of the device, and the model number. The IMEI
number can be found inside the device under the battery; additionally,
it can be retrieved by dialing *#06# if the device is on. Using IMEI can
provide all manufacturer information through several websites. For this
case, we use www.imei.info to show the device specifications using its
IMEI as in Figure 13-5. Basic device information is shown in the table
provided on the website. Additionally, more detailed information can be
provided if you click the More Details button.

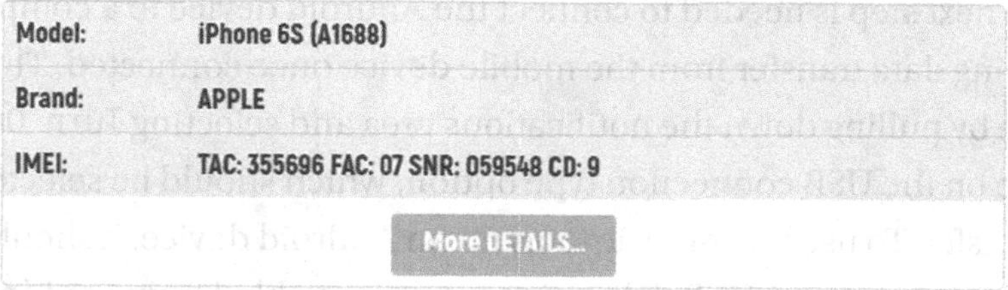

Model:	iPhone 6S (A1688)
Brand:	APPLE
IMEI:	TAC: 355696 FAC: 07 SNR: 059548 CD: 9

More DETAILS...

Figure 13-5. *Device type by IMEI*

Android Device Connection Setup

The device identification process for Android devices is very important for
forensic data acquisition. Manufacturer, model, and Android version all
determine the needed tools. Manufacturers can be known from looking at
the labels on the device mostly on the back of the device. From the Menu
➤ Settings ➤ About phone, the device model number can be identified
in addition to several useful pieces of information, including the Kernel
version. Additionally, the build number is located here, which is important
to enable the developer mode. There are tools to help in identifying the
device after connecting it to a digital forensic lab computer. The used
device in this case study is Huawei Y3 (2017) with Android version 6.0 and
kernel version 3.18.19.

To connect the device to a computer, a data cable is needed. The
required cable type can vary based on the device model. It can be a mini-
USB, micro-USB, or USB type C. Other types may appear in rare cases
like coaxial or D subminiature cables. For a successful connection to a
computer, the device drivers should be installed on that computer. On
Windows' new operating system, this process is done automatically by the
OS. In some cases, drivers must be downloaded from the manufacturer's
site and installed manually on the computer.

The next step is needed to connect the Android device to a computer. It is enabling data transfer from the mobile device once connected. This can be done by pulling down the notifications area and selecting Turn On USB storage on the USB connection type option, which should be selected as data transfer. To use the forensic tools on an Android device, it should be in USB debugging mode. USB debugging mode is enabled from Settings ➤ About phone by tapping several times continuously on the build number. A counter will start counting down until developer options are enabled. Now from Settings ➤ developer options, enable USB debugging. In some cases, the device should be checked for device administration settings. This will be enabled if a mobile device management application is installed on the device. Applications like Family link may disable accessing the device with USB debugging mode even if it is enabled on the device but disabled from the Family link.

Using Automated Tools

You can use any tools that used in previous chapters, such as Chapter 3's practical case to bypass the password or unlock Android devices. You can use free tools that utilize ADB and fastboot to automate the unlock processes such as *HalabTech* (halabtech.com), which is supported by a variety of digital forensic solutions and customized tools. Most of the commercial tools require the device to be in USB debugging mode. UFED user lock code recovery is one of the professional tools that require special connection cables as shown in Figure 13-6.

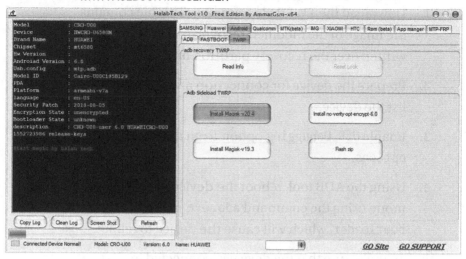

Figure 13-6. *Unlock Android device with HalabTech*

Gaining Root Access

From a forensic point of view, rooting Android devices is needed to access applications' data and to get more data when acquiring the rooted device. Rooting, as described in detail in Chapter 7, is granting access with the highest privileges on the OS level to perform actions and access partitions that are not allowed for normal users. Rooting makes unrecoverable changes to the evidence. It grants privileges that put the device at risk of vulnerabilities, malicious apps, and user misuse. For these reasons, rooting voids the warranty of the device, taking into consideration the risk of damaging the device during the process.

In this practical case, we need to get access to the FBM data partition in data that is protected by the OS and is not accessible in the unrooted mode. There is a forensic need to root the device to access FBM data. The following steps should be applied to the device in this case study, which is with Huawei Y3 [20].

1. Download the TWRP file from [20]. This file contains the image of the modified recovery partition to be written over the recovery partition on the device.

2. Prepare the device for connection and use ADB to list the device.

3. Enable USB Debugging option from the developer options.

4. Using the ADB tool, reboot the device in fastboot mode using the command adb.exe reboot bootloader, which will cause the device to reboot.

5. To make sure that the device is connected in fastboot mode, use the command fastboot.exe devices, which should show the device in the list.

6. Extract the recovery.img from the downloaded *TWRP* inside the ADB folder.

7. Write the image to the device using the command: fastboot flash recovery recovery.img. The result as shown in Figure 13-7 is to write on the recovery partition in the targeted device.

```
C:\WINDOWS\system32>cd c:/adb

c:\ADB>fastboot devices
6c750140              fastboot

c:\ADB>fastboot flash recovery recovery.img
target reported max download size of 536870912 bytes
sending 'recovery' (50140 KB)...
OKAY [  1.172s]
writing 'recovery'...
OKAY [  0.449s]
finished. total time: 1.621s

c:\ADB>fastboot reboot
rebooting...
```

Figure 13-7. *Writing recovery image*

8.   Download SuperSu file, paste the file to an SDcard,
power off the device, and then put it in the device.

9.   Power on the device in recovery mode by holding
volume up + power button.

10.   Choose backup data and then choose Install.

11.   Swipe the slide at the bottom of the screen.

12.   Reboot the device from the menu.

13.   Verify root by installing the app Root Checker.

Android Data Extraction Techniques

The preceding techniques will be discussed based on this case study
in investigating FBM data. The following subsections discuss the three
extraction techniques.

Manual Data Extraction

This technique involves accessing the device as a normal user and
browsing the data directly with documentation of each step with
screenshots. The disadvantage of this technique includes limited data
access and evidence changes. Limited data access is due to using the
interface as a normal user and seeing what is accessible to the regular user.
Evidence changes happen when opening unread messages or triggering
any action that may result in data loss. Based on the investigation case, this
may be the fastest data extraction technique with minimal preparation.
Even so, this method should not be considered unless it is an urgent life or
death case or for data verification for the other techniques.

In our case study, since the device is unlocked, we were able to open
the Messenger app and browse the conversations directly.

Logical Data Extraction

This technique, which involves using forensic acquisition tools to extract data and the file system from the device, works on most devices. The amount of data retrieved depends on the access level on the device. This means limited data will be retrieved for unrooted devices.

Several forensic applications support this technique: data can be acquired from an unrooted device by using Axiom, Belkasoft, and ADB command line. They all depend on using ADB backup. Normal user and system data can be retrieved but FBM data is located in /data, which is not accessible without root permission. The analysis and data extraction process may take a long time depending on the device specification as shown in Figure 13-8.

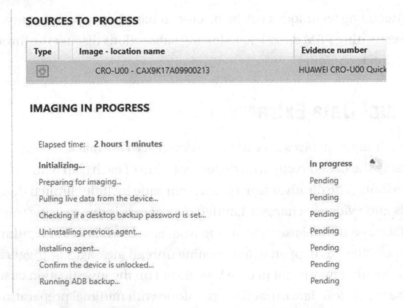

Figure 13-8. *Logical data extraction using AXIOM*

After finishing the logical ADB acquisition, we can browse the system and apps files, as shown in Figure 13-9.

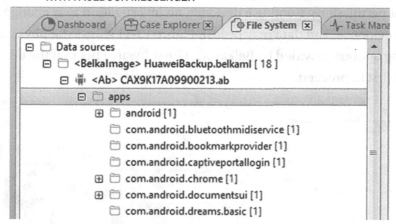

Figure 13-9. *File system browsing using Belkasoft*

Direct ADB data extraction is not allowed on the /data partitions, as it requires root access as shown in Figure 13-10; from that, we conclude that FBM data is not accessible without rooting the Android device.

```
shell@HWCRO-U6580M:/ $ cd data
shell@HWCRO-U6580M:/data $ ls
opendir failed, Permission denied
255|shell@HWCRO-U6580M:/data $
```

Figure 13-10. *ADB - data access denied*

Physical Data Extraction

This technique involves obtaining the exact binary image of the device's memory or external storage. This is done bit by bit for the entire memory. This technique is different from logical data extraction. With physical imaging, deleted files can be recovered in some cases. Additionally, hidden file leftovers can be retrieved from the slack space or unallocated space.

Most forensic software and imaging tools use the ADB command to perform the physical imaging process. This command requires a rooted device. Unrooted devices will not accept the ADB command due to the need

443

for root permissions. Rooting a device in an investigation may change data for the evidence, and data may be lost. Figure 13-11 shows the physical imaging options provided by Belkasoft. The software checks if the device is rooted first to proceed.

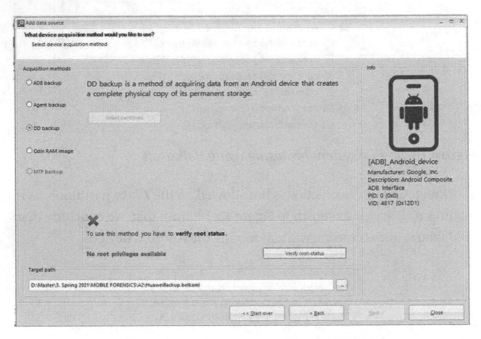

Figure 13-11. *Physical data extraction using Belkasoft*

For our case, the technique can be applied from the ADB tool using the following steps:

1. Connect the device to the computer and check the device connection using the command `adb devices` and make sure the device is listed.

2. Use a new empty SD card to store the image on it. It should be of an appropriate size and clean of data. The SD card should be attached to the device.

3. Use the mount command to list the partitions inside
    /div that contain the Android file system.

4. Execute the dd command to the partitions of
    interest. For the /data partition, it is located under
    /dev/block/<block number>. In front of the block
    number will be /data at the beginning of the
    comment. In the command, the input file is the
    targeted block, and the output file is the SD card
    partition as in the following:

```
dd if=/dev/block/<block number> of=/sdcard/imagename.img
```

To write the output image to the forensic computer, use the netcat
command. This is the method used by most forensic tools.

Practical Logical Data Extraction for iOS Devices

This experiment performs logical acquisition using iTunes backup, the
Libimobiledevice tool, Belkasoft Evidence Center, and Magnet AXIOM
Process.

Logical Data Extraction Using iTunes

iTunes backup is a type of logical acquisition for iOS devices. It is accessed
simply from the mobile summary tab on iTunes. After connecting the
mobile to iTunes, select *This Computer* from the Backups section and
make sure to select *Encrypted local backup*. Encrypted iTunes backups
include more artifacts. Click the *Back Up Now* button to start the process
as shown in Figure 13-12.

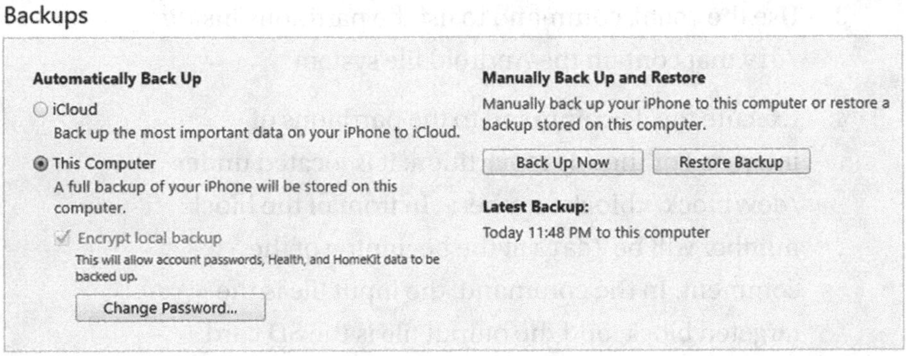

Backups

Figure 13-12. *iTunes backup*

In Our current case, the location of the iTunes backed-up image will be at `C:\Users\<User name>\Apple\MobileSync\Backup`. The Backup folder contains a folder named with the UDID of the iOS device. Each backed-up device will have its own UDID backup folder.

Logical Data Extraction Using Libimobiledevice Library

Two steps are required: enabling the encrypted backup option, and taking the logical image. We use the following command: `idevicebackup2.exe backup encryption on <Backup_Password>`.

After getting confirmation of enabling encryption, the following command is used to take the backup: `idevicebackup2 backup -full <Image_Path>`. The backed-up image will be ready in the destination image path, with the UDID folder name.

Logical Acquisition Using Belkasoft

After creating a new case, add a data source and select the Apple device.
Select the connected iOS device with its details shown. Select iTunes
backup and browse the path location to store the image as shown in
Figure 13-13.

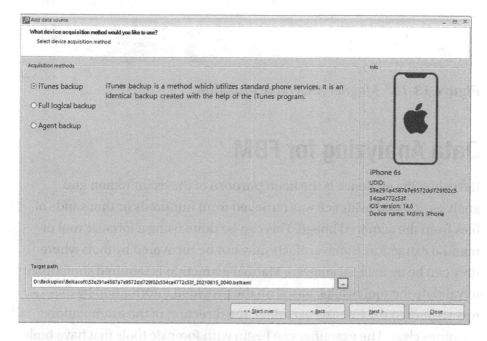

Figure 13-13. *Logical acquisition using Belkasoft*

Logical Acquisition Using Magnet AXIOM Process

After creating a new case, select *Mobile* from the *Evidence Sources* tab, then
iOS, and select Acquire evidence. Select the connected device as shown in
Figure 13-14 and click Next. Select the type of image; for this case *Quick* is
selected, whereas *Full* requires a jailbroken device.

447

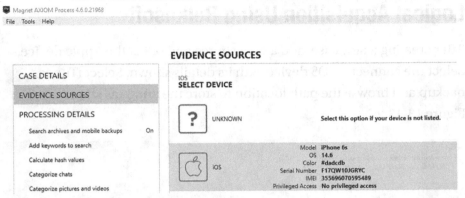

Figure 13-14. *Magnet AXIOM acquisition*

Data Analyzing for FBM

Revealing the evidence is the main purpose of the examination and
analysis. Related evidence was retrieved from hundreds or thousands of
files from the acquired image. This can be done using a forensic tool or
manual extraction. Some artifacts may not be recovered by tools where
they can be by manual analysis. Manual extraction is required sometimes
to validate the tool results. Based on the provided information by the
investigator to the forensic examiner, the direction of the examination
becomes clear. The examiner can begin with forensic tools that have built-
in filters related to the required application, and then prepare the files list
and databases to analyze.

FBM Data Analysis for Android

Apps data are stored in the /data partition, with each app being treated
as a user with permissions to its partition inside the /data partition.
Analyzing the db files in the subfolders of FBM will result in exploring
the related data; filenames indicate the contents of the db file. db files do

not have an extension but they can be opened normally in the SQLite
browser. The structure of the data is in BSON format with a key/value
pair. Additionally, a JSON file is found that contains the logged-in user
information. The main partition of FBM data can be found in /data/
data/com.facebook.orca/. Pictures can be found in /media/pictures/
messages/. Even though most FBM forensic investigations deal with the
messages in threads_db2 and contacts in contacts_db2, here is a list in
Table 13-3, of other sources of information in FBM [22], [23].

Table 13-3. *FBM Source of Information in Android*

Internal Path	File Name	File Type
/app_light_prefs/	logged_in_<User_ID>	JSON
/cache/audio/	*	Various
/cache/fb_temp/	*	Various
/cache/image/	*	Various
/databases/	call_logs_db	SQLite
/databases/	contacts_db2	SQLite
/databases/	omnistore_<User_ID>_v01.db	SQLite
/databases/	prefs_db	SQLite
/databases/	threads_db2	SQLite
/databases/	tican_db_<User_ID>	SQLite
/files/image/	*	JPG
/files/ExoPlayerCacheDir/	*	Various
/shared_prefs/	com.facebook.orca_preferences.xml	XML

FBM Data Analysis Using Magnet AXIOM for iOS

We examine the acquired image for iTunes. After selecting the image folder
(backup previously), the backup encryption password will be required.
After providing the password, click "CHECK" and then "OKAY" as shown
in Figure 13-15.

Figure 13-15. *AXIOM backup encryption password request*

After the evidence source is added to the case, click "Go to processing
details". In this section, the analysis can be tuned and categorized into
several techniques. Click "Go to artifact details"; from this section, artifacts
can be filtered based on category and application. This is an important
examination feature to comply with case requirements and keep the
evidence extraction process admissible in court. From this section, we
clear the selection from all categories, search for the FBM app, and select
it. The last step is clicking "Analyze" in the Analyze Evidence section. The
decryption process starts, and AXIOM Examine is launched. The artifact
analysis duration was 28 seconds, and the decryption process took 52
seconds for our case.

On AXIOM Examine, selecting the chat category shows all FBM
messages. Edit the time zone settings to modify the time parsing.
Figure 13-16 shows the results of the analysis.

Figure 13-16. *AXIOM Examine FBM analysis results*

By copying the provided URL for each message and opening it in a
browser, we retrieved all pictures, emojis, audio, and video messages
successfully, and all deleted messages are located as "unsent messages".
For our case, we used Belkasoft for data analysis and recovered FBM data
but the results show that we couldn't retrieve data related to our case. For
that, we recommend verification data using SQLite analysis.

FBM Data Analysis Using DB Browser for SQLite

Most mobile internal and third-party applications utilize SQLite databases
in their structure. Based on this, knowing the database location of the
required app will provide access capability to data stored in its tables.
For this FBM analysis case, DB Browser for SQLite was used. FBM
message artifacts are located in the "messages" table from the database
"4b6f02493291c174257c570cadf3b96d73c1a59f" inside the "4b" folder of
the decrypted iTunes backup. Browsing this table provided the required
messages, as shown in Figure 13-17.

| | Database Structure | Browse Data | Edit Pragmas | Execute SQL | | | | | | | | | | | |

Table: messages

	thread_key	timestamp_ms	message_id	offline_threading_id	text	se
	Filter	Filter	Filter	Filter	Filter	Filter
1	834654489	1622969646246	mid.$cAABbAxrKPaKAEczEpl54Id8mjp1S	6807228079078808914	Hi	834654
2	834654489	1622969564268	mid.$cAABbAxrKPaKAEcuEbF54IY7lS-x-	6807227734386535550	This is a first test message	100069
3	834654489	1622969550701	mid.$cAABbAxrKPaKAEctPbV54IYEnvnhd	6807227675371796573	Hi	100069
4	834654489	1623699461267	mid.$cAABbAxrKPaKAPUzck16DAeR58lwv	6810289142324300847	Test number 2	100069
5	834654489	1623699463796	mid.$cAABbAxrKPaKAPUzmdF6DAecrsz0C	6810289153896561922	NULL	100069
6	834654489	1623699468505	mid.$cAABbAxrKPaKAPUz42V6DAevGomO4	6810289173675795384	NULL	100069
7	834654489	1623699468670	mid.$cAABbAxrKPaKAPUz5fl6DAev4ImO4	6810289174506267576	NULL	100069
8	834654489	1623699468917	mid.$cAABbAxrKPaKAPUz6dV6DAew2omO4	6810289175554843576	NULL	100069
9	834654489	1623699480084	mid.$cAABbAxrKPaKAPU0mFF6DAfcS1uwV	6810289222198946837	Just sent an emoji	100069
10	834654489	1623699499777	mid.$cAABbAxrKPaKAPU1zAV6DAgkApxEJ	6810289299203232009	NULL	100069
11	834654489	1623699514958	mid.$cAABbAxrKPaKAPU2uTl6DAhkk4PsM	6810289368530483980	Sent an audio message	100069
12	834654489	1623699542646	mid.$cAABbAxrKPaKAPU4adl6DAjMjuTJ7	6810289480180249211	NULL	100069
13	834654489	1623699565249	mid.$cAABbAxrKPaKAPU5ywV6DAkfKzAhC	6810289568882624578	NULL	100069
14	834654489	1623699610560	mid.$cAABbAxrKPaKAPU8jwF6DAnZ6dxV5	6810289769398343033	Message after the deleted one	100069
15	834654489	1623699629214	mid.$cAABbAxrKPaKAPU9snl6DAol01ggu	6810289850908280878	مرحبا	834654
16	834654489	1623699638696	mid.$cAABbAxrKPaKAPU-RqF6DApK4hzdC	6810289890698671938	هذا نص باللغة العربية	834654
17	834654489	1623699644860	mid.$cAABbAxrKPaKAPU-pvF6DApi77mFF	6810289916525568325	Hello	834654

Figure 13-17. *Browsing messages table using DB Viewer for SQLite*

Additionally, SQLite data analysis helps in recovering deleted data in some cases as explained in the following section.

Recovering Deleted Evidence from SQLite Property Lists

Depending on the iOS version, the amount of defragmentation and database clean-up varies. Additionally, some user settings and device specs may affect that. Data records can be restored from SQLite tables if they are not overwritten or cleared. This happens when the record is marked as deleted even though it will be kept stored in the database. Using some forensic tools or manual extraction, we can recover such records. For example, the call history database has a limited size; when it is almost full, some of the oldest records are removed to provide space for new records.

If the new space is not overwritten yet, it can be recovered. This is
applicable for most SQLite tables such as messages, notes, emails, contacts,
and others that contain valuable evidence that might be intentionally
deleted by the criminal. From this, we conclude that it is not always possible
for AXIOM or Belkasoft to recover deleted records from SQLite databases.

Reporting

Reporting involves providing a summary of all the steps taken and
conclusions reached as part of the examination process for FBM on iOS
and Android devices. Details about all important actions performed in
this case study should be mentioned, including common information like
investigator name, reporting agency, and case identifier. The reporting
agency is the agency officially authorized by the judicial authorities to
investigate the seized devices for a specific investigation. It should have
forensic experts and the tools needed to issue an examination report.
The agency should issue a report that is admissible, authentic, complete,
reliable, and believable. The case identifier is the submission number of
the case. It is unique and makes it easy to reference the case.

Summary

Security enhancements to mobile operating systems make it harder
for forensic investigators to retrieve data. Devices now have full desk
encryption (FDE) features. This makes it almost impossible to retrieve the
data without knowing the unlock key. Jailbreaking and rooting devices are
necessary to extract data in some cases. Most Android applications data,
including FBM stored in partitions, requires root-level permissions to be
accessed. Rooting a Huawei Y3 device is not as simple as it looks. Several
factors may affect the rooting process including the binary image, the
forensic computer, the cables, and the device firmware. Applying different

rooting techniques to the device may result in damaging the device. For the case with iOS, there was no need for jailbreaking the device, as we were able to extract FBM data.

This case study focused on showing techniques required to forensically examine Apple iPhone 6 and Huawei Y3 devices for FBM artifacts. This study started by explaining Android and iOS architecture, then demonstrated the need for preparations for the data extraction phase, and finally explained the data extraction techniques and data analysis for FBM.

References

[1].   Statista, "Digital Population." https://www.statista.com/statistics/617136/digital-population-worldwide/ (accessed May 01, 2021).

[2].   Statista, "Most Popular Global Mobile Messenger Apps." https://www.statista.com/statistics/258749/most-popular-global-mobile-messenger-apps/ (accessed Apr. 29, 2021).

[3].   A. Yudhana, I. Riadi, and I. Anshori, "Identification of Digital Evidence Facebook Messenger on Mobile Phone with National Institute of Standards Technology (NIST) Method," *Kursor*, vol. 9, no. 3, Jan. 2019, doi: 10.28961/kursor.v9i3.152.

[4].   A. N. Ichsan and I. Riadi, "Mobile Forensic on Android-Based IMO Messenger Services Using Digital Forensic Research Workshop (DFRWS) Method," *International Journal of Computer Applications*, vol. 174, no. 18, Feb. 2021, doi: 10.5120/ijca2021921076.

[5]. Amer Shakir, Muhammad Hammad, and
      Muhammad Kamran, "Comparative Analysis &
      Study of Android/iOS Mobile Forensics Tools," 2021.

[6]. A. Akinbi and E. Ojie, "Forensic Analysis of Open-
      Source XMPP Multi-client Social Networking Apps
      on iOS Devices," *Forensic Science International:
      Digital Investigation*, vol. 36, Mar. 2021, doi:
      10.1016/j.fsidi.2021.301122.

[7]. M. S. Chang and C. Y. Chang, "Forensic Analysis
      of LINE Messenger on Android," *Journal of
      Computers (Taiwan)*, vol. 29, no. 1, 2018, doi:
      10.3966/199115992018012901002.

[8]. C. Alisabeth and Y. R. Pramadi, "Forensic Analysis
      of Instagram on Android," in *IOP Conference Series:
      Materials Science and Engineering*, 2020, vol. 1007,
      no. 1. doi: 10.1088/1757-899X/1007/1/012116.

[9]. P. Domingues, R. Nogueira, J. C. Francisco,
      and M. Frade, "Post-mortem Digital Forensic
      Artifacts of TikTok Android App," 2020. doi:
      10.1145/3407023.3409203.

[10]. T. Alyahya and F. Kausar, "Snapchat Analysis to
      Discover Digital Forensic Artifacts on Android
      Smartphone," in *Procedia Computer Science*, 2017,
      vol. 109. doi: 10.1016/j.procs.2017.05.421.

[11]. M. Kukuh, I. Riadi, and Y. Prayudi, "Forensics
      Acquisition and Analysis Method of IMO
      Messenger," *International Journal of Computer
      Applications*, vol. 179, no. 47, 2018, doi: 10.5120/
      ijca2018917222.

[12].   V. Jain, R. Sahu, and D. Singh Tomar, "Evidence
        Gathering of Line Messenger on iPhones," 2015.
        [Online]. Available: www.gtia.co.in

[13].   Google Developer, "Android Architecture." https://
        developer.android.com/guide/platform
        (accessed Jul. 15, 2021).

[14].   Android Authority, "Phone Storage Folders
        Explained." https://www.androidauthority.
        com/phone-storage-folders-explained-744100/
        (accessed Jul. 15, 2021).

[15].   Android Tutorials, "Android Filesystems." https://
        android.tutorials.how/android-file-system/
        (accessed Jul. 16, 2021).

[16].   Rohit Tamma, Oleg Skulkin, Heather Mahalik, and
        Satish Bommisetty, *Practical Mobile Forensics*,
        Fourth edition. Birmingham: Packt Publishing
        Ltd., 2020.

[17].   S. Chauhan, "Understanding Xamarin iOS - Build
        Native iOS App." https://www.dotnettricks.com/
        learn/xamarin/understanding-xamarin-ios-
        build-native-ios-app (accessed May 30, 2021).

[18].   R. Ayers, S. Brothers, and W. Jansen, "Guidelines on
        Mobile Device Forensics," Gaithersburg, MD, May
        2014. doi: 10.6028/NIST.SP.800-101r1.

[19].   Apple, "HT208200." https://support.apple.com/
        en-us/HT208200 (accessed Apr. 30, 2021).

[20].   androidgroup.net, "root-huawei-y3-2017-cro-u00."
https://www.androidgroup.net/2019/03/root-
huawei-y3-2017-cro-u00.html (accessed Jul.
16, 2021).

[21].   Apple, "Apple Guide." https://support.apple.com/
guide/security/secure-enclave-sec59b0b31ff/
web (accessed Jun. 14, 2021).

[22].   cheeky4n6monkey, "Facebook Messenger Android
App." http://cheeky4n6monkey.blogspot.
com/2014/01/facebook-facebook-messenger-
android-app.html (accessed Jul. 18, 2021).

[23].   freeandroidforensics, "Facebook for Android
Artifacts." http://freeandroidforensics.
blogspot.com/2015/02/facebook-for-android-
artifacts.html (accessed Jul. 18, 2021).

CHAPTER 14

Mobile Forensics for iOS and Android Platforms: Chrome App Artifacts Depending on SQLite

This chapter starts by comparing and contrasting the architectures of Android and iOS that are discussed in the first chapter. As a result, we implement and utilize mobile forensics methodology to analyze SQLite files from the applications that install on the mobile device, we discuss some of the techniques and tools used to extract information, and we present a case study of Chrome application. In terms of forensic analysis, the chapter will also emphasize the necessity of examining all SQLite files that come under the apps in order to extract the most amount of digital evidence feasible. We investigated practical forensic analysis for the Chrome app for iOS and Android, and forensic procedures were carried out using the three phases (seizure, acquisition, examination & analysis) methodology. This chapter aims to extract artifacts from

© Mohammed Moreb 2022
M. Moreb, *Practical Forensic Analysis of Artifacts on iOS and Android Devices*,
https://doi.org/10.1007/978-1-4842-8026-3_14

Chrome applications using many tools such as iBackup, iExplorer, iTunes, Belkasoft, and FINALMobile software for iOS. We use ADB, Belkasoft, AXIOM, FINALMobile, and MOBILedit for Android. SQLiteStudio is used to view SQLite database files extracted from both Android and iOS.

In this chapter, we will cover the following topics:

- Introduction to iOS Chrome App Forensics Using SQLite

- SQLite Acquisition Phase

- SQLite Forensic Tools

- SQLite Experimental Design

- Acquisition SQLite by iTunes and Belkasoft

- Android Chrome App Forensics Using SQLite

- Examination and Analysis Phase for Chrome App iOS and Android

- Comparison between Tools Used for iOS

iOS Chrome App Forensics Using SQLite

"SQLite is an in-process library that implements a self-contained, zero-configuration, serverless, transactional SQL database engine" (Bhosale et al., 2015). SQLite's evolution has made it one of the world's most commonly used database management systems, as well as a storage engine for browsers and mobile apps.

Seizure Phase

The digital equipment is seized before the beginning of the inspection
process. Seizure is carried out by law enforcement officers who have the
required competence and training to preserve evidence, ensuring that the
confiscated equipment is maintained in its original state. When seizing a
phone, it is critical to switch it to airplane mode. A seizure must be based
on a valid search warrant issued in line with the rules governing seizure
processes and purposes (Manendra Sai et al., 2015). In this study, work
will be done based on the Palestinian Cybercrime Law No. 10 of 2018,
especially Article 32.

I. **Agency**: including institutions that conduct the
forensics analysis and examination.

II. **Case identifier**: case number and some other
details for the case such as date and time.

III. **Forensic investigator**: information about the
forensics examiner including name, institution,
qualification, and experience.

IV. **Identity of the submitter**: details about the
submitter and how to hand it over to the examiner;
there can be pictures documenting the condition of
the device when it is handed over.

V. **Date of evidence receipt**: the date of delivery of the
devices to the forensic analysis department.

VI. **Details of the device seized for examination**:
including serial number, make, and model. In
this chapter, we will use Samsung Galaxy A7 with
Android 7.0, and Apple iPhone 6 with iOS 12.5.2.
Device specifications are shown in Table 14-1.

Table 14-1. *Suspected iPhone and Android Mobile Specifications*

iPhone Mobile Specifications

Make	iPhone 6	Model no.	MG482AA/A
IMEI	3592830694**29	Color	Silver
Jailbroken	No	Network	JAWWAL
Capacity	16 GB	Passcode	Provided (111111)
iOS version	12.5.2	Serial no.	C8QPM2RTG5MP
Mobile power	On	MEID	35928306947829
Airplane mode	On	Wi-Fi add.	D8:1D:72:E9:6F:0B
Bluetooth	D8:1D:72:E9:6F:0C	ICCID	89970281433296612949
Modem firmware	7.80.04	SIM no.	0594-4444***

Suspect Android Mobile Specifications

Make	Samsung Galaxy A7 2016	Model no.	SM-A710FD
IMEI (slot 1)	3581680770892**	Color	Black
Root	No	Network	JAWWAL-Ps
Capacity	16 GB	Passcode	Provided (123456)
Android version	7.0	Serial no.	RF8J72EJ*0R
Mobile power	On	Build no.	NRD90M.A710FXXS2CTJ1
Airplane mode	On	Wi-Fi add.	94:7B:E7:27:12:BC
Bluetooth	Unavailable	SIM no.	0593-333***

Acquisition Phase

Forensic Tools

The workstation and software used in this experiment to make acquisitions
for iOS and Android mobiles are shown in Table 14-2.

Table 14-2. *Experiment Tools and Devices*

No.	Tools/Devices	Description
1	iTunes, version 12.11.3.17	Used to get a backup for iPhone
2	Belkasoft Evidence center 9.9 Build 4662 x64	Forensic software used for acquisition and analysis, software
3	FINALMobile Forensics user version The file version is 2020.04.22. CDF version is 2020.04.22.	Forensic tool: used for extraction and analysis
4	SQLiteStudio v3.3.3	Open and view SQLite
5	AXIOM	Forensics SW used for acquisition and analysis
6	Odin3	SW used for root Android
7	Hp Zbook, windows 10, 64 bit, 24GB Ram, Intel(R) Core™ i7-7700HQ CPU@2.80GHz 2.81 GHz	Workstation
8	Original USB cable	Media to connect the smartphone with workstation
9	iPhone 6	Suspect smartphone X
10	Samsung Galaxy A7 2016	Suspect smartphone Y

Experimental Design

The experiment was prepared in terms of (a) activating mobile airplane
mode to isolate receiving and transmission signals, (b) connecting the
mobile device through a USB cable with the workstation, which is not
connected to the Internet and free of malware, (c) selecting trust computer,
(d) connecting iTunes for backup, (e) running Belkasoft to get backup
and to load iTunes backup for analysis and comparison, and (f) running
FINALMobile software to get another backup and later for analysis.

Acquisition by iTunes and Belkasoft

- **_iTunes backup_**: Create iPhone backup as shown in
  Figure 14-1. This backup will be analyzed forensically
  using Belkasoft. The backup data is stored in the
  following path: C:\Users\hp\AppData\Roaming\Apple
  Computer\MobileSync\Backup

Figure 14-1. *iTunes backup*

- **_Acquisition by Belkasoft_**: When doing acquisition
  for Apple mobile, Belkasoft offers three acquisition
  methods: iTunes backup; full logical backup, which

requires a jailbreak; and agent backup, which is
not supported for current iOS (12.5.3 for suspected
iPhone). Figure 14-2 shows selecting acquire Apple
mobile. In Figure 14-2 Belkasoft recognizes the iPhone
after connecting the iPhone with the workstation.
Figure 14-3 shows the starting backup process.

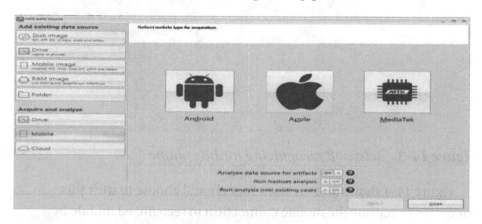

Figure 14-2. *Selecting acquire Apple mobile*

In Figure 14-2, mobile forensics examiners are required to choose
whether to add an existing data source or to acquire and analyze. As shown
in Figure 14-3, acquisition for mobile was selected and Apple mobile
was chosen.

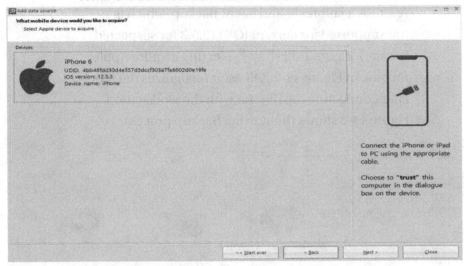

Figure 14-3. *Belkasoft recognizing mobile phone*

Figure 14-4 shows that the examiner should choose to trust this
computer to activate the mobile connection to recognized mobile by
Belkasoft.

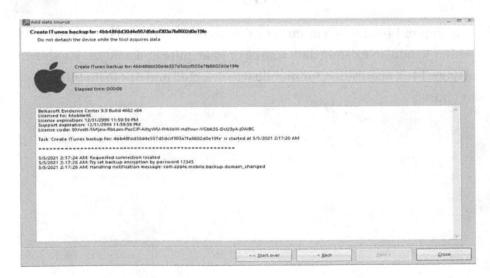

Figure 14-4. *Backup process*

For obtaining a logical image for targeted smartphones, it is not allowed to use Belkasoft without jailbreak as shown in Figure 14-5.

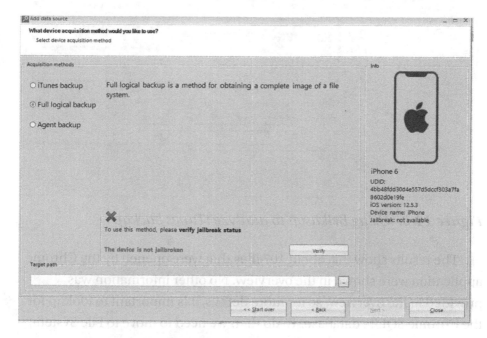

Figure 14-5. *Logical image required jailbreak*

As shown in Figure 14-8, when choosing full logical backup, it is required for the mobile to be jailbroken.

Examination/Analysis Phase

1. Using Belkasoft

iTunes backup, which was taken by Belkasoft, is open for analysis by Belkasoft as shown in Figure 14-6.

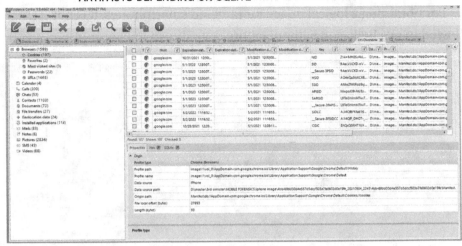

Figure 14-6. *Using Belkasoft to analyze iTunes backup*

The results show that about 107 files that were opened by the Chrome
application were shown in the overview. No other information was
provided in the overview, so for more details, it is important to lookup for
the Chrome SQLite database. To do that, we need to move to File System,
where we can locate related SQLite files as shown in Figure 14-7.

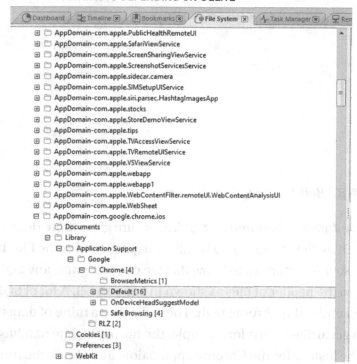

Figure 14-7. *Belkasoft file system*

As shown in Figure 14-8, all Chrome app SQLite database files are
located under the path AppDomain-com.google.chrome.os. Walk through
this path looking for SQLite database files. To open any SQLite files, we can
use the integrated SQLite viewer in Belkasoft as shown in Figure 14-9.

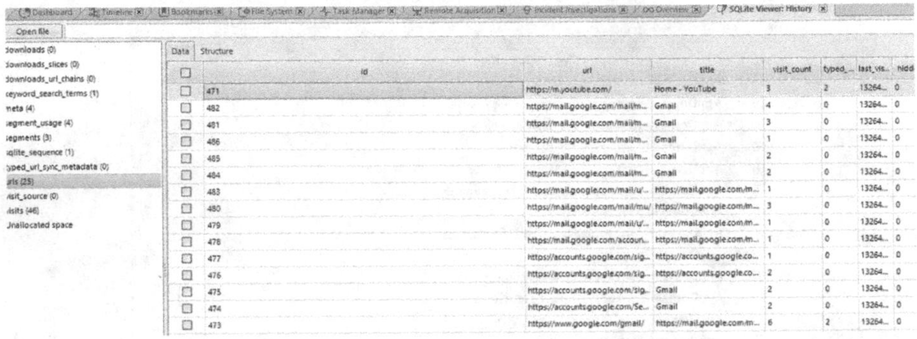

Figure 14-8. Belkasoft SQLite Viewer

Viewing data that is stored on SQLite for sure gives more details and artifacts. SQLite file format could be .db or .sqlite3, and some files have no extension, so it is important to know that we can recognize any SQLite file according to the header of files as shown in Figure 14-9. A lot of SQLite files were found under the Chrome path. These files are a mine of data that can be used to get artifacts. Just for example, the history SQLite database file provides the history for the Chrome application, and shows the number of times each site was visited. It provides a keyword search via Chrome application and many other details.

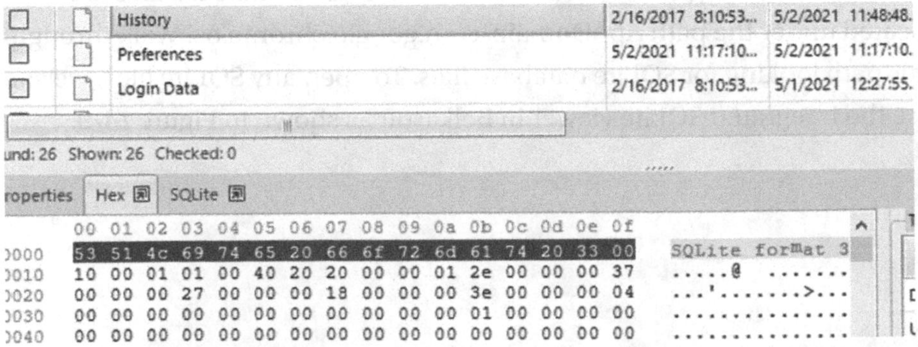

Figure 14-9. SQLite header

As shown in Figure 14-10, SQLite signature offset is zero and size is 16
bytes. Another example is the "Login data" SQLite database file, which is
saved by Belkasoft and viewed by SQLiteStudio as shown in Figure 14-10.
This table gives other artifacts about logins signed through the Chrome
application.

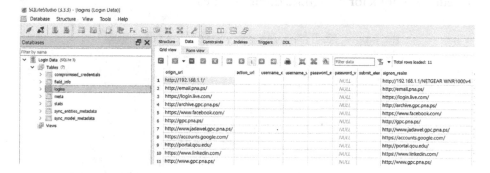

Figure 14-10. *Login data file through SQLiteStudio*

2. Using FINALMobile

iTunes backup was taken by iTunes and opened by the FINALMobile
forensics tool, as shown in Figure 14-11.

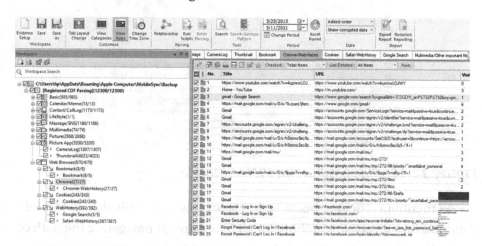

Figure 14-11. *FINALMobile interface*

It is clear at first glance that a program at the workspace directly displays some of the contents of the Chrome application; the display is done by the Chrome_WebHistory tap and all its contents are read directly from the history SQLite file. These tools also give us the ability to search all files manually through File Explorer as shown in Figure 14-12. We can use this feature to look for all SQLite database files.

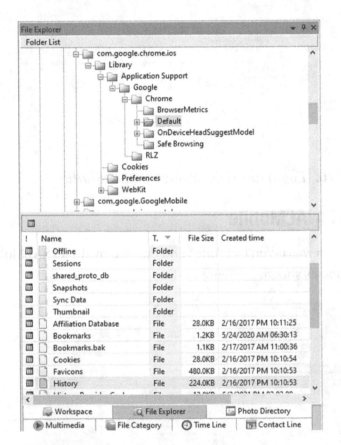

Figure 14-12. *File Explorer in FINALMobile*

As mentioned before, because forensic tools do not display all SQLite database files directly, searching for all files through navigating the path of desired application is extremely important to obtain the largest possible number of artifacts. FINALMobile also as Belkasoft gives us the ability for this search and also provides us with the ability to export SQLite database files to be opened later by any tool such as SqliteStudio, or we can directly open it without exporting as shown in Figure 14-13.

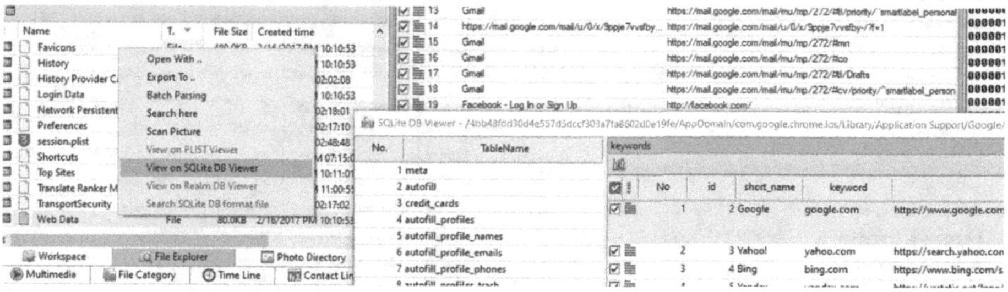

Figure 14-13. *View SQLite directly in FINALMobile*

3. Using iBackUp

iBackup will automatically find the iTunes backup as shown in Figure 14-17, or we can simply open the backup from the desired path. After that, it is easy to view all mobile content as shown in Figure 14-14. Also, these tools give us the ability to export any file including SQLite database files; in this practical case when we use iBackup tool it's can't able to recognize SQLite files, as it doesn't support hex dump to view the file header.

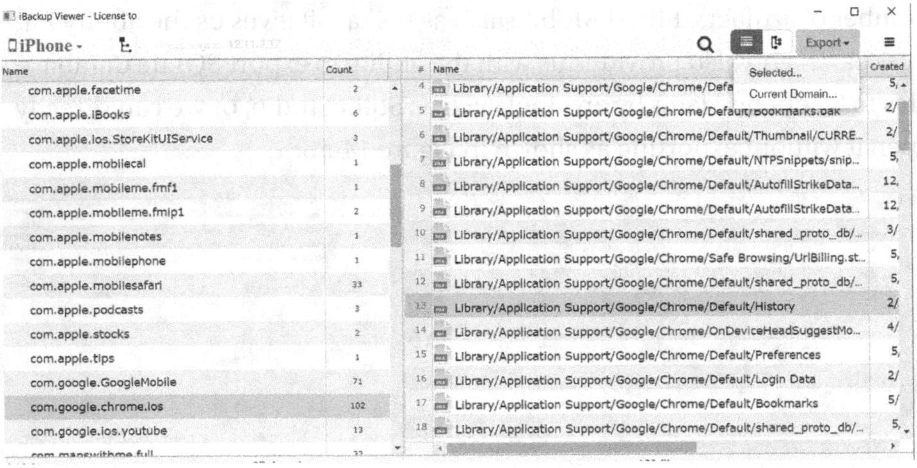

Figure 14-14. Export files using iBackup

4. Using iExplorer

Used to view iTunes backup and gather related SQLite files, this tool gives
us the ability to export any file including SQLite database files as shown in
Figure 14-15. In this tool, it is not possible to recognize SQLite files if they
have no extension or are without previous experience. In other words, it
doesn't support hex dump to view the file header.

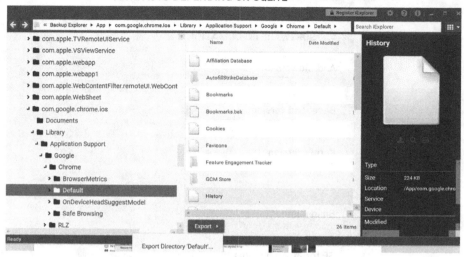

Figure 14-15. *Export files using iExplorer*

Android Chrome App Forensics Using SQLite

The experiment design was prepared in terms of (a) activating mobile airplane mode to isolate receiving and transmission signals; (b) connecting the mobile device through a USB cable with a workstation that is not connected to the Internet and is free of malware, (c) selecting the trust computer, (d) using ADB command to get backup, (e) running Belkasoft to get ADB backup and physical image (also used for analysis and comparison), (f) running FINALMobile software to get another backup and later for analysis, (j) using AXIOM to get the full image and later for analysis, and (h) using MOBILedit to get backup and analysis.

First, for the acquisition phase, to get backup or any type of acquisition, developer mode must be enabled. To enable developer mode for Samsung A7 2016: (1) go to settings, (2) About phone, (3) Software information (4) Click build number seven times to enable developer mode as shown in Figure 14-16.

475

Figure 14-16. *Enable developer mode*

Then it is required to enable USB debugging. For rooting the Android
mobile, we must enable OEM to unlock as shown in Figure 14-17.

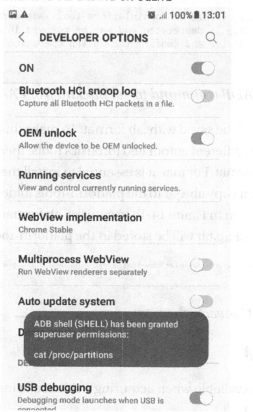

Figure 14-17. *Enable USB debugging mode*

Before Rooting

Using ADB Command

For everything you need, just download the Software Development
Kit (SDK), which includes an integrated development environment
(IDE), which is required for investigative tools like ADB and quick boot.
Figure 14-18 shows the adb command to get backup -shared -all, which is
used to get backup from external memory on the mobile.

```
C:\platform-tools_r31.0.2-windows\platform-tools>adb backup -shared -all
WARNING: adb backup is deprecated and may be removed in a future release
Now unlock your device and confirm the backup operation...
```

Figure 14-18. *ADB command to get backup from Android mobile*

The backup will be saved with .ab format. To make this backup universal format, open with different automated forensics tools; then it is required to convert it to .tar format. For that, it is essential to install the Java development kit (JDK), and then copy abe.jar to the platform-tools folder. Later we can use the command shown in Figure 14-19 to convert. ab format to .tar format. The backup.ab and backup.tar will be stored in the platform-tools folder.

```
C:\platform-tools_r31.0.2-windows\platform-tools>java -jar abe.jar unpack backup.ab backup.tar

C:\platform-tools r31.0.2-windows\platform-tools>
```

Figure 14-19. *Convert .ab to .tar*

Using AXIOM

Two options are available when acquiring evidence using AXIOM as shown in Figure 14-20.

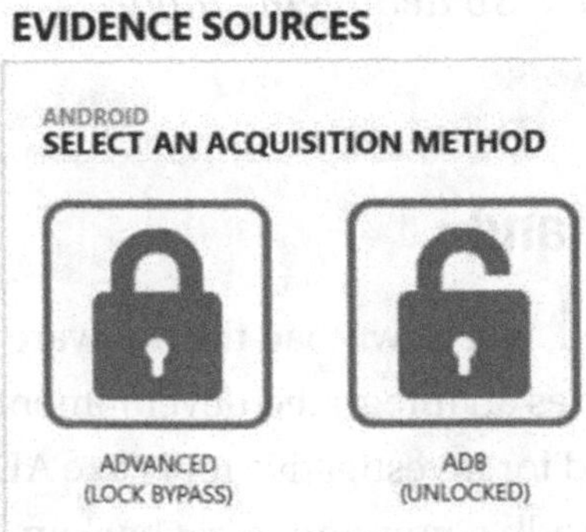

Figure 14-20. *AXIOM acquisition method*

ADB (Unlocked) is used when you have passcodes and patterns for the device and you can unlock it. Advanced (Lock Bypass) is used to bypass the lock screen. Figure 14-21 shows progress when choosing the ADB (Unlocked) option, which is used to acquire a quick or full image as shown in Figure 14-5, hence the full image requires the device to be rooting, and the quick image is stored as .zip format.

EVIDENCE SOURCES
PREPARING THE DEVICE
PROGRESS

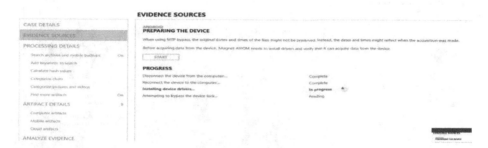

Figure 14-21. *ADB progress to acquire the quick image*

Figure 14-22 shows the progress of preparing the device including disconnecting and reconnecting the mobile to the workstation, installing the mobile driver, and attempting to bypass the device if it is locked. AXIOM provides two types of images: a full image, which means whole contents of the device, and a quick image.

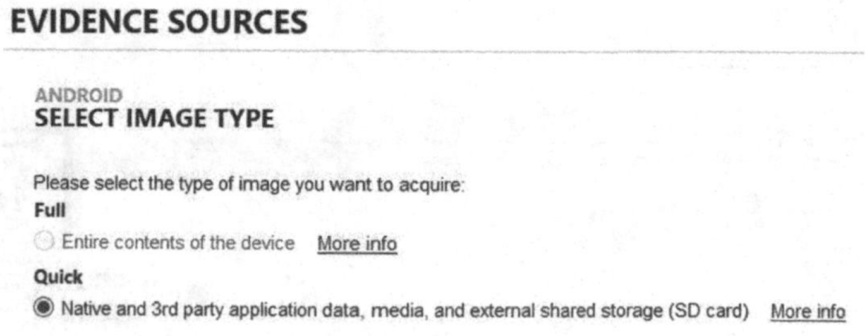

EVIDENCE SOURCES
ANDROID
SELECT IMAGE TYPE
Please select the type of image you want to acquire:
Full
Entire contents of the device
More info
Quick
Native and 3rd party application data, media, and external shared storage (SD card)
More info

Figure 14-22. *Quick image*

Using Belkasoft

We can get backup using Belkasoft by:

    a.   Choosing "Mobile" from Acquire and analyzing and
then select Android as shown in Figure 14-23.

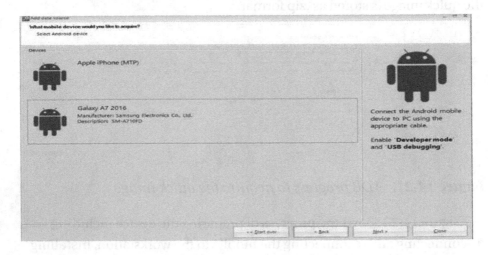

Figure 14-23. *Select mobile*

    b.   Selecting acquisition method as shown in
Figure 14-24.

Figure 14-24. *Acquisition methods*

480

Using FINALMobile

FINALMobile Forensics supports different platforms as shown in
Figure 14-25.

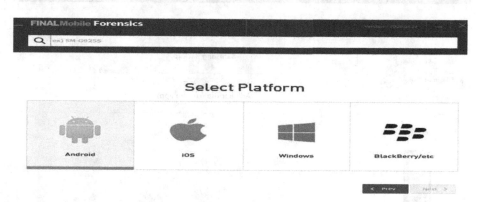

Figure 14-25. *Mobile platforms supported by FINALMobile*

To get a backup of Android using FINALMobile, we have to select
the Android platform, then choose the make and model as shown in
Figure 14-26.

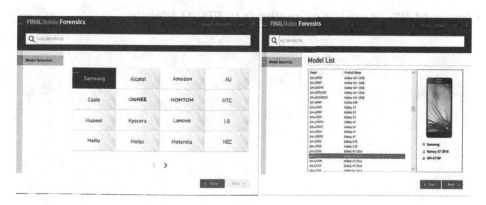

Figure 14-26. *The make and model*

There are two acquisition methods as shown in Figure 14-27. Both are given logical image.

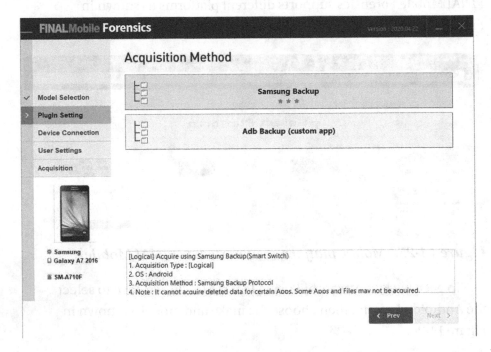

Figure 14-27. *Acquisition methods in FINALMobile*

Rooting

Odin3 software as shown in Figure 14-28 was used to root the mobile.

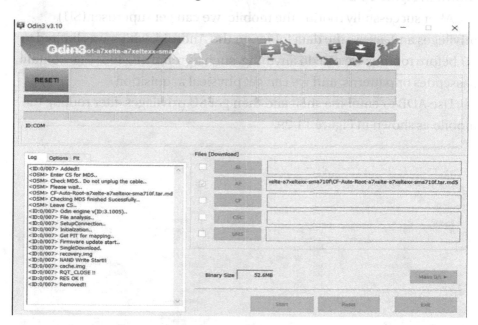

Figure 14-28. *Odin3 interface*

To root the mobile device using Odin3, first, we have to enable OEM to unlock as shown in Figure 14-17, turn off the mobile, and then log in to the download mode by holding and pressing power + volume down + home together until getting the warning screen, then pressing up the volume. After that, run Odin3 as administrator and connect the mobile device to the PC via USB cable; the Odin3 software will confirm the connection by showing "Added" as shown in Figure 14-29. If there is no confirmation, then there is a problem with the mobile driver and it is recommended to install the correct driver for the mobile.

Once the connection is confirmed, then locate the root file, which can be downloaded from samsungsfour.com [15] depending on the version

483

and model, add it to Odin3 by clicking AP, select the root file, which is
in the format of .tar.md5., and then choose to start rooting the device as
shown in Figure 14-28.

After successfully rooting the mobile, we can get superuser (SU)
privileges and access the data folder on the Android, which was limited to
SU before rooting; we can do anything, such as removing files that contain
passcodes or patterns, and we can get physical acquisition.

Use ADB to enter the shell and then get SU privileges after rooting the
mobile as shown in Figure 14-29.

```
C:\platform-tools_r31.0.2-windows\platform-tools>adb.exe shell
* daemon not running; starting now at tcp:5037
* daemon started successfully
a7xelte:/ $ su
a7xelte:/ # ls
acct           file_contexts.bin    init.rilchip.rc             oem                  sepolicy_version
bugreports     fstab.goldfish       init.rilepdg.rc             persdata             service_contexts
cache          fstab.ranchu         init.samsungexynos7580.rc   postrecovery.do      storage
config         fstab.samsungexynos7580 init.samsungexynos7580.usb.rc preload          su
cpefs          init                 init.supersu.rc             proc                 sys
d              init.baseband.rc     init.usb.configfs.rc        property_contexts    system
data           init.carrier.rc      init.usb.rc                 publiccert.pem       ueventd.goldfish.rc
default.prop   init.container.rc    init.wifi.rc                root                 ueventd.ranchu.rc
dev            init.environ.rc      init.zygote32.rc            sbin                 ueventd.rc
efs            init.goldfish.rc     knox_data                   sdcard               ueventd.samsungexynos7580.rc
etc            init.ranchu.rc       lib                         seapp_contexts       vendor
factory        init.rc              mnt                         sepolicy
a7xelte:/ # cd data
a7xelte:/data #
```

Figure 14-29. *SU privileges*

And now, let us remove password and pattern from the mobile using
SU privileges and using the files containing password and pattern, which
are found under /data/system, and then look for gatekeeper.password.
key and gatekeeper.pattern.key. by removing these two files, as shown in
Figure 14-30. Then there will be no passcode or pattern on the mobile.

```
a7xelte:/ # cd /data/system
a7xelte:/data/system # ls
AppOpsPolicy.xml          device_policies.xml          enterprise_nativecerts.bks    install_sessions        notification_policy.xml  reversestartingwindow     sync
OtpDatabase.db            deviceidle.xml               enterprise_untrustedcerts.bks install_sessions.xml    ovbt_bd.db               rut.db                    ucm_ce_cert
OtpDatabase.db-journal    displaysolution.db           enterprise_usercerts.bks      job                     ovbt_bd.db-journal       rut.db-journal            uiderrors.txt
SimCard.dat               displaysolution.db-journal   entropy.dat                   keyguardpreview         package-usage.list       screen_on_time            urigrants.xml
WifiHistory.db            dmappmgr.db                  gamemanager.db                last-fstrim             packages.list            sec_batterystats          usagestats
WifiHistory.db-journal    dmappmgr.db-journal          gamemanager.db-journal        locksettings.db         packages.xml             sec_batterystats-journal  users
appops.xml                dropbox                      gatekeeper.password.key       locksettings.db-shm     packages.xml.mbak        sec_batterystats_ext      wifipeofence.db
audioservice_sec.db-journal enterprise.conf          gatekeeper.pattern.key        locksettings.db-wal     pda.db                   sec_batterystats_ext-shm  wifigeofence.db-journal
batterystats-chockin.bin  enterprise.db                gms_bundling.data             log-files.xml           pda.db-journal           sec_batterystats_ext-wal  yas_lib.cfg
batterystats-daily.xml    enterprise.db-journal        gps                           ndebugsocket            pdaversion.txt           sensor_service
batterystats.bin          enterprise.db-shm            harmony_third_party_apps.xml  netpolicy.xml           phoneversion.txt         shortcut_service.xml
container                 enterprise.db-wal            heapdump                      netstats                pre_boot_csc.dat         slocation.db
cacversion.txt            enterprise_cacerts.bks       ifw                           notification_log.db     procstats                slocation.db-se
a7xelte:/data/system # rm getkeeper.password.key                                     notification_log.db-journal registered_ucm_services starting window
rm: getkeeper.password.key: No such file or directory
1|a7xelte:/data/system # rm gatekeeper.password.key
a7xelte:/data/system # rm gatekeeper.pattern.key
a7xelte:/data/system #
```

Figure 14-30. *Bypass passcode and pattern in Samsung A7 2016*

After Rooting

Using Belkasoft to get a physical copy, we need to select DD backup and
verify root status to continue as shown in Figure 14-31, then select the
partition or all partitions to get a backup physical in which the images are
logical, and then click Next to start the process of physical imaging.

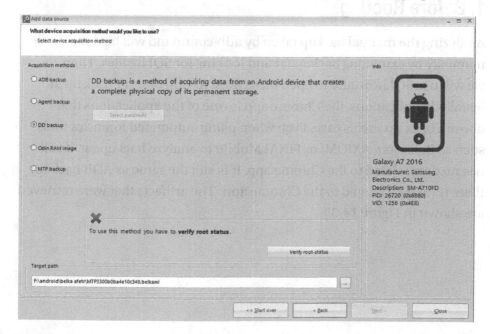

Figure 14-31. *Physical copy*

After rooting the mobile, using AXIOM the full image option will be available as shown in Figure 14-32.

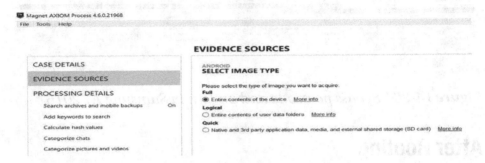

Figure 14-32. *AXIOM full image*

Examination and Analysis Phase for Android

1. Before Rooting

Analyzing the manual backup taken by adb command will be done manually by extracting backup.tar and looking for SQLite files. Then we will use SQLiteStudio to open these files. As adb doesn't back up all installed applications, the Chrome app is one of the applications that doesn't back up in this case. Even when using automated forensics tools such as Belkasoft, AXIOM, or FINALMobile to analyze backup.tar, it still has no data related to the Chrome app. It is still the same as ADB backup; there is no data related to the Chrome app. The artifacts that were retrieved are shown in Figure 14-33.

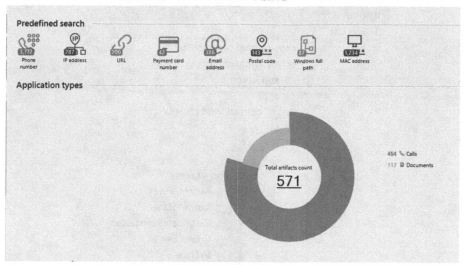

Figure 14-33. *Analyze ADB backup using Belkasoft*

Analyzing a logical image using FINALMobile, as shown in
Figure 14-34, shows analyzing results for the logical image that was taken
as "Samsung backup" and spotted on Chrome results.

Figure 14-34. *Analyzing results showing Chrome artifacts*

If we are looking for more artifacts, it will be necessary to look for every
single SQLite file located under Chrome. To achieve that, we navigate to
the File Explorer as shown in Figure 14-35.

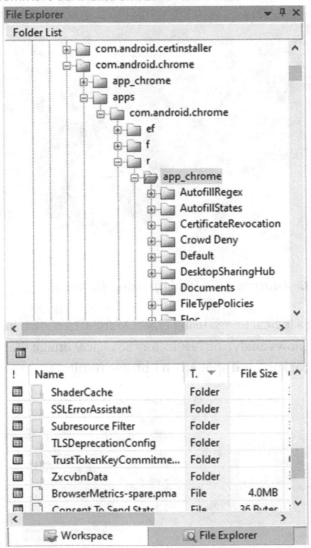

Figure 14-35. *File Explorer*

One more thing: it is important to look at all SQLite files depending on
file signature instead of looking at file extensions, as some SQLite files have
no extension. Figure 14-36 shows the SQLite signature.

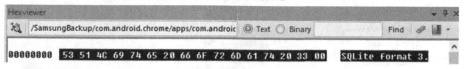

Figure 14-36. *SQLite file signature*

Analyzing Quick images using AXIOM, first we open the image by process and wait until we finish analyzing evidence. Figure 14-37 shows artifacts. No artifacts related to Chrome apps were found.

EVIDENCE OVERVIEW

samsung SM-A710F Quick Image.zip (2.722)

VIEW EVIDENCE FOR THIS SOURCE ONLY

Evidence number **samsung SM-A710F Quick Image.zip**

Description

Location **samsung SM-A710F Quick Image.zip**

Platform **Mobile**

No picture added

CHANGE PICTURE

PLACES TO START

ARTIFACT CATEGORIES

VIEW ALL ARTIFACT CATEGORIES

Evidence source **All**

Number of artifacts **2,722**

Media 1,567
Mobile 749
Refined Results 170
Documents 119
Operating System 108
Custom 9

TAGS AND COMMENTS

MAGNET.AI CATEGORIZATION

KEYWORD MATCHES   **PASSWORDS AND TOKENS**

PROFILES

Figure 14-37. *Case overview*

2. After Rooting

We try to find artifacts using Belkasoft and results show that no artifacts were acquired. By loading the image to the AXIOM process, and waiting until it finishes analyzing, Figure 14-38 shows artifact statistics for the full image after rooting.

Figure 14-38. *Artifacts for full image after rooting*

As shown in Figure 14-39, analyzing full images retrieves data related
to Chrome apps.

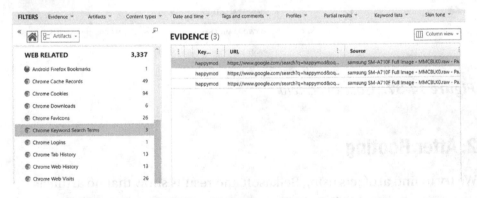

Figure 14-39. *Extract Chrome app data from full image*

Results and Discussion

iOS

The Chrome application used in iPhone mobiles is like any other application where many artifacts can be extracted. In the conducted experiment, acquisition of SQLite manually without jailbreaking the mobile is possible if the mobile is open (no passcode or pattern is given) using iTunes, iBackup, and iExplorer to get iTunes backup. We can easily export an SQLite file and then open it with any SQLite viewer such as SQLiteStudio. Or we can use Belkasoft and FINALMobile as forensics tools to get iTunes backup and do forensics analysis using tools features or export SQLite files to be opened by SQLiteStudio.

There are many SQLite database files under Chrome path, such as history, login data, top sites, affiliation database, cookies, favicons, shortcuts, web data, and more. Just for example, th history file contains information about all browsing such as downloads, keyword_searched_ items, URL, and so on. As shown in Figure 14-41, login data file contains information about all user logins, such as origin_url, password_element_ username_element, and so on as shown in Figure 14-40. Topsites: contains the most visited sites through Chrome application, as shown in Figure 14-40.

Figure 14-40. History SQLite file

491

All tables inside the History SQLite database files include login details through the Chrome app, and information about the top sites visited using Chrome app web browser, as shown in Figure 14-41.

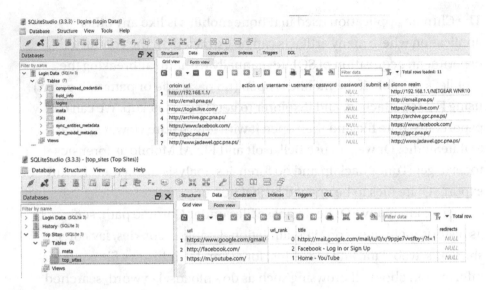

Figure 14-41. *SQLite database files for the Chrome app*

Android

Many applications exist for a specific purpose; for example, the purpose of the email application is to open the email, the purpose of the Facebook application is to open Facebook, and so on. Regardless of these applications that are designed for specific purposes, Internet browsers are still used to search and open an email, Facebook, and so on. The most used Internet browser is the Chrome app. Therefore, it is always recommended to check the artifacts in Chrome and the rest of the Internet browsers, if any. Like any mobile platform, Chrome is used in Android. Using Chrome can provide a lot of artifacts. And once more, if we are looking for more artifacts, it is required to look for all SQLite database files.

There are many methods to do acquisition for Android platforms. ADB manual extraction doesn't back up everything; for example, ADB didn't acquire Chrome data. To get Chrome data, we have to do logical acquisition by automated tools such as FINALMobile, AXIOM, and so on. There is no need to root Android mobile for the logical image. Logical images will never provide deleted files. After analyzing the logical image with FINALMobile as shown in Figure 14-42, we get 27 artifacts.

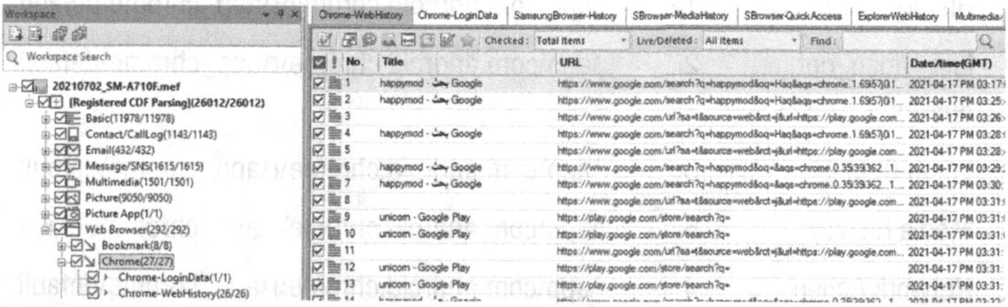

Figure 14-42. *Chrome app artifacts*

But if we go deeper and look for SQLite files by navigating File Explorer, we can find more artifacts. There are 22 SQLite files located under the Chrome app, as shown in Table 14-3.

Table 14-3. *SQLite Files Located under Chrome App*

No	SQLite file	No. of Tables	Description
1	Account Web Data	22	\app\com.android.chrome\r\app_chrome\default
2	Affiliation Database	3	\app\com.android.chrome\r\app_chrome\default
3	Cookies	2	\app\com.android.chrome\r\app_chrome\default
4	Favicons	4	\app\com.android.chrome\r\app_chrome\default

(continued)

Table 14-3. (*continued*)

No	SQLite file	No. of Tables	Description
5	Heavy_ad_ intervention_ opt_out.db	2	\app\com.android.chrome\r\app_chrome\default
6	History	12	\app\com.android.chrome\r\app_chrome\default
7	Lite_video_opt_ out.db	2	\app\com.android.chrome\r\app_chrome\default
8	Login Data	6	\app\com.android.chrome\r\app_chrome\default
9	Media History	6	\app\com.android.chrome\r\app_chrome\default
10	Network Action Predictor	4	\app\com.android.chrome\r\app_chrome\default
11	Origin Bound Certs	2	\app\com.android.chrome\r\app_chrome\default
12	QuotaManager	4	\app\com.android.chrome\r\app_chrome\default
13	Reporting and NEL	4	\app\com.android.chrome\r\app_chrome\default
14	Shortcuts	2	\app\com.android.chrome\r\app_chrome\default
15	Top Sites	2	\app\com.android.chrome\r\app_chrome\default
16	Trust Tokens	3	\app\com.android.chrome\r\app_chrome\default
17	Web Data	27	\app\com.android.chrome\r\app_chrome\default
18	Databases	2	\app\com.android.chrome\r\app_chrome\ default\databases
19	OfflinePages.db	3	\com.android.chrome\app_chrome\default\ offline Pages\metadata

(*continued*)

Table 14-3. (*continued*)

No	SQLite file	No. of Tables	Description
20	RequestQueue.db	1	\com.android.chrome\app_chrome\default\ offline Pages\request_queue
21	SyncData.sqlite3	5	\com.android.chrome\app_chrome\default\ Sync Data
22	Safe Browsing Cookies	2	\app\com.android.chrome\r\app_chrome

Rooting the Android platform is used to have SU privileges to do whatever we want. Android physical acquisition required the device to be rooted. After rooting the device, we can get a physical image. After doing a full image acquisition using AXIOM, we can do analysis for the full image using Belkasoft, because the image won't open with AXIOM. Since Belkasoft can deal with corrupted images, we will use Belkasoft to analyze the full image taken by AXIOM, as shown in Figure 14-43. A total of 204 Chrome artifacts were retrieved after rooting.

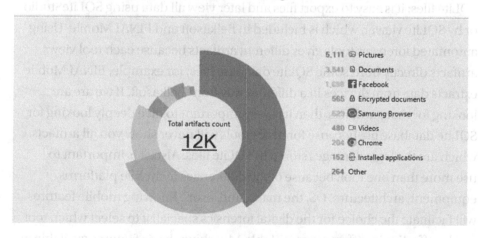

Figure 14-43. *Analyzing full image using Belkasoft*

495

Moreover, we still can navigate to the Chrome SQLite files as shown in Figure 14-44.

Figure 14-44. *Locating SQLite DB files for Chrome app*

After rooting Android, one more experiment is done when disabling Chrome apps. To disable the Chrome app go to Settings ➤ App ➤ Chrome ➤ Disable. After disabling Chrome, one more full image was taken by AXIOM. Analysis of this image returns nothing related to the Chrome app.

Comparison between Tools Used for iOS

In summary comparisons between data acquisition from iOS devices and iOS backups, we mainly used three tools to do data acquisition for the iOS device, iTunes, Belkasoft, and FINALMobile. No differences were found between the acquired data for the case study. All copies of backup contain the same SQLite files; it is easy to export files and later view all data using SQLiteStudio or by SQLite viewer, which is included in Belkasoft and FINALMobile. Using automated forensics tools gives different artifacts because each tool views artifacts directly from some SQLite database files; for example, FINALMobile extracts data from devices in a different way from Belkasoft. If we are are looking for more artifacts, then it is very important to dive deeply looking for SQLite database file because forensics tools will never show you all artifacts, which are the logical images stored in SQLite files. Also, it is important to use more than one tool, because of the differences in mobile platforms, equipment, architecture, OS, the make, and so on. Knowing mobile features will facilitate the choice for the digital forensics specialist to select which tool will be effective in different cases. Table 14-4 shows basic features available in each table for previous experiments.

Table 14-4. *Used Tool Features for iOS*

Tool	iTunes backup	Logical image	Required jailbreak for a logical image Yes/No	Export files	Include SQLite viewer	View SQLite directly	View hex dump	View SQLite structure
Belkasoft	✓	✓	Yes	✓	✓	✓	✓	✓
FINALMobile	✓	✓	Yes	✓	✓	✓	✓	✗
iTunes	✓	✗	--	✗	✗	✗	✗	--
iExplorer	--	--	--	✓	✗	✗	✗	--
SQLiteStudio	--	--	--	--	✓	--	✗	✓

Table 14-5 summarizes the comparison between tools used for Android in the acquisition phase.

Table 14-5. Comparison between Tools Used for Android in Terms of the Acquisition

Tool	ADB backup image	Logical image	Required root for a logical image Yes/No	Physical image	Export files	Required root for physical image	Include SQLite viewer	View SQLite directly	View hex dump	View SQLite structure
Belkasoft	✓	✓	Yes	Yes	✓	Yes	✓	✓	✓	✓
Final Data	✓	✓	No	No	✓	--	✓	✓	✓	✗
AXIOM	✓	✓	Yes	Yes	✓	Yes	✗	✗	✗	--
ADB command	✓	✗	--	--	Pull	--	--	--	--	--
SQLiteStudio	--	--	--	--	--	--	✓	--	✗	✓

Summary

In this chapter, we have investigated practical forensic analysis for the
Chrome app on iOS V.12 and Android v7.0, and forensic procedures were
carried out using the three phases (seizure, acquisition, examination/
analysis) methodology. This study aimed to extract artifacts from Chrome
applications. iBackup, iExplorer, iTunes, Belkasoft, and FINALMobile
software were used for iOS V.12.5.2. ADB, Belkasoft, AXIOM, FINALMobile
and MOBILedit were used for Android V 7.0. SQLiteStudio is used to
view SQLite database files extracted from both Android and iOS. The
results of the experiment have been presented, including artifacts such as
websites visited, top sites, login data, the email that was used, the words
searched, and so on. These artifacts help forensic investigators and law
enforcement agencies in the investigation and can be used as evidence
in court. Different tools provide different results, so it is recommended
to use more tools to do forensics analysis. These differences relate to the
differences in extraction evidence from different SQLite database files. It
is also recommended to view all SQLite database files located under any
application such as the Chrome app. Previous studies show some SQLite
database files, while in this study, all SQLite database files located under
the Chrome application are extracted.

References

[1].   Al-Hadadi, M., & AlShidhani, A. (2013). Smartphone
       Forensics Analysis: A Case Study. *International
       Journal of Computer and Electrical Engineering*,
       5(6), 576–580. https://doi.org/10.7763/
       ijcee.2013.v5.776

[2].   Al-Sabaawi, A., & Foo, E. (2019). A Comparison
Study of Android Mobile Forensics for Retrieving
Files System. *Ernest Foo International Journal
of Computer Science and Security (IJCSS), 13,*
2019–2148.

[3].   Aleem, F. (2019). *Layered Architecture Used by
iOS and Its Performance & Portability. July,* 0–19.
https://doi.org/10.13140/RG.2.2.22845.20968

[4].   *Android Architecture.* (2019). https://
androidframework.com/2019/04/27/android-
architecture/

[5].   Ashawa, M., & Ogwuche, I. (2017). Forensic
Data Extraction and Analysis of Left Artifacts on
Emulated Android Phones: A Case Study of Instant
Messaging Applications. *Circulation in Computer
Science, 2*(11), 8–16. https://doi.org/10.22632/
ccs-2017-252-67

[6].   Azfar, A., Choo, K. K. R., & Liu, L. (2016). An Android
Social App Forensics Adversary Model. *Proceedings
of the Annual Hawaii International Conference on
System Sciences, 2016-March,* 5597–5606. https://
doi.org/10.1109/HICSS.2016.693

[7].   Bhardwaj, D. (2021). *Download Odin Flash Tool for
Samsung Galaxy Devices (All Versions).* https://
www.thecustomdroid.com/download-odin-
flash-tool/

[8].   Bhosale, S. T., Patil, T., & Patil, P. (2015). SQLite:
Light Database System. *International Journal of
Computer Science and Mobile Computing, 44*(4),
882–885.

[9]. Castro, K. (2018). *How Are iOS and Android Similar? How Are They Different?* `https://www. tutorialspoint.com/how-are-ios-and-android- similar-how-are-they-different`

[10]. Chernyshev, M., Zeadally, S., Baig, Z., & Woodward, A. (2017). Mobile Forensics: Advances, Challenges, and Research Opportunities. *IEEE Security and Privacy, 15*(6), 42–51. `https://doi.org/10.1109/ MSP.2017.4251107`

[11]. Domingues, P., Frade, M., Andrade, L. M., & Silva, J. V. (2019). Digital Forensic Artifacts of the Your Phone Application in Windows 10. *Digital Investigation, 30*(June), 32–42. `https://doi. org/10.1016/j.diin.2019.06.003`

[12]. Faheem, M., Kechadi, T., & Le-Khac, N. A. (2015). The State of the Art Forensic Techniques in Mobile Cloud Environment: A Survey, Challenges and Current Trends. *Web-Based Services: Concepts, Methodologies, Tools, and Applications*, 2324–2344. `https://doi. org/10.4018/978-14.4666-9466-8.ch103`

[13]. Hamid, A., Ahmad, F., Ram, K., & Khalique, A. (2015). Implementation of Forensic Analysis Procedures for WhatsApp and Viber Android Applications. *International Journal of Computer Applications, 128*(12), 26–33. `https://doi. org/10.5120/ijca2015906683`

[14]. Hayes, D., Snow, C., & Altuwayjiri, S. (2017). Geolocation
Tracking and Privacy Issues Associated with the Uber
Mobile Application. *Proceedings of the Conference on
Information Systems Applied Research, 10*(4511), 1–11.

[15]. Thomas, A., 2022. How To Root Samsung Galaxy A7
(2016) On Android Nougat 7.0? All Models. [online]
Samsungsfour.com. Available at: <www.samsungsfour.
com/tutorials/how-to-root-samsung-galaxy-a7-2016-
on-android-nougat-7-0-all-models.html> [Accessed
26 March 2022].

[16]. Khan, J., & Shahzad, S. (2016). Android Architecture
and Related Security Risks. *Asian Journal of Technology
& Management Research, 5*(March), 2249–2892.

[17]. Kitsaki, T. I., Angelogianni, A., Ntantogian, C., &
Xenakis, C. (2018). A Forensic Investigation of
Android Mobile Applications. *ACM International
Conference Proceeding Series, December,* 58–63.
https://doi.org/10.1145/3291533.3291573

[18]. Lessad, J., & Kessler, G. C. (2013). Android Forensics:
Simplifying Cell Phone Examinations. *Small Scale
Digital Device Forensics Journal, 4*(1), 1–12.

[19]. Liu, S. (2020). *Market Share Held by Leading Mobile
Internet Browsers Worldwide from January 2012 to
September 2020.* Statista. https://www.statista.
com/statistics/263517/market-share-held-by-
mobile-internet-browsers-worldwide/

[20]. Liu, S. (2021). *Global Market Share Held by Mobile
Internet Browsers 2012-2021.* https://www.
statista.com/statistics/263517/market-share-
held-by-mobile-internet-browsers-worldwide/

[21].   Manendra Sai, D., G K Prasad, N. R., & Dekka,
        S. (2015). The Forensic Process Analysis of Mobile
        Device. *International Journal of Computer Science
        and Information Technologies, 6*(5), 4847–4850.
        www.ijcsit.com

[22].   *MOBILedit.* (n.d.). Retrieved July 3, 2021, from
        https://en.wikipedia.org/wiki/MOBILedit

[23].   Nemetz, S., Schmitt, S., & Freiling, F. (2018).
        A Standardized Corpus for SQLite Database
        Forensics. *DFRWS 2018 EU - Proceedings of the
        5th Annual DFRWS Europe, 24,* S121–S130.
        https://doi.org/10.1016/j.diin.2018.01.015

[24].   Rathod, D. (2017). Web Browser Forensics: Google
        Chrome Available Online at www.ijarcs.info.
        *International Journal of Advanced Research in
        Computer Science, 8*(December), 5–9. https://doi.
        org/10.26483/ijarcs.v8i7.4433

[25].   Umar, R., Riadi, I., & Zamroni, G. M. (2018).
        Mobile Forensic Tools Evaluation for Digital Crime
        Investigation. *International Journal on Advanced
        Science, Engineering and Information Technology,
        8*(3), 949–955. https://doi.org/10.18517/
        ijaseit.8.3.3591

Index

© Mohammed Moreb 2022
M. Moreb, *Practical Forensic Analysis of Artifacts on iOS and Android Devices*,
https://doi.org/10.1007/978-1-4842-8026-3

Printed in the United States
by Baker & Taylor Publisher Services

Printed in the United States
by Baker & Taylor Publisher Services